Development and Social Change

Eighth Edition

For all movements of progressive solidarity around this troubled world.

Development and Social Change

A Global Perspective

Eighth Edition

Philip McMichael

Cornell University

Heloise Weber

University of Queensland

Sage

FOR INFORMATION:

2455 Teller Road
Thousand Oaks, California 91320
E-mail: order@sagepub.com

1 Oliver's Yard
55 City Road
London, EC1Y 1SP
United Kingdom

Unit No. 323-333, Third Floor, F-Block
International Trade Tower
Nehru Place, New Delhi – 110 019
India

18 Cross Street #10-10/11/12
China Square Central
Singapore 048423

Acquisitions Editor: Erica DeLuca

Digital Content Editor: Kathy Moran

Production Editor: Vanshika Chauhan

Copy Editor: Colleen Brennan

Typesetter: diacriTech

Cover Designer: Candice Harman

Marketing Manager: Jennifer Haldeman

Printed in the United States of America

LCCN: 2024949387

SUSTAINABLE FORESTRY INITIATIVE
Certified Chain of Custody
At Least 10% Certified Forest Content
www.sfiprogram.org
SFI-01028

This book is printed on acid-free paper.

25 26 27 28 29 10 9 8 7 6 5 4 3 2 1

BRIEF CONTENTS

DETAILED CONTENTS

PREFACE TO THE EIGHTH EDITION

The eighth edition of this text updates and refines the narrative. The thread that weaves together this story is that *development* is a concept and practice stemming from the era of European colonization of the Americas, Asia, and Africa. The intersection of colonialism and capitalism (as part of the European project) as such embodies power relationships, including of race, gender, and class. It marks a dynamic process that has always been contested, from anticolonial struggles to struggles for labor protections and rights, the women's movement for equality and justice, and pushes for ecological sustainability. Such struggles, rooted in the history of the development project continue, revealing multiple crises and the urgent need for a sustainable development project. The world is at a crossroads. Our book traces these dynamics and guides critical reflection of possibilities for more humane futures.

In its most elemental form, the development project was advanced as a blueprint of progress across a diverse world through a singular lens of cultural evolution, problematically equating "civilization" with Europe and thereby discounting non-European cultures as well as masking the violence of European colonialism. At the same time, given the association of development with economic growth, the ecological foundations of human civilization have been seriously discounted. They are now undergoing recognition, but not necessarily in a uniformly effective direction, where decarbonization schemes are combined with continued fossil fuel consumption and extraction in short-term "net zero" offset maneuvers.

As a method of rule, development takes distinctive forms in different historical periods, and these are laid out here as changing sets of political-economic and political-ecological relations, animated by powerful discourses of progress, opportunity, enrichment, and sustainability. As such, development is examined here as a contested historical project rather than something to take for granted—operating through relationships of power among and within countries and world regions. Modern social thought identifies development as human progress, stemming from an Enlightenment ideal. It is, of course, an ideal not necessarily shared by the majority world, and yet it has become the dominant trope governing international relations via the project of development and its prioritization of the market. The limits of this secular ideal, as it shaped modern social thought, are becoming increasingly clear today, as the accumulation of environmental uncertainty and climatic crisis dramatically reveals the problematic implications of failing to respect the centrality of ecosystems to human life—and, therefore, also the illusion of unlimited economic growth.

This text engages critically with the persistent *economistic* association of development with material growth via market expansion, sanitized from socioecological violence and the enduring legacies of colonialism and class. To introduce the development project, as well as indicate where it comes from, it is necessary to trace its origins as well as how it has been shaped in recent world history. At the same time, it is important to de-fetishize the economic interpretation and reveal the social *relations* and processes, and the ecological consequences of development, as well as the power relations ordering this historic enterprise and reordering the world. This account of development focuses on these social and political transformations and the various ways in which development is realized through social and spatial inequalities. It also considers these processes from the perspective of social movements and how their resistances problematize, or question, the dominant vision of economism as a form of rule and as an increasingly evident threat to ecological stability.

The conceptual framework posits development as a political construct, devised by dominant actors such as metropolitan states, multilateral institutions, and political and economic elites to order the world and contain opposition. Development and its variant expressed through neoliberal globalization are presented as projects with clear ideological proclivities evident in their organizing principles (e.g., economic nationalism, market liberalization). However, they are highly problematic in their vision, approach, and realization through inequality and ecological deterioration.

The theoretical subtext of the development project is organized by extended Polanyian cycles of "market self-regulation" and resistance (countermovements). In the mid-twentieth century, a form of "embedded liberalism" (market regulation within a maturing nation-state system to contain labor and decolonization movements) informed social-democratic (developmentalist) goals within a Cold War context, including economic and military aid to what was then called the "Third World." This occurred as the former Third World states sought to steer a course of nonalignment and struggled through a strategy of solidarist internationalism aimed at changing the unequal international structures of world politics. That strategy was undermined by the capitalist bloc, and this "development era" ended with a "countermobilization" of corporate interests dedicated to instituting a "self-regulating market" on a global scale from the 1970s onward. The dominant discourse of neoliberalism advances market liberalization, privatization, freedom of capital movement and access, and so on. This globalization project was already "test run" during the debt regime of the 1980s and was institutionalized with the establishment of the World Trade Organization (WTO) in 1995.

A *further* countermovement, this time against the deprivations of the globalization project, has gathered momentum through maturing global justice movements in the 1990s, the Latin American and Arab rebellions of the new century, and globally connected social movements around, for instance, climate change, antiracism and austerity protests. All of these are in one way or another directed at a growing "legitimacy deficit" of the global development establishment. This is reflected in the reconstitution of the Washington Consensus following the 1997 Asian-originating global financial crisis, recovery of the trope of "poverty reduction" in the Millennium Development Goals (MDGs) initiative of 2000 and now in the 2030 Sustainable Development Goals agenda, stalemate at the WTO, and growing antipathy toward the World Bank and the International Monetary Fund (IMF) among countries of the global South.

Neoliberalism is at a crossroads, complicated by serious security concerns with social, ecological, and economic dimensions that are all related to and altering the politics of development, for instance, in deepening global impoverishment, evident not least in expanding slums and refugee camps; financial volatility and the casualization of employment; political conflict and violence, including rising authoritarian populism; and evidence of global climate change and the spread of deadly viruses. How the current cycle of opposition and creative development alternatives will unfold is yet to be determined, but we may see some kind of "sustainability project" emerge, with grassroots initiatives toward rethinking the values that define development, nevertheless contested by political and economic elites.

The major revisions in this edition are as follows. We have revised Chapter 1 (introduction) foregrounding contemporary challenges from rising material impoverishment and legitimacy questions regarding globalization's evident inequalities, to struggles for racial equality and justice and ecological sustainability. In line with our understanding of development as a historical framework, we connect these challenges to a critical engagement of the Eurocentric framing of development and its expression in modernization theory. And we make the case for applying a historical sensibility regarding the long-term, worldwide impact of colonial relations continuing into the present. Chapter 2 has been revised to incorporate recent critical revisions of the Eurocentric framing of development, and notions of progress and backwardness. Here we underscore how the development project rested on inverted normative premises. We draw attention to the link between knowledge and power, and the way in which strategic responses to anticolonial struggles and decolonization shaped the instituting of the development project. Chapter 3 has been revised to draw out Third World challenges to the colonial division of labor and how this was countered in ways that prefigured the neoliberal globalization project. We have included some additional case examples to illustrate some core political shifts. Chapter 4 re-emphasizes the construction of the institutional architecture of the globalization project, updating developments of institutional policy frameworks. Chapter 5 refocuses on the "Janus-faced" workings of neoliberal, market-based development, with its socioecological devastations.

The remaining five chapters (6–10) have been updated to encourage students to recognize and situate with contemporary expressions of crisis, juxtaposing "business-as-usual" responses with emergent shifts toward alternative and diverse understandings and practices of "development." *Pedagogically, the point here is to engage students with where they are, in the sense of how they interpret current challenges the world is facing and which they experience, and how they see and feel the future.*

The long-standing Chapter 6 on countermovements has been eliminated to maintain the temporal progression of the book, simply moving previous Chapter 7 on the austerity and legitimacy crises of the globalization project to Chapter 6, now including the rise of nationalist protectionism and right-wing populist authoritarianism, the role of southern debt encouraging extractivism by the global North, alongside de-globalization stirrings. Chapter 7 is now a new chapter, titled Global Reorderings, addressing the rise of multipolarity, China's Belt and Road Initiatives, India's enigmatic rise, the deepening of the Fourth Industrial Revolution, and new forms of green transitioning.

Chapter 8 uses the double entendre of the "development climate" to address and update how conventional developmentalism attempts to manage and/or take advantage of the climate emergency, noting the shortcomings of net zero policies, including carbon colonialism, and of governments and financial and corporate interests. This contrasts with Chapter 9 on public and local attempts to build forms of sustainable development in both urban and rural settings, alongside shortcomings of corporate "green technologies." The final chapter (Chapter 10) is an exercise in evaluating a range of emerging ideas pointing toward a sustainable development project, and the institutional limits to and possibilities for building a coordinated multilateral and just future for all peoples across the world. It is designed to offer hope at a time of substantial challenges and to encourage students to recognize that this moment offers new opportunities, precisely because the development crisis is revealing the truth of Albert Einstein's adage: "We can't solve problems by using the same kind of thinking we used when we created them."

The subject of development is difficult to teach. Living in relatively affluent surroundings, most university students tend to situate their society on the "high end" of a development continuum—at the pinnacle of human economic and technological achievement. And they often perceive the development continuum and their favorable position on it as "natural"—a well-deserved reward for embracing modernity. Development, thus, tends to be associated with problems of "developing" states rather than as a global project of which we are all a part. Such a recognition must include an understanding of the role of colonialism in shaping structural injustices that underpinned the formation of the development project. It is difficult to put one's world in historical perspective from this vantage point. It is harder still to help students grasp a world perspective that goes beyond framing their experience as an "evolved state"—the inevitable march of "progress." The current anti-immigrant politics, recent Black Lives Matter movements, and rising social solidarities globally, including Indigenous struggles, women's movements, and struggles over ecological integrity in the face of global elite rule, are powerful reminders of the uneven and contentious implications of development. They are also manifestations of relations of solidarity and inspire hope for more just development futures. We are at a crossroads.

In our experience, until students go beyond simple evolutionary views, they have difficulty valuing other cultures and social possibilities. When they do go beyond the evolutionary perspective, they are better able to evaluate their own culture sociologically and politically; appreciate the link between history, knowledge and power; and think reflexively about social change, development, and global inequalities. This is the challenge we face.

TEACHING RESOURCES

This text includes an array of instructor teaching materials designed to save you time and to help you keep students engaged. To learn more, visit **sagepub.com** or contact your Sage representative at sagepub.com/findmyrep.

ACKNOWLEDGMENTS

I wish to express my thanks to the people who have helped me along the way, beginning with the late Terence Hopkins (my graduate school mentor) and teachers James Petras and Immanuel Wallerstein. The late Giovanni Arrighi played a critical role in encouraging me to cultivate "analytical nerve." For the first three editions, which include acknowledgment of the various people who were so helpful, special mention still goes to the original editor in chief, Steve Rutter, for his remarkable vision and his enthusiasm and faith in this project, as well as friends and colleagues who made significant contributions to improving this project—the late Fred Buttel, Harriet Friedmann, Richard Williams, Michelle Adato, Dale Tomich, Farshad Araghi, Rajeev Patel, Dia Da Costa, Gayatri Menon, Karuna Morarji, Ian Bailey, Kathleen Sexsmith, and of course Heloise, whose worldly and pedagogical sensibilities have been critical to reworking these latest revisions. And finally, I express my gratitude to all the undergraduate students who taught me over the lifetime of this textbook, since 1996 (and particularly "my" remarkable graduate student Teaching Assistants) at Cornell.

Philip McMichael

I would like to express my thanks to everyone who has inspired me to think critically about politics and injustices. In particular I would like to thank my mentor and PhD supervisor, and dearly loved friend, Caroline Thomas. Special thanks to Tony McGrew and Julian Saurin. Special thanks to Heather Rae and Chris Reus-Smit for all the discussions, support, and friendship. Over the years, I have learned from and been inspired by wonderful colleagues and friends especially through the Global Development Studies (GDS) Section of the International Studies Association (ISA), for which I am very grateful. My former PhD students and friends, Kamil Shah, Kazi Rahman, Samid Suliman, Michael Spann, George Karavas, Aliya Abbasi, and Rajni Gamage have been frequent sources of inspiration. At POLSIS, UQ I would like to acknowledge the support of Roland Bleiker and friendship of Emma Hutchison. My thanks also to Gillian Whitehouse and Morgan Brigg. To Kate Lee Koo, thank you for being an exemplary Head of School. A very big thank-you to Martin Weber for all the constant discussions that I have benefited from, and for support, always.

My deep gratitude is to Philip McMichael—thank you for being such an outstanding inspiration, mentor, and educator over the past decades. Your intellectual, social, and political commitments have had a deep and lasting imprint on my work and outlook. I have tried to share this with numerous enthusiastic students who have benefited so much from engaging with *Development and Social Change*. Thank you, Phil and Karen, for your friendship and support.

Heloise Weber

For this eighth edition, we have been very fortunate to have ongoing encouragement and assistance from Erica DeLuca, Acquisitions Editor for Sociology at Sage, and sustained guidance from Kathy Moran, Content Project Manager. We are also grateful for the meticulous editorial work performed by Colleen Brennan on the whole manuscript.

Great thanks are also due to reviewers of previous editions.

ABOUT THE AUTHORS

Philip McMichael grew up in Adelaide, South Australia, completing undergraduate degrees in economics and in political science at the University of Adelaide. After traveling in India, Pakistan, and Afghanistan and doing community work in Papua New Guinea, he pursued his doctorate in sociology at the State University of New York at Binghamton. He has taught at the University of New England (New South Wales), Swarthmore College, and the University of Georgia, and he is presently Emeritus Professor of Global Development at Cornell University, in Ithaca, NY. Other appointments include Visiting Senior Research Scholar in International Development at the University of Oxford (Wolfson College) and Visiting Scholar, School of Political Science and International Relations at the University of Queensland.

His book *Settlers and the Agrarian Question: Foundations of Capitalism in Colonial Australia* (1984) won the Social Science History Association's Allan Sharlin Memorial Award in 1985. In addition to authoring *Food Regimes and Agrarian Questions* (2013), McMichael edited *The Global Restructuring of Agro-Food Systems* (1994), *Food and Agrarian Orders in the World Economy* (1995), *New Directions in the Sociology of Global Development* (2005) with Frederick H. Buttel, *Contesting Development: Critical Struggles for Social Change* (2010), *The Politics of Biofuels, Land and Agrarian Change* (2011) with Jun Borras and Ian Scoones, and *Finance or Food? The Role of Cultures, Values and Ethics in Land Use Negotiations*, with Hilde Bjørkhaug and Bruce Muirhead (2020).

He has served twice as chair of his department, as director of Cornell University's International Political Economy Program, as chair of the American Sociological Association's Political Economy of the World-System Section, and as president of the Research Committee on Agriculture and Food for the International Sociological Association. He is also an active member of the International Studies Association. He has worked with the Food and Agriculture Organization of the United Nations (FAO) and the Civil Society Mechanism of the FAO's Committee on World Food Security (CFS), the UN Research Institute for Social Development (UNRISD), the international peasant coalition *Via Campesina*, and the International Planning Committee for Food Sovereignty.

Heloise Weber was born in Colombo, Sri Lanka, where she spent her childhood before growing up and studying in England. She completed her undergraduate degree in International Politics from the University of Wales, Aberystwyth (now Aberystwyth University), and received her doctorate from the University of Southampton. She held a research fellowship and also taught at the University of Warwick and has held tenure track positions at the University of Aberdeen and the University of Sussex. Her current position is in International Relations and Development, at the School of Political Science and International Studies, the University of Queensland. She has been a Visiting Scholar at the Institute of Political Economy/Department of Political Science Carleton University (Canada), Department of Development Sociology, Cornell University, and with the Normative Orders Research Cluster, Goethe University Frankfurt am Main.

Her research interests are in the politics of global development and inequality, and critical approaches to international relations. Her publications include *Rethinking the Third World: International Development and World Politics* (coauthored with Mark T. Berger) and *Politics of Development: A Survey* (edited). She also coedited a special section of the *Review of International Political Economy* on the political economy of the GATS/WTO and development as well as a special issue of *Globalizations* on Rethinking Development: Beyond Recognition and Redistribution. She has published on the UN's 2030 Sustainable Development Goals Agenda in the *SAIS Review of International Affairs, Globalizations* and *World Development* (the latter coauthored with Martin Weber). Her work engaging international relations includes "Colonialism, Genocide and International Relations: Struggles for Restorative Relations" in the *European Journal of International Relations* (coauthored with Martin Weber).

She is an active member of the Global Development Studies (GDS) Section of the International Studies Association (ISA), and has served twice as GDS program and section chair.

A TIMELINE OF DEVELOPMENT

WORLD FRAMEWORK	**Developmentalism (1940s–1970s)**
POLITICAL ECONOMY	State-Regulated Markets (Keynesianism) Public Spending
SOCIAL GOALS	Social Contract and Redistribution National Citizenship
DEVELOPMENT [Model]	Industrial Replication National Economic Sector Complementarity [e.g., Brazil, Mexico, India]
MOBILIZING TOOL	Nationalism (Postcolonialism)
MECHANISMS	Import-Substitution Industrialization (ISI) Public Investment (Infrastructure, Energy) Education Land Reform
VARIANTS	First World (Freedom of Enterprise) Second World (Central Planning) Third World (Modernization via Development Alliance)

MARKERS				
		Cold War Begins (1946)	Korean War (1950–1953)	Vietnam War (1964–1975)
	Bretton Woods (1944)	Marshall Plan (1946)		Alliance for Progress (1961)
	United Nations (1943)	Non-Aligned Movement Forum: Bandung (1955)	Group of 77 (G-77) (1964)	World Economic Forum (1970)

FIRST DEVELOPMENT DECADE — SECOND DEVELOPMENT DECADE

1940 — 1950 — 1960 — 1970

INSTITUTIONAL DEVELOPMENTS			
	World Bank, IMF, GATT (1944) US$ as Reserve Currency	PL-480 (1954)	UNCTAD (1964) Eurodollar/offshore $ market
		COMECON (1947)	

Globalism (1980s–2000s)

Self-Regulating Markets (Monetarism)
Public Downsizing

Private Initiative and Global Consumerism
Multilayered Citizenship and Recognition

Participation in World Market
Global Comparative Advantage
[e.g., Chile, South Korea, Kenya; EPZs, NAFTA]

Markets and Credit
Financialization

Export-Orientation
Privatization
Extractivism
Public and Majority-Class Austerity

National Structural Adjustment (Opening Economies)
Regional Free Trade Agreements
Global Governance

Oil Crises | Cold War Ends (1989) | "New World Order" | Imperial Wars (2001–) | Rising Nationalism

Debt Regime | WTO Regime | Climate Regime? | China's BRI (2013–)

NIEO (1973) | Chiapas Revolt (1994) | World Social Forum (2001)

Group of 7 (G-7) (1975) | Earth Summit (1992) | Kyoto Protocol (1997) | Group of 20 (G-20) (1999) | MDGs (2000) | Stern Report (2006) | IAASTD Report (2008) | GGND (2009)

"LOST DECADE" | "GLOBALIZATION DECADE"

1970 | 1980 | 1990 | 2000

GATT Uruguay Round (1986–1994)
IPCC (1988)
UNFCCC (1988)

NAFTA (1994) SDGs (2015)
WTO (1995) UNFSS (2021)

Offshore Banking | Structural Adjustment Loans | "Governance"/HIPC Loans | Public–Private Partnerships

Glasnost/Perestroika

ABBREVIATIONS

AfDB	African Development Bank
AGRA	Alliance for a Green Revolution in Africa
ADB	Asian Development Bank
ALBA	Bolivarian Alternative for the Americas
AoA	Agreement on Agriculture (WTO)
APEC	Asia-Pacific Economic Cooperation
BAIR	bureaucratic-authoritarian industrializing regime
BIP	Border Industrialization Program
BRI	China's Belt and Road Initiative
BRICS	Brazil, Russia, India, China, and South Africa
CAFTA	Central American Free Trade Agreement
CBD	Convention on Biodiversity
CDM	Clean Development Mechanism
CEDAW	Convention on the Elimination of All Forms of Discrimination Against Women
CGIAR	Consultative Group on International Agricultural Research
COMECON	Council for Mutual Economic Assistance
COP	Conference of the Parties
ECA	export credit agency
ECLA	Economic Commission for Latin America
EOI	export-oriented industrialization
EPZ	Export processing zone
EU	European Union
FAO	Food and Agriculture Organization (UN)

FDI	foreign direct investment
FTA	free trade agreement
FTAA	Free Trade Area of the Americas
GAD	gender and development
GATS	General Agreement on Trade in Services
GATT	General Agreement on Tariffs and Trade
GDI	Gender Development Index
GDL	global division of labor
GDP	gross domestic product
GEF	Global Environmental Facility
GEM	gender empowerment measure
GGND	Global Green New Deal
GHG	greenhouse gas
GlobalGAP	a retailer produce working group on good agricultural practices
GNH	gross national happiness
GNP	gross national product
GPI	genuine progress indicator
HDI	Human Development Index
HIPC	heavily indebted poor countries
HYV	high-yielding variety
IAASTD	International Assessment of Agricultural Knowledge, Science and Technology for Development
ICT	information and communication technologies
IDA	International Development Association
IDB	Inter-American Development Bank
IDS	Institute for Development Studies
IEA	International Energy Agency
IFI	international financial institutions
IFPRI	International Food Policy Research Institute

IIED	International Institute for Environment and Development
IMF	International Monetary Fund
IPCC	Intergovernmental Panel on Climate Change
IPR	intellectual property rights
ISI	import-substitution industrialization
LDC	least developed countries
LDCF	Less Developed Countries Fund
MDGs	Millennium Development Goals
MEA	Millennium Ecosystem Assessment
MENA	Middle East North African states
MICs	middle-income countries
NAC	new agricultural country
NAFTA	North American Free Trade Agreement
NAM	Non-Aligned Movement
NAPA	National Adaptation Programme of Action
NEPAD	New Partnership for Africa's Development
NGO	nongovernmental organization
NIC	newly industrializing country
NIDL	new international division of labor
NIEO	New International Economic Order
NTE	nontraditional export
OAU	Organization for African Unity
ODA	overseas development assistance
OECD	Organisation for Economic Co-Operation and Development
PRSP	Poverty Reduction Strategy Papers
RAI	responsible agricultural investment
REDD	Reducing Emissions from Deforestation and Degradation
SAL	structural adjustment loan
SAP	structural adjustment programs

SDG	sustainable development goals
SEZ	special economic zone
SRI	System of Rice Intensification
TFN	transnational feminist network
TIE	Transnationals Information Exchange
TNB	transnational bank
TNC	transnational corporation
TPN	transnational policy network
TRIMs	trade-related aspects of investment measures
TRIPs	trade-related intellectual property rights
UBI	Universal Basic Income
UNASUR	Union of South American Nations
UNCED	United Nations Conference on Environment and Development
UNCTAD	United Nations Conference on Trade and Development
UNDESA	United Nations Department of Economic and Social Affairs
UNDP	United Nations Development Programme
UNEP	United Nations Environment Program
UNESCO	United Nations Educational, Scientific and Cultural Organization
UNFCCC	United Nations Convention on Climate Change
UNFSS	United Nations Food Systems Summit
USMCA	United States-Mexico-Canada Agreement (revised NAFTA)
WEEE	waste from electrical and electronic equipment
WEF	World Economic Forum
WHO	World Health Organization
WID	Women in Development
WSF	World Social Forum
WTO	World Trade Organization
ZBNF	Zero Budge Natural Farming

1 DEVELOPMENT

INTRODUCTION

How should we approach the subject of "development" in this moment, when most citizens across the world face economic deprivation with deepening forms of destitution, especially in the global South, and crises threaten the stability of environments and undermine human material improvements? The world is at a turning point regarding not only how to reverse these trends but also how to ensure sustainable life on Earth in coming decades. However, international solidarity and cooperation in the face of these challenges is lacking, especially as grievance politics over the recent elite project of globalization has catalyzed populist authoritarianisms in many countries, turning nations inward.

Yet, at the same time, we have countermovements advocating for social justice and meaningful sustainable development, also of transnational scope and reach. Among them are, for instance, growing sanctuary cities deliberately welcoming migrants on the basis of their "rightful presence," the global food sovereignty movement, and solidarity over insecurities of livelihoods expressed through alliances between those employed and those who are underemployed or unemployed. Simultaneously, decolonial thought and politics continue to push against dominant epistemic and political frames.[1] For instance, ongoing cases for reparations over colonial violence and injustices demonstrate the extent to which the past is in the present but also enabling and shaping struggles over more just social and political futures, including replenishing planet Earth.[2]

In this context there have been moves to supersede development at the world-economic scale, reducing reliance on trade and foreign investment by the private sector, and "revitalizing the state's economic role . . . in the interest of the common good."[3] Here, American economist Dani Rodrik advocates domestic cross-sectoral supply-side measures such as "the embrace of industrial policies to facilitate the green transition, rebuild domestic supply chains, and stimulate good jobs."[4] Such talk reflects rising interest in economic nationalism, in response to social unrest produced by unbridled global capital movements undermining stable employments, rural communities, and multilateralism. It also suggests the model for established economies in the **global North** but not necessarily for countries of the **global South**, whose economies depend on substantial export sectors organized for extraction of resources for the richer global North.

As we shall see, such world-economic patterning is the long-term consequence of Western colonialism, which was structured around capture of raw materials (such as rubber, timber, sugar, grains, palm oil, cotton, minerals) and, of course, labor. So remodeling "development" is a charged and contentious subject. And it is our subject here.

DEVELOPMENT AS A HISTORICALLY RELATIONAL PROCESS

Development, today, is increasingly about how we survive the present and future, rather than its claim to improve on the past. But what past, and how is this past represented? By Western convention, the past is viewed *normatively* as the baseline in framing development as a linear process from tradition to modernity. This convention reflects a Eurocentric narrative of *human* progress, even as its signifiers (e.g., rationalism, scientific discovery, technological change) were viewed as unique to the European experience. Such a narrative not only discounts non-European technologies and sciences, including early Pacific Islander navigation techniques, but alternative signifiers of being, such as the world's 350 million Indigenous peoples, whose lifeworlds value and protect 80 percent of Earth's remaining biodiversity.[5]

From this idealized Eurocentric account of progress, the non-European world has been represented as embodying the past. This baseline framing of "development" means that the violence of colonization by European states, slavers, and merchants is disarticulated from the history of development. It is reflected in contemporary political attempts to marginalize racial history from political discourse and some schooling curricula, to reinforce a linear, rather than a relational, understanding of human development. Here, what is made visible is at the expense of that which is rendered invisible[6]—producing a discriminatory development narrative.

Such disconnection has a double effect: First, it has produced knowledge conventions about development that override the devastating implications of colonialism for the non-European world and the dependence of European commercial wealth and "development" on that relationship. And such exploitation continues today as a form of **coloniality**, where, for example, the bottom 80 percent of humanity finances the richest 20 percent to the tune of approximately $660 billion per annum.[7]

Second, it promotes a sanitized understanding of development as a continuum, *within* each country, emulating the idealized European national path of industrialization. But it is more complicated than this: "development" has global dimensions, starting with European colonization and the violence of this project, profiting from trade in enslaved persons to extraction of resources from colonies through the organization of plantation economies. This has resulted in a palpably unequal, and an uneven, world of states in terms of living standards, voice, and power. Even as some southern states form cooperative relations to challenge the U.S.-centered world order,[8] their domestic economies remain highly unequal.

Accordingly, we seek to integrate the present with its historical past. This method underscores that the world we experience today has been profoundly shaped by colonial and postcolonial relations of power, including narratives of progress and consequences of exploitation. Much tension today around questions of development, sustainable development, and indeed sustainable life[9] stems from these relationships and how to manage the survival of the natural world, which is so fundamental to the survival of humans and all other beings. The 2023 fires in Maui exposed both the ecological consequences of development through colonial capitalism as well as the ongoing implications of colonial legacies. In particular, the spread of the fires have been linked to nonnative grasses left by previous corporate plantations in Hawaii.[10]

While the roots of such inequalities are colonial, the paths taken by non-Western postcolonial states have been shaped since the mid-twentieth century by new global forces. These include the World Bank and the International Monetary Fund in alliance with private interests to build economic infrastructures of a global capitalist economy. The resulting neoliberal "free market" international trade and financial relations have fostered global manufacturing and agricultural industries, serving to enrich corporate and financial elites. India is perhaps the exemplar (now the fifth largest economy in the world), where 90 percent of the population are by most measures poor, qualifying for free food rations intended to prevent malnutrition.[11] Former Nobel Prize winner and World Bank chief economist, Joseph Stiglitz, commented in 2024:

The neoliberal agenda was always partly a charade, a fig leaf for power politics. There was financial deregulation, but also massive government bailouts. There was "free trade," but also massive subsidies to big agriculture and the fossil-fuel industry. Globally this led to the creation of rules that preserve colonial trade patterns, with developing countries producing commodities and the advanced economies dominating high-value-added industries.[12]

The resulting inequality is both material and epistemic (how the world is viewed), and interlaced with enduring racial inequality. To be sure, the conditions and representations are always in contention, exemplified initially by anticolonial movements and continuing in postcolonial times in urban anti-austerity uprisings and international solidarity demands for sovereignty for farming cultures and Indigenous rights and, most recently, as authoritarian populist revolts against "neoliberal" economic deprivations, including anti-elite and anti-immigration politics.

Development today is in question, with deepening global inequality and environmental and climate emergency. A 2020 World Health Organization (WHO) commission reported, "Every country in the world is failing to shield children's health and their futures from intensifying ecological degradation, climate change and exploitative marketing practices."[13] Further, "today's children face an uncertain future," with every child confronting "existential threats," and "while the poorest countries need to do more to support their children's ability to live healthy lives, excessive carbon emissions—disproportionately from wealthier countries—threaten the future of all children."[14] In 2023, the WHO director-general emphasized, "The climate crisis is a health crisis, driving more severe and unpredictable weather events, fuelling disease outbreaks, and contributing to higher rates of noncommunicable diseases."[15] The year 2023 was the warmest year on record on land, as well as in the oceans, with multiple countries experiencing record-breaking heat waves, record-breaking wildfires, record-breaking rainstorms, or some combination.[16] These events are arguably the most dramatic consequences of a mode of development intensifying fossil fuel–dependent economic growth, alongside reduced public regulation, over the last half century.

In 2018, the *World Inequality Report* noted since 1980, net public wealth (state revenues) declined in almost every country. In China and Russia, public wealth declined from 60 to 70 percent of national wealth to 20 to 30 percent, and net public wealth recently became negative in the United States and the United Kingdom and only slightly positive in Japan, Germany, and France. This "limits government ability to regulate the economy, redistribute income, and mitigate rising inequality,"[17] as well as reducing emissions.

Development's outcomes are profoundly challenged, as we cross planetary boundaries (e.g., climate change, biosphere integrity, biogeochemical flows, fresh water, land system) and social effects of natural disasters accumulate. The question is how can, or why should, development maintain its goal of increased economic growth (and how does it serve to reinforce social inequalities)? This question animates a broad range of responses at all scales of political and social life, encountered in later chapters.

Development's economic focus on emulation of an idealized Western material lifestyle became the universal standard when in 1949 U.S. President Truman proclaimed the "era of development" as the alternative to Soviet communism. He defined it as achieving "the decent satisfying life that is the right of all people. Democracy alone can supply the vitalizing force."[18] *How, and how well, and with what implications development has addressed this goal is our subject.*

Fifty years after Truman's freedom doctrine, the United Nations General Assembly recycled the development quest on September 18, 2000, in *The Millennium Declaration*:

> We will spare no effort to free our fellow men, women and children from the abject and dehumanizing conditions of extreme poverty, to which more than a billion of them are currently subjected. We are committed to making the right to development a reality for everyone and freeing the entire human race from want.[19]

Not only has the entire human race not been relieved of want since the development era began, but also the trajectory of development has increasingly compromised its claims and possibilities. Across the past half century, annual consumption of global resources has outstripped Earth's carrying capacities (as depicted in Figure 1.1). Such consumption is hardly equal within and across societies.

FIGURE 1.1 ■ Humanity's Ecological Footprint

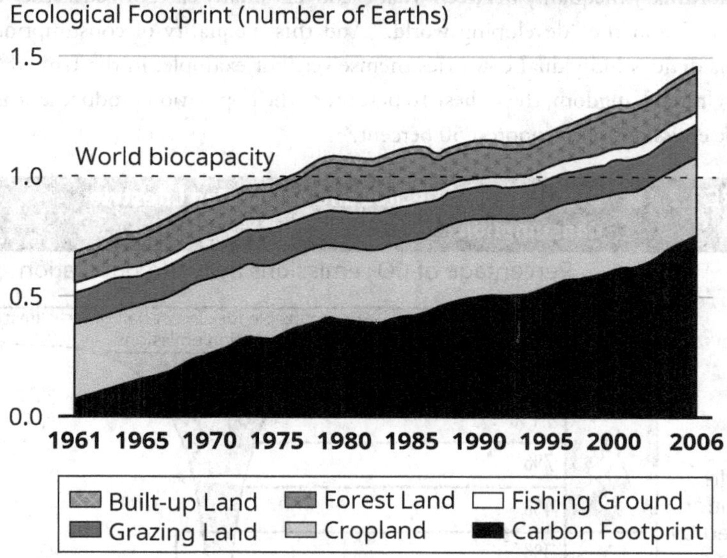

Source: Global Footprint Network, 2010 National Footprint Accounts.

As an orienting term, *emulation* is ideological and unrealistic—not only because of deepening inequalities in Western societies but also because Western (stratified) lifestyles depend so much on non-Western resources. Mass consumption, theorized as the ultimate goal of development, depends on a dense network of global supply chains delivering raw materials, foodstuffs, and manufactured goods produced with majority world resources (including exploited labor) for the world's minority with purchasing power (disproportionately in the so-called developed countries). Such products include timber from Indonesia and smartphone coltan from the Congo, quinoa from Peru and avocado from Mexico, and clothing from Bangladesh and Sri Lanka.

Behind these geographically dispersed relations stands the legacy of colonial exploitation, now compounded in new forms of global market exploitation by powerful corporate and financial interests. This is not to say non-Western societies do not have their affluent elite classes, but there are profound inequalities between the West and the rest of the world. For example, from a gender relations perspective, a 2020 Oxfam report noted that the world's 22 most affluent males combine more wealth than all 325 million women in Africa. Further, "women and girls across the globe contribute an estimated $10.8tn to the global economy with a total of 12.5bn hours a day of unpaid care work, a figure more than three times the worth of the global tech industry."[20] And such exploitation to source wealthy lifestyles generates an outsized ecological footprint, at substantial expense to non-Western habitats, resources, and weather patterning.

We know that the Western lifestyle footprint is responsible for the grossly uneven greenhouse gas emissions producing climatic disturbances with particularly devastating effect across the majority world. This is depicted in Figure 1.2,[21] reflecting the extraordinary inequality between what is conventionally categorized as the "developed world" and the "developing world." And this inequality of consumption and emissions divides individual countries themselves. For example, in the United States and the United Kingdom, the richest 10 percent of the population produce at least five times the emissions of the poorest 50 percent.[22]

FIGURE 1.2 ■ Global Income Deciles and Associated Lifestyle Consumption

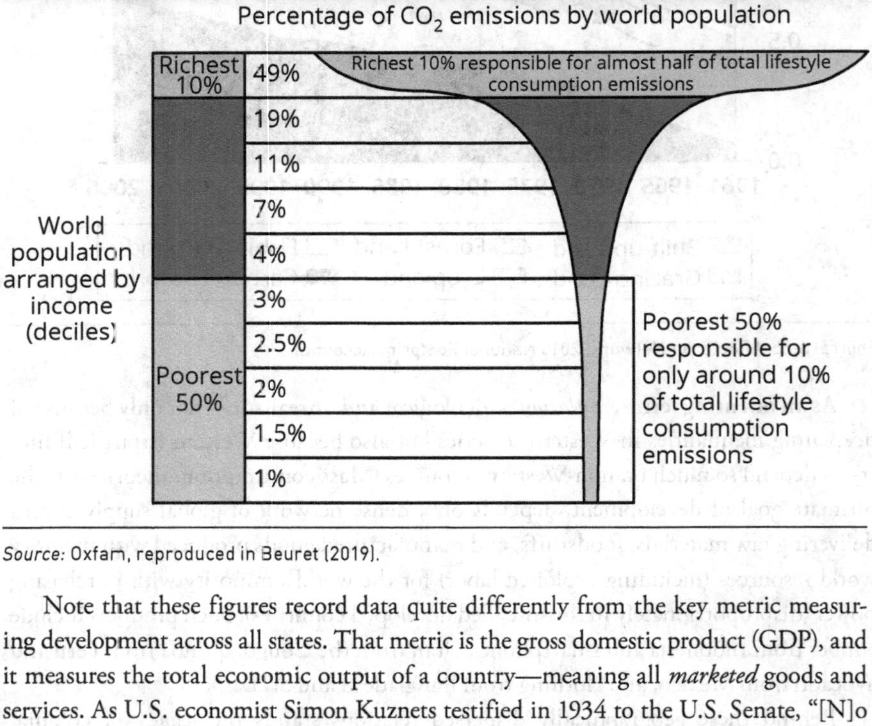

Source: Oxfam, reproduced in Beuret (2019).

Note that these figures record data quite differently from the key metric measuring development across all states. That metric is the gross domestic product (GDP), and it measures the total economic output of a country—meaning all *marketed* goods and services. As U.S. economist Simon Kuznets testified in 1934 to the U.S. Senate, "[N]o income measurement undertakes to estimate the reverse side of income, that is, the intensity and unpleasantness of effort going into the earning of income. The welfare of a nation can, therefore, scarcely be inferred from a measurement of national income as defined [in GDP statistics]."[23] Extrapolating, the "reverse side of income" suggests labor exploitation primarily but extends to nonmonetized activities such as domestic work and community care, as well as to the unpleasantness of environmental despoliation and public ill-health as effects of income-earning activities. In spite of this limitation, or blind spot, GDP was adopted internationally in the 1950s as the key standard measure of development. And it has remained the principal metric to the present day. As Joseph Stiglitz remarked in 2019,

> If our economy seems to be growing but that growth is not sustainable because we are destroying the environment and using up scarce natural resources, our

statistics should warn us. But because GDP didn't include resource depletion and environment degradation, we typically get an excessively rosy picture.[24]

As the standard, not only is GDP incapable of representing social and environmental well-being across a national society, but also it reinforces a one-dimensional understanding of development—invisibilizing the unequal social relations through which this growth is realized. Accordingly, GDP licenses a powerful and self-reproducing institutional (World Bank, United Nations, financial houses) and policy infrastructure, discounting the market's environmental impact—challenged in the UK *Stern Review on the Economics of Climate Change* (2006) as "the greatest market failure the world has ever seen."[25] Two years later the United Nations Environment Programme (UNEP) established the **Global Green New Deal (GGND)** in response to the combined food, fuel, and financial crises.

WHAT IS THE WORLD COMING TO?

Development, then, is a problematic term. Represented as a universal aspiration, its origins are overwhelmingly Eurocentric. It is a trope stemming from the era of European colonization of the Americas, Asia, Australasia, Middle East, and Africa. Colonization was in part justified through a European "civilizing" lens, as non-European cultures were devalued and redefined as "backward," as their habitats and resources were converted for commercial exploitation.

Destruction of the natural world is not the only source of development disillusion today. We see this all around us: in rebellions cascading across the world as economies stagnate and social services and stable jobs erode; in populist upsurges expressing dissatisfaction with political and economic elites captivated by global economic deals; in renewal of sustainable practices; in demands for race, class, and gender equality; in massive new global circuits of migrant labor; and in declining life expectancy from "deaths of despair" from rising precarity.[26] The response to the latter—closing the door to those impoverished by development processes—is perhaps the key allegory of our times. It rests on a disconnection of colonial legacies from the present postcolonial world's condition, expelling displaced people into migrant streams.

At face value, waves of immigration from the non-European world *appear* as masses of people seeking better lives in the "developed world." But this perception is based on erasure of the historical legacies of colonialism. To *reconnect histories relationally* means to deconstruct development as conventionally framed in terms of a simple dichotomy of "premodern" and "modern" societies. Rather, development remains an unequal world–socioeconomic *relationship*. And here, global development has been historically premised on, and productive of, unequal race relations. Racism is expressed across time in minority world exploitation, patronage, and exclusion of majority world peoples: through enslavement and forced labor, Indigenous genocide, and fear of yielding privilege to nonwhite migrants. Such fear is expressed by French author Renaud Camus, in a book titled *Le Grand Remplacement* (2011), claiming that "native 'white' Europeans . . . are being reverse-colonized by black and brown immigrants."[27]

When immigrants from the postcolonial "majority world" now come in waves, seeking redress (symbolically) for centuries of colonial disruption of their life-worlds, their presence triggers political "nativism" in the "minority world." Underlying this response is an implicit assumption that development is a national process and that racial groups have their place—forgetting white-settler colonization, trade in enslaved persons, historic Chinese and Indian diasporas, and even elite diasporas today, not to mention current freedoms of capital migration across borders versus limitations on people migrating.

To study "development," then, is to recognize its history, as an integrated and unequal process across world regions, states, and cultures. This is the underlying theme of this book. The historical process is subdivided into successive colonial, development, globalization, and potential sustainability projects—to distinguish key periods, or political conjunctures, in the making of the modern world. Each project shapes its successor, which in turn reconfigures what it inherits from the previous project. And the process of succession involves substantial/large-scale sociopolitical mobilizations.

Thus, the anticolonial mobilization across the nineteenth century and into the twentieth century shapes the **development project** (1940s–1970s), as decolonization and political independence nurtures "economic nationalism," within a United Nations internationalism. But this in turn was challenged by an increasingly powerful corporate and financial sector, championing a global economy, and hence a **globalization project** (1970s–2010s), opening world markets for trade and investment liberalization. The resulting ecological stress on Earth of intensifying global consumption patterns and a "race for resources" stimulates an array of environmental movements and sustainability initiatives, perhaps anticipating a sustainability project in coming years.

This book is a guide to the rise and transformation of "development" as a powerful instrument of global social change over several centuries. From one (long-term) angle, it appears increasingly cometlike: a brilliant lodestar for ordering the world but perhaps destined to burn out as its energy-intensive foundations meet their limits. From another (immediate) angle, the energy and inequality dilemma forces renewed critical thinking about how humans might live sustainably and equitably on the planet. These perspectives are the subjects of chapters to come.

DEVELOPMENT: HISTORY AND POLITICS

Development originated in the colonial era, as European domination came to be self-justified in terms of superiority and leadership along a development axis. Key to this relationship was power, vested in imperial states, and their military and mercantile operations dedicated to extending the realm of commercial and landed propertied classes. While development is represented in theory as a set of idealized outcomes (at the expense of devaluing other cultures), its implementation often has a violent history.

For example, the private enclosure of land and forests in the name of economic development dispossesses and displaces inhabitants. It also converts such habitats into "resources" to be marketed, thereby replacing one cultural life-world with a singular commodity culture, in the name of progress. Here, development's ends often justify its means, however socially and ecologically disruptive the process may be. And this process in turn is politically sanctioned and managed.

The distinction between development as an unfolding universal social *process* and development as a political *intervention* is useful here.[28] For our purposes it illuminates the ideological belief in "improvement" (European style), paired with distinct power relations to manage modern development. In Enlightenment terms, development was understood in Europe *philosophically* as improving humankind. Nineteenth-century European political elites interpreted development *practically*, as a way to socially engineer emerging national capitalist societies. Elites formulated government policy to manage the social transformations attending the rise of capitalism and industrial technologies. Development came to be identified with *both* industrialization *and* the regulation of its disruptive social impacts. These impacts began with the displacement of rural populations by land enclosures for cash cropping, a process generating impoverished individuals and families, such paupers who were in turn framed as menacing, restless proletarians ("undesirables"), as well as producing unhealthy factory towns.[29] Development, here, meant balancing technological change and the rise of new social classes, fashioning policies to manage wholesale social transformations. At the same time, such transformations became the catalyst of competing political visions—liberal, socialist, conservative—of the ideal society.

In Europe's colonies, the inhabitants appeared undeveloped—in European self-referential (evolutionary) terms—legitimizing imperial intervention. By the nineteenth century, social engineering underpinned European imperialism. While colonial resource extraction facilitated European industrialization, colonial administrators managed subject populations, as they experienced wrenching social transformations. Here, development came to be associated with an additional, normative meaning, namely, a "white man's burden"—the title of a poem by nineteenth-century English poet Rudyard Kipling. Such racist patronage remains a key legacy of European civilizing claims. When the leader of India's twentieth-century independence movement, Mahatma Gandhi, was asked what he thought of British civilization, reputedly he replied, "It would be a good idea."

Thus, development came to mean the extension of modern social engineering to colonies incorporated into the European orbit and through use of justifications steeped in racism. Subject populations were exposed to a variety of new disciplines, including forced labor schemes, schooling, and segregation in native quarters. Forms of colonial subordination differed across time and space, but the overriding object was either to adapt or marginalize the colonized in the processes of their dispossession. In this sense, development involved a relation of power. For example, British colonialism introduced the new English factory model "Lancaster school" to the (ancient) city of Cairo in 1843 to educate Cairo's emerging civil service. Egyptian students learned the new disciplines of a developing society that was busily displacing peasant culture with plantations of cotton for export to English textile mills and managing an army of migrant labor, which was building an infrastructure of roads, canals, railways, telegraphs, and ports.[30] Through the colonial relation, industrialism transformed both English and Egyptian society, producing new forms of social discipline among working- and middle-class citizen-subjects. And while industrialism produced new class and gender inequalities within each society, the racist underpinnings of colonialism added further and persisting forms of domination and inequality. In this way, new class and racial hierarchies within and across societies were introduced.

While development informed modern narratives in the age of industrialism and empire, it only became formalized as a *project* in the mid-twentieth century. This period was the high tide of **decolonization**, as the Western (British, Italian, German, French, Dutch, Portuguese, and Belgian) and Japanese empires succumbed to the moral force of anticolonial resistance and when development (associated with independence) became an emancipatory promise. The United States, identifying as a noncolonial power (disregarding its settler-colonial history) and strengthened by its New Deal, by which Keynesian public economic stimulus offered a model of "planned development," seized the post–World War II moment to proclaim a new (free) world project of development. Meanwhile, the United Nations, intent on expanding membership as colonies became independent as sovereign states, institutionalized the System of National Accounts. A universal quantifiable measure of development, the GDP, was born, as key to the development project, based on the ideal of self-governing states united by the ideology of nationalism. Here, formally, postcolonial *subjects* became *citizens*, in an era of U.S.-sponsored "development" that idealized modern society as composed of self-maximizing *consumers*. Western development culture contrasted with Soviet bloc socialism, where industrialism was driven not by consumerism but by central planning and social need—in part idealizing the worker-state and in part for self-defense against Western anticommunism.

DEVELOPMENT THEORY

Identifying development with rising consumption privileges the market as the vehicle of social change. The underlying philosophy—deriving from a popular (but limiting) interpretation of Adam Smith's *The Wealth of Nations*[31] and formalized in neoclassical economic theory—is that markets maximize individual preferences and allocate resources efficiently. Whether this theory reflects reality or not, it is a deeply held belief now institutionalized in much development policy across the world. Why is this the case?

Naturalizing Development

There are two ways to answer this question. First, a belief in markets is a central tenet of liberal Western philosophy. Hungarian philosopher Karl Polanyi noted that modern liberalism rests on a belief in a natural human propensity for self-gain. This translates in economic theory as the market principle.[32] Self-gain, via the market, drives the aspiration for improvement, aggregated as consumption. Second, as Polanyi noted, naturalizing market behavior as an innate propensity discounts other human traits or social values—such as cooperation, redistribution, and reciprocity, which are different organizing principles by which human societies have endured for centuries. For Polanyi and other classical social theorists, pursuit of individualism via an economic calculus is quite novel in the history and organization of human societies. That is, it is a social construct of modernity, rather than inherent in human social life.

Although individual improvement remains the ultimate goal of development, it is realized quite unevenly across gender, race, and class groupings, as well as across time. In this respect, the middle decades of the twentieth century saw powerful anticolonial, labor, and citizen movements pressing to temper private, with public, provisions, such as infrastructure, education, health, water supply, commons, clean air, and so forth. These measures were included in the United Nations Declaration of Human Rights in the 1940s and constituted the welfare state most clearly in Western societies in the postwar period. Postcolonial states faced the task of challenging the colonial division of labor and implemented social protections for their destabilized communities. This was the era of the development project, modeling these social protections to regulate uncertain markets. But, as noted earlier, such protections hamstrung increasingly powerful financial interests, whose combined power in policy circles contributed to intensifying **privatization** of public goods, and a pervasive discourse subordinating social-democratic states to market imperatives, as the medium of development in the subsequent globalization project.

This privatizing outcome was prefigured in one of the most influential theories of development emerging in the post–World War II world. In 1960, economist Walt Rostow published *The Stages of Economic Growth:* A *Non-Communist Manifesto*,[33] outlining a development theory celebrating the Western model of free enterprise in contrast to a state-planned economy. The "stages" traverse a linear sequence, beginning with "Traditional Society" (agrarian, limited productivity) and moving through "Preconditions for Take-Off" (state formation, education, science, banking, profit systematization), "Take-Off" (normalization of growth via industrialization), and "Maturity" (the second industrial revolution from textiles and iron to machine tools, chemicals, and electrical equipment)—and finally to the "Age of High Mass-Consumption," characterized by the movement from basic to durable goods, urbanization, and a rising level of white-collar versus blue-collar work, as in postwar America.

This evolutionary sequence, ostensibly distilled from the U.S. experience, represents the consumer society as the terminal stage of a complex historical process. Rostow viewed the U.S. model as the goal to which other (i.e., developing) societies should aspire; this partly explains his book's subtitle, which references the Cold War rivalry between the United States and the Soviet Union at the time. The theorization of development as a series of evolutionary stages naturalizes a process comprising unequal relations, framing it in terms of stages, whether with regard to a national (development era) or an international (globalization era) context. Mass consumption was a final goal to be realized through membership of the "free world" at the time, and, by implication, U.S. assistance would be available to spur **Third World** (postcolonial states) progress along the stages.

However, note that Rostow's "development blueprint" depended on a political context. Rostow's theory is premised on the convention of approaching development from the "baseline" we outlined earlier. It thereby served to disconnect colonialism and its legacies as an explanation for the conditions of development of the new states. Furthermore, it sought to naturalize liberal capitalism as the development dynamic. That is, markets are not natural; they require securing by **development states**. And development was neither spontaneous nor inevitable; rather, it was shaped by social struggle and required nurturing by an institutional complex on a world scale (a project), via trade, monetary, and investment rules; aid regimes; or a military umbrella—all of which were supplied through postwar, multilateral institutions and bilateral arrangements led by the United States, especially in the capitalist bloc. In this way, a theory of spontaneous markets diverges from reality. But reality was nonetheless shaped by this theory, informing public discourse and translated into implementation of policies governed by a market calculus. This is a central paradox explored in this book.

Global Context

Reality is more complicated than it first appears. For example, Rostow's prescriptions artificially separated societies from one another, perhaps expressing the idealism of mid-twentieth-century nationalism. But to assign stages of growth to individual societies, without accounting for their historic (and unequal) interdependence, discounts patterns of imperial wealth extraction. As we shall see, not only did European powers once depend on their colonies for resources and markets, but these patterns have continued in the postcolonial era. Because of continuing Western interests on maintaining their access to raw materials from the ex-colonial world, the latter struggled to challenge these historic structural inequalities.

This reality stimulated **dependency analysis** and **world-system analysis**. The concept of "dependency" (referring to unequal economic relations between Western and non-European states) emerged in the mid-twentieth century from several quarters: an empirical observation by economist Hans Singer that "peripheral" countries were exporting more and more natural resources to pay for increasingly expensive manufactured imports; an argument by Singer's collaborator, Argentinean economist Raul Prebisch, that Latin American states should therefore industrialize behind protective tariffs on manufactured imports; and earlier Marxist theories of exploitative imperialist relations between the European and the non-European world.[34] Dependency was, then, a relationship describing the development of Europe at the expense of the **underdevelopment** of the non-European world. Economist Andre Gunder Frank put it this way:

> [H]istorical research demonstrates that contemporary underdevelopment is in large part the historical product of past and continuing economic and other relations between the satellite underdeveloped and the now-developed metropolitan countries. . . . When we examine this metropolis-satellite structure, we find that each of the satellites . . . serves as an instrument to suck capital or economic surplus out of its own satellites and to channel part of this surplus to the world metropolis of which all are satellites.[35]

A similar imagery was used by political scientist Samir Amin, who drew the following conclusion based on an analysis of three case examples from the history of development in the African context: "We have to conclude that there are no traditional societies in modern Africa: there are only dependent peripheral societies."[36] This challenges the conventional baseline framing of traditional and modernity as reflected in Rostow's stages of development prescription. Complementing Amin, Walter Rodney provides a compelling critique of how Europe underdeveloped Africa,[37] detailing the economic, social, ecological, and political consequences. He identifies the European trade in enslaved persons as the key to enduring suffering and ongoing struggles for justice. Highlighting epistemic violence, Rodney critically discloses how the colonial education system was organized for subordination and exploitation.[38] Poignantly, he noted that "Cecil Rhodes could afford to leave a legacy of lavish scholarship to white students for study at Oxford University, having made a fortune from exploiting Africa and Africans."[39]

World-system analysis, advanced by sociologist Immanuel Wallerstein, deepened the concept of dependency by elevating the modern social system to a global scale. States became political units competing for, or surrendering, resources within a **world division of labor**. Here, regional labor forces occupy a skill/technological hierarchy, associated with state strength or weakness in the capitalist world economy.[40] From this perspective, the "core" concentrates capital-intensive or intellectual production and the "periphery" is associated with lower-skilled, labor-intensive production, whether plantation labor, assembly of manufactured goods, or routine service work (e.g., call centers). The point of a world division of labor emphasizes that labor everywhere has a global, rather than a national, locational value, with racist dimensions.

The concept of dependency challenges the assumption that societies are independently aligned on a "stages of growth" spectrum. But its binary, reflected in the framing of development/underdevelopment, rests on valuing Western-style development over other more collective, low-input life-worlds associated with non-Western cultures. Indian postcolonial theorist and political psychologist Ashis Nandy's critique of the conflation of "poverty" with both modern experiences of destitution and customary frugal lifestyles is instructive here. His point is that when we conventionally refer to poverty, we mean destitution "but are too clever by half to admit that."[41] Nandy argues this serves to justify a development industry premised on overcoming poverty but producing conditions of destitution, by undermining Indigenous life-worlds and the sovereignty of farm cultures.

While measuring all societies against a conception of (industrial) development may have seemed the appropriate goal for Modernization and Dependency Theory at mid-century, from the vantage point of the *twenty-first century* it is quite problematic. The growing recognition that the planet cannot sustain current Western-emulating socially unequal urban-industrial trends in China and India is one dramatic expression of this new reality.

Agrarian Questions

Urbanization is a defining outcome of development and the "stages of growth" metaphor, where "tradition" yields to "modernity" as industrialization deepens. As political scientist Samuel Huntington put it, "Agriculture declines in importance compared to commercial, industrial, and other non-agricultural activities, and commercial agriculture replaces subsistence agriculture."[42] Although this theoretical sequence has some validity (as urbanization deepens), informing policies discounting small-scale farming, there is a question as to whether and to what extent this trajectory is inevitable on a global scale. In fact, as we shall see, the demise of millions of small producers is an outcome of unequal global relations such as colonialism, targeted foreign aid, and policies favoring global agribusiness. How we perceive these relationships is important.

Agribusiness industrializes agriculture, with technologies and chemicals to promote food monocultures on a global scale. Meanwhile, low-input farming polycultures are gaining attention as they save seeds and local knowledge, promote biodiversity, and produce varieties of fresh foods with similar productivity as agri-monocultures per hectare.[43] Even so, the modernist preoccupation with large-scale technological change has fostered a broad international system of subsidies for agribusiness trading that discriminates against farming cultures, ostensibly to "feed the world," even as small-scale farmers produce two-thirds of the world's food.[44]

Ecological Questions

This example of conversion of farming into an industrial activity underscores a significant *ecological blind spot* in development theory. As is becoming clearer, where the displacement of small farming cultures by large-scale (commercial) agriculture is represented as improvement, or development, it is an insufficient claim if it does not account for what economists call "externals." These are the significant environmental impacts, such as disruption of agrarian cultures and their ecosystems, dependency on fossil fuels, and agriculture's responsibility for up to a third of greenhouse gas emissions. Such consequences challenge the wisdom of replacing long-standing knowledge-intensive farming culture/ecology with increasingly unsustainable industrial agriculture.

In 2011 the annual UNDP *Human Development Report* began adopting an ecological sensibility.[45] This new focus complemented the 2005 *Millennium Ecosystem Assessment*, which noted that the last half century of human action has had the most intensive and extensive negative impact on world ecosystems ever, and yet this has been accompanied by continuing global gains in human well-being.[46] And so the **"environmentalist's paradox"** was coined, where mastery of nature may be effective in the short term in generating rising consumption patterns but also effective in masking the long-term health implications of ecosystem stress, if these are "externalized." What such research suggests is that development needs a robust sustainability dimension, a possible **sustainability project**.

DEVELOPMENT PARADOXES

The environmentalist's paradox, when inverted, is, in fact, a **development paradox**. Former World Bank economist Herman Daly formulated this as an "impossibility theorem," namely, that the universalization of U.S.-style high mass consumption economy would require several planet Earths. Either way, the *ultimate paradox here is that the environment is not equipped to absorb its unrelenting exploitation by the current growth model of endless accumulation.* In other words, development as we know it is undermining itself.

Three of the nine designated planetary operational boundaries (i.e., climate change, biodiversity, and the nitrogen cycle) have been crossed already, whereas others (e.g., fresh water use and oceanic acidification) are at serious tipping points. Meanwhile, the costs of environmental degradation are borne disproportionately by the poor—the very same people the development industry claims to target. This is a key development paradox.

Other paradoxes include such questions as the following: Are low-carbon cultures that live with, rather than seek to master, nature backward? Are non-Western cultures judged poor in what makes Western cultures rich? Is frugality poverty? Why is malnutrition common to Western and non-Western cultures? Are non-Western cultures rich in what Western cultures are now poor (nonmonetized items such as open space, leisure, solidarity, ecological knowledge)? Should we measure living standards only in monetary terms?

Sources: Daly (1990); J. B. Foster (2011); Stern (2006).

SOCIAL CHANGE

As we have seen, development theory offers a blueprint, and justification, for universalizing a European-centered prototype. European industrialization depended on devaluing and displacing non-European knowledges and industry and capturing non-European resources (labor, minerals, raw materials, and foodstuffs). Of course, colonial subjects resisted; for example, there was the successful late-eighteenth-century uprising of the enslaved in the French colony of Saint-Domingue (forming the first, Haitian, postcolonial state in 1804), but also the unsuccessful Amritsar rebellion, put down savagely by British forces in India in 1919. Such uprisings (including by the enslaved in the southern United States) marked a long-term politics of decolonization, with colonial subjects articulating and gaining moral, material, and political power as **countermovements** to European empires. Resistance to colonialism, including substantial peasant mobilizations from China to Mexico to Kenya, was matched with labor uprisings and political organization during the late-colonial era. The British faced widespread labor strikes in their West Indian and African colonies in the 1930s, and this pattern continued over the next two decades in Africa as British and French colonial subjects protested conditions in cities, ports, mines, and on the railways.[47]

Colonial rule eventually surrendered to definitive anticolonial power struggles, animated by class and cultural mobilizations for independence. The **colonial project** reconfigured and subordinated communities and resources to service imperial needs, including through the creation of labor regimes. However, colonialism was rooted in and defended through racial politics that both justified subjugation (including enslavement) and fueled resistance across the colonial world. These struggles ushered in a postcolonial era, embedded in an expanding system of sovereign nation-states forming the United Nations organization.

The UN Security Council comprised China, France, the Soviet Union, the United Kingdom, and the United States, with new states joining through the 1940s and 1950s. During this period French demographer Alfred Sauvy coined the term *Third World*: the world region of postcolonial states distinct from the **First** (Western bloc) and **Second** (Soviet bloc) **Worlds**. Both First and Second Worlds were engaged in expanding their spheres of influence in the Third World with economic and military assistance. In this context, the Third World was also consolidating its power as a third force in world politics through the formation of the Non-Aligned Movement (NAM). In this political context President Truman identified the postcolonial states as "underdeveloped" countries, requiring access to Western largesse. This decree licensed the mid-twentieth-century global development project, facilitating the expansion of liberal capitalism and the application of the GDP price metric to measure national economic growth.

The transformation of material relations into commodities is represented in pricing. As Karl Marx pointed out, even human labor-power came to be commodified, as villagers lost their means of livelihood and were forced to work for monetary wages.[48] Karl Polanyi extended this observation to land and currency, noting that with the rise of nineteenth-century market society each of these substances came to be traded for a price. He argued that neither labor nor land nor money was *produced for sale*, and so they were really "fictitious commodities." When they are treated as commodities, workers, farmers, and firms are exposed to exploitative or uncertain conditions (as experienced in the 2008 world financial/debt crisis). That is, their labor, farming, or business is subject to competitive relations beyond their control by a market with seemingly independent authority. Accordingly, *social countermovements inevitably arise and advocate for protection from unregulated markets*.[49] This kind of "double movement" is definitive of the market system, where commodity relations appear to govern social relations, and people push back, as we see today across the world with a diverse range of mobilizations against wage stagnation, deteriorating commercial environments, austerity politics, and minority marginalization.

Such pushback defined the twentieth-century interwar period, marked by widespread economic depression and disorder, generating communist, labor union, and fascist interventions for market regulation. The eventual defeat of fascism, and containment of Russia, enabled progressive forms of social protection in postwar Western welfare/development states, regulating markets as the development project took hold. Notably, however, the development project did not facilitate such protective measures for communities in the global South. Today, countermovements, both left and right, are again in play for social protection from the market crises of the globalization project, as it produces labor precarity and migrant labor streams, ecosystem breakdown, and financial corruption in both private and public sectors. Notably, in 2019, the *Human Development Report* noted,

> The wave of demonstrations sweeping across countries is a clear sign that, for all our progress, something in our globalized society is not working . . . A connecting thread is deep and rising frustration with inequalities. . . . Too often, inequality is framed around economics, fed and measured by the notion that making money is the most important thing in life.[50]

The Projects as Historical Framework

This book frames the development story around three projects: colonialism, development, and globalization, with a sustainability project possible emerging. Each project models a specific kind of development as political-economic and environmental conditions transform. For example, the transition from development project to globalization project was provoked by increasingly powerful business and financial interests and their political allies engaging in a "countermovement" from above, to protect their expanding global markets from public regulations. This was accomplished with policies of market deregulation in the name of "globalization," legitimized by neoliberal economic theory. That countermovement pendulum swings the other way as social mobilization from below responds to economic destabilization and intensification of social inequalities as markets have largely escaped social controls.[51]

The current market malaise and combination of crises—food, energy, climate, social—suggest the world may transition toward another project, which we would term a *sustainability project*. The dynamic that links these projects and accounts for their succession can be thought of as a series of Polanyian "double movements" inflected with struggles for racial and gender justice: politicization of market rule (for or against) via social mobilization. The colonial project, accompanying the rise of capitalist markets, yielded to the development project, as social and decolonization countermovements challenged the ascendancy of the market in their respective territories. Then the development project yielded to a globalization project installed by a global power elite to restore market sway and *reduce* the power of states and citizens to the status of facilitators and consumers, respectively.

Currently, the crisis of the globalization project (see Chapter 6) stimulates a wide range of sustainability initiatives at all scales, geared to reducing environmental degradation and climate warming. How these may coalesce into some kind of world ordering is not yet clear. Whether we will see a more authoritarian world order built on energy and climate security claims or some decentralized, ecologically based social organization is among the possibilities informing debate. In the meantime, we can situate our condition via some "development coordinates."

The Development Experience

Contrary to the idealized version of development, which suggests Western citizens enjoy living standards that are the goal and envy of the rest of the world, the West appears to be "undeveloping," as jobs have relocated to the regions in the global South, as northern public infrastructure decays, as social services such as education and health care dwindle, and as ecosystems degrade. From this perspective, development does not look like a linear process.

In redistributing jobs to lower-wage regions, transnational firms enhance profitability and northern consumers with incomes enjoy access to low-cost goods produced offshore. In this sense, development is identified, for its beneficiaries, as consumption. This, of course, corresponds with Rostow's idealized final growth stage and not as the unequal *global relationship* it always was. Much of what we consume today has global origins. Even when a product has a domestic "Made in . . ." label, its journey to market probably combines components and labor from production and assembly sites located around the world. Sneakers, or parts thereof, might be produced in Indonesia or China, blue jeans assembled in the Philippines, a smartphone assembled in Singapore, a watch made in Hong Kong, and clothing in Kenya. The British savor organic vegetables from western China, the Chinese eat pork fed with South American soy, and North Americans consume fast foods that may include chicken diced in Mexico or hamburger beef from cattle raised in Costa Rica. Coffee is from Southeast Asia, the Americas, or Africa. We readers may not be *global citizens* yet, but we are certainly *global consumers.*

But global consumers are still a relative minority of the world's population, consuming the vast majority of global goods and services.[52] Over three billion people cannot, or do not, consume in the Western style. Uruguayan writer Eduardo Galeano observes,

> Advertising enjoins everyone to consume, while the economy prohibits the vast majority of humanity from doing so . . . . This world, which puts on a banquet for all, then slams the door in the noses of so many, is simultaneously equalizing and unequal: equalizing in the ideas and habits it imposes and unequal in the opportunities it offers.[53]

It is important also to note that while readers may be accustomed to a commercial culture and view it as the development "standard," other cultures and peoples are not (as) comfortable with commercial definition or are simply marginal (by choice or circumstance) to commercial life.

Nevertheless, the global marketplace binds consumers, producers, and even those marginalized by resource consumption. Consumers everywhere are surrounded, and often identified, by world products. The global economy is a matrix of networks of commodity exchanges, organized in a variety of cross-border chains. In any one network, there is a sequence of production stages, located across a number of countries at sites that provide inputs of labor and materials contributing to the fabrication of a final product. These networks are called **commodity chains** or supply chains. The chain metaphor illuminates the interconnections among producing communities dispersed across the world. And it allows us to understand that, when we consume a product, we often participate in a global process linking us to a variety of places, people, and resources. iPhones, for example, assembled in China, have used components produced across a network of countries, including Japan, South Korea, Singapore, Taiwan, Switzerland, and the Netherlands. Workers in these sites often have little security or few rights, as they constitute important but undervalued links in these chains stretching across an often unregulated global workplace, here conceptualized as "poverty chains."[54] Although we may experience consumption individually, it is a fundamentally social and environmental act realized through unequal relations. Not only does it bind us to producers elsewhere, but those producers may be disadvantaged by exporting potential local resources.

Global agribusiness, for example, transports food (or biofuels) to the global market, undermining local possibilities for food security. Supplying global consumers rather than improving local conditions is extroverted rather than introverted as in the Rostow schema. Globalization deepens development paradoxes by virtue of its sheer scale. Integrating the lives of consumers and producers across the world does not necessarily mean sharing the benefits of development globally. The distance between consumers and producers and their environments means it is virtually impossible for consumers to recognize the impact of their consumption on people and environments elsewhere.

CONCLUSION

In sum, this opening chapter introduces the multiple dimensions of development as a historically relational process. We connect to the world in multiple ways, with development organizing our lives and our thoughts and aspirations. Though we are its participants and agents, we are not its principal architects. The architects are the power brokers in state administrations, international organizations, and corporate/financial circles, in addition to a powerful discourse idealizing the market as natural and a neutral source of material benefits. This is why markets do not just appear; rather, they are instituted, enabled, and gamed by powerful interests. In this moment, such "market rule" is very much in contention, precisely because of deepening global inequalities and the climate emergency. As stated in the World Bank's *International Assessment of Agricultural Science and Technology for Development* 2008 report, "markets fail to adequately value social and environmental harm."[55] In other words, *externalizing* the market's unequal social impacts and related ecological footprints means human well-being takes a back seat to living standards measured in market values. *Well-being* has two distinctive meanings. Indian economist/philosopher Amartya Sen argues that development should pivot on a quality intrinsic to individuals, that the "appropriate 'space' is neither that of utilities (as claimed by welfarists), nor that of primary goods . . . but that of substantive freedoms—the capabilities—to choose a life one has reason to value."[56] Whereas this assumes individual agency, alternatively, the Spanish American term *buen vivir* ("living well"), derived primarily from Indigenous visions of well-being, promotes community, subordinating economy to ecology and human dignity.

Viewing development as a paradox encourages evaluation of how development is represented, how it works, and how it plays out, across disparate spaces. This is particularly so, given the looming threats to human and planetary health, over and above the automation of jobs and continuing socioeconomic inequalities.

Ultimately, it is important to link local effects and global context in such a way as to see the global in the local and vice versa. While development is conventionally assumed and measured as a national process, its coordinates are worldwide, and this has been so from the colonial era onward. Disconnecting European development from colonialism obscures its global history and transfer of wealth from exploited colonial subjects. Development, therefore, is more complex than its conventional measure (GDP). It comprises power relations that are always contested in one way or another.

Finally, development is not the same across time. We address this by identifying its projects as expressing particular world ordering by a dominant set of norms, practices, and instituted policies. The projects embody differential effects across space, as depicted in case studies of local impacts and initiatives, including resistances. In this sense, development is uneven within and among societies. It has been, and remains, contentious. This book illuminates this by emphasizing development paradoxes, offering a global perspective on development controversies, and enabling a more relational historical understanding.

KEY TERMS

Colonial project
Coloniality
Commodity chains
Countermovements
Decolonization
Dependency analysis
Development paradox
Development project
Development states
Environmentalist's paradox

First World
Global Green New Deal (GGND)
Global North
Global South
Globalization project
Privatization
Second World
Sustainability project
Third World
Underdevelopment
World division of labor
World-system analysis

FURTHER READING

Escobar, Arturo, Michal Osterwil, and Kriti Sharma. *Relationality: An Emergent Politics of Life Beyond the Human*. London: Bloomsbury, 2024.

Esteva, Gustavo, Salvatore Babones, and Philipp Babcicky. *The Future of Development: A Radical Manifesto*. Bristol, UK: Policy Press, 2013.

Galeano, Eduardo. *Upside Down: A Primer for the Looking-Glass World*. New York: Picador, 2000.

Kothari, Ashish, Ariel Salleh, Arturo Escobar, Federico Demaria, and Alberto Acosta, eds. Pluriverse. *A Post-Development Dictionary*. New Delhi: Tulika Books, 2019.

Patel, Raj, and Jason Moore. *History of the World in Seven Cheap Things. A Guide to Capitalism, Nature and the Future of the Planet*. Berkeley: University of California Press, 2017.

Prashad, Vijay. *The Poorer Nations: A Possible History of the Global South*. London: Verso, 2014.

Sen, Amartya. *Development as Freedom*. New York: Knopf, 1999.

Shilliam, Robbie. *Decolonizing Politics: An Introduction*. Cambridge: Polity Press, 2021.

Weber, Heloise, ed. *The Politics of Development: A Survey*. London: Routledge, 2014.

Wilson, Kalpana. *Race, Racism and Development: Interrogating History, Discourse and Practice*. London: Zed Books, 2012.

SELECT WEBSITES

Global Exchange: www.globalexchange.org

New Internationalist: www.newint.org

UNDP Human Development Reports: http://hdr.undp.org/en/

World Bank, World Development Report: https://www.worldbank.org/en/publication/wdr/wdr-archive

PART I

THE DEVELOPMENT PROJECT (LATE 1940s TO EARLY 1970s)

2 CONTEXTUALIZING THE DEVELOPMENT PROJECT

Colonialism, Anticolonial Struggles, and Decolonization

In this chapter we reconstruct and examine the historical relations that underpinned the emergence and consolidation of the post-1945 development project. We show that this project can only be adequately understood when examined in relation to the project of *colonialism*. European colonization of the non-European world significantly transformed social, political, cultural, economic, and ecological relations. It entailed the devaluing of other ways of knowing and being as it violently instituted Eurocentric conceptions of modernity and modernization. The disruptions and dislocations that were extended through the project of *colonialism* included genocidal violence, enslavement, the forced displacement of populations, the introduction of reservations, plantation monocultures, and ecological despoliation. Colonizers justified violence and exploitation inherent in this project claiming civilizational hierarchy, underpinned by racist ideas.[1] The colonial project rested on claims to moral authority and to advanced knowledge (epistemic superiority), alongside unremitting violence. This violence of colonialism was absent in the official and formal framing of the post-1945 development project.

The absenting of colonial violence from the formulation of the post-1945 development project was a deeply problematic abstraction: communities in former colonies, but also among the former colonizers, have been acutely aware of this abstraction and its legacies and implications. In 2020 this came once more into the limelight in the context of the Black Lives Matter movement and campaigns over monuments, museums, and exhibitions. Questions of race and the legacies of the project of *colonialism* are thus still central in struggles and contestations over relations of development today.[2]

COLONIALISM

Our appeal to history begins with a critical account of colonialism and the explicit and implicit justifications upon which it rested. Eurocentric racist premises served as a central justification of colonization, underpinning the idea that Europeans were more advanced technologically, morally, and ethically.[3] This assumption not only disregarded advanced scientific knowledge of other civilizations[4] but importantly rested on a "normative inversion" about claims to morality and ethical predispositions.[5] Thus, while colonialism often entailed barbaric acts of genocidal violence and enslavement, the colonizers justified such acts by framing the colonized as "barbarians" and uncivilized. This *inversion* was a key political strategy of the colonial project, and it has continued to shape institutional thinking and practices through the four projects we reconstruct. (*Colonialism* is defined and explained in the "What Is Colonialism?" box, and the European colonial empires are depicted in Figure 2.1.)

FIGURE 2.1 ■ European Colonial Empires at the Turn of the Twentieth Century

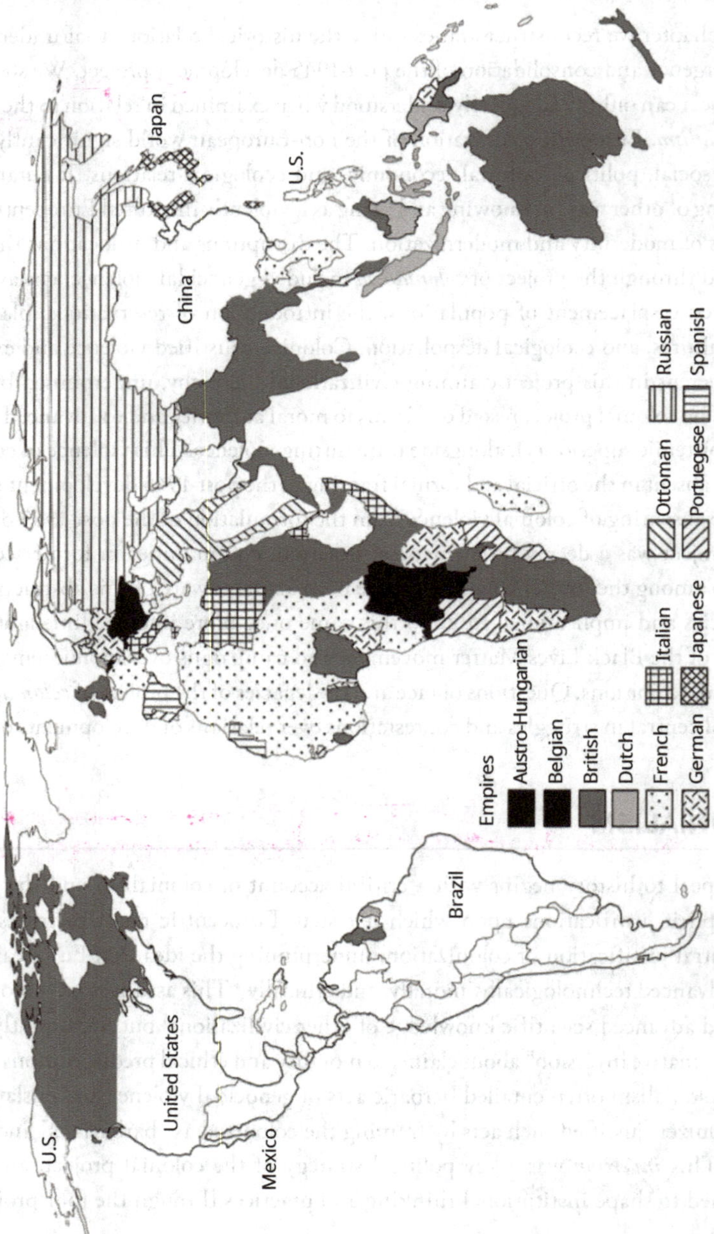

WHAT IS COLONIALISM?

Colonialism is the subjugation by physical and psychological force of one culture or race by another—a colonizing power—through military and economic conquest of territory and stereotyping the subordinated culture. It includes the era of European expansion (from the fifteenth century to the twentieth century) and extends to Japanese colonialism in the twentieth century and, most recently, Chinese occupation of Tibet and Israeli occupation of Palestinian territory. Colonialism was justified through the devaluing of other cultures and ways of being and rested on racist ideology and tropes of "backwardness" of the colonized. It took two forms: settler colonies, often genocidal against Indigenous people (such as the Spanish destruction of the Aztec and Inca civilizations in the Americas); and colonies of rule, where colonial administrators reorganized existing cultures by imposing new inequalities to facilitate their exploitation. Examples of the latter were the British creating local landlords, *zamindars*, to rule parts of India; confiscating personal and common land for cash cropping; depriving women of their customary resources; and elevating ethnoracial differences, such as privileging certain castes or tribes in the exercise of colonial rule. Implications are, first, the cultural genocide or marginalization of Indigenous people; second, the introduction of new tensions around class, gender, race, and caste that shape postcolonial societies; third, the extraction of labor, cultural treasures, and resources to enrich the colonial power, its private interests, and public museums; and fourth, responses by colonial subjects, ranging from internalization of inferiority to practices of resistances—from everyday forms to sporadic uprisings to mass political mobilization.

Such a powerful normative inversion, and the devaluing of other cultures, appears frequently in historical accounts. It is reflected in assumptions made by settlers about Indigenous people they encountered in the Americas and Australasia. Europeans perceived Native Americans and Aboriginal Australians as people who did not "work" the land they inhabited. Consequently, for European colonizers the native populations had no right of "property"—a European concept in which property is private and alienable. This was a powerful self-justification that disregarded centuries of Indigenous custodianship of nature and elaborate systems of law, diplomacy, and justice.[6] Their displacement from their ancestral lands is a bloody reminder of the combined military power and racism with which the European powers pursued colonization.

In precolonial Africa, communities relied on ancestral ecological knowledge and Earth-centered cosmologies to sustain themselves and their environment. These methods were at once conservative and adaptive because, over time, African communities changed their composition, scale, and location in a long process of settlement and migration through the lands south of the equator. European colonists in Africa, however, framed these as superstitious cultures, as static, and as only occupying, rather than improving, the land. Such perceptions denigrated and disregarded the complex social and political systems Africans had created in their exchanges with local ecology.[7] In these contexts, Europeans viewed themselves as bringing civilization to the nonwhite races. French historian Albert Sarraut, ignoring non-European inventions such as gunpowder, the compass, the abacus, moveable type printing, and the saddle, claimed,

> It should not be forgotten that we are centuries ahead of them, long centuries during which—slowly and painfully, through a lengthy effort of research, invention, meditation and intellectual progress aided by the very influence of our temperate climate—a magnificent heritage of science, experience, and moral superiority has taken shape, which makes us eminently entitled to protect and lead the races lagging behind us.[8]

The ensuing colonial exchange was captured in the postcolonial African saying, "When the white man came, he had the Bible and we had the land. When the white man left, we had the Bible and he had the land." Under colonialism, when non-Europeans lost control of their land, their spiritual life was compromised not least insofar as it was connected to their landscapes. It was difficult to sustain material and cultural integrity under these degrading extractive processes and conditions. At the same time, European colonization of nature converted land, water, cultivars, and food into economic categories, discounting their complex regenerative capacities and ecological interdependencies.

The systematic oppression of non-Europeans has remained largely unacknowledged, just as non-European scientific, ecological, and moral achievements, and their impact on European culture, were generally ignored or denied. At the same time it is important to note that *despite* the dominance and oppressive force of European colonialism, resilience and resistance were cultivated among the colonized, including through transnational networks.[9]

WHAT ARE SOME CHARACTERISTICS OF PRECOLONIAL CULTURES?

All precolonial cultures had their own ways of satisfying their material and spiritual needs. Cultures varied by the differentiation among their members or households according to their particular ecological endowments and social contact with other cultures. They ranged from small communities of subsistence producers, who lived off the land or the forest, to extensive kingdoms or states. Subsistence producers, organized by kin relations, usually subdivided social tasks between men, who hunted and cleared land for cultivation, and women, who cultivated and processed crops, harvested wild fruits and nuts, and performed household tasks. These cultures were highly skilled in resource management and production to satisfy their material needs. They generally did not produce a surplus beyond what was required for their immediate needs, and they organized cooperatively. By contrast, the Mogul empire in seventeenth-century India had a complex hierarchical organization, based on local chiefdoms in which the chief presided over the village community and ensured that surpluses (monetary taxes and produce) were delivered to a prosperous central court and "high culture." Village and urban artisans produced a range of metal goods, pottery, and crafts, including sophisticated muslins and silks. Caste distinctions, linked to previous invasions, corresponded to divisions of labor, such as trading, weaving, cultivating, ruling, and performing unskilled labor. Colonizers typically adapted such social and political hierarchies to their own ends, alienating Indigenous cultures from their natural ecologies and their political systems from their customary social functions, incubating tensions that have been inherited by postcolonial states. It is important to note that Indigenous communities across the world have been engaged in processes of retrieval of cultural practices, languages, and knowledges and in practices of resistance.

Sources: Bujra (1992); Coulthard (2014); Rowley (1974); Watson (2015).

The Colonial Division of Labor

From the sixteenth century, European colonists and traders traveled along African coasts to the New World and across the Indian Ocean and the China seas, seeking fur, precious metals, labor (including through enslavement), spices, tobacco, cacao, potatoes, sugar, and cotton. The principal European colonial powers—Spain, Portugal, Holland, France, and Britain—and their merchant companies exchanged manufactured goods such as cloth, guns, and implements for these products and for Africans taken into enslavement and transported to the Americas. In the process, they reorganized the world.

The basic pattern was to establish in the colonies specialized extraction of raw materials and production of primary goods that were unavailable in Europe. In turn, these products fueled European manufacturing as industrial inputs and foodstuffs for its industrial labor force. On a world scale, this unequal specialization between European economies and their colonies came to be termed the **colonial division of labor** (see Figure 2.2).

While the colonial division of labor stimulated European industrialization, it forced non-Europeans into primary commodity production. Specialization at each end of the exchange set in motion a transformation of social and environmental relationships, underpinned by a relocation of resources and energy from colony to metropolis: an unequal ecological exchange.[10] This captures the practice of indebted countries of the global South producing agricultural monocultures (with imported chemicals and fertilizers) for exports to the global North. Consequently, in parts of the global North it *appears* that the pressures on the natural environment have abated, when such abatement comes at the expense of ecological destruction in the global South.

FIGURE 2.2 ■ Distinguishing Between an International and a National Division of Labor

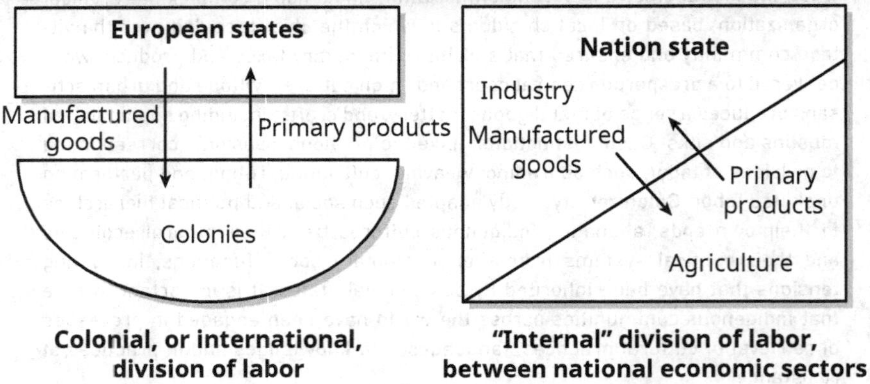

Through the colonial division of labor, non-European cultures and ecologies were subjected to profound disorganization, as colonies were reorganized to serve primarily as supply zones of labor and resources. Local crafts and mixed farming systems were undermined, alienating land and forests for commercial exploitation and rupturing the ecological balance. Not only were non-European cultures forced to surrender their handicraft industries in this exchange, but also their agriculture was often reduced to a specialized **export monoculture**, where local farmers produced a single crop, such as peanuts or coffee, for export, or plantations (sugar, cotton, tea, rubber, bananas) were imposed on land expropriated from those who were consequently forced to become plantation laborers. Systems of export agriculture interrupted centuries-old patterns of diet and cultivation, creating the all-too-familiar commercial food economy, in which "what was grown became disconnected from what was eaten, and for the first time in history, money determined what people ate and even if they ate."[11]

Handicraft decline was often deliberate and widespread. Perhaps the best-known destruction of native crafts occurred through Britain's conquest of India. Until the nineteenth century, Indian cotton muslins and calicos were luxury imports into Europe (as were Chinese silks and satins). By that time, however, the East India Company (which ruled India for the British Crown until 1858) undermined this Indian craft and, in its own words, "succeeded in converting India from a manufacturing country into a country exporting raw produce."[12] The company had convinced the British government to use tariffs of 70 percent to 80 percent against Indian finished goods and to permit virtually free entry of raw cotton into England. In turn, British traders flooded India with cheap cloth manufactured in Manchester. Industrial technology (textile machinery and the steam engine) combined with political power to impose the colonial division of labor, as British-built railway systems moved Indian raw cotton to coastal ports for shipment to Liverpool and returned across India selling machine-made textiles—and undermining a time-honored craft.

THE COLONIAL DIVISION OF LABOR AND UNEQUAL ECOLOGICAL EXCHANGE

The ecological dimension of the colonial division of labor reminds us that industrialism is premised on transforming nature from a regenerative system to mere "raw material." Prior to industrial society and colonialism, the majority of humans depended on their local ecosystem to supply their various needs via a multiplicity of locally produced materials, harvesting just what was necessary. Overharvesting resources wastes energy, reducing an ecosystem's capacity and thereby threatening the sustainability of the human community. The colonial division of labor depended on overharvesting.

For instance, the early Portuguese colonists, enslaving Indigenous labor, extracted luxury goods from the Amazon, such as cacao, rosewood, spices, caimans, and turtle eggs—all of which had high value-to-volume ratios in European markets. Wealthy Europeans prized turtle oil for perfume and lighting their lamps, but wasteful harvesting of turtle eggs for the oil severely depleted protein supplies and Amazonian aquatic environments on which populations depended for their material reproduction.

By the nineteenth century, European and North American extraction focused on industrial inputs such as rubber, further disrupting Amazonian habitats and ecology and exposing local industry to competition from commodities imported cheaply in the ample cargo space on the return leg of the rubber transport ships. As demand for rubber intensified later in the century, rubber plantations were established in Southeast Asia and Africa, by the British and the Americans, respectively, in turn transforming those ecologies by introducing monocultures and also impoverishing the Amazonian economy as feral rubber extraction declined.

What are the consequences of the developmentalist focus on trade merely in terms of exchange of commodities, ignoring the unjust human relations as well as the exchange with nature?

Sources: Bunker and Ciccantell (2005: 34–47); Sheller (2003: 81); E. Wolf (1982).

Social Reorganization under Colonialism

The colonial division of labor devastated producing communities and their craft- and agriculture-based systems. When the British first came to India in the mid-eighteenth century, Robert Clive described the textile city of Dacca as "extensive, populous, and rich as the city of London." By 1840, Sir Charles Trevelyan testified before a British parliamentary committee that the population of Dacca "has fallen from 150,000 to 30,000, and the jungle and malaria are fast encroaching upon the town . . . . Dacca, the Manchester of India, has fallen off from a very flourishing town to a very poor and small town."[13]

While native industries declined under colonial systems, local farming cultures lost their best lands to commercial agriculture supplying European consumers and industries. Plantations and other kinds of cash cropping proliferated across the colonial world, producing specialized tropical exports ranging from bananas to peanuts, depending on local agroecologies (see Table 2.1). Non-European societies were fundamentally transformed through the loss of resources and craft traditions, as colonial subjects were forced to labor in mines, fields, and plantations to produce exports sustaining distant European factories. Enslaved persons, peasants, and laborers in the colonies provisioned European industrial classes with cheap colonial products, such as sugar, tea, tropical oils, and cotton for clothing. The legacy of this relationship continues today. For example, in 2018 Mali (ranked 184 out of 189 on the UN **Human Development Index**) derived half of its export revenues from cotton, with 40 percent of its population depending on this crop for their livelihoods, but the country is in unequal competition with highly subsidized cotton producers in the United States, the European Union, and China.[14]

TABLE 2.1 ■ Selected Colonial Export Crops

Colony	Colonial Power	Export Crop
Australia	Britain	Wool, wheat
Brazil	Portugal	Sugar, coffee
Congo	Belgium	Rubber, ivory
Egypt	Britain	Cotton
Ghana	Britain	Cocoa
Haiti	France	Sugar
India	Britain	Cotton, opium, tea
Indochina	France	Rice, rubber
Indonesia	Holland	Rubber, tobacco
Côte d'Ivoire	France	Cocoa
Kenya	Britain	Coffee, tea, sisal
Malaya	Britain	Rubber, palm oil
Senegal	France	Peanuts
South Africa	Britain	Gold, diamonds

Colonial systems of rule focused on mobilizing labor from the colonized. For instance, a landed oligarchy (the hacendados) ruled South America before the nineteenth century in the name of the Spanish and Portuguese monarchies, using an institution called encomienda to create a form of native serfdom. Settler colonialism also spread to the Americas, Australasia, and southern Africa, where settlers used military force, legal constructs, and economic power to wrest land from the natives for commercial purposes, using enslaved, convict, and indentured labor.[15] As the industrial era matured, colonial rule (in Asia and Africa) grew in terms of organizational and administrative power. By the end of the nineteenth century, colonial administrations were financed by the colonized subaltern classes, with revenues collected through the use of military force, taxation (hut and poll taxes), and the loyalty of local princes and chiefs, tribes, and castes (note that the British presence, for example, never exceeded 0.5 percent of the Indian population).[16] Native rulers were also bribed with titles, land, or tax-farming privileges to recruit male peasants to the military and to force them into cash cropping to pay the taxes supporting the colonial state.

Male entry into cash cropping disrupted patriarchal gender divisions, creating new gender inequalities. Women's customary land-user rights were often displaced by new systems of private property, circumscribing food production, traditionally women's responsibility. For example, British colonialism in Kenya fragmented the Kikuyu culture as peasant land was confiscated and men were forced to migrate to work on European estates, reducing women's control over resources and lowering their status, wealth, and authority.[17]

In India, production of commercial crops such as cotton, jute, tea, peanuts, and sugar cane grew by 85 percent between the 1890s and the 1940s. In contrast, in that same period, local food crop production declined by 7 percent while the population grew by 40 percent, a shift that spread hunger, famine, and social unrest.[18] Using tax and irrigation policies to force farmers into export agriculture, Britain came to depend on India for almost 20 percent of its wheat consumption by 1900. Part of the reason that "Londoners were in fact eating India's bread" was the destruction of Indian food security by modern technologies, converting grain into a commodity. New telegraph systems transmitted prices set by London grain merchants, prying grain reserves from villages along railway networks for export to Britain. Thus, new global market technologies undermined the customary system of grain reserves organized at the village level as protection against drought and famine. For example, during the famine of 1899 to 1900, 143,000 peasants in Berar starved to death as the province exported tens of thousands of cotton bales in addition to 747,000 bushels of grain.[19] Starvation in the colonies was not simply due to conversion of resources into export commodities. British rule in India, for example, converted the "commons" into private property or state monopolies.

By the end of the 1870s, Britain had enclosed all Indian forests, previously communally managed. Ending communal access to grassland resources ruptured "the ancient ecological interdependence of pastoralists and farmers," and age-old practices of extensive crop rotation and long fallow, to replenish soils, declined with the expansion of cotton and other export monocrops.[20] Export monocultures displaced Indigenous irrigation systems with canals, which blocked natural drainage and thus exacerbated water salinity and pooled water in swamps, the perfect host environment for the dreaded malarial anopheline mosquito. A British engineer reported to the 1901 Irrigation Commission, "Canals may not protect against famines, but they may give an enormous return on your money."[21]

The colonial division of labor was organized to serve European capitalist societies (with food and raw materials) at the same time that it undermined non-European cultures and ecologies. As European industrial society matured, the rapidly increasing urban populations relied on ever-increasing imports of sugar, coffee, tea, cocoa, tobacco, and vegetable oils from the colonies, and the expanding factory system relied on ever-increasing inputs of raw materials such as cotton, timber, rubber, and jute, employing forced and enslaved labor.

As the trade in enslaved persons from Africa subsided, the Europeans created new schemes of forced, or indentured, labor. Indian and Chinese peasants and handicraftsmen, impoverished by colonial intervention or market competition from cheap textiles, were forced to move to sugar plantations in the Caribbean, Fiji, Mauritius, and Natal; to rubber plantations in Malaya and Sumatra; and to British East Africa to build the railways that intensified the two-way extraction of African resources and the introduction of cheap manufactured goods. In the third quarter of the nineteenth century alone, more than one million indentured Indians went overseas. Today, Indians still outnumber native Fijians; they also make up 50 percent of the Guyanese population and 40 percent of the residents of Trinidad. In the same period, 90,000 Chinese indentured laborers went to work in the Peruvian guano fields, and 200,000 went to California to work in the fruit industry, on the gold fields, and on the railways.[22] Displacement of groups and individuals from their societies and their dispersion to resolve labor shortages elsewhere in the colonial world have had a lasting global effect—notably in the African, Indian, and Chinese diasporas. This cultural mosaic undergirds modern expressions of race, ethnicity, and nationality. Either lack of awareness of this history and/or the continued prevalence of racism continues to generate ethnopolitical tensions that shape national politics across the world today and question the modern ideal of the secular state.

European exercise of power in the colonies revealed the hard edge of the modern state, premised on class structuring via racism, expressing the injustices and inequalities it engendered.[23] Such methods produced resistances among subject populations, whether laborers, peasants, soldiers, or civil servants. This resistance underpinned the politics of decolonization, dedicated to molding inchoate resistance to colonial abuses into coherent, nationalist movements striving for independence.

How Understanding the Colonial Project Unlocks a Development Puzzle

The colonial project was far-reaching and multidimensional in its effects. We focus here on rendering how the colonial project and the colonial division of labor helps us to come to grips with a development puzzle. Unless we account for structural inequalities created through colonialism and its enduring legacies, it is easy to take our unequal world at face value and view it as a natural continuum, accepting the narrative of the post-1945 development project that some states simply *are* "advanced," while others have to "catch up." Viewing world inequality as relational (unequally connected) rather than as sequential (catch-up) calls this conventional modern understanding of development into question. The conventional understanding is that individual societies experience or pursue development in sequence, on a "development ladder." If, however, industrial growth in Europe depended on agricultural monoculture in the non-European world, then development was more than simply a national process, even if represented as such. What we can conclude from the colonial project is that development historically depended on the unequal relationships of colonialism. This included an unequal and unjust division of labor and unequal ecological exchanges, both of which produced as a legacy the conditions of "underdevelopment" as well as the institutional conditions through which inequality would be sustained and reproduced in the colonial and postcolonial worlds.

DECOLONIZATION

Anticolonial resistance, though always present during colonialism across the Americas, Asia, and Africa, gained momentum and explicitly challenged the European colonial project. In the French sugar colony of Saint-Domingue, the late-eighteenth-century "Black Jacobin" revolt powerfully exposed its double standards. Turning the sovereignty rhetoric of the French Revolution successfully against French colonialism, the revolt of the enslaved from the sugar plantations became the first to achieve independence in the newly established nation of Haiti, sounding a massive warning to defenders of enslavement everywhere.[24]

Resistance to colonialism, while always present, gained increasing momentum across the next two centuries, from the early-nineteenth-century independence of the Latin American republics (from Spain and Portugal) to the dismantling of South African apartheid in the early 1990s. Although decolonization has continued into the present day (with the independence of East Timor in 2002 and the Kurds and Palestinians still struggling for a sovereign homeland), the worldwide decolonization movement peaked as European colonialism was successfully challenged in the mid-twentieth century, when World War II sapped the power of the French, Dutch, British, and Belgian states to withstand anticolonial struggles. The vehicle for decolonization became the *nation-state*, because committing to this offered the only pathway to formal political independence. Substantively, however, the sovereignty of independent states was somewhat compromised by the racial, cultural, and economic legacies of colonialism.

Anticolonial Struggle

Freedom included overcoming the social-psychological scars of colonialism. The racist legacy of colonialism penetrated the psyche of the colonist and the colonized and remains with us today. In 1957 at the height of African independence struggles, Tunisian philosopher Albert Memmi wrote *The Colonizer and the Colonized*, dedicating the American edition to the (colonized) American Negro. In this work (published in 1967), he claimed this:

> Racism . . . is the highest expression of the colonial system and one of the most significant features of the colonialist. Not only does it establish a fundamental discrimination between colonizer and colonized, a *sine qua non* of colonial life, but it also lays the foundation for the immutability of this life.[25]

In directly confronting this colonial system as described by Memmi, West Indian psychiatrist Frantz Fanon, writing from Algeria, responded with *The Wretched of the Earth*, a manifesto of liberation. It was a searing indictment of European colonialism and a call to people of the former colonies (the Third World) to transcend Eurocentric modernity and forge a new path for humanity. He wrote,

> It is a question of the Third World starting a new history of Man, a history which will have regard to the sometimes prodigious theses which Europe has put forward, but which will also not forget Europe's crimes, of which the most horrible was committed in the heart of man, and consisted of the pathological tearing apart of his functions and the crumbling away of his unity. . . . On the immense scale of humanity, there were racial hatreds, slavery, exploitation and above all the bloodless genocide which consisted in the setting aside of fifteen thousand millions of men. . . . Humanity is waiting for something other from us than such an imitation, which would be almost an obscene caricature.[26]

Decolonization was rooted in a liberatory upsurge, expressed in mass political movements of resistance. In Algeria (as in Palestine today), the independence movement incubated within and struck at the French occupation from the native quarter. Fanon provides detailed accounts of the violence directed against anticolonial struggle in Algeria, as well as the psychological hardships experienced by the native population (brilliantly portrayed in Gillo Pontecorvo's film, *Battle of Algiers*).

Other forms of resistance included militarized national liberation struggles (e.g., Portuguese African colonies, French Indochina) and widespread colonial labor unrest. British colonialism faced widespread labor strikes in its West Indian and African colonies in the 1930s, and this pattern continued over the next two decades in Africa as British and French colonial subjects protested conditions in cities, ports, mines, and on the railways.[27] In this context, development became configured by the colonizers as a pragmatic effort to preserve the colonies by improving material conditions. British Colonial Secretary MacDonald observed the following in 1940:

> If we are not now going to do something fairly good for the Colonial Empire, and something which helps them to get proper social services, we shall deserve to lose the colonies and it will only be a matter of time before we get what we deserve.[28]

Anticolonial resistance brought forth eloquent international appeals to justice in the language of rights and freedom by the representatives of colonized peoples. A new world order was in the making. From 1945 to 1981, 105 new states joined the United Nations (UN) as the colonial empires crumbled, swelling UN ranks from 51 to 156 (now 193). The reclaiming of political sovereignty by millions of non-Europeans (more than half of humanity) ushered in the era of development.[29] The idealism of the development era was reflected in the proclamation of equality as a domestic and international goal, informed by the UN Universal Declaration of Human Rights (1948).

The UN declaration represented a new world paradigm of fundamental human rights of freedom, equality, life, liberty, and security to all, without distinction by race, color, sex, language, religion, political opinion, national or social origin, property, birth, or other status. The declaration also included citizenship rights—that is, citizens' rights to the **social contract**: everyone was "entitled to realization, through national effort, and international co-operation and in accordance with the organization and resources of each State, of the economic, social and cultural rights indispensable for his dignity and the free development of his personality."[30]

THE TENSIONS AND LESSONS OF THE INDIAN NATIONALIST REVOLT

Mahatma Gandhi's model of nonviolent resistance to British colonialism affirmed the virtue of the ideal-typical premodern solidarities of Indian village life. Rather than embrace the emerging world of nation-states, Gandhi argued, didactically, that Indians became a subject population not only because of colonial force but also through the seduction of modernity. Gandhi's approach flowed from his philosophy of transcendental (as opposed to scientific or historical) truth, guided by a social morality. Gandhi disdained the violent methods of the modern state and the institutional rationality of the industrial age, regarding machinery as the source of India's impoverishment, not only in destroying handicrafts but in compromising humanity.

Gandhi's method of resistance included wearing homespun cloth instead of machine-made goods, avoiding use of the English language, and mistrusting the European philosophy of self-interest. Gandhi viewed self-interest as undermining community-based ethics and advocated the decentralization of social power, appealing to grassroots notions of self-reliance, proclaiming the following:

> Independence must begin at the bottom. Thus, every village will be a republic or panchayat having full powers. It follows, therefore, that every village has to be self-sustained and capable of managing its affairs even to the extent of defending itself against the whole world.

While Gandhi's politics, anchored in a potentially reactionary Hindu religious imagery, galvanized rural India, Indian nationalism actually rose to power via the Indian National Congress and one of its progressive democratic socialist leaders,

Jawaharlal Nehru. Nehru represented the formative national state, viewing the Gandhian philosophy as inappropriate to the modern world but recognizing its mobilizing power. Infusing the national movement with calls for land reform and agrarian modernization to complement industrial development, Nehru declared this:

> It can hardly be challenged that, in the context of the modern world, no country can be politically and economically independent, even within the framework of international interdependence, unless it is highly industrialized and has developed its power resources to the utmost.

Together, Gandhi and Nehru are revered as fathers of Indian independence and the Indian national state, respectively. Note that the struggle against empire was woven out of two strands: an *idealist* strand looking back and looking forward to a transcendental Hinduism anchored in village-level self-reliance, as well as a *realist* strand looking sideways and asserting that Indian civilization could be rescued, contained, and celebrated in the form of a modern state. (Hinduism today is expressed as a dominant right-wing ideology of Hindutva versus India's minority populations.)

Did Gandhi's and Nehru's opposing visions of development at the time of Indian independence foreshadow today's rising tension between sustainability and maximum economic growth?

Source: Chatterjee (2001: 86, 87, 91, 97, 144, 151).

DECOLONIZATION AND DEVELOPMENT

Decolonization gave development new meaning, linking it to the ideal of sovereignty, inclusive citizenship, and the pursuit of economic development for social justice. Already independent Latin American states adopted similar goals of state building via national education systems, national languages and currencies, and modern armies and voting citizens, though the franchise was not extended to Indigenous peoples in many contexts, as in the case of Peru. The ideology of development also informed the twentieth-century movements in Asia and Africa for decolonization, coinciding with the rise of the United States to global power and prosperity. Eager to reconstruct post–World War II Europe and to expand markets and the flow of raw materials, the United States led an international project, at the same time prefiguring development as a *national* enterprise to be repeated across a world of sovereign states, while strategically planning to ensure its own reliance on resources of the global South would not be undermined.

Despite relentless destruction of Native American cultures as the continent was claimed (*settler colonialism*), the revolt of the North American colonies against British colonialism in the late eighteenth century contributed to the United States' self-image as an "anticolonial" power. Once enslavement was abolished, the New South was incorporated into a national economic dynamic, articulating agricultural and industrial sectors. Figure 2.2 depicts the difference between the colonial and the national division between industry and agriculture.

The United States' model of development was premised on this national division of labor between industry and agriculture. Chicago traders, for instance, purchased midwestern farm products for processing, in turn selling machinery and goods to those farmers. This mutual prosperity of city and countryside is a *model*—that is, it *prescribes an ideal version*, even as foreign trade and investment continued. But it did industrialize agriculture as a series of specialized crops, requiring endless inputs of chemical fertilizers and hybrid seeds, with corrosive effects on soils and water cycles. The export of this developmental model of capital-intensive industrial farming has defined agricultural modernization, with global ecological consequences.[31] It is important to note that U.S. modernization and development continued to rely on raw materials procured through international trade, especially from the global South (postcolonial states). The foreign policy of the United States during that period reflected the preoccupation with securing access to these resources. To this end, its *internal* development concerns and policies were linked to *external* political-economic integration.[32]

POSTWAR DECOLONIZATION AND THE RISE OF THE THIRD WORLD

In the era of decolonization, the world came to be subdivided into three geopolitical segments. These subdivisions emerged after World War II (1939–1944) during the Cold War, dividing the capitalist Western (First World) from the Communist Soviet (Second World) blocs. The Third World included the postcolonial bloc of nations. Of course, there was considerable inequality across and within these subdivisions, as well as within their national units.

Ranged against the United States were the Soviet Union and contiguous Eastern European Communist states. This Second World was considered the alternative to First World capitalism. The Third World, the remaining half of humanity—most of whom were still food-growing rural dwellers but also workers on plantations as well as in some urban areas—was represented in economic language as impoverished and needing to catch up. Their conditions were not conventionally explained in terms of structural injustices of colonialism and its legacies.

Whereas the First World had 65 percent of world income with only 20 percent of the world's population, the Third World accounted for 67 percent of world population but only 18 percent of its income. Whereas some believe the gap in living standards between the First and Third Worlds registers differential rates of growth, others believe that much of it was a result of colonialism.[33] Still others are skeptical of distinguishing cultures via a uniform standard based on income levels, since non-Westernized cultures value non-cash-generating practices.

Seizing the moment as leader of the First World, President Harry S. Truman included in a key speech on January 20, 1949, the following proclamation:

> We must embark on a bold new program for making the benefits of our scientific advances and industrial progress available for the improvement and growth of underdeveloped areas. The old imperialism—exploitation for foreign profit—has no place in our plans. What we envisage is a program of development based on the concepts of democratic fair dealing . . . . Only by helping the least fortunate of its members to help themselves can the human family achieve the decent, satisfying life that is the right of all people. Democracy alone can supply the vitalizing force.[34]

The following year, a Nigerian nationalist voiced the following sentiments at a Union of Democratic Control conference, "The Crisis in Africa," in London:

> Self-government will not necessarily lead to a paradise overnight . . . . But it will have ended the rule of one race over another, with all the humiliation and exploitation which that implies. It can also pave the way for the internal social revolution that is required within each country.[35]

The latter sentiments express a different set of concerns from Truman's. President Truman's paternalistic proclamation articulated a new paradigm for the postwar era: the division of humanity into developed and undeveloped regions. This division of the world projected a singular destiny for all nations. Mexican intellectual Gustavo Esteva commented,

> Underdevelopment began, then, on January 20, 1949. On that day, two billion people became underdeveloped. In a real sense, from that time on, they ceased being what they were, in all their diversity, and were transmogrified into an inverted mirror of others' reality: a mirror that defines their identity . . . simply in the terms of a homogenizing and narrow minority.[36]

In other words, the proclamation by President Truman divided the world between those who were modern and those who were not. *Development/modernity* became the discursive benchmark. Note how this directly leads to a *disarticulation* of the historical (colonial) underpinnings of pre-WWII world inequality and injustices, a problem we discussed earlier.

Through this framing, First World power and privilege were inscribed within the new institutional structure of the postwar international economy. In the context of the Cold War between First and Second Worlds (for the hearts and resources of the ex-colonial world), development was simultaneously the restoration of a capitalist world market to sustain First World wealth, through access to strategic natural resources, and the opportunity for Third World countries to emulate First World civilization and living standards. Because development was both a blueprint for the world of nation-states *and* a strategy for world order, we call this enterprise the **development project.** The epithet *project* emphasizes the political content of development, as a global organizing principle. It also underlines the self-referential meaning of development, as defined by those with the means to make the dominant institutional rules.

The power of the new development paradigm arose in part from the way in which it was framed and presented as universal, "natural," and "scientific"— obliterating its colonial roots. By acknowledging the colonial roots of European and Western development, a just response would have seen a commitment to redressing the colonial division of labor, as well as working toward repairing the injustices through which it was realized. It would have also provided the opportunity to embark on alternative, more humane development projects as called for by Frantz Fanon and other anticolonial thinkers and activists. Instead, the presentation of the post-1945 development project in terms of an aura of inevitability once more devalued non-European cultures and discounted what the West learned and could have learned from the non-European world. Gilbert Rist observed of postcolonial states, "Their right to self-determination had been acquired in exchange for the right to self-definition,"[37] suggesting little choice but to choose the Western-centered future for the world. Of course, each state imparted its own particular style to this common agenda, drawing on regional cultures such as African socialism, Latin American bureaucratic authoritarianism, or Confucianism in East Asia. As we will see, these differences also comprised some (significant) resistance to the development project and its obliteration of colonialism and its legacies.

INGREDIENTS OF THE DEVELOPMENT PROJECT

The development project was a political and intellectual response to the condition of the world at the historic moment of decolonization. Here, development assumed a specific meaning. It imposed an essentially economic (reductionist) understanding of social change, universalizing an instrumental form of development across multiple cultures as a single market culture, driven by the nation-state and economic growth.

The Nation-State

The **nation-state** was to be the framework of the development project. Nation-states were territorially defined political systems based on the government–citizen relationship that emerged in nineteenth-century Europe. This political model (with its military shell) became the preeminent one, framing the politics of the decolonization movement, even where national boundaries made little sense. The UN Economic Commission for Africa, for example, argued in 1989 that the root causes of underdevelopment in Africa are "the colonial origins of African economies."[38] The following box illustrates the effects of these arbitrarily drawn boundaries.

HOW WAS AFRICA DIVIDED UNDER COLONIALISM?

The colonial powers inflicted profound damage on Africa, driving frontiers straight through the ancestral territories of nations. For example, a line was drawn through Somalia, separating off part of the Somali people and placing them within Kenya. The same was done splitting the great Maasai nation between Kenya and Tanzania. Elsewhere, of course, we created the usual artificial states. Nigeria consists of four principal nations: the Hausa, Igbo, Yoruba, and Fulani peoples. It has already suffered a terrible war, which killed hundreds of thousands of people and which settled nothing. Sudan, Chad, Djibouti, Senegal, Mali, Burundi, and of course Rwanda are among the many other states that are riven by conflict.

Source: Quoted from Goldsmith (1994: 57).

During the 1950s, certain leading African anticolonialists challenged the appropriateness of the nation-state form to postcolonial Africa. They knew that sophisticated systems of rule had evolved in Africa before colonialism. They advocated a pan-African federalism, whose territories would transcend the arbitrary borders drawn across Africa by colonialism.[39] However, decisions about postcolonial political arrangements were made in London and Paris where the colonial powers, looking to sustain spheres of influence, insisted on the nation-state as the only appropriate political outcome of decolonization. Indeed, a British Committee on Colonial Policy advised this to the prime minister in 1957:

> During the period when we can still exercise control in any territory, it is most important to take every step open to us to ensure, as far as we can, that British standards and methods of business and administration permeate the whole life of the territory.[40]

Economic Growth

The second ingredient of the development project was *economic growth*. A mandatory UN System of National Accounts institutionalized a universal quantifiable measure of national development. The UN Charter of 1945 proclaimed "a rising standard of living" as the global objective. This "material well-being" indicator is measured in the commercial output of goods and services within a country: capita gross national product (GNP), or the national average of per capita income. Although per capita income was not the sole measure of rising living standards (others included health, literacy, etc.), it has been the key criterion of measurable progress toward the "good society," popularized by U.S. presidential adviser Walt Rostow's idea of the advanced stage of "high mass consumption."[41]

In the minds of Western economists, precommitted to the problematic assumptions of Modernization Theory, Third World underdevelopment required a jump-start to realize development. Cultural practices of wealth sharing and cooperative labor—dissipating individual wealth but sustaining the community—were perceived as *traditional* and an obstacle to making the "transition" to development. The solution was to consolidate a market system based on private property and wealth accumulation. A range of modern practices and institutions designed to sustain economic growth, such as banking and accounting systems, education, stock markets, and legal systems, and public infrastructure (transport, power sources), was required.

The use of the *economic growth* yardstick of development, however, is fraught with problems. Average indices such as per capita income obscure inequalities among social groups and classes. Aggregate indices such as rising consumption levels in and of themselves are not accurate records of improvement in quality of life. Air conditioner use is measured as increased consumption, but it also releases harmful hydrocarbons into the warming atmosphere. Economic criteria for development have normative assumptions that often marginalize other criteria for evaluating living standards relating to the quality of human interactions, physical and spiritual health, and so on.

The emphasis on converting human interactions into measurable (and taxable) cash relations discounts the social wealth of nonmonetary activities (nature's processes, cooperative labor, and people growing their own food, performing unpaid household labor, and doing community service).

The *other* implication of the dominant approach to development is that it once more disarticulated the fact that the new states were not starting on a level playing field but instead had to deal with the impoverishing effects of decades or centuries of colonial expropriation.

FRAMING THE DEVELOPMENT PROJECT

Perhaps the most compelling aspect of the development project was a powerful perception by planners, governmental elites, and citizens alike that development was destiny. Both Cold War blocs understood development in these terms, even if their respective paths of development were different. Each bloc took its cue from key nineteenth-century thinkers. The West identified free-enterprise capitalism as the endpoint of development, based in Jeremy Bentham's utilitarian philosophy of the common good arising out of the pursuit of individual self-interest. Communist orthodoxy identified the abolition of private property and central planning as the goal of social development, deriving from Karl Marx's collectivist dictum: "From each according to their ability, and to each according to their needs."

Although the two political blocs subscribed to opposing representations of human destiny, they shared the same modernist paradigm. *National industrialization* would be the vehicle of development in each.

National Industrialization: Ideal and Reality

National industrialization had two key assumptions. First, it assumed that development involved the displacement of agrarian civilization by an urban-industrial society. For national development policy, this meant a deliberate shrinking of the agricultural population as the manufacturing and service sectors grew. It also meant the transfer of resources such as food, raw materials, and redundant labor from the agrarian sector as peasant livelihoods would be overcome and agricultural productivity grew. Industrial growth would ideally feed back into and technicize agriculture. These two national economic sectors would therefore condition each other's development, as in the U.S. case discussed earlier in this chapter and illustrated in Figure 2.2.

Second, the idea of national industrialization assumed a *linear direction* for development—for example, catching up with the West. Soviet dictator Joseph Stalin articulated this doctrine in the 1930s, proclaiming, "We are fifty or a hundred years behind the advanced countries. We must make good this distance in ten years. Either we do it or they crush us."[42] Stalin's resolve came from the pressures of military (and therefore economic) survival in a hostile world. The Soviet Union industrialized in one generation, "squeezing" the peasantry to finance urban-industrial development with cheap food.

Across the Cold War divide, industrialization symbolized success. Leaders in each bloc pursued industrial development to legitimize their power; the reasoning was that as people consumed more goods and services, they would subscribe to the prevailing philosophy delivering the goods and would support their governments. *In this sense, development is not just a goal; it is a method of rule.*

ECONOMIC NATIONALISM

Decolonization involved a universal nationalist upsurge across the Third World, assuming different forms in different countries, depending on the configuration of social forces in each national political system. Third World governments strove to build national development states—whether centralized like South Korea, corporatist like Brazil, or decentralized and populist like Tanzania. **The development state** organizes national economic growth by mobilizing money and people. It uses individual and corporate taxes, along with other government revenues, such as export taxes and sales taxes, to finance public transport systems and state enterprises, such as steel works and energy exploration. And it forms coalitions to support its policies. Elites within the state often use their power to accumulate wealth and influence in the state—whether through selling rights to public resources to cronies or capturing foreign-aid distribution channels. As Sugata Bose remarked of the Indian state, "Instead of the state being used as an instrument of development, development became an instrument of the state's legitimacy."[43] Either way, the development state was a central pillar of the postwar development era.

Import-Substitution Industrialization

Just as political nationalism was linked to consolidating sovereignty for Third World populations, so **economic nationalism** sought to reverse the colonial division of labor—as governments encouraged and protected domestic industrialization with tariffs and public subsidies, reducing dependence on primary exports ("resource bondage").

Economic nationalism was associated with Raul Prebisch, an adviser to the Argentine military government in the 1930s. During that decade's world depression, world trade declined and Latin American–landed interests lost political power, as shrinking primary export markets depleted their revenues. Prebisch proposed an industrial protection policy. Import controls reduced dependency on expensive imports of Western manufactured goods, shifting resources into domestic manufacturing.[44] This policy was adopted in the 1950s by the **UN Economic Commission for Latin America (ECLA)**, under Prebisch's lead as executive secretary.

Import-substitution industrialization framed initial economic development strategies in the Third World as governments subsidized "infant industries." The goal was a cumulative process of domestic industrialization. For example, a domestic automotive industry would generate parts for manufacturing, road building, service stations, and so on, in addition to industries such as steel, rubber, aluminum, cement, and paint. In this way, a local industrial base would emerge. Import-substitution industrialization became the new economic orthodoxy in the postwar era.[45]

To secure an expanding industrial base, Third World governments constructed political coalitions among different social groups to support rapid industrialization—such as the Latin American **development alliance**.[46] Its social constituency included commercial farmers, public employees, urban industrialists, merchants, and workers dependent on industrialization, organized into associations and unions. Policymakers used price subsidies and public services such as health and education programs, cheap transport, and food subsidies to complement the earnings of urban dwellers, attract them to the cause of national industrialization, and realize the *social contract*.

CONCLUSION

The idea of development emerged during, and within the terms of, the era of the *colonial project*. A problematic conception of a global hierarchy, resting also on the normative inversion discussed in this chapter, informed the understanding of development as a European achievement, disarticulating its colonial dimension. Colonialism was a violent project that expropriated non-European societies by reconstructing their labor systems around specialized, ecologically degrading export production and by disrupting the social psychology of colonial subjects. However, the colonial project could never be comprehensive, and this was reflected in everyday, as well as more organized, anticolonial resistance and political struggle, locally and transnationally.[47]

The political independence of the colonial world was countered by the institution of the *development project.* Third World states became independent, but they were collectively defined by Western political representatives and intellectuals as "underdeveloped." As we will see in the next chapter, the Third World constituted a new political force in world politics and worked collectively to redress the colonial division of labor.

The pursuit of rising living standards, via industrialization, inevitably promoted Westernization in political, economic, and cultural terms. Thus, the development project undercut Frantz Fanon's call for a non-European way, qualifying the sovereignty and diversity that often animated the movements for decolonization. It also undermined the pan-African insight into alternative political organization. These ideas and struggles over more just social and political relations could never be dissipated, though, and are reemerging, with increasing resonance even amid neoliberal development trajectories.

The next chapter examines the development project in action.

KEY TERMS

Colonial division of labor
Development alliance
development project
development state
Economic Commission for Latin America (ECLA)
Economic nationalism
Export monoculture
Human Development Index
Import-substitution industrialization
Nation-state
Social contract

FURTHER READING

Achebe, Chinua. *Things Fall Apart.* London: William Heineman, 1958.

Davis, Mike. *Late Victorian Holocausts: El Niño Famines and the Making of the Third World.* London: Verso, 2001.

Doty, Roxanne Lynn. *Imperial Encounters: The Politics of Representation in North-South Relations.* Minneapolis: University of Minnesota Press, 1996.

Escobar, Arturo. *Encountering Development: The Making and Unmaking of the Third World.* Princeton, NJ: Princeton University Press, 1995.

Fanon, Frantz. *The Wretched of the Earth.* Harmondsworth, UK: Penguin, 1967.

Getachew, Adom. *World Making After Empire: The Rise and Fall of Self-Determination.* Princeton, NJ: Princeton University Press, 2019.

Leys, Colin. *Underdevelopment in Kenya: The Political Economy of Neo-Colonialism.* Berkeley: University of California Press, 1975.

Memmi, Albert. *The Colonizer and the Colonized*. Boston: Beacon Press, 1967.

Mitchell, Timothy. *Colonizing Egypt*. Berkeley: University of California Press, 1991.

Shilliam, Robbie. *The Black Pacific: Anti-Colonial Struggles and Oceanic Connections*. London: Bloomsbury Academic, 2015.

Watson, Irene. *Aboriginal Peoples, Colonialism, and International Law: Raw Law*. London: Routledge, 2015.

3 THE DEVELOPMENT PROJECT

An International Framework in Global Context

The development project instituted in the post-1945 era was organized around the idea and practice of "national development," with the United States now as the hegemonic Western power. The pursuit of national development in this context was to be mediated through newly established international institutions, which became key sites of contestation over development. This is because the development project intersected with anticolonial struggles and post-1945 Cold War politics. With decolonization, the membership of the new states in international institutions and organizations, such as the United Nations, significantly altered international political dynamics and power relations.

A key challenge remained for postcolonial states: to bring about a just settlement to the legacies of colonial exploitation and expropriation, while charting more humane development pathways in the context of the emerging geopolitics of the Cold War between U.S.-led Western capitalism and the Soviet Union communist empire. Integral to this power conflict was access to non-Western postcolonial resources, and undermining local and national resistance and liberation struggles, thereby sustaining the colonial division of labor *after* the formal end of colonialism. At the same time, the United States and its allies sought to prevent newly independent (postcolonial) states from pursuing socialist or even "mixed" development models and aligning with the Soviet bloc.

In this chapter, we outline how these dynamics played out in the context of the institution of the development project. Throughout, we keep these dynamics in view, even though our primary focus is on the liberal approach advanced by the United States and its allies, which we discuss and summarize as the development project. This is not least because it was the institutionally dominant model. The development project reinforced international economic inequalities and put in place new constrictions on the development trajectory of the postcolonial states. Consequently, socioeconomic inequalities were sustained and reinforced, embedded in race, gender, and class relations.

We introduce and examine the development project. We concentrate in particular on the construction of the Bretton Woods system and how its multilateral arrangements shaped national development strategies and international political relations. We then briefly outline how the development project facilitated the conditions for the next phase: the globalization project. The term *globalization project* does not imply that development was only then becoming a global process; rather, it refers to its distinctive neoliberal dynamics and the paradoxes and contention it engenders.

THE DEVELOPMENT PROJECT: WHAT WERE ITS MAIN OBJECTIVES AND HOW WERE THEY REALIZED?

The development project was an internationally organized strategy for stimulating nationally managed economic growth. As colonialism was successfully challenged, political elites of newly independent states embarked on development programs to pursue inclusive growth, revenue generation, and legitimacy. This occurred in many ways in parallel with the rebuilding of economies and societies in post-WWII Europe (and East Asia) on the one hand, and what emerged as the Soviet bloc on the other. The two blocs of the Cold War associated development with modernization but pursued different political-economic models—one capitalist, the other socialist. Development served as an organizing concept with universal claims (e.g., development as rising living standards, rationality, and scientific progress). Broadly, whether socialist or capitalist, the pursuit of development was modeled on the following:

- A national framework for economic growth
- A formal comparative method that distinguished states in terms of "developing" (the new postcolonial states and the Soviet bloc) and "developed" (the Western states [former colonial powers])
- An international framework of aid (military and economic) binding the "developing" world to the "developed" world and securing continuing access to its natural and human resources
- A growth strategy favoring industrialization
- An agrarian reform strategy encouraging agro-industrialization
- Development-state initiatives to manage investment and mobilize multiclass political coalitions into a development alliance supporting industrial growth

THE DEVELOPMENT PROJECT: AN INTERNATIONAL FRAMEWORK FOR NATIONAL DEVELOPMENT

The development project was instituted on the basis of the strategic objectives of the United States and its allies. Following the severe 1930s depression and the devastation of World War II (1939–1945), the United States spearheaded two initiatives to reconstruct the world economy: the bilateral **Marshall Plan** with Europe and the multilateral **Bretton Woods** program. The development project emerged within the Marshall Plan and was formalized under the Bretton Woods program, but it did not become a full-fledged operation until the 1950s, the peak decade of what became referred to as Third World political independence.

U.S. Bilateralism: The Marshall Plan (Reconstructing the "First World")

In the post–World War II years, the United States focused on European reconstruction as the key to stabilizing the Western world and securing capitalism against the socialist bloc. European grain harvests in 1946 would reach only 60 percent of prewar levels. Scarcity of labor skills and certain goods depleted transport and communication networks. There was also a growing popular desire for social reform.[1] Returning from Europe in 1947, U.S. Assistant Secretary of State for Economic Affairs Will Clayton stated,

> Communist movements are threatening established governments in every part of the globe. These movements, directed by Moscow, feed on economic and political weakness. . . . The United States is faced with a world-wide challenge to human freedom. The only way to meet this challenge is by a vast new programme of assistance given directly by the United States itself.[2]

In these political circumstances, the United States hoped to use financial aid to stabilize discontented populations and rekindle economic growth in strategic parts of the world. Central to this strategy was containing communism—primarily in Europe, where the Soviet Union had laid claim to territories including what became (until 1989) East Germany (excluding West Berlin), but also in the Far East, where communism had gained ground, first in China and then in North Korea. The United States courted nations' allegiance to the Western free enterprise system with financial assistance. Hence, the Marshall Plan was a *bilateral* transfer of billions of dollars to Europe (and Japan). The plan restored trade and price stability and expanded productive work to undercut socialist movements and labor militancy. Dollar credits, allowing recipients to purchase U.S. goods, and a massive rearmament effort closely integrated these countries' economies with that of the United States, solidifying political loyalty to the Western "free world."

Europeans desired social peace and full employment, to be achieved through closely regulated national economies, but the U.S. government wanted an open world economy. The Marshall Plan solved this dilemma, using bilateral aid to facilitate international trade and encourage U.S. direct investment in European national economies.[3]

Multilateralism: The Bretton Woods System

The idea for an international bank was part of the plan to initially reconstruct Europe and then the world economy in the 1940s. Trade was to be restored by disbursing credit to regions devastated by war or colonialism. The famous July 1944 conference of 44 financial ministers at Bretton Woods, New Hampshire, provided the opportunity to create such an international banking system. Here, the U.S. Treasury steered the conference toward chartering the foundation of the "twin sisters": the **World Bank** (originally the International Bank for Reconstruction and Development [IBRD]) and the **International Monetary Fund (IMF)**.

Each institution was based on member subscriptions. The World Bank would match these subscriptions by borrowing in international capital markets to raise money for development (which was in turn provided to states with interest). The IMF was to disburse credit where needed to stabilize national currency exchanges.

The key functions of the Bretton Woods agencies in this context were

- to stabilize national finances and revitalize international trade (IMF),
- to underwrite national economic growth by funding Third World imports of First World infrastructural technologies, and
- to expand Third World primary exports to earn foreign currency for purchasing First World exports.

The World Bank's mandate was for large-scale loans to states for national infrastructural projects such as dams, highways, and power plants, complementing smaller-scale private and public investments. In its first 20 years, two-thirds of the World Bank's loans purchased inputs to build transportation and electric power systems. At the same time, the World Bank invested in large-scale cash crop agriculture, such as cacao, rubber, and livestock, deepening the legacy of the colonial division of labor.[4]

Expanded trade stimulated economic growth across the First World–Third World divide. These agencies disseminated the technologies of the development project, encouraging Third World states to adopt the capital-intensive methods of the West. Whereas Europe had taken several centuries to industrialize, significantly through colonial exploitation, Third World governments generally expected to industrialize rapidly with multilateral loans, substituting capital-intensive for labor-intensive production technologies despite substantial populations already displaced from their customary habitats.

The Bretton Woods system was unveiled as a universal and *multilateral* attempt to promote rising living standards on a global scale. Of the 44 nations in attendance at Bretton Woods, 28 were from the Third World. Nevertheless, the institutions had a decided First World imprint. First, the World Bank was, and is, controlled by its five largest First World shareholders. Second, the president of the World Bank is selected by the U.S. president, and the managing director of the IMF is appointed by the largest European nations (the United Kingdom, France, and Germany).[5] Third, the World Bank finances foreign exchange costs of approved projects, encouraging import dependence (in capital-intensive technologies) in development priorities. Finally, the IMF adopted a "conditionality" requirement (subsequently also adopted by the World Bank), requiring applicants to have economic policies that met certain criteria for them to obtain loans. International banks (including the World Bank) and other lenders inevitably adopted IMF conditionality as their criterion for Third World loans. In this way, Third World development priorities were tailored toward external (i.e., First World) evaluation and objectives.[6]

The World Bank emphasized "productive" investments, such as energy and export agriculture, rather than "social" investments, such as education, health services, water and sanitation facilities, and housing. In addition, it focused on investing in large-scale, capital-intensive projects that might, for example, have common technological inputs and similar appraisal mechanisms.[7] Not only has the World Bank sponsored Western **technology transfer**, but it has also established an *institutional presence* in Third World countries. When the World Bank finances infrastructural projects, these are often administered through agencies with semiautonomous financial and political power within host countries.

The World Bank has been the key multilateral agency responsible for underwriting Third World development. Overall, the World Bank framed development priorities via onsite project agencies and by encouraging large-scale power generation and transport projects, stimulating industrialization on a Western scale. It also channeled loans into intensive agriculture, requiring fossil fuel, energy-dependent technical inputs such as chemical fertilizers, pesticides, and hybrid seeds. And it created the Economic Development Institute in 1956 to train Third World officials (soon-to-be prime ministers or ministers of planning or finance in their own countries).[8]

In short, multilateralism, World Bank style, characterized the Bretton Woods system—World Bank policy set the parameters for development. Third World representatives found themselves more often than not forced to accede to them. When governments adopted redistributive policies, loan funds would shrink, trade would become constricted, and aid would be withheld. The structural power of the development project significantly circumscribed the ability of the decolonized states to shape their social and economic development. Nevertheless, there were concerted efforts to come together and call for transformations of international political relations to reflect a more just and equitable multilateralism.

Political Strategies and the Development Project

As the realm of free enterprise expanded, the political dynamics of the Cold War deepened. While the United States and the Soviet Union were busy attempting to divide the world, the countries of the Third World came together, asserting a collective political project in solidarist internationalism.[9] Here we explore the interplay of all these forces.

Foreign Aid

Cold War rivalry governed much of the political geography of the development project. The Soviet Union was expanding economic and political relations with Third World states, especially newly independent states in Asia and Africa. By 1964, the Soviet

Union had extended export credits to about 30 states, even though eight received the most aid. Under the Soviet aid system, loans could be repaid in local currencies or in the form of traditional exports, a program that benefited states short of foreign currency. Not only was the Soviet Union offering highly visible aid projects to key states such as Indonesia and India, but aid policies also clearly favored states pursuing policies of **central planning** and public ownership in their development strategies.[10]

For the United States and its First World allies, the development project was more than a transmission belt for Western technology and economic institutions. First World security was deemed to be at stake as long as Third World countries pursued plausible alternatives to realize security and development on their own terms. In 1956, this view was articulated clearly by Walt Rostow, the influential development economist and national security adviser to the U.S. president: "The location, natural resources, and populations of the underdeveloped areas are such that, should they become effectively attached to the Communist bloc, the United States would become the second power in the world."[11] The United States' foreign aid patterns between 1945 and 1967 confirm this view of the world.[12]

The Non-Aligned Movement and the Bandung Conference

Against this world ordering was an emerging bloc that came to be referred to as the Third World advocating a more independent vision. As decolonization proceeded, the composition of the United Nations shifted toward a majority of non-European member states. In 1955, the growing weight of the Third World in international politics produced the first meeting of "nonaligned" Asian and African states at Bandung, Indonesia. Both the Bandung conference (also referred to as the Asian-African Conference of 1955) and the final Bandung communiqué sent a powerful message globally. It called for an immediate end to colonialism and racism, celebrated the civilizational and cultural achievements of Asia and Africa, and committed to "work for closer cultural cooperation."[13] It also called for the stabilization of international commodity prices and recommended that they adopt (as far as possible) a unified position at the United Nations on commodity trade. This stance already reflected a challenge aimed at redressing the unjust colonial division of labor. Bandung also called for nuclear disarmament and human rights to be upheld. It was the first declaration on development, peace, and security that was underpinned by a sensibility of development that was not tied to economic growth or equality of opportunity. Rather, it reflected a commitment to a more humane alternative grounded in a sensibility of solidarist internationalism, which was a counterpoint to the liberal version. The final Bandung communiqué made a commitment to nonalignment during the Cold War.

The Bandung conference led to the forming of the **Non-Aligned Movement (NAM)** by 1961. Key players were the leaders of Yugoslavia (Tito), Indonesia (Sukarno), India (Nehru), Ghana (Nkrumah), North Vietnam (Ho Chi Minh),

Egypt (Nasser), and China (Zhou Enlai). The NAM used its collective voice in international fora to forge a political project centered on noninterference in international relations. President Nyerere of Tanzania articulated this position in terms of economic self-reliance:

> By non-alignment we are saying to the Big Powers that we also belong to this planet. We are asserting the right of small, or militarily weaker, nations to determine their own policies in their own interests, and to have an influence on world affairs. . . . At every point . . . we find our real freedom to make economic, social and political choices is being jeopardized by our need for economic development.[14]

The thrust of this statement, following the final Bandung communique, challenged the legitimacy of the model of development embedded in the multilateral institutional order. The first bone of contention was the paucity of multilateral loans. By 1959, the World Bank had lent more to the First World ($1.6 billion) than to the Third World ($1.3 billion). Third World members of the UN pressed for expanded loans, with concessions. The First World's response was to channel this demand toward the World Bank, where the International Development Association (IDA) was established to make loans at highly discounted rates (called "soft loans") to low-income countries. In addition, several regional banks were established, including the Inter-American Development Bank (IDB) in 1959, the African Development Bank (AfDB) in 1964, and the Asian Development Bank (ADB) in 1966.[15]

The Group of 77

International trade remained contentious. The **General Agreement on Tariffs and Trade (GATT)**, founded in 1947, enabled states to negotiate reciprocal trade concessions but without adjusting for the uneven effects of colonialism.[16] During the 1950s, the Third World's share of world trade fell from one-third to almost one-fifth, with declining rates of export growth and declining terms of trade.[17]

Third World political initiative led to the foundation of the **United Nations Conference on Trade and Development (UNCTAD)** in 1964—the first international forum in which Third World countries, caucusing as the **Group of 77 (G-77)**, collectively demanded world-economic reforms. They demanded stabilized and improved primary commodity prices (a concern already raised at the Bandung conference), opening First World markets to Third World manufacturers and provisions for technology and finance. This culminated in a United Nations Resolution for a **New International Economic Order (NIEO)** in the 1970s.

The NIEO was much more radical and explicit in its call for significant restructuring of the international economic order. Point 1 of the NIEO included the critical and explicit linking of the political economy structures established through colonialism and its enduring legacies in the postcolonial context.

FROM THE NIEO DECLARATION

The developing countries, which constitute 70 per cent of the world's population, account for only 30 per cent of the world's income. It has proved impossible to achieve an even and balanced development of the international community under the existing international economic order. The gap between the developed and the developing countries continues to widen in a system which was established at a time when most of the developing countries did not even exist as independent States and which perpetuates inequality.

Point 4 of the Declaration proclaimed the following:

Full permanent sovereignty of every State over its natural resources and all economic activities. In order to safeguard these resources, each State is entitled to exercise effective control over them and their exploitation with means suitable to its own situation, *including the right to nationalization or transfer of ownership to its nationals, this right being an expression of the full permanent sovereignty of the State.* No State may be subjected to economic, political or any other type of coercion to prevent the free and full exercise of this inalienable right;

The right of all States, territories and peoples under foreign occupation, alien and colonial domination or *apartheid to restitution and full compensation for the exploitation and depletion of, and damages to, the natural resources and all other resources of those States, territories and peoples*;

Just and equitable relationship between the prices of raw materials, primary commodities, manufactured and semi-manufactured goods exported by developing countries and the prices of raw materials, primary commodities, manufactures, capital goods and equipment imported by them with the aim of bringing about sustained improvement in their unsatisfactory terms of trade and the expansion of the world economy.[18]

Point 4 of the NIEO called for the right of states to nationalize their industries and key economic sectors as well as the transfer of foreign ownership to its nationals. The UN resolution for the NIEO was translated into the Charter of Economic Rights and Duties of States (CERDS) in December 1974. The CERDS was a somewhat qualified statement of the NIEO resolution; for example, the CERDS included a clause for adequate compensation in the event of nationalization or state expropriation of foreign-owned corporations. While not a radical program, the CERDS was designed to codify a commitment to global reform along neo-Keynesian lines (public initiatives).

Widely perceived as "the revolt of the Third World," the NIEO/CERDS initiative was a culmination of collectivist politics growing out of the Non-Aligned Movement (NAM). Its prime movers were the presidents of Algeria, Iran, Mexico, and

Venezuela—all oil-producing nations distinguished by their very recently acquired huge oil rents.[19] Ultimately, though, political power dynamics underpinning the structural inequality underscored by colonialism and its legacies could not be redressed by the CERDS. Subsequently, the Third World's united front strategy unraveled in large part due to the international political strategies of the United States and its European allies (former colonial powers). Although some attempts to achieve and implement the objectives of the NIEO, including price controls of commodities, had some success, they were ultimately thwarted. Notably, the "bloc" of key capitalist countries (including Denmark, the United Kingdom, the Federal Republic of Germany, Belgium, and the United States) voted against the CERDS, with other allies abstaining in the General Assembly.[20]

The Group of 7: The Capitalist Bloc and the Globalization Project

A counterpoint to the NIEO episode involved a strengthening of a First World core: the formation of the **Group of Seven (G-7)** states. The finance ministers of the United States, the United Kingdom, France, West Germany, Japan, Italy, and Canada held secret meetings annually, performing crisis management, including undermining the NIEO and its politics of solidarist internationalism. The backdrop to the NIEO episode and its aftermath was the Cold War strategic stand-off. This was interlaced with efforts by the sponsors of the development project to sustain international political economy conditions beneficial to Western powers. This meant that alongside the entrenchment of institutional arrangements, there were numerous cases of military interventions aimed at securing strategic interest.

In general, intervention involved more than two decades of military and financial disciplining of Third World policies that restricted foreign corporate access to Third World resources and markets, exemplified by the installation of General Suharto in Indonesia (1965).

In 1965, Indonesian President Sukarno and his brand of economic nationalism were overthrown in a bloody coup led by General Suharto. Declassified documents reveal that a 1964 British Foreign Office file called for the defense of Western interests in Southeast Asia because it is "a major producer of essential commodities. The region produces nearly 85 percent of the world's natural rubber, over 45 percent of the tin, 65 percent of the copra, and 23 percent of the chromium ore." Two years earlier, a CIA memo recorded an agreement between British Prime Minister Harold Macmillan and U.S. President John F. Kennedy to "liquidate president Sukarno, depending on the situation and available opportunities."[21]

Time-Life, Inc., sponsored a 1967 meeting in Geneva between General Suharto, his economic advisers, and corporate leaders representing "the major oil companies and banks, General Motors, Imperial Chemical Industries, British Leyland, British-American Tobacco, American Express, Siemens, Goodyear, the International Paper Corporation, and US Steel." With Ford Foundation help, General Suharto reformulated a development partnership with foreign investment. James Linen, president of Time-Life, Inc., expressed the *birth of this new global order* in the following opening remarks:

> We are here to create a new climate in which private enterprise and developing countries work together . . . for the greater profit of the free world. This world of international enterprise is more than governments. . . . It is the seamless web of enterprise, which has been shaping the global environment at revolutionary speed.[22]

The war waged in Vietnam by a U.S.-led coalition during the next decade confirmed this policy, followed by strategic interventions in Chile, El Salvador, Nicaragua, Panama, Grenada and Iraq, as well as disbursements of military and economic aid to secure the perimeter of the "free world" and its resource empire. Militarization was critical, securing and prying open the Third World to an emerging project of global development orchestrated by the United States as the dominant power.

CHILE: THE ORIGINAL MODEL OF ECONOMIC LIBERALIZATION

Chile is perhaps the founding model of economic liberalization, prefiguring the policies of the globalization project. A military coup in 1973 eliminated the democratically elected socialist president Salvador Allende, implementing detention, torture, and execution of thousands of Chileans as part of an eight-year period of debilitating authoritarian rule. General Augusto Pinochet pursued a radical free-market reform, otherwise known as "shock treatment," masterminded by economists trained at the University of Chicago, a center of neoclassical economics. Over the next two decades, 600 of the country's state enterprises were sold; foreign investment expanded into strategic sectors such as steel, telecommunications, and airlines; trade protection dwindled; and the dependence of the Chilean GDP on trade grew from 35 percent in 1970 to 57.4 percent in 1990. In other words, *Chile was structurally adjusted before* **structural adjustment** *became a central strategy of the Bretton Woods Organizations.* Sergio Bitar, Allende's minister of mining, remarked that privatization was "the greatest diversion of public funds that has occurred in our history, without the consultation of public opinion or accountability to a congress."

Chile was one of the most democratic of Latin American nations prior to the assault on its parliamentary and civil institutions. Debt restructuring in the 1980s increased social polarization. Social spending continued to fall, wages were frozen, and the peso was seriously devalued. Deindustrialization set in, unemployment levels rose to between 20 and 30 percent, and real wages suffered a 20 percent reduction. Meanwhile, an export boom occurred, retiring debt and earning the Chilean experiment a reputation as a miracle. U.S. President George H. W. Bush declared in Chile in 1990, "You deserve your reputation as an economic model for other countries in the region and in the world. Your commitment to market-based solutions inspires the hemisphere."

By 1990, about 40 percent of the 13 million Chilean people were impoverished in a country once known for its substantial middle class. In consequence, a sustained grassroots movement, centered in the *poblaciones* (slums), succeeded in regaining elections in 1988 when Pinochet was defeated.

As the original laboratory for neoliberalization policies, how did the Chilean experiment foreshadow the globalization project?

Sources: Bello (1994: 42, 44–45, 59); J. Collins and Lear (1996: 157, 162); George (1988: 131–32); Schneider, quoted in Chomsky (1994: 184); C. L. Schneider (1995: 3, 194, 201); Taffet (2007: 67–93).

Interventions were, of course, not limited to the use of overt military force, or the sponsorship of coups. An example is the experience of **Jamaica**, which gained independence from British rule in 1962 with a trading deficit of 15 million pounds sterling, which had grown to 85.6 million by 1971.[23] This deficit had built mainly as a result of decreasing capital inflows but had been compounded by the size of the food import bill. Jamaica experienced a deterioration of its terms of trade, as the export-oriented banana and sugar industries were exposed to falling international prices. Rising inequality and racial divisions ushered in a new government under Michael Manley, who sought to address these issues through a democratic socialist program, committed to meeting the "social and economic needs of the majority of the population."[24]

As part of this strategy, he levied a tax on bauxite mining and the aluminum industry. The business community and international partners, such as U.S. multinationals Revere and Alcoa, reduced or temporarily suspended production, forcing President Manley to reduce the levy in order to restore production to fixed levels. Manley's government also nationalized Barclay's Bank in an effort to create a commercial banking sector under public ownership in Jamaica, precipitating a backlash. Attempts to balance a rising deficit alongside social welfare provision led to Jamaican dependence on the IMF for access to finance. The IMF in turn mandated *conditionalities*, many of them directed specifically toward winding back the welfare measures that Manley had successfully implemented.[25] Ultimately, Manley was not prepared to choose furthering social suffering through IMF conditionalities and economic efficiency.

REMAKING THE INTERNATIONAL DIVISION OF LABOR

Given the ideological and strategic objectives of the development project, it certainly had some success when measured in conventional terms, including with regard to *some* Third World industrialization. In the case of some countries, as we demonstrate in our discussion in this section, it was a result of U.S.-led strategic interventions in the context of the Cold War. The result was uneven, however, and in some respects industrialization, along with broader modernization objectives (including infrastructure), remained incomplete with constrictions on democracy.

The Newly Industrializing Countries (NICs)

The average growth rate for the Third World in the 1960s was 4.6 percent; however, six Third World **newly industrializing countries (NICs)**[26] grew at rates of 7 to 10 percent.[27] These six countries were Hong Kong, Singapore, Taiwan, South Korea, Brazil, and Mexico. The rise of the NICs revealed two sides of the development project. The NICs fulfilled the expectation of rising living standards for some and upward mobility in the international system, *legitimizing the development project as showcases.* The other middle-income countries—especially Malaysia, Thailand, Indonesia, Argentina, and Chile—expected to follow the same path (as depicted in Figure 3.1, where Thailand, Malaysia, and Indonesia replace textile exports of the NICs). On the other hand, the NICs demonstrated the *selectivity* of the development project. They cornered the bulk of private foreign investment and considerable (Cold War–driven) military aid sustaining authoritarian regimes.[28] Much of this was concentrated in developing export production facilities in textiles and electronics in South Korea, Taiwan, Mexico, and Brazil. In 1969, for instance, most of the foreign investment in electronic assembly centered on the Asian NICs—Hong Kong, South Korea, Taiwan, and Singapore.[29] Between 1967 and 1978, the share of manufactured exports from the NICs controlled by transnational corporations was 20 percent in Taiwan, 43 percent in Brazil, and 90 percent in Singapore.[30] Distribution of industrial growth in the Third World was also highly concentrated. Between 1966 and 1975, more than 50 percent of the increase in value of Third World manufacturing occurred in only four countries, while about two-thirds of the increase was accounted for by only eight countries: Brazil, Mexico, Argentina, South Korea, India, Turkey, Iran, and Indonesia.[31]

Across the Third World, countries and regions differed in their levels of industrialization. The manufacturing portion of the gross domestic product (GDP) in 1975 was 5 percent in Africa, 16 percent in Asia, and 25 percent in Latin America and the Caribbean.[32] Meanwhile, the European First World lost its core manufacturing position in this period. Japan and a middle-income group of Third World states improved their share of world manufacturing, from 19 percent to 37 percent.[33] In agriculture, the Third World's share of world agricultural exports fell from 53 percent to 31 percent between 1950 and 1980, while the American breadbasket consolidated its critical role in world agricultural trade.[34] By the 1980s, the United States was producing 17 percent of the world's wheat, 63 percent of its corn, and 63 percent of its soybeans; its share of world exports was 36 percent in wheat, 70 percent in corn, and 59 percent in soybeans.[35] On the other side of the globe, between 1961 and 1975 Third World agricultural self-sufficiency declined everywhere except in centrally planned Asian countries (China, North Korea, and Vietnam). In all regions except Latin America, self-sufficiency dropped below 100 percent. Africa's self-sufficiency, for instance, declined from 98 percent in 1961 to 79 percent in 1978.[36]

FIGURE 3.1 ■ Textiles, Clothing, and Footwear Exports From Newly Industrializing Countries

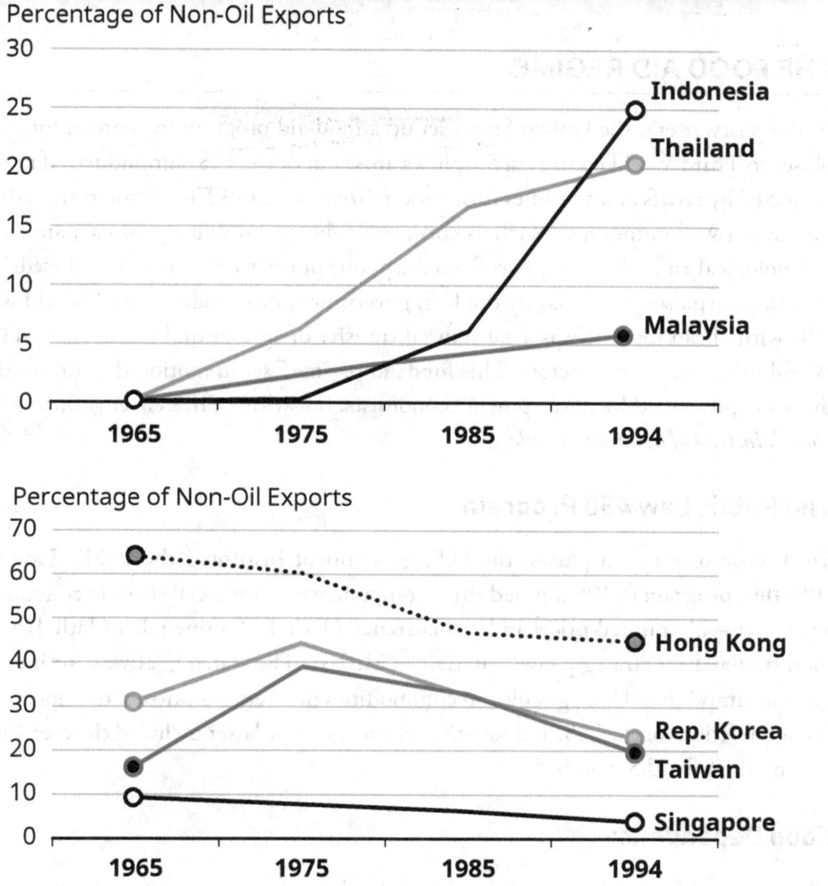

Sources: Adapted from graphs in Ransom (2001a: 103); data retrieved from UNCTAD (1996: 118–119).

Two questions arise:

- Why did commercial agriculture concentrate in the First World, while manufacturing dispersed to the Third World?
- Is there a relation between these trends?

The answers lie in the political structures of the development project. While import-substitution industrialization protected some Third World "infant" industries, farm subsidies protected First World agriculture under the terms of the GATT. These policies complemented one another, whereby American food surplus aid reshaped the international division of labor by subsidizing Third World manufacturing with cheap food for industrial workforces. Central to this process was a "food aid regime," which demonstrated the profoundly international character of the development project as a strategy of ordering the world under the guise of promoting development.

THE FOOD AID REGIME

In the postwar era, the United States set up a food aid program to channel food surpluses to Third World countries. Surpluses arose out of the U.S. agroindustrial model, protected by tariffs and subsidies (institutionalized in the GATT). Farmers specialized in one or two commodities (such as corn, rice, wheat, and dairy products) and, with technological and subsidy support from the public purse, routinely overproduced. The resulting surpluses were used by the U.S. government to subsidize Third World wage bills with cheap food. It was a substantial transfer of agricultural resources to Third World urban-industrial sectors. This **food aid regime**[37] set in motion the rural–urban dynamic prescribed by development economists, but with a difference: *operating on a global, instead of a national, scale.*

The Public Law 480 Program

To dispose of farm surpluses, the U.S. government instituted the **Public Law 480 (PL-480) program** in 1954. It had three components: commercial sales on concessionary terms—discounted prices in local currency (Title I); famine relief (Title II); and food bartered for strategic raw materials (Title III). The stated goal was "to increase the consumption of U.S. agricultural commodities in foreign countries, to improve the foreign relations of the U.S. and for other purposes." The latter included the creation of new markets for U.S. goods.[38]

Food Dependency

The impact of food aid varied across the world, depending on the resources of particular countries and their development policies. South Korea was a success story largely because the government centralized management of its rice culture and the supply of labor to the industrial centers. By contrast, urbanization in Colombia followed the collapse of significant parts of its unprotected farm sector under the competitive impact of food aid and commercial imports of wheat. Stimulated by the food aid program, imports of discounted wheat grew tenfold between the early 1950s and 1971, reducing by half the prices obtained by Colombian farmers. Displaced peasants contributed to the characteristic urban underemployment and low-wage economy of Third World countries.[39]

Between 1954 and 1974, major recipients of U.S. food aid were India, South Korea, Brazil, Morocco, Yugoslavia, South Vietnam, Egypt, Tunisia, Israel, Pakistan, Indonesia, Taiwan, and the Philippines (see Figure 3.2). Usually, it was cheaper and easier for governments to import wheat to feed their growing urban populations than

FIGURE 3.2 ■ Food Shortage Regions and Food Aid Recipients

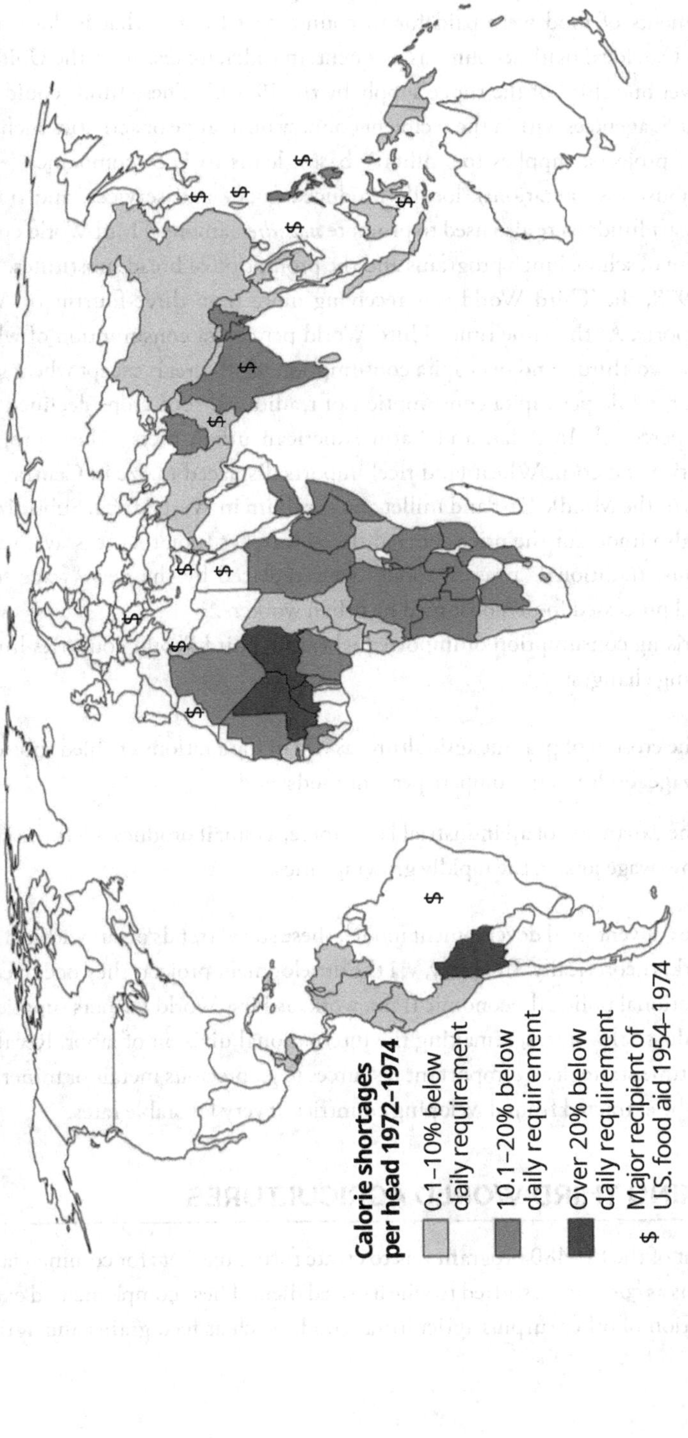

Source: Kidron and Segal (1981).

to bankroll long-term improvements in the production, transportation, and distribution of local foods.[40] Food aid allowed governments to purchase food without depleting scarce foreign currency, but it built "food dependency."

Shipments of food were paid for in counterpart funds—that is, local currency placed in U.S. local bank accounts as payment; in India, for example, the United States owned over one-third of the rupee supply by the 1970s.[41] These funds could be spent only by U.S. agencies within the recipient country on a range of activities such as infrastructural projects, supplies for military bases, loans to U.S. companies (especially local agribusiness operations), locally produced goods and services, and trade fairs. Counterpart funds were also used to promote *new diets* among Third World consumers in the form of school lunch programs and the promotion of bread substitutes.

By 1978, the Third World was receiving more than three-fourths of American wheat exports. At the same time, Third World per capita consumption of wheat rose by almost two-thirds, and per capita consumption of all cereals except wheat increased 20 percent, while per capita consumption of traditional root crops declined by more than 20 percent.[42] In Asian and Latin American urban diets, wheat progressively replaced rice and corn. Wheat (and rice) imports displaced maize in Central America and parts of the Middle East and millet and sorghum in West Africa. Subsidized grain imports also undercut the prices of traditional starches (potatoes, cassava, yams, and taro). Thus, traditional "peasant foods" were replaced by the new "wage foods" of grains and processed foods consumed by urban workers.[43]

The rising consumption of imported wheat in Third World countries linked two far-reaching changes:

- the erosion of peasant agriculture, as urban food rations enabled subsidized wage foods to out-compete peasant foods; and
- the expansion of an industrial labor force, as small producers left the land for low-wage jobs in the rapidly growing cities.

In the conventional development model, these social trends occur within a national framework, theoretically. In reality, via the development project, they occurred within an international political-economic framework, as First World farmers supplied Third World industrial workers, remaking the international division of labor. Recall that at the same time strategically important resources (e.g., precious metals or minerals) continued to be extracted from developing countries at very favorable rates.

REMAKING THIRD WORLD AGRICULTURES

The intent of the PL-480 program was to create future markets for commercial sales of U.S. grains as consumers shifted to wheat-based diets. These complemented expanding consumption of other surplus agricultural goods, such as feed grains and agricultural technology. Behind this stood the massive state-sponsored expansion in American agricultural productivity, which outstripped manufacturing from the 1950s to the 1970s. Disposal of surpluses was a matter of government policy. At this point, it is important to reflect on the longer-term consequences of this "food empire" strategy. Such public support of "petro-farming"—where petroleum fuels industrial agriculture via mechanization, inorganic fertilizers, pesticides, herbicides, and seed varnishes, abandoning agriculture's natural biological base—undermines nature's intrinsic ecological qualities over time. In the process, intensive agriculture annually loses two million acres of farmland to erosion, soil salinity, and flooding, in addition to consuming groundwater 160 percent faster than it can be replenished.[44] An unsustainable agribusiness model is one of the key export legacies of the development project.

The Global Livestock Complex

During the food aid regime, surplus grain was sufficiently cheap and plentiful to feed livestock rather than people. Expanding supplies of feed grains stimulated the growth of commodity chains, linking specialized feed producers with specialized animal protein producers across the world. Beyond a wheat-based diet, more affluent consumers shifted up the food chain, from grain to animal protein (beef, poultry, pork, and shrimp). Such "dietary modernization" followed rising incomes, converting rainforest to pasture for cattle in turn converted into hamburger, as a fast-food industry emerged, with environmental consequences. The contributions of beef production to global warming, via carbon dioxide, nitrous oxide, and methane, are significant.

The grain companies that formerly sold and processed wheat diversified into processed feeds (corn, barley, soybeans, alfalfa, oats, and sorghum) for cattle and hog feedlots as well as poultry motels. Consumption of animal protein became identified with "the American way of life," as meat accounted for one-quarter of the food bill by 1965.[45] Beef consumption roughly doubled between the turn of the century and 1976, and poultry consumption more than tripled between the 1930s and 1970.[46]

Through the food aid program, exports of feed grains also flourished as animal protein consumption spread among Third World middle classes. The U.S. Feed Grains Council routinely channeled counterpart funds, via over 400 agribusinesses, into the development of local livestock and poultry industries.[47] In 1969, four South Korean firms entered into joint ventures with U.S. agribusinesses (including Ralston-Purina and Cargill) to acquire technical and marketing expertise.

A global livestock complex formed, with livestock production expanding across the Third World and specialized feed grain supply zones concentrating in the First World and in "middle-income" countries such as Brazil and Argentina. Between the late 1940s and 1988, world production of soybeans increased sixfold. At the same time, maize production was revolutionized as a specialized, capital-intensive agroindustry, outstripping the value of the world wheat trade by a factor of six.[48]

The Green Revolution

The other major contribution to the remaking of Third World agriculture was the **green revolution**. This involved a "package" of plant-breeding agricultural technologies originally developed by the Rockefeller Foundation in Mexico—increasing production of corn, wheat, and beans in the two decades after 1943 by 300 percent and, in a combined venture with the Ford Foundation in the Philippines in the 1960s, in tropical centers in Nigeria and Colombia. In 1971, it culminated in the formation of the Consultative Group on International Agricultural Research (CGIAR), sponsored by the **Food and Agricultural Organization (FAO)**, the **United Nations Development Programme (UNDP)**, and the World Bank, with research facilities and gene banks across the world.[49] The green revolution was also the principal medium through which the U.S. model of chemical agriculture was introduced into the Third World—a technology transfer involving specific political choices and consequences.

Green revolution advocacy symbolized the idealized prescriptions of the development project, with its focus on output, despite known social and ecological consequences.[50] In the development narrative, rural population shrinkage is inevitable as agriculture "modernizes." The question is, why accept the retrenchment of large rural populations where industry is either capital-intensive or not extensive and slumdwellers constitute 50 percent of Third World populations?

"Productivism" has been a central development theme. It was promoted heavily by the U.S. land-grant university system, with an extension program geared to a model of commodity-specific research, supporting large, capitalized farmers.[51] Within the development project, the "entire argument for increasing yields was framed by the specter of increasing population." This argument lent moral and political legitimacy to a technological solution (despite the consequences); it represented population as an independent variable (we have seen how the case study of Egypt questions this); and, finally, the green revolution program appealed to "economic nationalism," a central ingredient of developmentalism at the time.[52]

Even more compelling were the political implications of the Chinese model where, following the 1949 Communist revolution, about 45 percent of total cultivated land monopolized by landlords was redistributed to small and landless peasants. Collectivization of land mobilized underemployed surplus labor and investment in water management and local enterprises and extended basic health and rural education through a decentralized process supplemented with central government assistance—albeit with a goal of squeezing agriculture to finance industrial growth and the Communist Party.[53] Whether or not this vast social experiment ultimately succeeded, the Chinese model loomed large in countries such as India, where Prime Minister Nehru was determined to match the Chinese.[54]

Meanwhile, the United States, with the leverage of its counterpart funds in India, was encouraging India to substitute green revolution technology for land redistribution.[55] Pressure to extend chemical agriculture stemmed from the conversion of wartime nitrogen production (for bombs) to inorganic fertilizer, displacing nitrogen-fixing legumes and manure, and the development of insecticides, stemming from World War I nerve gases, with advances in petroleum refining and organic chemistry.[56]

The new high-yielding varieties (HYVs) of hybrid seeds were heavily dependent on disease- and pest-resisting chemical protections in the form of fungicides and pesticides. Intensive irrigation and fertilization were necessary to optimize macronutrient yields, eliminating traditional leafy greens (with micronutrients such as vitamin A) now redefined as "weeds" and targeted by herbicides. The HYVs produced "wage foods" for urban consumers, displacing "peasant foods" produced with methods of crop rotation to maintain soil fertility. In 1984, an Indian farmer commented on the stronger, healthy soils promoted by manure-based fertilizer: "Chemical fertilizer makes the crop shoot up . . . whereas organic manure makes for strength. Without strength, no matter how much fertilizer you put, the field won't give output."[57] The hybrid seed ruptured the ecological cycle of natural regeneration and renewal, replacing it with linear flows of purchased inputs and commodified outputs, and incorporated farmers into the "chemical treadmill."[58] Long-term economic and ecological impacts have been blamed for as many as 100,000 farmer suicides in India between 1993 and 2003.[59]

From an *international* perspective, the food aid program helped to spread green revolution technology. Counterpart funds routinely promoted agribusiness and green revolution technologies, complemented with loans from institutions such as the U.S. Agency for International Development and the World Bank.[60] These agencies aimed to weave First World commercially oriented agricultural technologies into Third World commercial farming.

The green revolution was realized through the increase of rural income inequalities. In parts of Latin America, such as Mexico, Argentina, Brazil, and Venezuela, as well as in irrigated regions of India (Punjab and Haryana), this high-input agriculture promoted economic differentiation among—and often within—farming households. Within households, typically women have less commercial opportunity. Hybrid seeds and supporting inputs had to be purchased; to buy them, participants needed a regular supply of money or credit. Women tended to be excluded—not only because of the difficulty of obtaining financing but also because of agricultural extension traditions of transferring technology to male heads of households.[61]

Among farming households, the wealthier ones were more able to afford the package—and the risk—of introducing the new seed varieties. They also prospered from higher grain yields—often with easier access to government services than their poorer neighbors, who lacked the political and economic resources to take full advantage of these technologies. Rising land values often hurt tenant farmers by inflating their rent payments, forcing them to rent their land to their richer neighbors or to foreclose to creditors. Finally, the mechanical and chemical technologies associated with the green revolution either reduce farmhand employment opportunities for poor or landless peasants (where jobs were mechanized) or degrade working conditions where farmhands are exposed to toxic chemicals, such as pesticides and herbicides.[62]

Anti-Rural Biases of the Development Project and Peasant Struggles

Within the framework of the development project, Third World governments strove to feed growing urban populations cheaply, for political support, for lowering wages, and for national security. The term **urban bias** has been coined to refer to the systematic privileging of urban interests, from health and education services through employment schemes to the delivery of food aid.[63] This bias was central to the construction of development alliances based in the cities of the Third World. It also expressed the modernist belief in peasant redundancy (now challenged by the global food sovereignty movement).

Urban bias did not go unnoticed in the countryside. Growing rural poverty, rural marginalization, and persistent peasant activism over the question of land distribution put **land reform** on the political agenda in Asia and Latin America. When the Cuban Revolution redistributed land to poor and landless peasants in 1959, land reforms swept Latin America. Between 1960 and 1964, Brazil, Chile, Costa Rica, the Dominican Republic, Ecuador, Guatemala, Nicaragua, Panama, Peru, and Venezuela all enacted land reforms. Whatever transformative potential this represented was swiftly counteracted. The **Alliance for Progress** (1961)—a program of nationally planned agrarian reform coordinated across Latin America—provided an opportunity for the United States to use land reforms to undercut radical insurgents and stabilize rural populations via a U.S.-inspired family farming model.[64]

The land reform movement exempted commercialized farmland, redistributing what was left, including frontier lands. Indeed, considerable "re-peasantization" occurred during this period. In Latin America, two-thirds of the additional food production between 1950 and 1980 came from frontier colonization, and the number of small farmers with an average of two hectares of land grew by 92 percent. Overall, arable land increased by as much as 109 percent in Latin America and 30 percent in Asia but possibly declined in Africa.[65] Resettlement schemes on frontiers, including forests, were typically financed by the World Bank, especially in Indonesia, Brazil, Malaysia, and India, and they usually privileged males as household heads—"one of the principal mechanisms of exclusion of women as direct beneficiaries."[66] These strategies sometimes simply relocated rural poverty. In Brazil between 1960 and 1980, roughly 28 million small farmers were displaced by industrial farming for export to enhance foreign exchange earnings. The displaced farmers spilled into the Amazon region, burning the forest for new and often infertile land.[67]

Through a combination of food dumping and institutional support of commercial and export agriculture, the long-term assault on peasant agriculture begun in the colonial era intensified. Priority given to import and production of "wage foods"—compromising soil fertility and hydrological cycles—undermines the viability of household food production as a livelihood strategy for peasants and a subsistence base for the rural poor. One significant result has been a swelling migration of displaced peasants to overcrowded urban centers of Latin America, Asia, and Africa, creating a "planet of slums."[68]

CONCLUSION

The development project was multilayered, as national strategies of economic growth dovetailed with international multilateral and bilateral assistance. Importantly, the fundamental premises upon which this project rested were directed at achieving strategic objectives to consolidate the legacy of colonial capitalism. The aim was to integrate the Third World *as a whole* into a *singular* project, despite national/regional variations in resources, starting point, and ideological orientation. And it proceeded on the basis of discounting the colonial relations that had underpinned and unequally created these variations, including the economic wealth of the United States and its European (Western) allies.

Military and economic-aid programs shaped the geopolitical contours of the "free world," integrating Third World countries into the Western orbit. They also shaped patterns of development through technological transfer and food subsidies to industrialization programs. Food aid was significant in securing geopolitical alliances, as well as in reshaping the international division of labor via support of Third World manufacturing. As development economists predicted, Third World industrialization depended on the transfer of rural resources. But this transfer was not confined to national arenas, as exports of First World food and agricultural technology constituted a *global* rural–urban exchange.

The development project was instituted through unequal *global* relations, consolidating rather than completely eliminating the unjust colonial division of labor. In the context of the Cold War, this compounded struggles for a just settlement to decolonization. Throughout, Third Worldism gathered momentum as a political project, directed toward a more solidarist and humane global order. It is this that Indian historian and journalist Vijay Prashad captures when he asserts that the "Third World was not a place. It was a project."[69] We cannot detail national varieties here, and that is not the point of this story. Rather, the focus is on understanding how the development project intersected with the dynamics we outlined in the beginning. The framing of development in terms of *national* development was premised on *ideal* rather than existing relations, deriving from the colonial era, which were compounded through strategic programs.

In this chapter, we have examined one such example. First World agricultural expansion was linked with the rise of new industrial classes in the Third World. At the same time, the export of green revolution technology to Third World regions stimulated social differentiation among men and women and among rural producers, laborers, and capitalist farmers. Those peasants unable to survive the combined competition of cheap foods and high-tech farming in the countryside migrated to the cities, further depressing wages. Not surprisingly, this scenario stimulated a massive relocation of industrial tasks to the Third World, reshaping the international division of labor. In short, it laid the groundwork for the political-economic, institutional, and legal structures of what we call the globalization project.

KEY TERMS

Alliance for Progress
Bretton Woods
Central planning
Food aid regime
Food and Agriculture Organization (FAO)
General Agreement on Tariffs and Trade (GATT)
Green revolution
Group of Seven (G-7)
Group of 77 (G-77)
International Monetary Fund (IMF)
Jamaica
Land reform
Marshall Plan
New International Economic Order (NIEO)
Newly industrializing countries (NICs)
Non-Aligned Movement (NAM)
Public Law 480 (PL-480) program
Structural adjustment
Technology transfer
United Nations Conference on Trade and Development (UNCTAD)
United Nations Development Programme (UNDP)
Urban bias
World Bank

FURTHER READING

Chang, Ha-Joon. *Kicking Away the Ladder: Development Strategy in Historical Perspective*. London: Anthem Press, 2002.

Gupta, Akhil. *Postcolonial Developments: Agriculture in the Making of Modern India*. Durham, NC: Duke University Press, 1998.

Kloppenburg, Jack R, Jr. *First the Seed: The Political Economy of Plant Biotechnology, 1492–2000*. Cambridge, UK: Cambridge University Press, 1988.

Prashad, Vijay. *The Poorer Nations: A Possible History of the Global South*. London: Verso, 2012.

Rich, Bruce. *Mortgaging the Earth: The World Bank, Environmental Impoverishment and the Crisis of Development*. Boston: Beacon, 1994.

SELECT WEBSITES

Consultative Group on International Agricultural Research (CGIAR): www.cgiar.org

Food and Agriculture Organization (FAO), UN: www.fao.org

International Monetary Fund (IMF): www.imf.org

The South Centre: https://www.southcentre.int

United Nations Conference on Trade and Development (UNCTAD): www.unctad.org

The World Bank: www.worldbank.org

PART

II

THE GLOBALIZATION PROJECT (1980s TO 2000s)

4 INSTITUTING THE GLOBALIZATION PROJECT

The globalization project can be identified as a qualitatively different phase marked by the ascendancy of a distinctive neoliberal ideology of development. This project, while rooted in latter phases of the 1970s and early 1980s, has been consolidated through a number of interconnected trends and transformations in world politics, and together they comprise the institutional architecture for globalization. A core feature of this architecture is the new international organizations set up to advance and deepen the global scope and reach of neoliberalism. Key here are the World Trade Organization (WTO) and regional free trade agreements such as the United States–Mexico–Canada Agreement (USMCA, formerly the **North American Free Trade Agreement [NAFTA]**). Their emergence has been accompanied by changes in the mandates and objectives of the Bretton Woods institutions aimed at integrating development policies comprehensively with WTO agreements. The resulting framework of interagency governance expresses the institutionalization of the expanding and deepening of neoliberal ideology. This has been reflected concretely, for instance, in the push for the privatization and liberalization of public goods and services, reframed as commodities. While privatization of public services, such as water and health services, had been underway since the early 1980s, from the 1990s onward and under trade-led global governance "reform," this became significantly intensified.

The neoliberal globalization project was ushered in by a coalition of state and non-state actors with a shared commitment to the distinctively liberal capitalist ideal of what Karl Polanyi had identified as "market society." The state sponsors of this project included the United States as the preeminent leader, its Western allies, and governments in the global South it supported (e.g., Pinochet's Chile). Among notable non-state actors was the Trilateral Commission, an informal body composed of representatives from Japan, Western Europe, and the United States and founded by, among others, Jimmy Carter, David Rockefeller, and Zbigniew Brzezinski. Its purpose was to forge closer ties between the three blocs and harmonize commercial and political interests. Similarly, we had the emergence and ascendancy of the World Economic Forum, the annual gathering of leading figures primarily from the corporate world.

Taken together, *this constellation characterizes how development is reconfigured in the context of the globalization project.* As part of this context, international aid underwent a transformative shift. Aid became bracketed directly with achieving the objectives of establishing a global market society. For example, the 2011 Busan Declaration on Aid Effectiveness (a high-level meeting concerned with the coordination of international aid) redefined conceptions and practices of aid by recontextualizing the conventionally used concept of "aid effectiveness" within a broader agenda, which it called "effective development co-operation." The latter was conceived to privilege commercial interests behind the core objectives of the neoliberal globalization project, explicitly advocating for the "promotion of approaches that mitigate risks faced by the private sector." In contrast, it broadly adopted the premise communities ought to embrace and manage rather than avoid risk.[1] These objectives are also reflected in the wide use of the policy framework of Aid for Trade (AfT). The AfT is linked to the Sustainable Development Goals agenda, specifically through Goal 17 "Means of Implementation."

In this chapter, we take a closer look at how this neoliberal institutional architecture of development has been organized and configured through the globalization project, and the social changes it inaugurated and consolidated. It is pertinent to recall the Polanyian lesson that "market society" is inherently destabilizing and always contested. Such resistances exemplify Polanyi's "double movement," whereby subordination of social life to market relations generates protective countermovements.

NEO-CLASSICAL ECONOMICS AND NEOLIBERALISM: GLOBAL MARKET SOCIETY

Theoretical justification for liberalization of national economies derives from nineteenth-century English political economist David Ricardo's concept of **comparative advantage**—linking economic growth to optimizing trading advantage through economic specialization, reflecting a nation's relative resource endowments. The theorem stated that when countries exchange their most competitive products on the world market, national and international economic efficiency results.[2] This theorem contradicts the development project's ideal of a series of integrated national economies while affirming the globalization project's focus on the global economy as the unit of development. But the theorem did not allow for capital mobility, which today is central to the construction of a *corporate-based* comparative advantage, so the original *market-based* theorem has lost the plausibility of its simplistic appeal.

Until the 1970s, "comparative advantage" represented a minority strand of economic thought, being out of step with mid-twentieth-century social history. As the welfare state's wage and social program costs affected their profits, a corporate countermovement resuscitated neoclassical market theory, relegating Keynesian ideas of state intervention and public investment to the background. The welfare state was reconfigured as the "competition state."[3] The political form of neoclassical economic theory, **neoliberalism**, took universal shape in welfare reform/reversal, wage erosion, relaxing trade controls, and privatization schemes—the underpinnings of the globalization project.

The neoliberal development project has been organized in terms of what has been aptly described critically as "new constitutionalism,"[4] namely, the establishment of legal frameworks designed to be conducive to trade and investment interests, and to protect investor and trader rights.[5] In effect, the corporate countermovement shifted economic burdens and risks away from owners, investors, and traders and turned them into social risks and burdens for workers and ecological ones for all, if differentially. Another way of formulating this would be with Harvey's coinage of "accumulation by dispossession."[6]

This is evident in the enlargement of the global labor force at the base of ubiquitous supply chains (foodstuffs, manufactures, services) and in the deepening of natural resource extraction. Where the latter threatens habitats, displaced peasants, fisherfolk, and forest dwellers join the swelling pool of labor, some of whom find work in export production. This doctrine, represented as the new development strategy for countries to find their world market niche, has been interpreted as a *selective development* device, where local and global firms mobilize cheap land and labor for export production to provision distant consumers:

> Millions of acres once used to feed poor families in poor countries are now used to grow kiwis, asparagus, strawberries, and baby carrots for upper-middle-class consumers who can now eat what was once the fare of kings—365 days a year.[7]

The consequence is a *selective* realization of "high mass consumption," an expanding consumer class, and its "insatiable appetite for energy, private automobiles, building materials, household appliances, and other resource-intensive commodities."[8]

Under these circumstances, fueled by "freeing" markets to supply relatively cheap resources, commercial extraction of natural resources has intensified globally, threatening environments and resource regeneration. The close correlation between debt, export liberalization, and high rates of deforestation, as depicted in Figure 4.1, is well known.[9] In Chile, timber exports doubled in the 1980s, reaching beyond industrial plantations to the logging of natural forests. Chile's export boom overexploited the country's natural resources beyond their ability to regenerate.[10] In Ghana—the World Bank's African *model* of structural adjustment—the exports of mining, fishing, and timber products were accelerated to close the widening gap between cocoa exports and severely declining world prices of cocoa. From 1983 to 1988, timber exports increased from $16 million to $99 million, reducing Ghana's tropical forest to 25 percent of its original size.[11] The NGO Development GAP (Group for Alternative Policies) reported that deforestation

> threatens household and national food security now and in the future. Seventy-five percent of Ghanaians depend on wild game to supplement their diet. Stripping the forest has led to sharp increases in malnutrition and disease. For women, the food, fuel, and medicines that they harvest from the forest provide critical resources, especially in the face of decreased food production, lower wages, and other economic shocks that threaten food security.[12]

FIGURE 4.1 ■ Debt and Deforestation

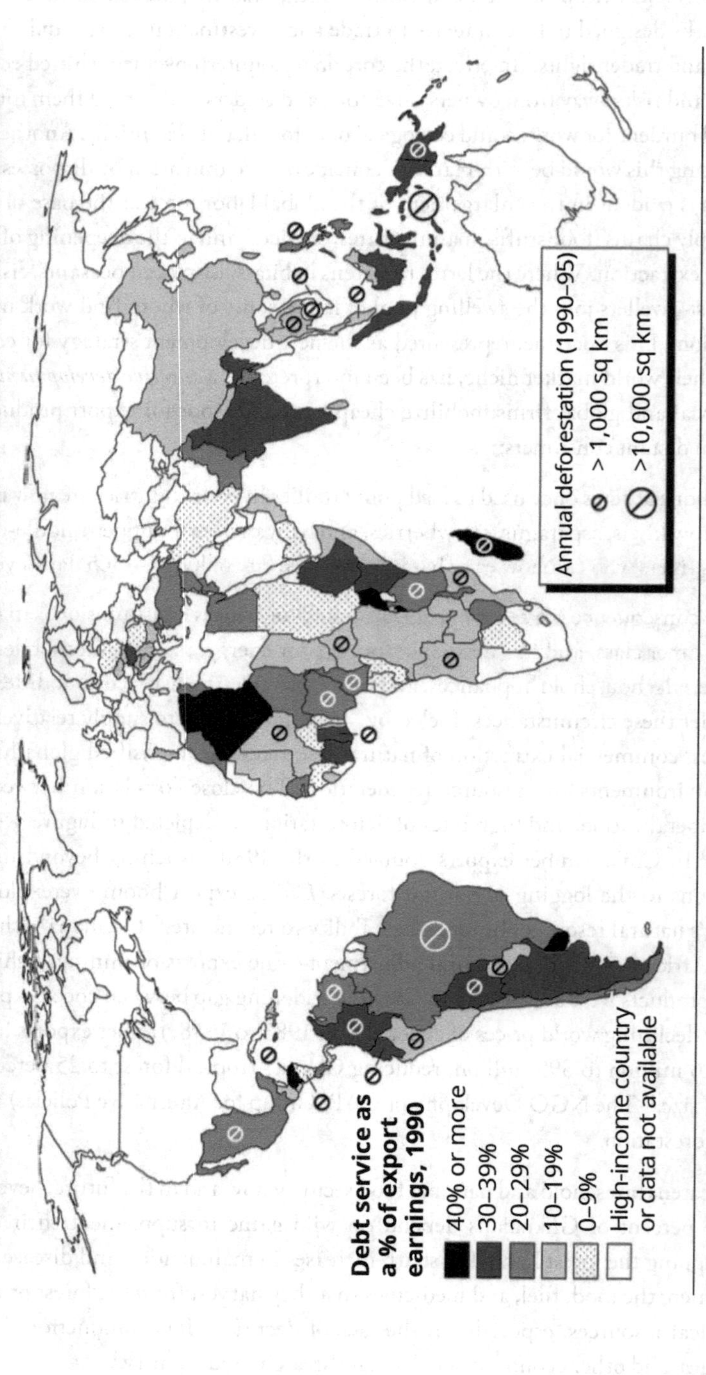

Sources: A. Thomas and Crow (1994); World Bank (1998–1999).

How did proponents of neoliberal development manage to establish it as a new orthodoxy, and what made it possible for the project to assume the transformative (and destructive) forces we have discussed so far? In the next section, we take a closer look at the circumstances that led to neoliberalism's ascendancy and its impact on development.

THE DEBT CRISIS AND STRUCTURAL ADJUSTMENT PROGRAMS: ORGANIZING NEOLIBERAL DEVELOPMENT

The 1980s debt crisis instituted a new era of *global governance* in which individual national policies were subjected to external, rule-based procedures that strengthened the grip of the First World through the international financial institutions (the IMF and the World Bank). In other words, the debt crisis spawned a **debt regime.** The divisions in the Third World enabled global political and economic elites to argue that a country's debt stress stemmed from failure to copy the newly industrializing countries' (NICs') strategy of export diversification in the world market.[13] Although represented and celebrated as examples of market virtue—to justify neoliberal ideology—the NICs were in fact state-managed economies and also the recipients of strategic support from the United States and allies during the Cold War.

The debt crisis began in 1980 when the U.S. Federal Reserve Board moved to stem the fall in the dollar's value from its overcirculation in the 1970s lending binge—reducing dollar circulation with an aggressive monetarist policy.[14] The contraction of credit raised interest rates as banks competed for dwindling funds. Lending to Third World states slowed, and shorter terms were issued—hastening the day of reckoning on higher-cost loans. Some borrowing continued, nevertheless—partly because of rising oil prices. Higher oil prices actually accounted for more than 25 percent of the total debt of the Third World.[15]

Third World debt totaled $1 trillion by 1986. Even though this amount was only half of the U.S. national debt in that year, it was significant because countries were devoting new loans entirely to servicing previous loans.[16] Unlike the United States, cushioned by the dollar standard (the de facto international reserve currency preferred by countries and traders), Third World countries were unable to continue debt servicing; their dollar reserves lost value as real interest rates spiked, First World recession reduced consumption of Third World products, and Third World export revenues collapsed as primary export prices declined 17 percent relative to First World manufactured exports.[17]

Third World countries were suddenly mired in a *debt trap:* debt was constricting their economies and landing them in a double bind. To repay the interest (at least), they had to drastically curtail imports and drastically raise exports. But reducing imports of technology jeopardized growth. Expanding exports was problematic, as commodity prices were at the lowest in 40 years—a result of the expansion of commodity exports to reduce debt. The market alone could not solve these problems.

Debt Management

The chosen course of action became debt management. The Bretton Woods institutions were back in the driver's seat, even though 60 percent of Third World debt was with private banks. The IMF assumed a supervisory status, implementing structural adjustment programs (SAPs) in the mid-1980s: a comprehensive restructuring of production priorities and government programs in a debtor country. Working with the World Bank and its structural adjustment loan (SAL) facility, the IMF levied restructuring conditions on borrowers in return for loan rescheduling—demanding *policy restructuring*, whereby debtor states received austere prescriptions for political-economic reforms.

In 1989, the executive director of UNICEF, James P. Grant, observed,

> It is hardly too brutal an oversimplification to say that the rich got the loans and the poor got the debts.[18]

Under this regime, debt was defined as an individual liquidity problem (i.e., the shortage of foreign currency) rather than a systemic problem; that is, the debt managers blamed debtor policies rather than the unequal historical structural conditions that underpinned Third World debt (see the example of Jamaica in Chapter 3). These conditions were compounded by the development project, which facilitated the consolidation of a financial system that subsequently produced the "debt crisis."

Mexico was the first "ticking bomb" in the global financial structure, with an $80 billion debt in 1982. Over 75 percent of this was owed to private banks. Mexican political forces were divided between a "bankers' alliance" and the "Cardenas alliance"—representing a nationalist coalition rooted in the labor and peasant classes.[19] The outgoing president, José López Portillo, allied with the latter group, opposed debt management proposals by nationalizing the Mexican banking system and installing exchange controls against capital flight.

However, Portillo's conservative successor, Miguel de la Madrid, agreed to a bailout, in which the IMF put up $1.3 billion, foreign governments $2 billion, and the banks $5 billion in "involuntary loans." In 1986, Mexico was rewarded for resisting a regional effort to form a debtors' club.[20]

The Mexican bailout became a model. In other middle-income nations (e.g., Brazil, Thailand, Turkey) as in Mexico, development alliance constituencies—particularly ruling elites and middle classes benefiting from the original loans—used their power to shift repayment costs on to the working poor via austerity cuts in social services. As World Bank chief economist Stanley Fischer noted in 1989, "Most of the burden has been borne by wage earners in the debtor countries."[21]

Structural Adjustment Programs and Austerity

Through the debt regime, social protections were reconceptualized from line item subsidies in national policies to the status of "emergency social funds"—subsequently mainstreamed by the World Bank as **social funds**, ostensibly targeted to soften the impact of austerity in the Caribbean, Latin America, and Africa. These "social safety nets," such as the Bolivian Fondo de Emergencia Social and the Egyptian Social Fund, were administered by **nongovernmental organizations (NGOs)** through decentralized feeding and microcredit programs that often bypassed communities with the least resources to propose programs and neglected gender differences.[22] In the meantime, rescheduling bought time for debt repayment, but it came at a heavy cost.

Adjustment measures included

- drastic reduction of public spending (especially social programs and food subsidies);
- currency devaluation (inflating prices of imports and reducing export prices to improve trade balances);
- export intensification (to earn foreign exchange);
- privatization of state enterprises (to "free" the market);
- reduction of wages to attract foreign investors and reduce export prices; and
- mandating industrial relations reform (to supress unions, or de-unionize workforces).

Most of these measures fell hardest on the poorest and least powerful social classes—those dependent on wages and subsidies. While some businesses and export outfits prospered, poverty rates climbed. Governments saw their development alliances crumble with deindustrialization and shrinking funds for subsidizing urban constituencies.

IMF/World Bank adjustment policies in Africa reduced food subsidies and public services, leading to urban demonstrations and riots in Tanzania, Ghana, Zambia, Morocco, Egypt, Tunisia, and Sudan (see Figure 4.2). In Zambia, for example, the price of cornmeal—a staple—rose 120 percent in the mid-1980s following adjustment. Between 1980 and 1986, average per capita income declined by 10 percent, and unemployment almost tripled.[23] In effect, all the "development" indicators, including infant mortality, took a downturn under the impact of adjustment policies. The NGO Oxfam reported in 1993 that World Bank adjustment programs in sub-Saharan Africa were largely responsible for reductions in public health spending and a 10 percent decline in primary school enrollment.[24]

From 1978 to 1992, more than 70 countries undertook 566 stabilization programs and SAPs to manage their debt.[25] The debtor countries collective entered the 1990s with 61 percent more debt than they held in 1982.[26]

As a consequence of growing debt, many countries found themselves under greater scrutiny, in addition to surrendering greater amounts of their wealth to global agencies. The turning point was 1984. In that year, the direction of capital flows reversed—that is, the inflow of loan and investment capital into the former Third World was replaced by an *outflow* in the form of debt repayment (see Figure 4.3). The (net) extraction of financial resources from the Third World during the 1980s exceeded $400

FIGURE 4.2 ■ Locations of Riots against Austerity Programs

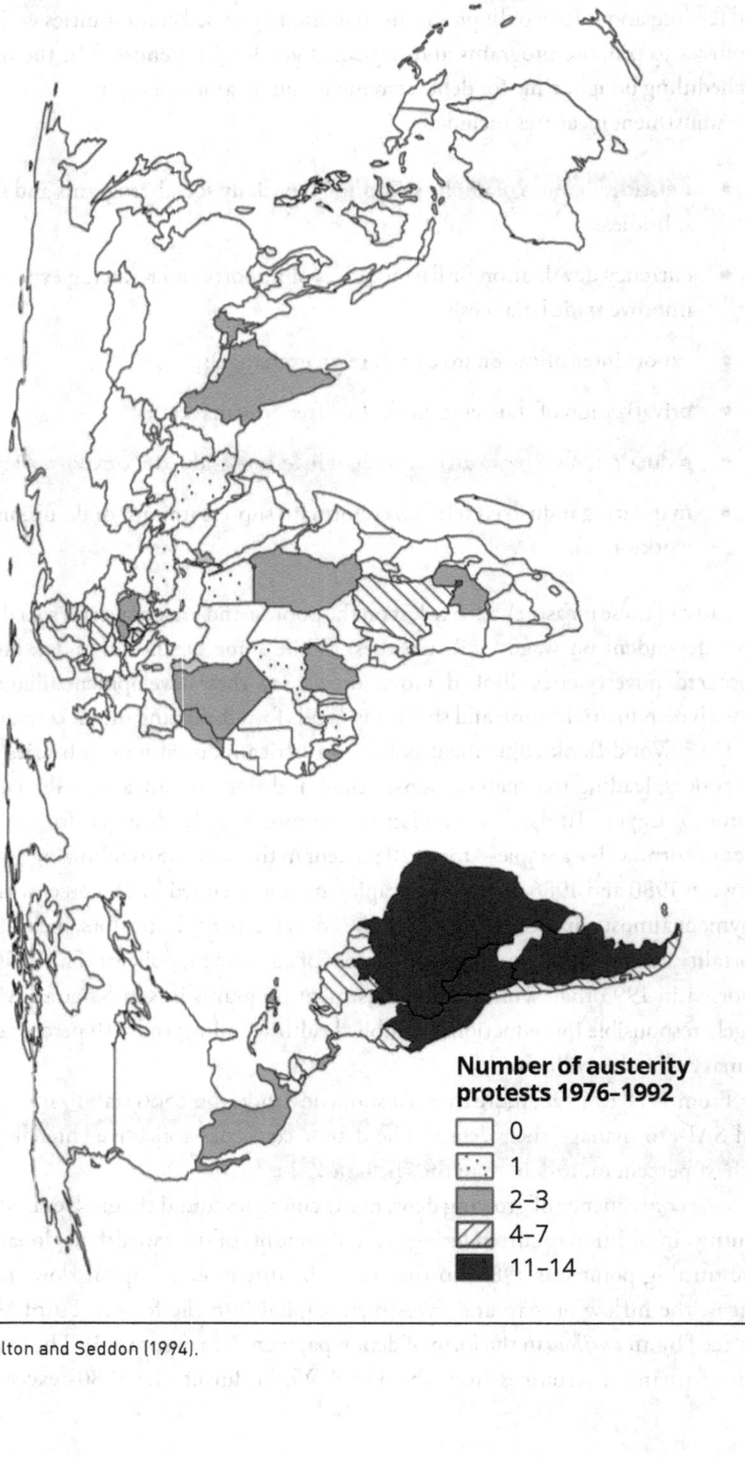

Source: Walton and Seddon (1994).

billion.[27] The debt crisis opened up the Third World—now recategorized as the global South[28]—to northern-imposed disciplines, foreign investment, and unsustainable export production to defray debt.

FIGURE 4.3 ■ Net Transfers of Long-Term Loans to Third World States

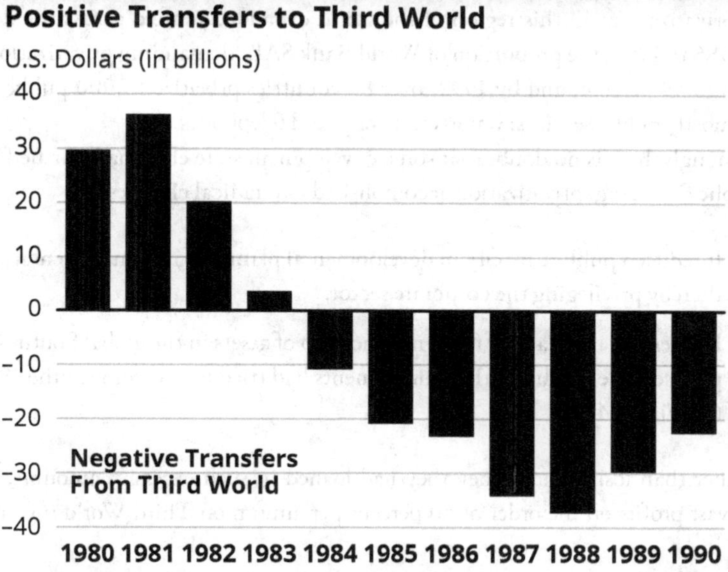

Source: United Nations (1997: 64).

IMF RIOTS: CITIZENS VERSUS STRUCTURAL ADJUSTMENT

The so-called IMF riots registered the impoverishing effects of austerity. Between 1976 and 1992, some 146 riots occurred in 39 of the approximately 80 debtor countries, including Romania, Poland, Yugoslavia, and Hungary. These large-scale, often coordinated, urban uprisings protested the public austerity measures, with rioters often breaking into food banks. Collapsing social entitlements included a range of subsidized services to members of hyper-urbanized environments, including food, health care, education, transportation, and housing. Riots sought to restore basic mechanisms of **social reproduction**. They also targeted the International Monetary Fund (IMF) as the source of policies undermining national public capacity, and therefore, popular sovereignty. Björn Beckman claimed that the logic of the structural adjustment program was to "further weaken the motivation of the state to respond to the popular demands that have been built into the process of postcolonial state formation."

Sources: Beckman (1992: 97); Kagarlitsky (1995: 217); Walton and Seddon (1994).

Privatization and Enabling New Actors and Interests

As neoliberalism consolidated its orthodoxy in the 1980s, debt managers demanded a *shrinking* of Third World states' commitments to public welfare through reductions in social spending and the privatization of state enterprises. As a condition of debt rescheduling, governments were forced to sell off their public assets. The average number of privatizations in this region of the world expanded tenfold across the decade. From 1986 to 1992, the proportion of World Bank SALs demanding privatization rose from 13 to 59 percent, and by 1992, over 80 countries privatized 7,000 public enterprises, mostly public services: water, electricity, and telephones.[29]

Although there is no doubt that some development state elites had pursued excessive public financing, privatization accomplished two radical changes:

- It reduced public capacity in developmental planning and implementation, thereby privileging the corporate sector.
- It extended the reach of foreign ownership of assets in the global South—precisely the condition that governments had tried to overcome in the 1970s (see Figure 4.4).

Rather than losing the money they had loaned in such excessive amounts, banks earned vast profits on the order of 40 percent per annum on Third World investments

FIGURE 4.4 ■ Select Private Foreign Direct Investment Flows in the 1990s

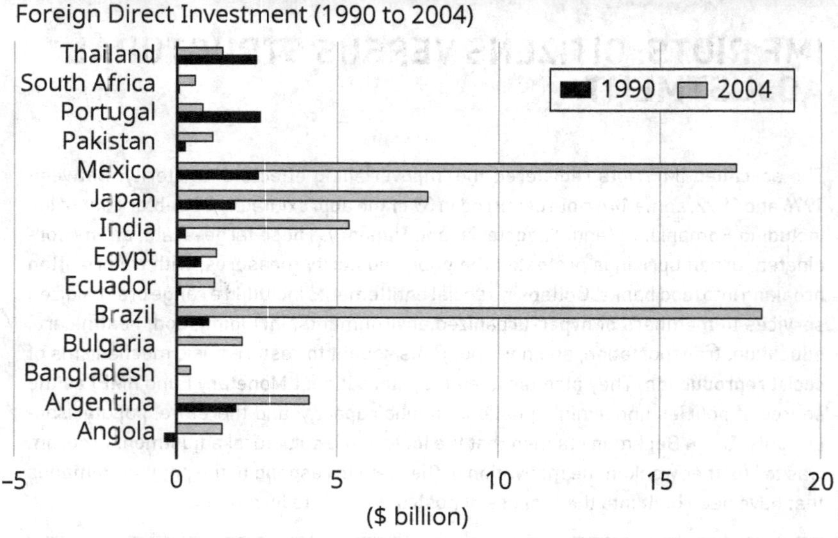

Source: World Bank (2006).

alone.[30] Foreign investment in the Third World resumed between 1989 and 1992, increasing from $29 billion to $40 billion (especially in Mexico, China, Malaysia, Argentina, and Thailand).[31] The restructured (now) global South was yet quite profitable for private investment: wages were low, governments were not competing in the private capital markets, and an export boom in raw materials, manufactures, and foodstuffs was underway.

During the debt regime, the World Bank established local agencies (known as *parastatals*) to administer its SAPs. SALs restructure national economies and redistribute power within the state—privileging the central bank and trade/finance ministries over program-oriented ministries (social services, agriculture, education), thus weakening the political coalitions and goals of the national development state.[32] This power shift removes resources from state agencies that support and regulate economic (e.g., import-substitution industrialization [ISI]) and social sectors affecting the majority of the citizenry, especially the poorer classes. These resources are shifted to the agencies more directly connected to global enterprise; thus, global economic criteria override national social criteria (see Figure 4.5).

FIGURE 4.5 ■ Government Spending on Foreign Debt and Social Services (Selected Countries, 1995)

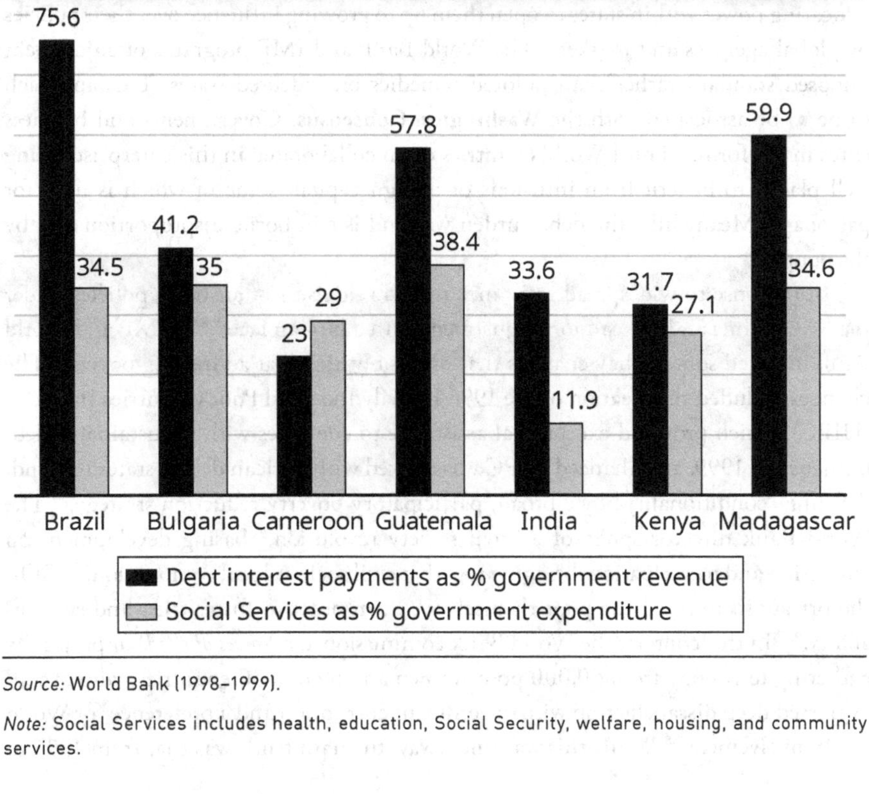

Source: World Bank (1998–1999).

Note: Social Services includes health, education, Social Security, welfare, housing, and community services.

The World Bank's premise for the policy shift was that development states were overly bureaucratic and inefficient on one hand and unresponsive to their citizenry on the other. Some of these observations were credible, confirmed by authoritarian government, corruption, and "hollow" development financing—such as Zaire President Mobutu's lavish global, jet-set lifestyle and Côte d'Ivoire President Felix Houphouet-Boigny's construction in his home village of a larger-than-life-size replica of St. Peter's Basilica in the Vatican. Nevertheless, the solutions proposed and imposed by the World Bank substituted growing external control of these countries in the name of financial orthodoxy.[33] Noting what he considered a form of revival of "trusteeship" in the 1990s, economist Jeffrey Sachs observed,

> Not unlike the days when the British Empire placed senior officials directly into the Egyptian and Ottoman finance ministries, the IMF is insinuated into the inner sanctums of nearly 75 developing-country governments around the world—countries with a combined population of some 1.4 billion. These governments rarely move without consulting the IMF staff, and when they do, they risk their lifelines to capital markets, foreign aid, and international respectability.[34]

When states become unaccountable, citizens may withdraw into a "shadow" economy and society, as has been illustrated in the case of Tanzania.[35]

In summary, the debt regime reformulated the terms of economic management, relocating power within states to open them up to growing influence over their policies by global agencies and markets. The World Bank and IMF programs of adjustment imposed standard rather than tailored remedies on indebted states. This approach came to be associated with the **Washington Consensus**. Governments and business elites in the former Third World countries often collaborated in this enterprise, being well placed to benefit from infusions of foreign capital, some of which is used for patronage. Meanwhile, the debt burden was and is still borne disproportionately by the poor.

In response to widespread resistance to and criticisms of austerity policies under the SAP regime and the call for "adjustment with a human face," the IMF and World Bank initiated some policy changes that ostensibly aimed at addressing poverty. The changes included the creation of the 1996 Heavily Indebted Poor Countries Initiative (HIPC), which provided exceptional assistance to countries with unsustainable debt burdens. By 1999, an enhanced HIPC was created with African debtor states in mind, defining "conditionality" by a broad, participatory poverty reduction strategy.[36] The World Bank director spoke of a "civil society revolution," basing development on "inclusion and participation, bringing together civil society, local competition, NGOs, the private sector, and the poor themselves . . . in order to foster trust and sustainability."[37] In this context, the World Bank commissioned a *Voices of the Poor* project by gathering testimony from 60,000 poor women and men in 50 countries, who overall expressed deep dissatisfaction with government corruption and a preference for World Bank involvement.[38] While this was underway, the hard truth was that from 1996 to

1999, HIPC-eligible country debt had quadrupled—from $59 billion to $205 billion—mobilizing northern activists, in particular, the Jubilee 2000 organization dedicated to debt forgiveness.[39]

In this context, SAPs were refashioned as "partnerships," with states ostensibly required to author their own development plans, on which loans, debt rescheduling, and debt forgiveness can be made. With these plans, known as **Poverty Reduction Strategy Papers (PRSPs)**, compiled as "performances" in order "to meet the charge that imposing conditions is undemocratic, the international financial institutions (IFIs) then insisted that other stakeholders, such as NGOs, churches, unions, and business, rather than just governments, are involved in writing the plans."[40] Under the slogan "country owned and country driven," the PRSPs were represented as a major shift in policy, reflecting a move toward new *process* conditions for loans.[41]

The World Bank and the IMF characterized the PRSP program in 2002 as "a new approach to the challenge of reducing poverty in low-income countries based on country-owned poverty reduction strategies."[42] Such procedures, in holding states accountable for poverty reduction, embed public priorities in market relationships—in effect fashioning "governance states."[43]

REFRAMING SAPS THROUGH THE PRSPS

Structural adjustment programs (SAPs) created a legitimation crisis for the international financial institutions (IFIs) due to the impoverishing effects of austerity. Austerity had been mandated through *conditionalities*, that is, prescriptions jointly imposed on indebted countries by the IMF and the World Bank. In response to criticisms of conditionalities, the IFIs shifted to center the language and discourse of poverty reduction, exemplified by the Poverty Reduction Strategy Paper (PRSP) initiative. In reality the PRSP framework continued the neoliberal agenda.

- All PRSPs had to be aligned with World Bank policy frameworks and operational directives and endorsed by the World Bank executive.
- If countries had not no implemented a comprehensive SAP, they would have to go through an "interim PRSP" before qualifying for the full process.

Together, these provisions mean that the SAP conditionality architecture continued to underpin the IFIs' approach.

Source: Weber (2006).

Governing development and poverty in this way also involves coordinating international NGOs with access to information and resources, enabling them to leverage initiatives within states. As Oxfam, for example, observes, "PRSPs offer Oxfam and other NGOs major opportunities to influence policy and practice at local, national, and international levels, both at the formulation and implementation stage."[44] The privatization of state responsibilities has also been shaped by transnational policy networks. Thus, in Africa the African Policy Institutes Forum was created by the World Bank to establish professional training program centers and sites for preparation of PRSPs.[45] In what became known (misleadingly) as the **Post–Washington Consensus**, the influence such agencies gained remained fundamentally contingent on compliance with the neoliberal institutional architecture of the globalization project. This reconstruction of the state–civil society relation was, as we will see below, matched by the implications of the focus on market access.

GEOPOLITICS AND THE GLOBALIZATION PROJECT

Alongside the debt regime, during the 1980s the United States led an attempt to build a free-market global consensus—focusing on breaking down the resistance of the Soviet empire (the Second World) to market capitalism. This was a central geopolitical strategy of the emerging globalization project.

As it happened, Eastern European countries, borrowing from the West to finance consumer items demanded by restive citizens, came under IMF supervision. By 1986, Soviet President Mikhail Gorbachev was formulating plans for *perestroika* (restructuring) in exchange for membership in the Bretton Woods institutions. IMF policies required replacement of central planning by "market-responsive" enterprises and reduced food, transport, heating fuel, and housing subsidies (i.e., economic rights of the socialist systems). *Social equality* was redefined as the equality of private opportunity, which was exploited by former public officials who enriched themselves as public property was privatized. Once the Soviet Union and empire fell in 1989, Western shock treatment methods (austerity policies) were deployed, leading to a precipitous decline in Russian living standards and an explosion of organized crime. But the world was now unipolar—instead of the bipolarity of the Cold War era—and cleared for the globalization project proper.[46]

The advocates of neoliberalism construed the focus on national development as an obstruction to the transnational mobility of goods, money, and firms and as preventing the efficient (i.e., private) allocation of global resources. As early as 1971, at the inception of the (corporate and elite-based) World Economic Forum, its first publication declared, "Nationalism is economically indefensible."[47] This reflects an early push to implement neoliberal policies privileging private investors, the private sector, and market forces. Recall here that this comes against the backdrop of rising political pressure toward reorganizing the world economy differently, as epitomized soon after by the call for a New International Economic Order (see Chapter 3).

Representing transnational corporations (TNCs) are institutions, such as the WTO, that have governed this global project. The director-general of the WTO, Renato Ruggiero, expressed this in 2000 in the following way:

> It is a new world. . . . The Cold War is over. Even more significant is the rise of the developing world as a major power in the international economy as a result of the shift to freer markets and open trade—an event that could rank with the industrial revolution in historical significance.

In this vision, the future of development lay with the world market, linked by the rules of neoclassical economic discourse. Ruggiero continued,

> If we want real coherence in global policymaking and a comprehensive international agenda, then coordination has to come from the top, and it must be driven by elected leaders. . . . Progress in resolving the challenge of the new century will hinge on our ability not just to build a coherent global architecture, but to build a political constituency for globalization. . . . Without the WTO, we will go back to a world of national barriers, protectionism, economic nationalism, and conflict.[48]

This was the vision of the globalization project: the implementation of "market rule" via the restructuring of policies and standards across the nation-state system. The globalization project did not begin on any particular date, but it signifies a new way of thinking about development. Among the political and economic elites, a consensus emerged, redefining development in private terms as "trade, not aid."

The globalization project involved political choices to (re)define the bearings and future of states and their civic responsibilities. If competing in the world market requires policies of cutting public expenditures that may reduce safeguards and standards of employment, health care, and education, then neoliberal *globalization was a decision, not an inevitability*. And it centers on "governance," overriding and reformulating government.

Global Governance

In the shift from the development to the globalization project, governments faced a world order in which global institutions assumed a more powerful governing role. This role is by no means absolute, and it requires compliance from the states themselves, guaranteed by consensus or coercion (which can backfire, as demonstrated by the Arab Spring of 2011 and the EU/Greek struggle of 2015).

Ultimately, the most effective way of guaranteeing compliance is to institutionalize market rule, where individual governmental functions are recomposed as global governance functions and enforced through multilateral protocols. Indeed, at the first ministerial meeting of the WTO in December 1996, Director-General Ruggiero remarked that preparing a global investment treaty was similar to "writing the constitution of a single global economy."

Global circuits (of debt, money, investment, and pension funds) are so embedded in national economies (and vice versa) that stabilizing these destabilizing financial relations (as evidenced by domino-like financial crises: Asia in the late 1990s, Europe in the late 2000s) dominated national policy making. While adopted by countries (in varying fashion), governance protocols favoring open markets reflect requirements of, or conditions favored by, the **global managers**—officials of the international financial institutions of the IMF and the World Bank, G-7 political elites, executives of TNCs, and global bankers. Indebted states restructure their political-economic priorities to obtain creditworthiness in the eyes of the global financial community. Paradoxically, an agroexport priority, which may negatively affect national food security, nonetheless conforms to the requirements of sound financial policy. It may enhance foreign exchange earnings for a time, but it reorients agriculture to supplying foreign consumers. Thus, global governance essentially deepens global market relations within states, compromising their sovereignty and accountability to citizens.

MEXICAN SOVEREIGNTY EXPOSED—FROM ABOVE AND BELOW

Mexico's admission into the Organisation for Economic Co-operation and Development (OECD) via its participation in the North American Free Trade Agreement (NAFTA) precipitated the 1994 Zapatista uprising in Chiapas (see Chapter 6), a region of intensive resource extraction by foreign companies. Protesting President Salinas's decision, Zapatista spokesperson Subcomandante Marcos claimed it was a "death sentence for Indigenous peoples."

The Zapatistas suggested that NAFTA was a confidence trick of the globalization project:

> At the end of 1994 the economic farce with which Salinas had deceived the Nation and the international economy exploded. The nation of money called the grand gentlemen of power and arrogance to dinner, and they did not hesitate in betraying the soil and sky in which they prospered with Mexican blood. The economic crisis awoke Mexicans from the sweet and stupefying dream of entry into the first world.

The Mexican peso lost 30 percent of its value in December 1994, generating a negative "tequila effect" throughout Latin American financial markets. International financiers hastily assembled a financial loan package of $18 billion to stabilize the peso: The United States committed over $9 billion, while the European Central Banks provided $5 billion; Canada also contributed $1 billion, and a dozen global banks, including Citibank, added a $3-billion line of credit. Finally, the IMF was called in to lend both money and its stamp of approval to restore investor confidence in the Mexican economy. U.S. President Bill Clinton remarked in 1995, "Mexico is sort of a bellwether for the rest of Latin America *and* developing countries throughout the world." Confidence in NAFTA was also at stake.

If the Mexican bailout was to stabilize the global economy and legitimize the globalization project, the question remains why the Mexican federal army occupied Chiapas. What is it about the globalization project that would make it value foreign investment over human rights?

Sources: Bradsher (1995: D6); Starr (2000: 104).

The Making of a Free Trade Regime

From 1986 to 1994, the whole world became the target of the Uruguay Round of the General Agreement on Tariffs and Trade (GATT). The Uruguay Round was to establish a set of new and binding rules concerning free trade, freedom of investment, and protection of **intellectual property rights**. Once formulated, these rules framed the WTO.

The United States engineered the creation of the GATT in 1948 as an alternative to the International Trade Organization (which included provisions from the **UN Universal Declaration of Human Rights** concerning full employment, working conditions, and social security).[49] Through GATT, trade expansion was *delinked from the social contract.* From 1948 through 1980, GATT reduced tariff rates on trade in manufactured goods by more than 75 percent.[50] Agriculture was excluded from the GATT. In the 1980s, at a time of recession and declining industrial leadership, the United States initiated the Uruguay Round, with the aim of liberalizing agriculture and services (such as banking, insurance, telecommunications), in which the North held a competitive advantage. Northern pressure and the promise of open markets for southern products, including agricultural goods, won acceptance from the South.[51]

The liberalization movement was supported by an activist lobby of "free trader" agroexporting states (the Cairns Group), TNCs such as IBM and American Express, and agribusinesses such as Cargill, Ralston-Purina, General Mills, Continental Grain, RJR Nabisco, and ConAgra, looking to reduce trade barriers, domestic price supports, and supply-management policies restricting demand for farm inputs such as fertilizer and chemicals. Corporations produce and sell farm products across the world—they take advantage of seasonal variation and dietary variation. Alternatively, family farmers are spatially fixed and depend on national farm policy—input and price subsidies, farm credit, risk insurance, and import controls—for their economic viability.

Given the competitive dumping of surplus foods by the United States and Europe, depressing agricultural prices by 39 percent (1975–1989),[52] GATT proposed an "urgent need to bring more discipline and predictability to world agricultural trade."[53] Southern farm sectors were adversely affected by dumping, deepening food import dependency, especially in sub-Saharan Africa. However, whereas liberalization was expected to stabilize markets, it has not stabilized farming in the global South since markets are controlled by huge agribusiness corporations, which dictate prices at the expense of family farmers. The United States challenged GATT's Article XI food security provisions, arguing for comparative advantage:

> The US has always maintained that self-sufficiency and food security are not one and the same. Food security—the ability to acquire the food you need when you need it—is best provided through a smooth-functioning world market.[54]

In short, the making of a free trade regime reconstructed "food security" as a market relation, privileging and protecting corporate agriculture and placing small farmers at a comparative disadvantage. Food security would now be "governed" through the market by corporate, rather than social, criteria.

The World Trade Organization

The singular achievement of the GATT Uruguay Round was the creation of the World Trade Organization (WTO) on January 1, 1995. The WTO, with over 160 voting members, assumes unprecedented power to enforce GATT provisions. It was unprecedented because the WTO is arguably less about trade rule consistency than about governing member states via liberalization. *Free trade* is a misnomer for the reach of WTO rules. In combination, they challenge national democratic processes, removing decision making to nontransparent tribunals located in Geneva, Switzerland, using "market logic" to override individual government policy where it interferes with "free trade."

Unlike the GATT (a trade treaty only), the WTO has independent jurisdiction. It claimed the power to enforce its rulings on member states, and these include rulings going beyond simply cross-border trade into the realm of "trade-related" issues. This means setting rules regarding the movement of goods, money, and productive facilities across borders—rules that restrict countries from enacting legislation or policies discriminating against such movement. WTO rules, in advancing trade freedoms, privilege corporate rights to compete internationally, ensuring that TNCs receive treatment equal to that received by domestic firms and reducing or removing local restrictions (e.g., labor, health, environmental laws) on trade and investment that might interfere with corporate competitiveness in the global marketplace. The WTO staff are unelected bureaucrats and their proceedings are secret, thus denying citizen participation in making and evaluating policy. In 1994, World Bank economist Herman Daly warned that establishing rules to override national governments' capacity to regulate commerce "is to wound fatally the major unit of community capable of carrying out any policies for the common good."[55]

The WTO formed with an *integrated dispute settlement* mechanism. If a state was perceived to be distorting trade obligations in one area, such as curbing investments in timber cutting to protect a forest, it can be disciplined through the application of sanctions against another area of economic activity, such as some of its manufactured exports. Member states can lodge complaints through the WTO, whose decision holds automatically unless every member of the WTO votes to reverse it. Should states refuse to comply, the WTO can authorize the plaintiff to take unilateral action. Martin Khor, director of the Third World Network, suggests that, in claiming to reduce "trade-distorting" measures, the WTO becomes "development-distorting."[56] The very *threat* of such challenges has already had the effect of diluting national laws protecting human and environmental health.

The WTO, in enforcing market freedoms, has *depoliticized* their profound social impact. Thus, the 1996 Singapore Ministerial Declaration invites objection to labor rights laws: "We reject the use of labor standards for protectionist purposes, and agree that the comparative advantage of countries, particularly low-wage developing countries, must in no way be put into question."[57] This implies a *general* challenge to national laws and regulations regarding the environment, health, preferential trade relations, social subsidies, labor legislation, and so on. While the challenge does not eliminate all laws, it seeks to *harmonize* regulation internationally, lowering the ceiling on democratic initiatives within the national polity. As we shall see, the goal of depoliticizing the economy can backfire, and this explains in large part the mushrooming global social justice movement.

In this sense, although implementation is uneven, the WTO expresses the essence of the globalization project. That is, global managers assumed extraordinary powers to govern the web of global economic relations lying across nation-states, privileging corporate over democratic rights. Below we outline three of the key mutually reinforcing protocols of the WTO: the Agreement on Agriculture (AoA), Trade-Related Aspects of Intellectual Property Rights (TRIPs), and the General Agreement on Trade in Services (GATS).

The Agreement on Agriculture (AoA)

The 1995 Agreement on Agriculture advocated universal reductions in trade protection, farm subsidies, and government intervention. Countries with the capacity to pay (the United States and European states) retained concealed subsidies at the expense of much larger southern farm populations who are threatened daily with imports (i.e., "dumping") of cheap farm commodities from the North.

With liberalization, farmers everywhere are under pressure to compete by selling cheap. Corporate farmers survive by subsidized "scale economy." Between 1998 and 1999, UK farm income fell by about 75 percent, driving 20,000 farmers out of business, and U.S. farm income declined by almost 50 percent between 1996 and 1999. In the global South, conservative estimates are that in the 1990s between 20 and 30 million farmers lost their land from the impact of AoA trade liberalization.[58]

Liberalization is evidently less about freeing trade than about consolidating a corporate food regime.[59] Under the AoA, states no longer have the right to self-sufficiency as a national strategy. Rather, the minimum market access rule guarantees the "right to export" (therefore the requirement to import), even under conditions of subsidized exports. "Food security," then, is not food self-reliance but rather food import dependency for a large minority of southern states. By the mid-1990s, half of the foreign exchange of the 88 low-income food-deficit countries went to food imports.[60]

THE AOA—REINFORCING INEQUALITY AND UNDERMINING DEMOCRATIC PROVISIONS?

In the context of the AoA under the WTO, it may be tempting to assume that members from the global South could, in principle, benefit from the provisions for market access of the global trading system. Proponents of trade liberalization for agricultural goods point to the potential for dismantling subsidy regimes that favor producers in wealthy countries.

However, in practice, few challenges in the WTO are made on behalf of increasing export prospects for poorer agriculturalists. This is because of a chilling effect: development aid–receiving countries are unlikely to jeopardize relationships with donors by initiating a WTO dispute.

Instead, the majority of cases around the AoA involve market access concerns between wealthy countries.

For example, the case under file number DS26 involved the United States challenging EU regulation against imports of beef from cattle treated with growth hormones, a case that the EU lost. To maintain the regulation, the EU had to accept U.S. retaliatory tariffs worth almost US$ 117 million annually. The case was ongoing between 1999 and 2009. This confirms the case about the WTO's role in undermining the democratic provision and also its role in the selective empowerment of actors biased toward economic clout.

Source: Glauber and Xing (2020).

Trade-Related Intellectual Property Rights (TRIPs)

The TRIPs protocol was defined by a coalition of 12 major U.S. corporations, a Japanese federation of business organizations, and the agency for European business and industry. Based on a synthesis of European and U.S. patent laws, intellectual property rights protection is to be administered by the WTO. Advocates claim that it simplifies the protection of property rights across national borders and protects and promotes innovation for everyone by guaranteeing profits from technological developments, such as computer software, biotechnological products and processes, and pharmaceuticals. But critics contest this corporate definition of intellectual rights, arguing that biodiverse and generic knowledge should remain available to humankind as a global "commons."[61]

Many commercial drugs these days derive from chemicals found in tropical flora and fauna. The northern lifestyle is directly connected to the extraction of these sorts of resources, such as drugs from the rosy periwinkle of Madagascar to fight childhood leukemia and testicular cancer; Brazzein, a powerful sweetener from a West African berry; biopesticides from the Indian neem tree; and human cell lines to identify genes causing illnesses such as Huntington's disease and cystic fibrosis.[62]

The global South contains 90 percent of global biological wealth, and scientists and corporations of the North hold 97 percent of all patents. Patents on biological wealth give patent holders exclusive control over the use of the genetic materials. Corporations have often patented genetic material obtained from a southern country without payment or obligation, turned it into a commodity such as a medicine, and then charged a fee for use of the genetic resource in local production or high prices for the commodity—even to the country where the material originated, often over centuries. Critics view this appropriation of genetic material by foreigners as **biopiracy**.[63]

General Agreement on Trade in Services (GATS)

Services, unlike goods, are defined as "anything you cannot drop on your foot."[64] They include public and financial services. The 1994 GATS regime opened markets for trade in services by establishing the rights to corporate "presence" in member countries for the delivery of a service in the areas of finance, telecommunications, and transport. "GATS 2000" is a fundamentally more far-reaching protocol to compel governments to provide unlimited market access to foreign service providers, without regard for social and environmental impacts of the service activities. As Tony Clarke notes, GATS 2000 involves the following:

- A "necessity test" requiring government proof that regulations on service provision are the "least trade restrictive," imposes severe constraints of governments' abilities to protect environmental, health, and other public interest standards.
- WTO "national treatment" protocols on government procurement and subsidies that impede the role of government funds for public services, making them equally available to foreign-based private service corporations.
- The guaranteed access of private service corporations to domestic markets in all sectors, including health, education, and water, is accelerated by permitting commercial presence in GATS member countries.[65]

In other words, *GATS threatens the social contract between state and citizen with a private contract between corporation and consumer.* The democratic claims of the citizen-state (expressed in municipal contracts for construction, sewage, garbage disposal, sanitation, and water services) would yield to the private capacities of the consumer-citizen at the expense of the public interest and its development expressions. In the GATS we see the elimination of all vestiges of the development-state and its replacement by corporate services globally. As Krajewski has shown other routes outside of the GATS to realizing the objectives of trade in services agenda are being negotiated, such as the Trade in Services Agreement (TiSA), the aim of which "is to further deepen liberalization commitments among countries with a strong interest in liberalizing trade in services and to adopt an agreement which could potentially be integrated into the WTO framework."[66] As he notes, though, "health education and water services do not seem to be at the core of the TiSA negotiations."[67] These sectors have already been liberalized fairly comprehensively, engendering much social suffering across the world.

WATER, WATER, EVERYWHERE? UNLESS IT'S A COMMODITY . . .

When a service is commodified, it becomes the property of only those who can afford to buy it. Its availability on the market for some makes it scarce for others. Water is understood to be the last infrastructure frontier for private investors. Only 5 percent of water services are in private hands, and expansion opportunities are estimated at a trillion dollars. Water privatization is dominated by two French TNCs: Vivendi SA and Suez Lyonnaise des Eaux. Other TNCs involved include Bechtel, Enron, and General Electric. The GATS protocol favors privatization of this public good. Meanwhile, the IMF and the World Bank demand privatization of water services as a funding condition.

Struggles over water in Bolivia and other parts of Latin America came to be known as the "water wars" with communities claiming the "right to define their rights" to the commons. Water struggles have proliferated everywhere, including in Europe and North America, where privatization has been pushed through.

More recently, water privatization has come under increased scrutiny with the case of the United Kingdom, the only country to have privatized its entire water service sector. "Since privatization in 1983, water bills across Britain have increased 360%." Meanwhile, the world faces a water crisis, with demand outstripping fresh water supply by 40 percent by 2030, according to the Global Commission on the Economics of Water.

Should the availability and distribution of a basic and precious resource such as water or food be governed by market forces, which tend to favor only those with purchasing power and compromise human rights?

Sources: India Resource Center, www.indiaresource.org; Amenga-Etego (2003: 20–21); Barlow (1999: 2, 7, 14, 18, 27, 33, 38); Conca (2006: 215–55); Godrej (2003: 12); Morgan (2011: 85–117); Vidal (2003: 24); Mazzucato et al. (2022); Almeida (2024); Moore (2023).

CONCLUSION

The development project incubated an economic nationalism that became increasingly limiting to TNCs. At the same time, a rising debt crisis enabled new direction in world ordering via the debt regime. The new direction was the globalization project, a neoliberal approach to organizing economic growth, corresponding to the growing scale and power of the transnational banks and corporations. The increasing volume of economic exchanges and the greater mobility of money and firms required forms of regulation beyond the reach of the nation-state even if imposed through the system of nation-states. The WTO represents one such form of interstate-system regulation. It is important to note here that the WTO has lost some power, or presence, more recently, even as it laid the institutional foundations for the globalization project. This began with a challenge to the WTO by the key states of the G-20 (Brazil, Russia, India, and

China: BRIC nations) in 2006 on grounds of U.S. and EU hypocrisy (continuing to subsidize their farm sectors while requiring all other states to reduce farm sector protections), which led to multilateral stalemate and the rise of multipolarity (as discussed in Chapter 7). Further, President Trump challenged the WTO's trade dispute mechanism in 2019, on account of Chinese state support of its global corporations. However, the logic of WTO agreements has not been undermined, with private actors, corporations, and investor rights still privileged.

Under these conditions, globalization is everything but universalist in its consequences. It assigns communities, regions, and nation-states new niches or specialized roles (including marginalization) in the global economy. The development project proposed social integration through national economic growth under individual state supervision and according to a social contract between government and citizenry. Nevertheless, it manipulated an unequal international political and economic structure inherited from colonialism, to the advantage of the capitalists in the West and elsewhere. As these structures were being challenged, the architects of the development project shifted to organizing a new phase: the globalization project offers new forms of authority and discipline governed by the market, reconfiguring inequalities globally and engendering new forms of resistance.

KEY TERMS

Biopiracy
Comparative advantage
Debt regime
Global managers
Intellectual property rights
Neoliberalism
Nongovernmental organizations
North American Free Trade Agreement (NAFTA)
Post–Washington Consensus
Poverty Reduction Strategy Papers (PRSPs)
Social funds
Social reproduction
United Nations Universal Declaration of Human Rights
Washington Consensus

FURTHER READING

George, Susan. *The Debt Boomerang: How Third World Debt Harms Us All*. Boulder, CO: Westview Press, 1992.

Hopewell, Kristen. *Breaking the WTO: How Emerging Powers Disrupted the Neoliberal Project*. Stanford, CA: Stanford University Press, 2016.

Mgbeoji, Ikechi. *Global Biopiracy: Patents, Plants, and Indigenous Knowledge*. Ithaca, NY: Cornell University Press, 2006.

Rosset, Peter M. *Food Is Different: Why We Must Get the WTO Out of Agriculture*. Halifax, NS: Fernwood, 2006.

Soederberg, Susanne. *Global Governance in Question: Empire, Class, and the New Common Sense in Managing North-South Relations*. London: Pluto, 2006.

Soederberg, Susanne. *Debtfare States and the Poverty Industry: Money, Discipline and the Surplus Population*. Abingdon, UK: Routledge, 2014.

Sylla, Ndongo Samba. *Imperialism and the Political Economy of Global South's Debt*. Leeds UK: Emerald Publishing, 2023.

Wallach, Lori, and Patrick Woodall. *Whose Trade Organization? A Comprehensive Guide to the WTO*. London: New Press, 2004.

SELECT WEBSITES

Public Citizen Global Trade Watch (USA): www.citizen.org/trade

Structural Adjustment Participatory Review International Network: www.saprin.org

UN Capital Development Fund: www.uncdf.org

World Health Organization (WHO): www.who.int/en

World Trade Organization (WTO): www.wto.org

5 EXPERIENCING THE GLOBALIZATION PROJECT

Processes and Implications

The globalization project has been Janus-faced. It has consolidated "market rule" at the same time intensifying its socially harmful implications: informalization, displacement, marginalization, and impoverishment. The cost of prioritizing market relations involves many people working on the fringes of the formal economy, performing casual and unregulated (often outsourced) labor, working in cooperative arrangements, street vending, or pursuing what are deemed illegal economic activities. Those who are bypassed or marginalized by this form of development often form protective social projects or resistance movements to market society.

In this chapter, we disclose the unequal social relations through which modalities of the globalization project circulate and take shape. Our historical relational analytic introduced in Chapter 1 allows better understanding of how distinctive features of the globalization project intersect with and compound historical injustices of colonialism. Unequal relations underpin what are termed global supply chains (or global commodity chains) from an economic perspective, which from a social-relational perspective operate as "poverty chains,"[1] given their integration of dis-organized and closely surveilled low-cost labor forces in the prototypical world factory.

This new social form of the globalization era has reproduced the exploitative relations of the colonial era, in rubber and cotton and tea plantations, and mining and logging industries, for example, all of which now contribute to contemporary assembly lines of world factories producing garments, shoes, automobiles, or technology. Global agribusiness, alongside the international retailing industry, elaborates monocultures combined with chemicals and preservative inputs to market increasingly processed food products across the world. Images of abundance and universal availability simultaneously harm landscapes, farm cultures, and farmworkers (and often consumers). Furthermore, such offshore industries have undermined manufacturing and labor unions and family farmers in the global North, underlining the Janus-face of globalization, and engendering ongoing resistances to exploitation and displacement in both areas[2] and rising grievances against global elites (increasingly taking the form of authoritarian populism).

These vignettes speak to the magnitude of the contradictions of the neoliberal globalization project. Increasing urbanization has been accompanied by an unprecedented rise in sprawling informal settlements across the global South. At the same time, homelessness and destitution have been on the rise in wealthy countries of the global North as well, evidenced, for instance, by tent cities and rising numbers of street sleepers.[3] As the World Cities Report (2022) noted, chronic homelessness in London and persistent concentrated poverty in Baltimore (Maryland) highlight urban poverty and inequality in so-called developed countries.[4]

All of these adverse experiences integral to the globalization project are today exacerbated by global heating and its climate change corollaries. As current scenarios model global temperature increases to potentially reach 2 degrees Celsius in 2050, an expected 2.9 billion people (or 29 percent of the world population) are expected to experience high climate-related risks.[5] For example, industrial agriculture often has unsustainably high water-usage patterns, but in the context of rising temperatures and wildfires, this now trends toward potentially catastrophic outcomes.[6] In all these contexts, socially disadvantaged communities are exposed to much greater risks and vulnerabilities, even as everyone potentially deals with some consequences of these changes.

Even with these conditions now firmly on everyone's radar, the globalization project continues the historic "colonial" relationship of **extractivism**. With this, it augments the depletion of the very resources that all life as well as livelihoods depend on. Notably:

> The environment (is) simultaneously a means of accumulation of capital, and a means for the reproduction of the conditions that make such accumulation possible. The environment's joint function applies to units of production at all scales. At the level of a rural household, land and water are central to the possibility of petty accumulation, but the continued existence of fertile land and clean, available water resources are also essential for the reproduction of the rural household as a social unit.[7]

Depletion, as critical feminist scholarship has shown,[8] can therefore be used to understand the experiences of households subjected to exploitation and to being inserted differentially into neoliberal relations of wealth accumulation. At the same time, from everyday forms of resistance to more organized movements, the neoliberal globalization project continues to be contested.

THE (NEW) GLOBAL DIVISION OF LABOR AND OUTSOURCING

The institutionalization of the neoliberal globalization project reflected a significant shift in the organization of development globally. In this section, we discuss some key processes through which the globalization project has been advanced, the experiences it has engendered, and some of its social, political, and ecological implications.

Notably, transnational corporations (TNCs) began to outsource production processes to the global South, or, more accurately, *around* the global South. They were looking to capitalize on weak labor regulations and environmental standards, on favorable taxation regimes, or on arrangements such as tightly controlled export processing zones. The pursuit of such objectives enabled dramatic cuts in production costs, at the expense of labor exploitation, social deprivation, and ecological despoliation. Another distinguishing feature of changing South–North dynamics has been the rise of the service sector, and in particular the ascendancy of the financial services industry (banking, insurance, credit rating agencies, consulting services) in the global North, with allies, partners, and branches in the global South, especially in East and South Asia.

Outsourcing relocates the production of goods and services as a cost-reduction strategy and a means to increase operational flexibility of an organization. It includes offshoring, as firms shift production overseas.[9] Outsourcing has become significant for two reasons: (1) the hypermobility of capital in an era of deregulation and expanding access to unprotected labor (in terms of rights, conditions, and wages) and (2) the privatization of state responsibilities to provide public goods and services to citizens. Under neoliberalism, in addition to corporate outsourcing, governments have outsourced service contracts to reduce public expenditure and/or privilege the private sector.

When the South African government outsourced Telkom, the state telephone company, in 2003, it completed the privatization of this essential service, which already had increased tariffs for poor households while slashing rates for rich families and firms, and cut 80 percent of new land lines because of the inability of poor subscribers to pay.[10] Meanwhile, in health care, the World Bank has made loans to outsource public health to private managed care initiatives in the name of reducing public sector inefficiencies. As a result, neoliberal policy brings about these three characteristic effects:

1. Access to health care for the poor shrinks while investments grow—"between 1996 and 1999, revenues of multinational health care corporations grew much faster in Latin America than in the United States."[11]
2. Outsourcing and cutbacks in public sector budgets reduce preventative programs, allowing banished diseases such as cholera, dengue fever, and typhus to reemerge as epidemics.
3. As has happened in a dozen states in the United States, after profiting through the privatization of public health care systems, managed care organizations and health insurance companies move on when profit margins fall.[12]

Corporate outsourcing has become virtually synonymous with globalization. It has been facilitated by the emergence of the world factory.

The World Factory

The expanding belt of export industries in the global South, led by the newly industrialized countries, provides a clue to a broader transformation occurring within the world at large. There was a new "fast track" in manufacturing exports, superseding the traditional track of exporting processed resources. It heralded the rise of the **world factory**: proliferating manufacturing export platforms producing world, rather than national, products. Often, production steps are separated and distributed among geographically dispersed sites in assembly-line fashion, producing and assembling a completed product. World products—including automobiles, cell phones, computers, jeans, and electronic toys—emerge from a single site or a **global assembly line** of multiple sites (commodity chains) organizing disparate labor forces of varying skill, cost, and function.[13]

The phenomenal growth of export manufacturing using labor-intensive methods in the East Asian region, as well as regions such as Mexico's border-industrial zone, signaled the rise of a *global production system*. In Asia, the stimulus came from the relocation of the Japanese industrial model of hierarchical subcontracting arrangements to sites across the region. The Mexican Border Industrialization Program (BIP) paralleled this "decentralization" of industrial production, importing unfinished components for local assembly as a world market product. In 1965, the Mexican government implemented the BIP to allow entirely foreign-owned corporations to establish labor-intensive assembly plants (known as **maquiladoras**) within a 12-mile strip south of the U.S. border. The geographic restrictions were progressively relaxed, and dropped entirely in the early 1990s.[14] Concessions to firms employing Mexican labor at a fraction of U.S. wages and paying minimal taxes and import duties to the Mexican government were part of a competitive world factory strategy. The *maquiladoras* have earned about one-third of Mexico's scarce foreign currency income.

The cost calculus driving the relocation of manufacturing to the global South includes avoidance of stringent environmental regulations. Over a quarter of factory operators in the city of Mexicali, close to the California border, cited Mexico's lax environmental enforcement as a condition of relocation. The impact is both physical and environmental. Electronics factories commonly include open and toxic fume-emitting containers of carcinogenic acids and solvents; this results in chronic illness, such as headaches, sore throat, and drowsiness, among the workforce. Chemical discharges from *maquiladoras* into open ditches adjacent to shantytowns have been linked to cancer, birth defects, and brain damage, and factories in export processing zones have been associated with the dumping of pollutants into local waters, affecting drinking water and fisheries.[15]

The Export Processing Zone

Export processing zones (EPZs), or free trade zones (FTZs), are specialized manufacturing export zones, with minimal customs controls, and usually exempt from labor regulations and domestic taxes (see Table 5.1). EPZs serve firms seeking lower wages as well as the interests of governments of "developing" countries seeking capital investment and foreign currency to be earned from exports.

EPZs typically serve as *enclaves*—in social as well as economic terms. Often physically separate from the rest of the country, walled in with barbed wire, locked gates, and special security guards, EPZs are built to receive imported raw materials or components and to export the output directly by sea or air. Workers are bused in and out

TABLE 5.1 ■ Estimated Number of Workers in EPZs by Selected Country, 2014

Geographical area	Estimated number of workers	Number of zones
Asia	55,741,147	900+
Central America and Mexico	5,252,216	155
Middle East	1,043,597	50
North Africa	643,152	65
Sub-Saharan Africa	860,474	90+
United States	340,000	713
South America	459,825	43
Transition economies	1,400,379	400
Caribbean region	546,513	250
Indian Ocean	182,712	1
Europe	364,818	50
Pacific	145,930	14
TOTAL (estimations)	**65,980,763**	**3500+**

Source: International Labour Organization (2014: 3).

daily or live in the EPZ under a short-term labor contract. Inside the EPZ, whatever civil rights and working conditions exist in the society at large are usually denied to the workforce. At the same time, resistance by and protection of this workforce spawned a "transnational gender and trade network" (drawing attention to the gendered nature of this workforce), as well as mobilizations of civil society organizations "to monitor and participate in trade policy debates."[16]

EPZs provided an early portal for some women in the global South to enter the formal global workforce, just as young English and American farm girls staffed early textile mills. They earned in one week approximately what their First World counterparts earned in one hour. In the early 1980s, 80 to 90 percent of zone workers were females between 16 and 25 years old. Dominant patriarchal representations frame women as best suited to the tasks. Women are depicted to have "natural patience" and "manual dexterity." A personnel manager of a Taiwanese assembly plant claimed, "Young male workers are too restless and impatient to be doing monotonous work with no career value. If displeased, they sabotage the machines and even threaten the foreman. But girls, at most they cry a little."[17] Appealing to Orientalist stereotypes, a Malaysian investment brochure stated the following:

> The manual dexterity of the oriental female is famous the world over. Her hands are small and she works fast with extreme care. Who, therefore, could be better qualified by nature and inheritance to contribute to the efficiency of a bench-assembly production line than the oriental girl.[18]

GENDERING THE GLOBAL LABOR FORCE

The expectation of endless supplies of unprotected labor, especially in the global South, affects women in particular. Much labor-intensive work is feminized, depending on complex patriarchal and subcontracting hierarchies. Labor-intensive export platform industries prefer young, unmarried, and relatively educated women. While employers argue that women are suited to the jobs because of their dexterity and patience, these qualities are required as much by the jobs themselves as by patriarchal assumptions and practices reproduced within the factories, sweatshops, and home work units.

Women are typically subjected to long workdays and lower wages compared with men. High turnover, lack of union rights, sexual harassment, and poor health characterize the female workforce that has mushroomed across the Asian, Central American, and Middle Eastern regions. Under these conditions, patriarchal states—competing for foreign investment—encourage women to enter the workforce at the same time as the new female workforce may be under official scrutiny for loose morals, and governments withhold maternity benefits, child care, and education opportunities on the grounds that they are "secondary workers" in a male-dominated labor market.

Where young women and children work in family production units (a widespread practice), subcontractors rely on patriarchal pressures to discipline the workers. In the workplace, teenage girls are often forced to take birth control pills to eliminate maternity leave and payments or are forced to have abortions if they get pregnant. Labor contractors and managers routinely demand sexual favors from young women for awarding them jobs, giving rise to a "factory harem mentality." The endless nature of the supply of female labor comes from their short working life in many of these jobs because of the eye–hand coordination of girls that peaks at age 16; the physical deterioration from low wages, poor health, and poor nutrition; the high turnover due to harassment; the steady experience of having the life sucked out of them by long working hours and no advancement in skills; and the steady stream of new cohorts of younger women to follow, whether from the countryside, the children of the working poor, or international traffickers in labor.

Are women working under these conditions better off, empowered, or further devalued?

Sources: Agarwal (1988); Fernández-Kelly (1983: 129); Gunawardana (2016).

The world factory emerged on a foundation of the new global division of labor as a forerunner of the era of neoliberal integration. This pattern, amplified by trade-related aspects of investment measures, has consolidated as the **global division of labor**, now extending to high- and low-paid services and perishable agricultural commodities. Outsourcing of production has depended on the deepening of information and communication technologies, especially microprocessing power and developments in fiber optics. For example, in the first decade of the twenty-first century, "e-mailing a 40-page document from Chile to Kenya cost less than 10 cents, faxing it about $10 and sending it by courier $50." By the twenty-first century, "more information was sent over a single cable in a second than over the entire Internet in a month in 1997."[19] This compression of space by time enhances the ability of firms to manage far-flung and fragmented outsourcing operations—coordinating movement of components through the supply chain and of foods shipped across seasonal and time zones.

Between 1996 and 2000, U.S. corporate outsourcing grew from $100 billion to $345 billion, concentrating in call centers, graphic design, computer programming, and accountancy.[20] Many of the new jobs in the Caribbean, for example, have involved data processing positions that large U.S. insurance, health industry, magazine subscription renewal, consumer credit, and retailing firms have shifted offshore at a lower cost. Swissair, British Airways, and Lufthansa relocated much of their reservation operations to Indian subcontractors in Bangalore, where "the staff are well educated at English-speaking universities, yet cost only a fraction of what their counterparts are paid in the North."[21]

With outsourcing upgrades in India into product research and development, financial analysis, and handling insurance claims and payrolls, call center employee wages increased by 50 percent, providing an opportunity for the Philippines, where call center jobs rose 100 percent over five years to 200,000 in late 2006.[22] Indian companies now outsource in order to capture an expanding back-office industry as Indian wages rise, and China, Morocco, and Mexico challenge India's successful model.

Information technology (IT) services have expanded in India at a rate of between 30 and 60 percent annually (contributing to 60 percent of Indian GDP now), with new frontiers of "virtual services" beyond customer service centers beckoning to TNCs—"health care, where a scan may be carried out in one country, processed in another, and sent to a third for another opinion before being sent back home again, is one example."[23] The economics profession may be another mobile "virtual service."

Barbados, with a literacy rate of 98 percent and a reputation for social stability and polite service, used its English-speaking tradition to turn itself into a haven for offshore information-based data processing work, globally sourced by subsidiaries of British and U.S. telecommunication corporations. While such work is unskilled and gendered, Carla Freeman found that, despite better pay in the sugar cane fields, these women find "pink-collar" jobs attractive because of the identification with office work and informatics technology, and because the Barbados Development Plan—development via information-based exports—includes guarantees of basic employment benefits such as maternity and sick leave and paid vacations and because differentiation from field and factory work through dress codes and consumption styles enables them to "experience class as gendered Afro-Caribbean subjects within a distinctly feminized arena."[24]

For India, with an English-speaking tradition, as in parts of the Caribbean, South Africa, Pakistan, and the Philippines, language became a "comparative advantage" for this kind of service outsourcing. At the SpectraMind call center in Delhi, in addition to a two-hour seminar on the royal family, one set of recruits would receive "a 20-hour crash course in British culture, watching videos of British soap operas to accustom them to regional accents, [and learning] about Yorkshire pudding." Another set of recruits, exposed to American TV shows and sporting slang, learn "the nuances of baseball."[25]

Since 1991, foreign corporations have established subsidiaries in India to outsource jobs in IT, financial services, business processes, pharmaceuticals, and automotive components, generating thousands of new jobs and annual rates of growth that are twice those in the North. Bangalore, Hyderabad, Delhi, and Mumbai displayed their newfound wealth as emerging "global cities."[26] One-third of Bangalore's population are slum dwellers, and half "lack piped water, much less cappuccino, and there are more ragpickers and street children (90,000) than software geeks (about 60,000)."[27] Not only are two-thirds of the populace (230 million) still residing in publicly neglected and deteriorating rural habitats, but the IT sector generates less than 2 percent of national income and employs one million in an economy where eight million join the labor force annually.[28] Outsourcing generates clusters of prosperity networked more often across national borders than within them.

Rural land appropriation for outsourcing industries is routine (though not without resistance). In China in Dongguan City (site of Reebok and Nike shoe manufacturers), local farmers now live off factory rents while tens of thousands of migrants from the hinterland swell the workforce.[29] Datang, a rice-farming village in the late 1970s, with a cottage industry in socks, now produces nine billion socks annually. Renamed "Sock City," Datang is one of many new coastal cities: southeast is Shenzhou, the world's necktie capital; west is Sweater City and Kids' Clothing City; and to the south, in the low-rent district, is Underwear City.[30]

The global supermarket revolution is founded on an outsourcing model of "buyer-driven commodity chains," linking contract farmers with centralized food processing and retailing operations.[31] Transnational firms such as Ahold, Carrefour, and Walmart constitute 70 to 80 percent of the top five supermarket chains in Latin America, centralizing procurement from farmers across the region (and their own processing plants) and, together with Nestlé and Quaker, supplying regional consumer markets throughout the Mercosur trading bloc in the eastern part of Latin America. In Guatemala, where three supermarkets control about 30 percent of food retailing,[32] "their sudden appearance . . . brought unanticipated and daunting challenges to millions of struggling, small farmers," lacking binding contractual agreements, rewarded only if they consistently meet new quality standards, and facing declining prices as they constitute a virtually unlimited source for retailers.[33]

GLOBAL LABOR–SOURCING POLITICS AND MIGRATION

While outsourcing is typically associated with firms "going global," there are growing migrant circuits across the world contributing to the sourcing of labor on a global scale and serving all facets of industry (manufacturing, agriculture, construction, and services). Ironically, as northern manufacturing has moved offshore, southern labor has found its way north in the form of farmworkers and food workers, as well as construction workers, especially to the Middle East. In Europe, the "great turnaround" describes the reversal of patterns of migration, where southern European states formerly supplied migrant labor to industrialized centers of northern Europe, but now southern Europe is the destination for inflows of North African migrant labor, where a growing proportion of farm labor in Italy is foreign.[34] In the United States 73 percent of farmworkers are foreign.[35] Migrant labor conditions are always precarious because of issues of documentation, exploitation, racism, sexism, and employment uncertainty (not to mention separation from family and community back home).

Displacement

As we can see from the previous discussion, in the shadow of globalization lurks a rising dilemma: the casualization of labor and growing redundancy.[36] Despite, and perhaps because of, an expanding global economy, numbers of unemployed (including hard-to-count long-term unemployed) in the global North rose from 10 million to almost 50 million between 1973 and the early twenty-first century.[37] This is the dilemma of structural unemployment, where automation and/or outsourcing of work sheds stable jobs and where workers made redundant cease rotating into new jobs. It has been matched across the world by other forms of displacement, including SAP-mandated dismantling of import-substitution industrialization sectors and privatization of public enterprise, forced resettlement by infrastructural projects (e.g., 1.2 million peasants resettled in China's Three Gorges Dam project),[38] civil wars, and the destabilization of rural communities by privileging and deepening market forces (dumping of cheap food, land concentration, and decline of farm subsidies). At the turn of the twenty-first century, one billion workers (one-third of the world's labor force, mainly southern) were either unemployed or underemployed.[39]

Displacement begins either with colonization or depeasantization, even though agriculture is the main source of food and income for the majority of the world's poor. In the twenty-first century over three billion people across the world directly depend on the agricultural sector, and more than half of the South's population is agrarian.[40]

As we saw in Chapters 3 and 4, the neoliberal vision of food security means privileging food importing over local farming for many southern states, displacing small farmers. The transnational peasant coalition Via Campesina notes, "The massive movement of food around the world is forcing the increased movement of people."[41] Under the WTO's Agreement on Agriculture, decoupling of (northern) subsidies from prices removes the price floor, establishing a *low* "world price" for agricultural commodities and undercutting small/family farmers everywhere, resulting in displacement. Liberalization policies are rooted in IMF–World Bank structural adjustment measures, which have routinely required "free markets" in grain—for example, in formerly self-sufficient countries such as Malawi, Zimbabwe, Kenya, Rwanda, and Somalia.

Global economic integration intensifies displacement as the global economy stratifies populations across, rather than simply within, national borders. At the same time, conflict within states (often rooted in development processes), war, and persecution have expelled 60 million people, half of whom are children.[42] With provocative imagery, in 1991 Jacques Attali distinguished *rich nomads* ("consumer-citizens of the privileged regions") from *poor nomads* ("boat people on a planetary scale").

Migration is often associated with fears of terrorism, underlying the concern of many northerners to stem the tide of global labor migration. Consequences range from the spread of "gated communities" to a rollback of civil rights in the global North and outbreaks of racist violence toward "guest workers." This attitude has spread in Europe, where millions of so-called "illegal" migrants (from Eastern Europe, Turkey, Central Asia, China, and Francophone West Africa) work in restaurants, construction, and farming—they "enjoy none of the workers' rights and protections or social benefits of the state . . . are paid less than the legal wage, and are often paid late, with no legal recourse."[43]

In the global North, continuing immigration is in the interests of firms that need cheap labor and of the privileged who require domestic workers. But such organized migration has led to the *displacement of love* via the feminization and export of care workers from the South to care for children of working women in the North; it has been termed the *global heart transplant* and linked to the "care drain" from the South via "chains of love," whereby migrant women work as "global nannies" at considerable emotional cost to their own children, who in turn are cared for by relatives or teenage girls at home.[44]

MIGRANT LABOR IN THE GLOBAL ECONOMY: THE PRODUCTION OF ECONOMIC AND ENVIRONMENTAL REFUGEES

As the twenty-first century proceeds, as many as 232 million people are estimated to be living as expatriate laborers around the world. Asian women are the fastest growing group of foreign workers, increasing by about one million each year. In 2021 the International Labour Organization (ILO) reported that almost 80% of domestic workers are women.

Environmental migration is increasingly significant, with reports that one billion people could be displaced by climate change by 2050:

- 135 million people whose land is being transformed into deserts (desertification);

- 900 million of the world's poorest, existing on less than a dollar a day and living in areas vulnerable to soil erosion, droughts, desertification, and floods;
- 200 million people facing rising sea levels due to climate change;
- 50 million people in famine-vulnerable areas subject to climate change; and
- 550 million people already suffering from chronic water shortage.

Sources: Boyd, S. (1998: 17); Baird (2002: 10); Perrons (2005: 211); Swing (2015); Vidal (2007a); International Labour Organization (2021).

Migrant Labor: The New Export

The mobility rights for capital guaranteed by neoliberalism do not extend to labor. Nevertheless, labor increasingly circulates, seeking employment opportunities—whether "legal," "illegal," or indentured/bonded labor. Migration is not new to this century. The separation of people from the land is etched into the making of the modern world. Colonialism propelled migrations of free and unfree people.

During the 1980s, spurred by debt regime restructurings, there was an internal migration in the former Third World of between 300 and 400 million people.[45] This pool of labor has contributed to global migration from overburdened cities to northern regions as migrants seek to earn money for families back home. In excess of 100 million kinfolk depend on remittances of the global labor force. In 2013, remittances were over three times larger than Overseas Development Assistance[46] (see Figure 5.1).

FIGURE 5.1 ■ Remittance Flows Are Large and Growing

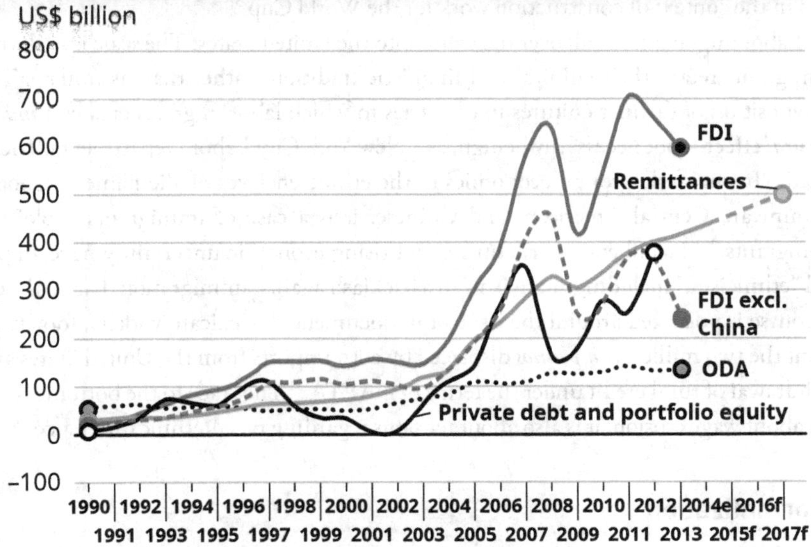

Source: World Bank (2014).

The global pandemic has of course slowed the growth of remittances by about 20 percent, as labor migration has declined, but recovered immediately.[47] The influx of foreign exchange not only supplies much-needed hard currency, but in an era of structural adjustment and privatization, remittance money also supplements or subsidizes public ventures. Thus, in Indonesian villages, remittances finance schools, roads, and housing in lieu of public funding.

Spurred by debt, labor export has become a significant foreign currency earner: in the early 1990s Filipino overseas earnings amounted to about $5.7 billion, for example, with about six million Filipino/as working overseas in 130 countries as contract workers (seamen, carpenters, masons, mechanics, or maids).[48] The government of the Philippines has included labor export in its development strategy.[49] Much labor is exported to the oil-rich Middle East, where contractors organize the ebb and flow of foreign labor. One contractor, Northwest Placement, a privately run recruiting agency, receives 5,000 pesos ($181)—the maximum allowed by the Labor Department—from Filipino applicants on assurance of a job; this covers the costs of a medical check, visas, and government clearance fees. Not surprisingly, there are also plenty of unlicensed agencies operating.[50]

International labor circulation combines formal policies with decidedly informal working conditions. Migrant workers are routinely denied human rights. Recent examples include accounts of the conditions experienced by migrant workers who had been recruited under the *kafala* migration sponsorship system to build the stadiums and facilities for the 2022 FIFA World Cup in Qatar. Under pressure from international reports, Qatar eventually discontinued the *kafala* system and introduced labor rights reforms; however, by 2021 it was reported that over 6,500 migrant workers had died in the context of construction work for the World Cup.[51]

Labor migrates from all over the world into the United States. The scale is such that immigrants retain their cultural and linguistic traditions rather than assimilate. The juxtaposition of distinct cultures in countries to which labor migrates creates a *multicultural* effect—not necessarily benign, as a New York City Labor Department Official noted: "In the underground economies of the ethnic enclaves of Vietnamese, Cuban, Dominican, Central American, and Chinese, it is a case of immigrants exploiting immigrants."[52] Neoliberal restructuring and rising economic uncertainty have amplified "ethnicism," including "nativism" in a backlash against immigration. U.S. political discourse is polarized around the issue of undocumented Mexican workers, forgetting about the two million *campesinos* displaced by corn imports from the United States and withdrawal of rural credit under the terms of NAFTA.[53] The "race to the bottom" is not just about wage erosion; it is also about tensions regarding racial/ethnic difference.

Informalization

The globalization project also has pushed more people out of stable employment and forces them to adopt self-help measures. In some cases, a revival of subsistence farming may improve living standards over working as a rural laborer or existing on the urban fringe, as long as land is available.[54] However, marginalization is closely associated with forms of displacement—for example, cycles of expansion and contraction of formal economic activity or the concentration of resources in fewer corporate hands generate **informalization**, producing the idea of a "**precariat**": a highly vulnerable class of casual proletarians.[55] It is important to note that "precarity" is not new. As Scully reminds us, "In Southern Countries these are not recent products of contemporary precarity, but longstanding features of wage-work; they have shaped workers' politics from the colonial era, through the period of post-independence development, and into the neoliberal present."[56] This point notwithstanding, new alliances have emerged between workers and nonworkers, from the UK to Mexico, in order to counteract and challenge the socially corrosive effects of neoliberal market society.[57]

Informalization is a politico-cultural process. With the rise of market societies, the boundaries of the formal economy were identified and regulated by the state for tax purposes, but they have always been incomplete and fluid, often by design and certainly by custom. An army of servants and housecleaners, for example, routinely works "off the books." Casual labor has always accompanied small-scale enterprise and even large-scale harvesting operations where labor use is cyclical.

Distinguishing between a formal economy (with its legal/moral connotations) and an informal sector (with its illegal or immoral connotations) is either artificial or political. We make the distinction here because it reveals the limits of official, formal development strategy and identifies alternative, informal livelihood strategies—often intimately connected and mutually conditioning. Economists and governments make the distinction because national accounting measures legal cash transactions. By ignoring informal activity, development policy discounts and marginalizes substantial mechanisms of social reproduction on which the formal "productive economy" depends.

The "informal economy" comprises two related domains: forms of social reproduction complementing production (as previously mentioned) and informal "productive" activity off the books. For example, one of the world's largest slums, Dharavi, has an "informal" output of $1.25 billion a year, largely from the work of 250,000 people recycling the discarded waste of Mumbai's 16 million citizens.

Slum dwellers now comprise at least *a third* of the global urban population and 50 percent of the population of the global South (see Figure 5.2). UN-Habitat, an agency for human settlement and sustainable urban development, suggests for instance that in 2020 49 percent of the urban population of India lived in slums, while the figure for Chad was 82 percent.[58]

In effect, neoliberal development and the generation of a "planet of slums" go together. Of course, these *peri-urban* communities, as they are known, have been expanding throughout the twenty-first century, as the world's urban population surpassed that of the countryside in 2006.[59]

Informalization as a process has two related aspects: the casualization of labor via corporate restructuring and new forms of individual and collective livelihood strategies.

FIGURE 5.2 ■ Growth of World's Largest Cities, 1950 and 2007

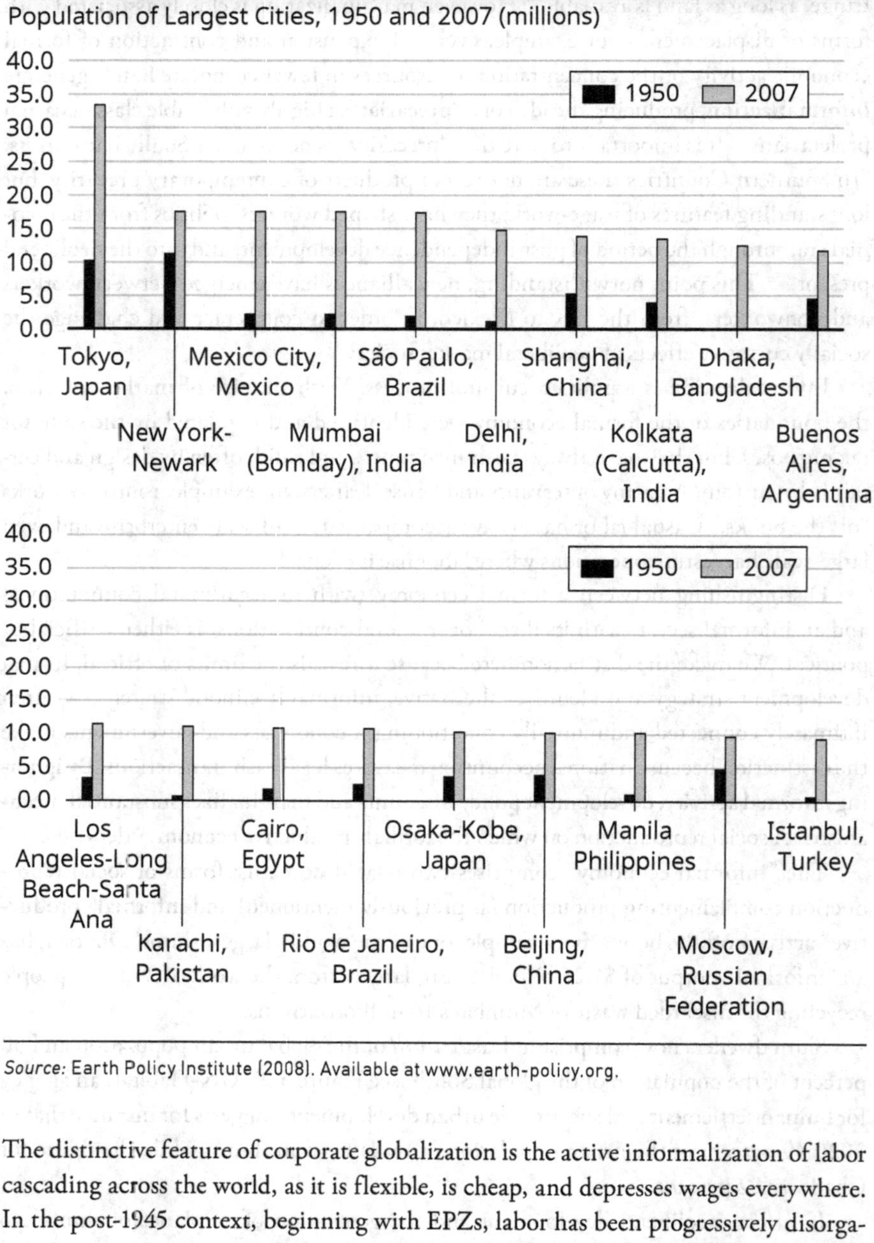

Source: Earth Policy Institute (2008). Available at www.earth-policy.org.

The distinctive feature of corporate globalization is the active informalization of labor cascading across the world, as it is flexible, is cheap, and depresses wages everywhere. In the post-1945 context, beginning with EPZs, labor has been progressively disorganized via weakening and dismantling of labor regulations, incorporating vulnerable first-generation labor forces as depeasantization has proceeded. International Labour Organization (ILO) estimates show some variation in the percentage of informalization of nonagricultural employment: 48 percent in North Africa, 51 percent in Latin America, 65 percent in Asia, and 72 percent in sub-Saharan Africa.[60]

China has shown an interesting variation on labor informalization. Given the draconian agricultural tax system in China and an urban/rural differential greater than anywhere else, between 1996 and 2000 over 176 million peasants migrated to cities for work, but they went without the social benefits extended to urban residents. This itinerant labor force works mainly in newly zoned export factories and cost foreign corporations one-third the wage (itself a fraction of northern wage costs) of city-born workers. During this migration, the female percentage of informal workers rose from 45 percent to over 65 percent.[61] Li Quiang's study of Beijing migrants (2002) revealed that one-quarter were unpaid, almost two-thirds worked over 10 hours a day—with a sizable percentage working over 16 hours a day (over and above rush order episodes)—and health care was nonexistent.[62]

Meanwhile, in export agriculture from the global South, millions of women, constituting between 50 and 90 percent of workers employed in producing, processing, and retailing high-value horticultural crops (roses, apples, snow peas, green beans, and avocados), experience informalization. TNCs organize these global supply chains, using their market power to pass business costs and risk on to suppliers, who in turn displace these onto their workforce. The ILO reports that rights violations of agricultural workers are "legion" and that women suffer weak labor rights, casualization, low wages, long hours, lax health and safety practices, gender stereotyping, and sexual harassment.[63]

The other face of informalization is the expanding range of activities of production and social reproduction occurring in the "shadow economy," comprising over 50 percent of the population of the global South. Commercial agriculture and habitat degradation routinely expel peasants and laborers from rural livelihoods; they migrate to urban centers where—as they hear on the radio and through migrant networks—jobs and amenities may be available.

Under these conditions, regions of informality may become anomic, deepening human exploitation such as child prostitution and organ selling, with Chennai (India) having become world renowned for its "kidney farms."[64]

NEOLIBERAL DEVELOPMENT AND EXTRACTIVISM: RECONFIGURING INTERNATIONAL RELATIONS

The neoliberal globalization project is also mirrored in South–South cooperation, regarding extractivism. As an example, we consider relations between China and countries in Africa. The United Nations Conference on Trade and Development (UNCTAD) noted in 2003 that 12 African countries depended on a single export commodity: crude petroleum (Angola, 92 percent; Congo, 57; Gabon, 70; Nigeria, 96; and Equatorial Guinea, 91), copper (Zambia, 52 percent), diamonds (Botswana, 91 percent), coffee (Burundi, 76 percent; Ethiopia, 62; Uganda 83), tobacco (Malawi, 59 percent), and uranium (Niger, 59 percent).[65] In 2004, foreign direct investment in

Africa was $15 billion (up from $2 billion in 1986), with most new investment concentrated in mineral extraction, especially in Angola, Equatorial Guinea, Nigeria, and Sudan, and in deepwater oil fields off the West African coast—sourcing 25 percent of North American oil imports by 2015.[66]

In an era of Chinese ascendancy, the resource grab intensifies. Once self-sufficient in oil (1990), China was the second largest importer of oil after the United States by 2003, accounting for 40 percent of rising demand for oil between 2001 and 2005.[67] One-third of its oil is African. The Chinese National Petroleum Corporation (which overtook Shell in 2006 as the world's sixth largest oil company) and two other large Chinese oil firms operate in 17 African countries, including Sudan (Darfur notwithstanding), where a Chinese state-owned company owns 40 percent of the oil concession in the South (with 4,000 Chinese troops protecting Beijing's oil interests).[68] In 2006, China made a $1.4-billion deal to develop new oil fields in Angola, which became the largest supplier to China ahead of Saudi Arabia. The deal included China rebuilding Angola's railway and bridges, inland roads, irrigation systems, hospitals, and schools.[69]

For controversial anti–foreign aid economist Dambisa Moyo, the "explosive development of infrastructure" is a "transformational moment for Africa," leading to a maturing civil society as the middle class expands. But such "resource for infrastructure" development, while boosting economic growth statistics (and a middle class linked to state patronage), raises questions about an infrastructure of dependency. A Congolese lawyer remarked, "Six billion dollars in infrastructure is not development. . . . China is taking the place of the West. . . . Our cobalt goes off to China in the form of dusty ore and returns here in the form of expensive batteries."[70]

China surpassed the United States as Africa's largest trading partner in 2009 and has concentrated on infrastructural investment. The stock of Chinese investment in Africa rose from 2 percent of U.S. levels to 55 percent between 2000 and 2014, with the McKinsey report estimating that Chinese investments will surpass U.S. levels by 2030. Meanwhile, the Council on Foreign Relations reported, "China is acquiring control of natural resource assets, outbidding Western contractors on major infrastructural projects and providing soft loans and other incentives to bolster its competitive advantage."[71] That same year, exploiting a "South–South" rhetoric, China claimed its growing interests as a "strategic partnership with Africa, featuring political equality and mutual trust, economic win-win cooperation," implying that China does not require governance reforms and anticorruption initiatives as a condition for aid and trade, as do the IFIs.[72] Sociologist Ching Kwan Lee cautions that these relations are not monolithic and the Chinese impact depends on local political conditions and the learning curve of Chinese firms. She remarks, "China has become a compelling and effective conduit of capitalism in Africa. Its unparalleled rise . . . achieved largely independent of international financial institutions, [has] lent it enormous credential as a model of development for many African countries."[73]

In the wake of debilitating neoliberal reforms, endless debt servicing, and NEPAD (New Partnership for Africa's Development), African countries now have access to a superwealthy southern state, lacking northern colonial baggage. Yet these relations are not unproblematic. South Africa, where 86 percent of clothing imports are from China, has lost 300,000 textile jobs since 2002. Since 2000, Nigeria has lost 350,000 jobs directly and 1.5 million indirectly due to Chinese competition.[74] Cheap imports of Chinese manufactured goods are matched by Chinese investment in the sectors such as commercial aviation, agricultural machinery, urban transportation, and telecommunications.[75] Human Rights Watch claims Chinese policies in Africa (following the historic lead of the West) have "propped up some of the continent's worst human-rights abusers." Exploitation of natural resources have raised concerns over "the environmental impact of various Chinese-run mining operations in Africa, including copper mines in Zambia and Congo and titanium sands projects in ecologically sensitive parts of Mozambique, Kenya, Tanzania, and Madagascar."[76]

While contemporary extractivism reflects new geopolitical constellations, it is important to remember the ongoing social, ecological, and political crisis of historical cases with present implications. Indicatively, consider the ongoing conflicts in the Niger Delta region. As Obi reminds us, "the Nigerian oil industry was built to serve the extractive and exploitative interests of the world's largest international oil companies."[77] The militarization around extractivism coalesces around livelihood insecurities for many, justified in terms of national security and development.

The Global Land Grab

Land enclosure is a time-honored process, from the colonial era to the present. In the twenty-first century, enclosure by the **global land grab** has intensified as investors and companies and states acquire land for profit and/or access to new food and fuel supplies. In its 2011 report, *Rising Global Interest in Farmland*, the World Bank noted that global investors acquired 111 million hectares of agricultural lands over four years, 75 percent of which were in Africa.[78] China and the Middle Eastern countries were the first players in the land rush. Since 2008, China, Saudi Arabia, Egypt, Bahrain, the Gulf countries, Jordan, Kuwait, Libya, Qatar, United Arab Emirates, India, Malaysia, Japan, and South Korea have been on a land rush to Africa, South and Southeast Asia, Central Asia, Australia, and South America.

Aside from these food-insecure states (insofar as they do not produce sufficient food), other investors include agribusiness firms, investment houses, private equity funds, and fund managers. They work either through local private partners, host governments, or their own governments in joint ventures with target countries. Host governments, with World Bank assistance, alter national laws, policies, and land-owning practices to facilitate foreign acquisition for food or biofuels, usually leasing or selling land at low prices. The Japanese firm Mitsui, for example, has purchased 100,000 hectares of land in Brazil for soybean production. Meanwhile, Chinese firms are shifting their focus from mining to financing agricultural infrastructure in Western Australia to develop grain and beef lands as offshore farms for Chinese consumers.[79]

Not only have the food and energy crises propelled and justified investment in land offshore in the name of addressing food shortages and alternative energy, but also investment in agriculture offers a new profit frontier for investors at a time of jobless growth, when they (investors) also may prefer speculative versus real investments.[80] Susan Payne, founder and CEO of the UK firm Emergent Asset Management, raising $450 million to $750 million for investment to consolidate and industrialize farmland in sub-Saharan Africa for food and biofuels, stated the following:

> Farmland in Sub-Saharan Africa is giving 25% returns a year and new technology can treble crop yields in short time frames. . . . Agricultural development is not only sustainable, it is our future. If we do not pay great care and attention now to increase food production by over 50% before 2050, we will face serious food shortages globally.[81]

The cost of land may be low for investors but not to the locals. And governments are typically classifying lands, whether common lands or privately used, as "idle" or "unproductive." Ethiopia's "land lease project," intended to develop large-scale commercial farming (mainly for export of food and fuel), allocated three million hectares of "idle land" (about 20 percent of currently cultivated land). An Indigenous Anuak from the fertile Gambella region of Ethiopia observed, "All the land 'round my family village of Illia has been taken over and is being cleared. People now have to work for an Indian company. Their land has been compulsorily taken and they have been given no compensation."[82]

The commitment of states to this "modernizing" perspective via neoliberal development obscures the intrinsic cultural, spiritual, and survival value of such land to its inhabitants; instead, it is viewed as an opportunity for capitalization, usually for export production of food or biofuels to supply affluent appetites elsewhere.

AGRICULTURAL GLOBALIZATION

With both the food aid regime and the green revolution incorporating former Third World countries into global circuits of food and agribusiness technologies, the **world farm** emerged alongside the world factory. In this process, many Third World country development profiles switched from a focus on modernizing agriculture as a domestic industry toward developing agriculture as a world industry. A second green revolution facilitated this switch.

Beginning in the 1960s, the green revolution encouraged agribusiness in the production of "wage foods" for urban consumers in the Third World. Beyond that *national* project, agribusiness technology has spread from basic grains to other grains—especially feedstuffs—to livestock and to fresh fruit and vegetable horticultures.

Further, agribusiness has created feed grain substitutes such as cassava (corn gluten feed) and citrus pellets, and biotechnology is creating plant-derived "feedstocks" for the chemical industry, as well as an expanding array of biofuels. This kind of industrial agriculture depends on hybrid seeds, chemical fertilizers, pesticides, animal antibiotics and growth-inducing chemicals, specialty feeds, and, most recently, genetically modified plants. It is a specialized, high-input agriculture servicing high-value markets in addition to food processing and agrochemical firms. It has been called the "second green revolution."[83] A distinguishing feature is that whereas the first green revolution was a *public* initiative geared to *national* markets (for staples), its successor is a *private* initiative increasingly geared to *global* markets (for higher-value foods).[84]

Global supermarket firms in the United States, such as Dole, Chiquita, and Del Monte, moved beyond their traditional commodities of bananas and pineapples into other fresh fruits and vegetables. By coordinating producers scattered across different climate zones, these firms reduce the seasonality of fresh fruits and vegetables. Year-round produce availability is complemented with exotic fruits, vegetables, and salad greens.[85]

In this new division of world agricultural labor, TNCs typically subcontract with or hire smallholders to produce specialty horticultural crops and off-season fruits and vegetables for export processing (canning, freezing, gassing, boxing, juicing, and dicing) to supply expanding consumer markets located primarily in Europe, North America, and the Asia-Pacific. As the conversion of agriculture into a global, increasingly feminized industry proceeds, it impinges on women's livelihoods, their food security, and that of their families. Much of the food consumed across the world is produced by women, averaging about 50 percent in Africa, across Asia ranging from 35 percent in South Asia to 50 percent in East and Southeast Asia, and averaging 20 percent in Latin America.[86] Women's lack of security and rights in land means that commercialization easily erodes women's role in and control of food production. As small farming is destabilized, women must work in the agribusiness sector on plantations and in processing plants as planters, pickers, and packers, feminizing the global agricultural labor force and adding to women's workday, despite income benefits and associated "empowerment."

GLOBAL LABOR IN AGRICULTURE AND THE QUESTION OF FOOD SECURITY

The global fruit and vegetable industry depends on flexible contract labor arrangements. Coordination of multiple production sites for a year-round supply of fresh produce is achieved through information technologies. These supply chains disconnect producers and consumers across space, with interesting consequences: consumers are ignorant of the conditions under which their goods are produced, while producers increasingly grow food for distant consumers rather than for their own communities.

Deborah Barndt's research retraces the journey of the "corporate tomato" from Mexico to the ubiquitous fast-food and retailing outlets of North America. Naming it "Tomasita" to underline its ethnic and gendered-labor origins, she describes a plant of one of Mexico's largest agroexporters, Santa Anita Packers, which in peak season employs more than 2,000 pickers and 700 packers. The improved seed varieties need heavy doses of pesticides, but health and safety education and the required protective gear are lacking. Perhaps a more visually striking indicator of monocultural production is the packing plant, employing hundreds of young women whom the company moves from one site to another as a kind of "mobile *maquiladora*":

> The only Mexican inputs are the land, the sun, and the workers. . . . The South has been the source of the seeds, while the North has the biotechnology to alter them. . . . The workers who produce the tomatoes do not benefit. . . . They now travel most of the year—with little time to grow food on their own plots in their home communities. . . . With this loss of control comes a spiritual loss, and a loss of a knowledge of seeds, of organic fertilizers and pesticides, of sustainable practices such as crop rotation or leaving the land fallow for a year—practices that had maintained the land for millennia.

The food security of northern consumers depends on Mexican food insecurity. Displaced *campesinas* (especially Indigenous women) work in the *agromaquilas* or in North American orchards or plantations, earning in a day what takes a week to earn in Mexico.

What are the long-term consequences of a global food system that destabilizes peasant communities and exacerbates southern food dependency for private profit and a year-round supply of tasteless tomatoes?

Source: Barndt (2008: 59–62).

CONCLUSION

The experiences of the neoliberal globalization project has had many social and political dimensions. We have examined several of its vectors: international institutional policy on neoliberal development and poverty, outsourcing, displacement, informalization, extractivism, land grabbing, and world farming. None of these is unique to the globalization project. They have all appeared in previous eras in different forms but not on the scale found today. They are linked—indeed, they are mutually conditioning processes, being dimensions of a single process of global restructuring affecting all countries, although with local variation. The social and environmental consequences are substantial (see Chapters 6 and 8).

Neoliberal policies have significantly reconfigured development: altering South–North relations and South–South relations in ways that deepen market relations and privilege affluent consumers and powerful investors and corporations. With policies of privatization and liberalization, states have strengthened the neoliberal globalization project but with unequal outcomes (as discussed in Chapter 4). Informalization, displacement, and the worldwide creation of impoverishment, for instance, exemplify how the project of globalization is realized through inequalities and exploitation. Yet, there have been relations of solidarity and movements for social protection and meaningful ecological sustainability emerging. We address these issues in the following chapters.

KEY TERMS

Export processing zones (EPZs)
Extractivism
Global assembly lines
Global division of labor
Global land grab
Informalization
Maquiladoras
Outsourcing
Precariat
World factory
World farm

FURTHER READING

Anantharaman, Manisha. *Recycling Class: The Contradictions of Inclusion in Urban Sustainability*. Cambridge, MA: MIT Press, 2024.

Boo, Katherine. *Behind the Beautiful Forevers: Life, Death and Hope in a Mumbai Undercity*. New York: Random House, 2012.

Bremen, Jan, Kevan Harris, and Ching Kwan Lee, eds. *The Social Question in the 21st Century*. Oakland: University of California Press, 2019.

Caraway, Teri L. *Assembling Women: The Feminization of Global Manufacturing*. Ithaca, NY: Cornell University Press, 2007.

Davis, Mike. *Planet of Slums*. London: Verso, 2006.

Ferguson, James. *Global Shadows: Africa in the Neoliberal World Order*. Durham, NC: Duke University Press, 2006.

Guerrero, Dorothy-Grace, and Firoze Manji, eds. *China's New Role in Africa and the South*. Capetown, South Africa: Fahamu & Bangkok: Focus on the Global South, 2008.

Munck, Ronaldo. *Social Transformation and the Global Economy. Labour, Latin America, and the Lefts*. London & New York: Routledge, 2024.

Standing, Guy. *The Precariat: The New Dangerous Class*. London: Bloomsbury Academic, 2011.

SELECT WEBSITES

China Labor Watch: www.chinalaborwatch.org

Farmlandgrab.org

Global Labor Justice–International Labor Rights Forum: www.laborrights.org

International Labour Organization (ILO): www.ilo.org

Maquila Solidarity Network (Canada): www.maquilasolidarity.org

Transparency International: www.transparency.org

UNI Global Union: www.uniglobalunion.org

United Nations High Commissioner for Refugees (UNHCR): www.unhcr.org

PART III

MILLENNIAL RECKONINGS (2000s TO PRESENT)

6 THE GLOBALIZATION PROJECT IN CRISIS

The globalization project is experiencing a multifaceted legitimacy crisis, as the Western-centered geopolitical order unravels. It is accompanied by contention over the neoliberal-inspired world trade regime and recent global supply-chain vulnerabilities. Communities in both global North and global South have felt neglected, contributing to widespread alienation and distrust of global economic liberal elites, and the effects of "the ambition for market sovereignty over the entire world."[1] In this vortex, **illiberalism** has metastasized internationally, expressed in cascading labor and austerity protests combined with growing authoritarianism, as well as multipolar challenges to the Western "rule-based order." What new global order might emerge is not yet clear, but what is quite clear is that the economic and social crisis is also fueling a political crisis across the world, including reevaluation of "development."

The world is at a critical turning point—economically, politically, and environmentally. *Economically*, the globalization project is unraveling as the so-called free market has destabilized economies, generating widespread public austerity, precarious employment, social crisis, and waves of migration. *Politically*, this conjuncture is expressed in a cumulating politics of unrest in left- and right-wing national populisms—the former championing increased wages, environmental justice, and social welfare programs via renewal of the public sector, and the latter promoting authoritarian ethnonationalism. *Environmentally*, market deregulation, resource extractivism, and global consumerism have intensified longer-term emissions of greenhouse gases and ecological deterioration, generating widespread rural and urban displacement and public ill-health.

Worldwide processes of (economic and environmental) displacement foment migration, particularly from the global South. The UN International Organization for Migration anticipates "as many as 1.5 billion environmental migrants in the next 30 years."[2] In response, political elites (many beholden to financial elites) use immigration as a threat, via racist appeals, to distract from shrinking employment and deteriorating public services. And nationalist politics in turn deepens international disorder as U.S. global hegemony weakens and its associated institutions (embodied in the United Nations [UN], international financial institutions [IFIs—the World Bank, and the IMF], and the World Trade Organization [WTO]) fragment. As Louise Haagh, social policy specialist, notes:

> The IMF [International Monetary Fund] has conceded states put too much trust in the market: corporations have reneged on the public's trust by not diverting resources into productive investment. Extraordinarily, the IMF is admitting that the economic theory behind regulatory policies of the last four

decades, which gave corporations more power to structure employment and set wages, was simply wrong.[3]

Here, deregulation policies promoted inordinate corporate and financial restructuring with much investment favoring intercompany mergers and acquisitions rather than production facilities. The result has been deepening inequality across the world with the enriching of economic elites and substantial job loss (disappearing or offshoring), and wages declining alongside rising unemployment. And such tensions and contradictions of the globalization project were laid bare during the Covid-19 pandemic. As Oxfam International noted, in 2023:

> "We are living through an unprecedented moment of multiple crises. Tens of millions more people are facing hunger. Hundreds of millions more face impossible rises in the cost of basic goods or heating their homes . . . . Poverty has increased for the first time in 25 years. At the same time . . . the very richest have become dramatically richer and corporate profits have hit record highs, driving an explosion of inequality . . . . Since 2020, the richest 1% have captured almost two-thirds of all new wealth—nearly twice as much money as the bottom 99% of the world's population."[4] (See Figure 6.1.)

FIGURE 6.1 ■ Rich people in the global North still own the world. Share of wealth concentration in the global North compared to the rest of the world (%).

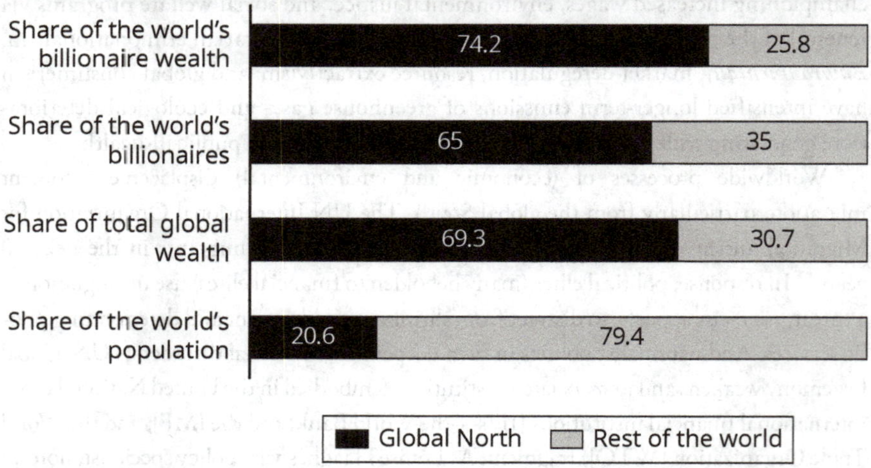

Source: Oxfam. (January 2024). Inequality Inc.: How corporate power divides our world and the need for a new era of public action (Davos 2024 Report). Lead authors: Rebecca Riddell, Nabil Ahmed, Alex Maitland, Max Lawson, and Anjela Taneja. Retrieved from https://www.oxfamamerica.org/explore/research-publications/inequality-inc/

We are grateful to Oxfam for their continued dedication to addressing global inequality and for providing the data and insights that form the basis of Figure 6.1: Rich People in the Global North Still Own the World. This material is reproduced with permission from Oxfam. For further information, please visit oxfamamerica.org.

Just as the development project unraveled as large corporations and banks went global—precipitating a debt crisis with what came to be referred to as a "lost decade" in the South (reversing public welfare provisioning) and crafting a trade regime to undo "economic nationalism"—so the globalization project unravels in its own way. The world is in a transition toward a reworking of the development paradigm.

The globalization project's policies of financial deregulation have exposed citizens to greater uncertainty with increasingly volatile financial markets and job instabilities. In 2015, *The Guardian Weekly's* report "Has Globalisation Hit the Wall?" argued that "failure to shield workers from foreign competition has . . . undermined faith in Globalization," that "the impact of the [2008] financial crisis has led the public to feel they need protection from the ravages of the markets."[5]

The unpopularity of a casino-like global economy, rendering employment everywhere precarious with drastic *human* consequence, is one signal of crisis. The other is the erosion of the network of international rules and institutions first established by the U.S.-orchestrated development project in the post–World War II era. This has led to a growing **multipolarity** as new regional and bilateral trade alliances complement the liberalizing world-economic order instituted in the World Trade Organization.

Much of this chapter suggests a cumulative crisis stemming from continuing attempts by corporates and financiers to use their power to shape state policy in their interests. This is evident, for example, in the repeated recourse to austerity policy in both global South and global North. Economist Clara Mattei suggests that *austerity* is the name of the ideological regime required under capitalism for maintaining social order, such as it is, and imposing a "scarcity of *imagination* as well as of the material requirements of everyday life."[6] This entails exploiting the inertia of political and economic structures and mindsets:

> It should not be surprising that the ideologies that led us here, those that have guided the postindustrial age—techno-lust and hyper-individualism, conflation of growth with progress, unflagging faith in unfettered markets—are the same ones many now rely on as we try to find a way out.[7]

That comment was made over a decade ago and still has relevance. This chapter examines various dimensions of the crisis of the globalization project, expressed in part in groundswells of resistance to shortcomings and injustices of global development.

SOCIAL CRISIS

A straightforward way of understanding the source of social crisis in the globalization project is to recognize that this project changed the conditions of development drastically by creating a global labor force targeted by corporations competing to invest in places where protections for environments and labor are weak (including where unionization is suppressed or banned). This resembled the patterning of European empires, redeploying colonial labor to produce minerals, fibers, and foods for Western consumption. But in the late-twentieth century a truly international labor force was created by liberalization and the "race to the bottom" phenomenon. Here wages for southern laborers have been progressively undermined by host states and transnational corporations competing to produce export commodities for revenues and profits, respectively.

Between 1980 and 2000, the global labor force trebled, as the ex-Soviet bloc joined the global economy alongside China's and India's expanding workforces. The newcomers earned low wages, *weakening the bargaining position of workers elsewhere*, and since 2000 additional states with emerging manufacturing capacity—including Vietnam, Indonesia, Cambodia and Thailand, and Bangladesh—have expanded their (cheapened) labor forces.[8] Under these circumstances, corporations have extracted concessions from northern labor with the threat of offshoring jobs. Job insecurity became the new normal, with the IMF and World Bank advocating labor flexibility policies in the global South to enhance "participation in the world market," weakening employment protections across the world.

While Rostow's "age of high mass consumption" serves a global minority, it is hardly a trajectory for the *global* majority, many of whom experience destabilized or stagnant livelihood possibilities, with no evident national path to development.

The global social crisis, then, is twofold:

> First, it is a *crisis of the development promise.* For the global North, what has been a fairly stable region of relatively prosperous citizenries, its foundation of secure employment has steadily eroded. Those jobs not offshored have lost considerable ground, with, for example, U.S.-based firms reducing health care benefits and cutting pension obligations and other social entitlements won by organized labor during the development project. With the gig economy, such freelance work does not often come with health benefits or workplace protections.
>
> Northern worker expectations of improvement as members of the so-called high mass consumption society have foundered on a trade regime that has weakened their employment security to labor-force cheapening across an unequal world. The effect has been to expose the myths of national development proclaimed in a postcolonial, nevertheless imperial age. The social crisis is comprehensive, with the global South experiencing declining wage share of wealth of 10 to 20 percentage points since 1994, while the northern wage share has fallen by 9 percentage points since 1990. And alongside 10 million stateless people, the rights of the world's 258 million global migrants, and about another 800 million internal migrants, remain largely unprotected.[9] As the patterning in Figure 6.2 suggests, a majority of the stateless and migrant laborers join global slum dwellers and the rural poor as populations excluded from stable livelihoods.

FIGURE 6.2 ■ Transnational Distribution of Global Population by Relative Inclusion/Exclusion

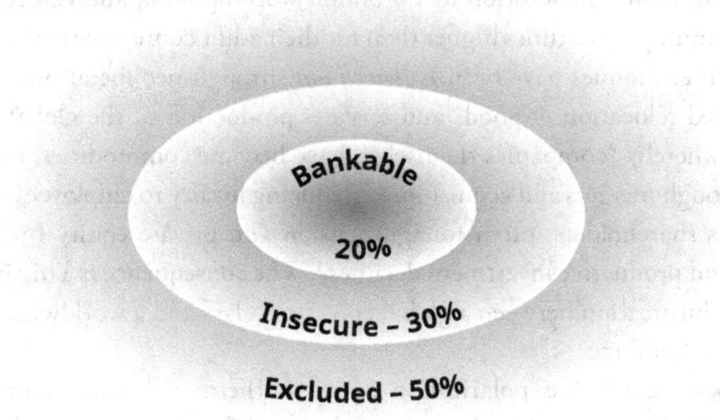

Source: Hoogvelt (2006: 164).

Second, *northern economies now host the very same structural adjustments* visited upon the global South from the 1980s. Public debt is endemic, and the global pandemic has not helped (on top of looming climate emergencies). This recalls the 1980s debt regime, in which southern governments were required by the IFIs to privatize their public assets to stabilize the financial sector. This anti-welfare-state ideology spread to the North, ideological claims of the development project. When the debt crisis hit the global North in the first decade of the twenty-first century, privatization and new financial disciplines rolled back northern public services, and public employees faced retrenchment as public sector downgrading became "part of the post-2008 adjustment across all industrialized countries."[10] Here, the argument for public austerity was market-based, with advocates of neoliberal policy claiming the private sector would fill the gap as the state retreated as provider of public welfare and regulator the private sector. This did not happen significantly—because investing in financial instruments and speculation became more attractive than productive investments.

In consequence, a growing proportion of working populations, with insecure jobs and insecure access to housing and compelled to trade off work and child care, represent the new precariat in the global North.[11] This substantial reversal of the development promise was increasingly evident in a rising politics of frustration across the world, with progressive demonstrations in support of demands of the poor, the young, students, workers, minorities, the Indigenous, women, trade unionists, and migrants, countered by conservative protests in the global North against religious and racial minorities, migrants, and refugees. Notable uprisings occurred in the so-called **Arab Spring**, followed by mushrooming of the **Occupy Movement** in the 2010s across North

America, Europe, Nigeria, and Australia.[12] Unemployment has become the great leveler across the North–South divide. By 2016, global unemployment was running at around 200 million,[13] in addition to 1.4 billion working poor, and youth unemployment rates running three times higher than for their adult counterparts.[14]

Northern economies have been *hollowed out* through neoliberal policies in ways that facilitated relocation of goods and services production to the global South and the process whereby "companies themselves have become commodities, to be bought and sold through mergers and acquisitions," reducing loyalty to employees (skilled and unskilled) as shareholders (often foreign pension and private equity funds) assume ownership and productive investment declines.[15] The consequence is a distinctive (and politicizing) bifurcation between a global consumer class and a worldwide casual and unemployed labor force.

In Europe, social-class polarization of its southern perimeter (Portugal, Italy, Greece, and Spain) occurred in the wake of the 2008 financial crisis, and deep structural-adjustment deflationary policies. In consequence, new political parties emerged: Podemos in Spain, and Syriza in Greece, challenging the *unaccountability* of the EU and the European Central Bank's austerity regime.[16] The rising impoverishment of southern European citizens stimulated new forms of political mobilization to restore social rights via alliance building. That is, since so many life experiences were subjected to commodification, alliances have spread among renters, teachers, gig workers, students, farmers, Indigenous peoples, feminists, environmentalists and extinction rebels, food justice seekers, health care workers, and others. In Spain, with youth unemployment at 43 percent in 2011,[17] Podemos mobilization combined an anti-eviction network to support mortgage victims, the Marca Blanca movement to preserve health services, and the Marca Verde movement to defend public education.[18] Podemos (which assisted the socialist leader, Pedro Sánchez, to the prime ministership in 2018) is a new kind of "party movement": "thousands of citizens have come together in a networked approach to politics that is fresh and engaging in defying, above anything else, the hierarchical approach favoured by vested interests."[19]

The turmoil in southern Europe mirrored waves of popular anti-authoritarian/anti-corruption struggles across the global South—in Brazil, Bolivia, Ecuador, Venezuela, Chile, Colombia, Mexico, Guatemala, Turkey, South Africa, and elsewhere. Citizens, generally, have been losing faith in liberal representative democracy and its unholy alliance with financial and corporate oligarchies corrupting states and entire political systems.

The bottom line is that the globalization project has had the effect of undermining social provisioning in order to maximize corporate competitive advantage and has enabled elites to favor financial interests over public needs, reversing social contracts in both North and South. Countless mobilizations for social rights and public integrity across the globe have ensued. The social crisis of the globalization project has universal reach with politically contentious impact. All of these struggles are strands of what Karl Polanyi would describe as a countermovement against "market rule."

LEGITIMACY CRISIS

If the development project started with the aim of international poverty alleviation, as early as the end of the twentieth century it became clear that development was not working and faced a crisis of legitimacy. In 2000, World Bank president James Wolfensohn said, "We have yet to solve old problems—above all, that of the yawning gulf between the haves and the have-nots of the world."[20] Accordingly, the United Nations coordinated a response in the form of the **Millennium Development Goals (MDGs)**, with the key goal of halving world hunger by 2015, as well as halting the spread of HIV/AIDS, addressing gender inequality, and providing universal primary education. A decade later the 2010 *MDGs Report* stated that despite gains in reducing malnutrition in the 1990s, the 817 million undernourished in 1990 approached one billion in 2010, following the food price and financial crises of 2008,[21] and that figure remained through the next decade, worsened by the pandemic crisis.

The gulf was yawning wider (see Figure 6.3). Despite a general reduction in the proportion of the world's population living in absolute poverty (the China effect), there has been a widely observed expansion of global inequalities between and within countries. The 2023 *Global Wealth Report* noted: "For the first time since 2008, global household wealth in US dollar terms decreased on aggregate as well as on a per adult basis, both in nominal and real terms. Wealth per adult also recorded the second-largest reduction since 2000."[22]

FIGURE 6.3 ■ The Global Wealth Pyramid, 2022

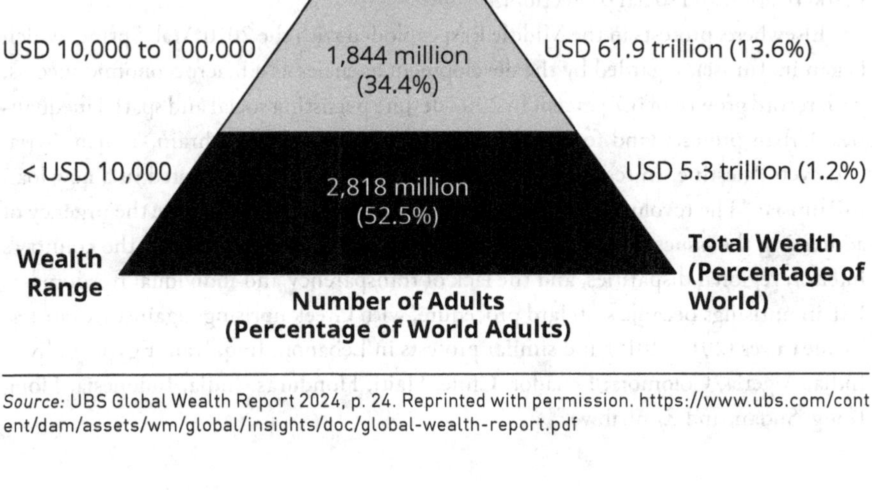

Source: UBS Global Wealth Report 2024, p. 24. Reprinted with permission. https://www.ubs.com/content/dam/assets/wm/global/insights/doc/global-wealth-report.pdf

Since 1980, with the inception of the globalization project, very substantial transfers of national wealth from public to private sectors occurred across the world of states, tying the hand of governments in addressing inequality. A 2016 Pew Research Center survey in 44 nations found that majorities perceive inequality as a big problem, and majorities in 28 nations consider it a *very* big problem. It reported that "elites are worried about this issue, too"—likely from the perspective of a crisis in their legitimacy.[23]

The legitimacy crisis of neoliberal development was clearly visible in Latin America, in the so-called pink wave. Early in the twenty-first century, a democratic revolution swept the continent, as this broad "double movement" pushed back from market rule toward the restoration of social rights and the development state. New social-democratic presidents were elected in 11 countries—Venezuela, Brazil, Argentina, Uruguay, Bolivia, Chile, Ecuador, Nicaragua, Guatemala, Paraguay, and El Salvador—alongside Cuban socialism. More pragmatic and populist, these governments espoused a social egalitarianism, drawing on the deepening frustration and protests of poor and Indigenous citizens with the deprivations of the globalization project and Latin America's extremely high levels of inequality.[24] Social movements demanded independence from foreign corporations, banks, and U.S. military involvement across the continent—forming the **Union of South American Nations (UNASUR)**, pursuing economic integration around a single currency (the *sucre*), destined to be an international reserve currency, centered on the Bank of the South (*Banc del Sur*), as an alternative to the IMF. A regional economic bloc named the **Bolivarian Alternative for the Americas (ALBA)** formed, based on the concept of "cooperative advantage"—fostering mutual cultural and economic exchanges, such as Venezuelan cheap oil for Cuban doctors and teachers, and building a form of cooperative development to encourage collective interest in sharing material goods and social services.[25]

While such initiatives served as regional counterweights to the globalization project, by the end of the second decade they had been blunted by right-wing political reaction in states such as Brazil, Ecuador, and Bolivia, and U.S. intervention to undermine ALBA, reversing the so-called double movement in the dialectical relation between marketization and social protection.[26]

Elsewhere, protests in the Middle East exploded with the 2010 Arab Spring, which began in Tunisia, regarded by the development agencies as a macroeconomic success, with record growth of 6.7 percent in 2007 despite persisting social and spatial inequalities. Urban protests (and food riots) spread to Egypt, Libya, Bahrain, Yemen, Syria, and even Palestine. In response, the African Development Bank noted in a new loan to Tunisia: "The revolution and the ensuing social protest demonstrate the urgency of addressing the issues of unemployment, especially among the youth in the country's interior, regional disparities, and the lack of transparency and individual freedoms."[27] Urban uprisings became standard procedure, with Greek uprisings against EU austerity measures (2014–2015) and similar protests in Lebanon, Iraq, Iran, Egypt, Bolivia, India, Algeria, Colombia, Ecuador, Chile, Haiti, Honduras, India, Indonesia, Hong Kong, Sudan, and Zimbabwe.[28]

In this moment of global unrest, the World Economic Forum (WEF), representing the world's "outstanding firms" with a primarily U.S. and European membership (the Davos Class), staged a Global Redesign Initiative (GRI) between 2009 and 2011. It proposed global governance reform as a solution to growing legitimacy problems for private, corporate power —involving a watershed moment in the global double movement between profit and protest.

Accordingly, WEF founder and executive, Klaus Schwab, initiated an MOU with the United Nations to establish a new space for partnership with transnational corporations in global food governance. The WEF envisaged a flexible governance system replacing governments "when a core group of corporate executives decide they could be effective in their own terms in addressing a global challenge,"[29] instituting the 2019 Davos Manifesto, which made a point of positioning "private corporations as trustees of society."[30]

In 2020, Schwab's *The Great Reset*, addressed the widespread social unrest, which "has been on the rise globally," with the pandemic intensifying "the macro challenges of social inequalities," and with citizens denouncing "a breakdown of the social contract, expressing more and more forcefully a general loss of trust in institutions and leaders."[31] It also emphasized the unravelling of multilateralism in "a vacuum of global governance and the rise of various forms of nationalism" as a sign of governing morbidity. *The Great Reset* prepared the way for the 2021 UN Food System Summit (UNFSS), by which the UN enabled food governance capture by the transnational corporate sector.

In this vortex the WEF/UN partnership staged the UNFSS with the president of the Alliance for a Green Revolution in Africa (AGRA), Agnes Kalibata, as special envoy. It was an assertion of corporate leadership in global food governance.[32]

Hundreds of civil society organizations (CSOs), including La Vía Campesina, warned that the WEF "emerged as the key space for decision makers and corporate leaders to roll out initiatives around global public goods—water, food and climate . . . seeking to shape the future of a wide range of services." While grassroots agrarian and food movements, and their representatives in the UN's Committee on World Food Security, were initially excluded and then invited as an afterthought, the civil society organizations' response anticipated this was in fact a WEF-instigated legitimacy exercise on behalf of corporate control of future food systems:

> The UN-WEF strategic partnership agreement signed in June 2019 casts a cloud on the integrity of the United Nations (UN) as a multilateral system. . . . We believe that this agreement is fundamentally at odds with the UN Charter and with intergovernmental decisions on sustainable development, the climate emergency, and the eradication of poverty and hunger. It will provide transnational corporations (TNCs) preferential access to the UN system and permanently associate the UN with TNCs, some of whose core activities have caused and/or worsened the social, economic and environmental crises the world faces.[33]

Following this showdown over the restructuring of global food governance, the extended UNFSS+2 has institutionalized the summit's privatizing preferences—contravening the UN Charter and Human Rights framework (to serve public interest) and eliminating intergovernmental multilateralism. Here, individual member states are enjoined to elaborate "national pathways" to food security, even as foreign investment in national landscapes and food production continues, supported by a Scientific Advisory Committee excluding frontline small-scale farmer practitioner knowledges.

GEOPOLITICAL TRANSITIONS

Consistent with our overall theme of the paradox of "development," crisis in the globalization project was imminent from the 1980s on, with mushrooming civic unruliness in the new century and geopolitical regrouping to challenge U.S. supremacy and northern power overall. As fallout from the 1997 Asian financial crisis, the **Group of 20 (G-20)** formed, combining original members of the G8 with significant states from the global South, including Argentina, Brazil, Mexico, China, India, Indonesia, South Korea, Saudi Arabia, South Africa, and Turkey (altogether accounting for about 90 percent of the global economy). Meanwhile, key southern states—Brazil, India, and China—led an effective opposition to northern attempts to retain their unequal economic power through WTO protocols in the "Development Round," which first met in 2001. The southern states objected to the undemocratic procedures of the North, its aggressive attempts to dominate southern markets, and the hypocrisy of continuing farm subsidies in the North while the WTO outlawed them in the South.

The G-20's appearance signaled a *turning point in the balance of global forces* (see Figure 6.4). Not only did the politics of the WTO precipitate a solidarity group from the global South, but that solidarity group *imprinted its economic rise and recognition* in the G-20. Its leading edge, the so-called **BRICS** countries (Brazil, Russia, India, China, South Africa), represented an attempt to break out of the neocolonial system through mutual trade and political cooperation. Due in part to the 2008 financial crisis, the United States' "share of global economic power fell from 50% to just 15% in 2017."[34]

Following the 2008 financial crisis, *Financial Times* columnist Martin Wolf declared:

> The west has dominated the world economically and intellectually for at least two centuries. That epoch is over. Hitherto, the rulers of emerging countries disliked the west's pretensions, but respected its competence. This is true no longer. Never again will the west have the sole word. The rise of the Group of 20 leading economies reflects new realities of power and authority.[35]

FIGURE 6.4 ■ Changing of the World-Economic Guard?

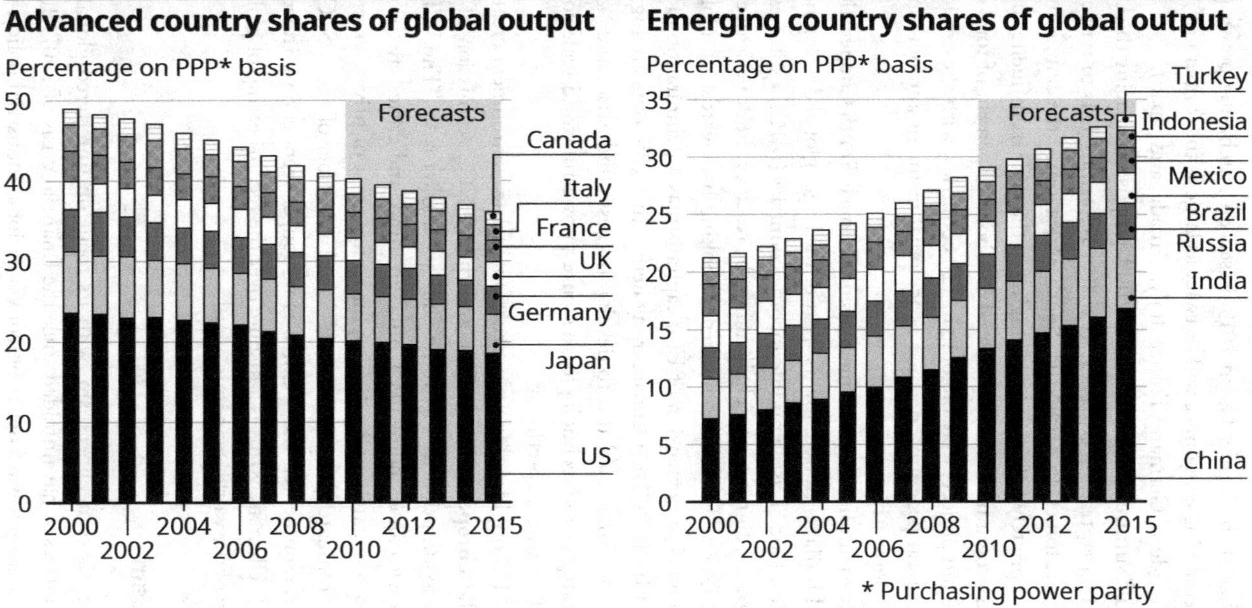

Source: IMF, Federal Reserve, and Schroders, via Martin Wolf, "Three Years On, Fault Lines Threaten the World Economy," *Financial Times*, July 14, 2010: 7. https://www.ft.com/content/39c67712-8eb1-11df-8a67-00144feab49a#ixzz1QDmJRJWk

These new realities of power produced what is now called a *multipolar world*. A 2018 Price Waterhouse Cooper report, *The World in 2050*, noted: "the GDP of the 7 new emerging economies (Brazil, China, India, Indonesia, Mexico, Russia and Turkey) already equals that of the former G7 in 2015, based on purchasing power parity. By 2040, the seven emerging economies will be twice as large as the former G7"[36] (United States, United Kingdom, Germany, France, Italy, Canada, and Japan).

The first BRIC summit, held in Russia in 2009, proposed replacing the U.S. dollar as the world's principal trading currency, as well as reforming IFIs to reflect the new balance of economic forces. In April 2011, South Africa joined the club, rounding out the acronym appropriately (BRICS) and bringing to the table its influence in Africa.[37] South–South aid programs already accounted for about 10 percent of total aid,[38] and by 2016 over 500 aid projects were ongoing in 120 countries, with the explicit goal of replacing northern aid programs, deemed neocolonial in intent and outcome, rather than focused on cooperative relations.[39]

With its mainstreaming in government agendas,**South-South Cooperation (SSC),** led by China and India, is viewed now as "part of the larger global development architecture."[40] The new bloc of rising middle-income countries (MICs) expresses a geopolitical shift of growing significance, challenging the reach of the American empire. In 2011, sociologist Göran Therborn remarked, "Looking backwards . . . globalization does not look so much an extension of U.S. capitalism as a delimitation of it, by the rise of China and India."[41] The ultimate irony here is that U.S. outsourcing of industrial production to China enabled it to develop domestic industries and "go global" via importing strategies and technologies to secure a powerful world-scale commodity export platform (see next chapter).

Recall the WTO originated in an international trade environment created by the United States, the **European Union (EU)**, and their TNCs. Admission of China in 2001 was on the assumption that it would embrace market rule: "The WTO's rules were not written with an economy like China's in mind, and critics say the organization has failed to adequately police Beijing for using a mix of private enterprise and state support to dominate global industries."[42] And a member of the U.S. Council of Foreign Relations commented that "China is no longer seen as on a trajectory that favours the US."[43] Ultimately this is a dispute over the reconfiguring of globalization and the changing of the world-economic guard.

Neo-Illiberalism

The legitimacy crisis of neoliberalism, with its focus on unfettered global markets favoring private interests, has unfolded since the financial crisis of 2007–2008, with governments gravitating toward development via national industrial policy, including trade protections. In 2023, the World Bank and IMF decreed: "country ownership of development and climate-transition strategies is essential, with each country charting its own path according to its specific national circumstances."[44] U.S. President Biden's 2021 Bipartisan Infrastructure Bill exemplified this redirection, in its plan to "rebuild America's roads, bridges and rails, expand access to clean drinking water, ensure every American has access to high-speed internet, tackle the climate crisis, advance environmental justice, and invest in communities that have too often been left behind."[45]

As former World Bank chief economist and Nobel Laureate in Economics Joseph Stiglitz remarked at the time, regarding the crisis of neoliberalism's unfettered markets: "We can thank that ideology for the past 40 years of weak growth, rising inequality, and inaction against the climate crisis. Its proponents have always argued vehemently against industrial policies."[46] In consequence, he claimed the failure of neoliberal ideology provided even more fertile ground for populist demagogues to sow the seeds of resentment and discontent. . . . Across every dimension, including the economy, the greatest threat to well-being today is political. Over half the world's population lives under authoritarian regimes. . . . Those ideas have put us on a truly dangerous course: the road to a twenty-first century version of fascism.[47]

Neoliberalism is by now widely recognized as being in transition. What is called a "*mutating* transatlantic neoliberalism—an emergent *neo-illiberalism*,"[48] refers to a remnant neoliberal economic infrastructure (e.g., selective corporate global supply chains) coupled with rising political authoritarianism.

The waning of neoliberalism is symptomatic of the crisis of the globalization project. Why? Because rising nationalism and political authoritarianism embody a long-term southern sense of betrayal by northern liberal elites' institutionalized global market appropriation of southern resources. For much of the global South, as Philippines University professor Walden Bello suggested,

> the chronic crisis of underdevelopment . . . exacerbated by neoliberal "reforms" since the 1980s, had already shredded the legitimacy of key institutions of globalization like the World Bank, International Monetary Fund, and World Trade Organization, even before the 2008 crisis.[49]

The free trade regime's unbundling of domestic manufacturing systems via a multiplicity of corporate global production chains, taking advantage of cheap labor offshore, produced de-industrialization, collapse of trade unions, increased labor precarity, and deepening austerity. Related social crises, uprisings, and migrant waves have in turn encouraged various forms of authoritarianism, across both global North and global South, including "demagogic authoritarian capitalism" emerging in Turkey, the Philippines, Russia and Hungary, as well as "bureaucratic authoritarian capitalism" represented by China and Vietnam.[50]

Here we invoke our theme of "history as present." Pankaj Mishra has suggested mid-twentieth-century liberalism concealed Western colonialism's history of racist, anti-Semitic and misogynist complicity, unmasked now in the neoliberal crisis, which he calls *Age of Anger*.[51] Here, "market rule" has enlisted unequal states in deepening transnational flows of capital and commodities, subjecting labor forces and farming cultures to globally competitive relations, fomenting migrations and intensifying resentment, xenophobia, and sociopolitical unrest. Indian author Arundhati Roy claims: "The specter of an endless flow of unwanted immigrants with the wrong skin color or the wrong religion is now being used to rally fascists and ethnonationalists across the world."[52]

Such circumvention of social protections on a world scale spawns neo-illiberalism, in responding to national crises with policies of nativist discrimination against immigrants, threats to human rights, and increased private corruption of state administrations.[53] It is accompanied by breakdown of the system of multilateral governance, the international order framed by the United Nations, and premised on the development project's advocacy of partnerships between capitalism and democracy (as Cold War doctrine in the postcolonial age). We see this in the growing acceptance of authoritarian states, in neo-illiberal narratives as well as in recent multipolar groupings of states lacking democratic institutions and values. Historian Quinn Slobodian notes, "The formula of right-wing alter-globalization is: yes to free finance and free trade. No to free migration, democracy, multilateralism and human equality."[54]

Rising nationalism is symptomatic of increasing illiberalism, as the liberal architecture of the postwar U.S.-centered international order unravels. For British social scientist Colin Crouch, it takes two related forms. The *first* is an aversion to the *erosion of certainty*, as employment stability has declined with globalization, which has meant "the loss, not just of individual jobs, but of entire long-established industries and the communities and ways of life associated with them, spiraling into further disorientation as foreign customs and large numbers of persons from other cultures invade and obscure life's familiar landmarks."[55] While the original UN architecture promoted a cooperative multilateralism, nowadays contemporary conservative nationalism does not offer security through redistribution, but through the assertion of values, old certainties [e.g., "Make America Great Again"'] . . . the main offence committed against conservative values by liberal elites is that they support various ethnic, sexual, and cultural minorities, disturbing an earlier, ostensibly more comfortable world.[56]

The *second* form of illiberalism is an aversion to southern immigrants threatening social cohesion/national identity and (seemingly) northern jobs. Such *nativism* is a visceral response often incited, with racist appeals, by opportunistic national elites to distract from austerity and market volatility on their watch. White supremacist politics echo in Hungarian Prime Minister Viktor Orbán's hostility toward a "mixed race society." This sentiment ignores European historical responsibility for political-economic and climate refugees from the global South—ironically intimated in French novelist Renaud Camus' reference to "reverse-colonization" of whitened Europe by "black and brown immigrants."[57]

While European colonization created world minorities of largely agrarian populations (whether exterminated, enslaved, subordinated, or dispossessed), its legacies of discrimination continue today with a vengeance, both internationally and domestically. This is clearly represented in the current, and deepening, debt crisis in the global South. And it is generating demands for a new development paradigm, including "deglobalization."

DEGLOBALIZATION?

There is now a broad debate on whether globalization is over, reconfiguring, or retreating, especially in the shadow of mushrooming opposition, likely pandemics, and certain climate emergencies. Globalization backlash, registering social malaise and loss of faith in its uneven development trajectory, has been cumulative. Anti-austerity IMF riots in the 1980s were a harbinger, followed in 1994 by the Indigenous Zapatista uprising in Mexico anticipating peasant mobilization for national food sovereignty at the 1996 World Food Summit, capped off by the alliance of progressive labor and environmental movements in the 1999 anti-globalization Battle of Seattle. Global uprisings in the midst of the 2007–2008 food and financial crisis registered job loss and deepening austerity with eroding public welfare systems and inflated food prices (with food export restrictions). Government responses to the transatlantic financial crisis led to bank bailouts with expansionary monetary policies and new regulations underpinning public economic management. Trade protectionism in the wake of continuing austerity protest consolidated movement toward forms of economic nationalism. With growing tensions between China and the United States, trade restrictions almost doubled from 2016 to 2021.[58]

By the twenty-first century's third decade, a new frontier of **deglobalization** agitation had emerged. In addition, COVID-19's disruption of trade revealed the *fragility of dependence* on strategic medical equipment, pharmaceuticals, and food products, as substantial food surplus producers such as Russia, Romania, and Kazakhstan (wheat) and Cambodia, Thailand, and India (rice) imposed export restrictions, and Russian war on Ukraine devastated its grain bowl, affecting 25 food-importing African countries. As COVID-19 gripped the world in 2020, the heads of the WTO, the WHO, and the FAO declared that because "millions of people around the world depend on international trade for their food security and livelihoods," governments should refrain from taking measures to "disrupt the food supply chain."[59]

While security of food supplies was certainly necessary at the time, the political-ecological question of the future of *global* food supply chains remains. And this holds for manufacturing and services alike (see subsequent chapters). As we know, corporate and financial power has deepened this century. Large corporations, controlling 80 percent of world trade, claim the means to restore and manage global economic relations.[60] This claim shaped the WEF-led corporate mobilization in the 2021 UN Food System Summit (UNFSS) to strengthen corporate capture of the global food system.

THE ATLAS NETWORK

If the World Economic Forum is the overt promoter of corporate governance versus multilateral governance, the Atlas Network is the covert operative. Founded in 1981, its goal is spreading "innovative, market-based perspectives to issues of public policy" globally. To "win the long-term policy battles that will shape history, we need freedom champions to create credible institutes."

The Atlas Network is a Washington, DC–based nonprofit organization that supports a network of over 500 free market organizations in nearly 100 countries. In the United States it includes the Cato Institute (Koch think tank), and the Heritage Foundation (which prepared a Mandate for Leadership dossier for Donald Trump), and oil and coal interests across the world, including an Ottawa-based think tank, the Macdonald-Laurier Institute (MLI), which recruited pro-industry Indigenous representatives in its campaign to undercut Indigenous claims to territorial sovereignty in Canada. Member Atlas think tanks have supported climate science denial and campaigned against legislation to limit greenhouse gas emissions. Journalist George Monbiot notes the Atlas Network, with its funding networks, is "a highly effective means of disguising and aggregating power. They are the channel through which billionaires and corporations influence politics without showing their hands, learn the most effective policies and tactics for overcoming resistance to their agenda, and then spread these policies and tactics around the world. This is how nominal democracies become new aristocracies."

A recent example might be Argentina, where, in December 2023, in the midst of widespread citizen protests, Argentina's newly installed right-wing President Milei announced initiatives to transform a sluggish and heavily regulated economy with large-scale privatization of public industries, demolishing public services, sacking civil servants, centralizing political power, criminalizing protest, and reducing protections for renters, employees and consumers: "The goal is start on the road to rebuilding our country, return freedom and autonomy to individuals and start to transform the enormous amount of regulations that have blocked, stalled and stopped economic growth in our country." Milei's program, which was heavily influenced by Argentinian neoliberal think tanks belonging to the Atlas Network, illustrates how problems are recycled as the solution.

There are two issues here: (1) the consolidation of private power to mobilize against public needs during the era of neoliberal globalization, and, via think tanks, global organizations like the WEF, and dark money associated with the Atlas Network; and (2) the collapse of multilateral initiatives, individualizing (mainly southern) states' means to address deteriorated social contracts, and exposing them to vastly unequal world-economic power, which limits their options.

Sources: Atlas Network: https://www.desmog.com/atlas-economic-research-foundation/; Monbiot (2024); Dembicki (2022); Associated Press (2023).

Decolonizing global relations in response to myriad public needs, would start by including strict regulations of the corporate and financial sectors, including taxing cross-border capital movements, closing offshore banking and corporate tax evasion to restore public financial viability, as well as massive financial support and debt forgiveness for much of the global South.[61] In the period 1990–2019, southern external debt rose on average roughly 90 percent of GDP to 170 percent, with the pandemic accelerating the crisis. In 2022, author George Monbiot noted, "135 out of 148 nations in the poorer world are now classed as 'critically indebted'"[62] (see Figure 6.5).

FIGURE 6.5 ■ Rising Debt Distress in Low-income Countries (Percent of DSSI Countries)

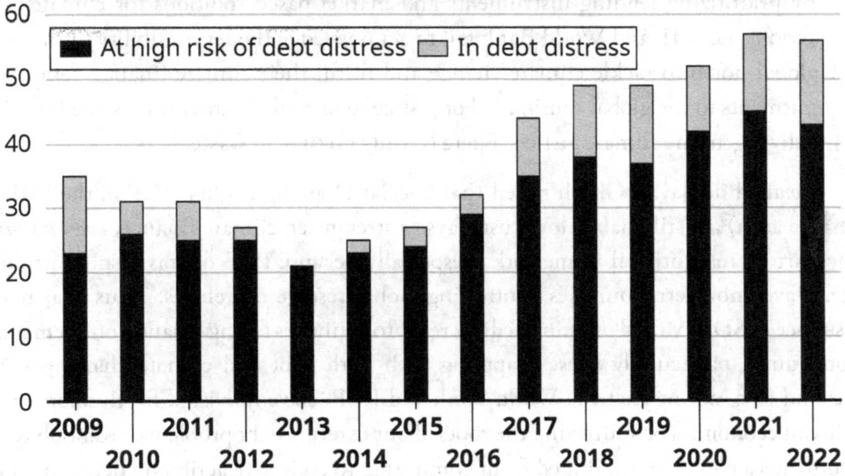

Sources: IMF (2022a). *Annual Report 2022*. Washington, DC: International Monetary Fund. www.imf.org/external/pubs/ft/ar/2022/in-focus/debt-dynamics/; Fischer, A. M., and Storm, S. (2023), The Return of Debt Crisis in Developing Countries: Shifting or Maintaining Dominant Development Paradigms? *Dev Change*, 54: 954–993. https://doi.org/10.1111/dech.12800

Private lending to southern governments became the norm in the new century, with public debt to private creditors rising from 46 percent to 61 percent between 2010 and 2021. In Lebanon, for example, "external debt reached . . . 381% of gross national income in 2021."[63] In a report titled "Decolonising the Global Economic Architecture," Fadhei Kaboub of the Global Institute for Sustainable Prosperity, claimed, "The Global South faces severe structural economic deficiencies that weaken its economic sovereignty and put it at the mercy of a neo-colonial international trade, finance and investment architecture [where] the global economic architecture annually extracts $2 trillion of net financial flows from the Global South to the Global North."[64]

In response to the IMF declaring in its 2023 *Global Financial Stability Report* the debt crisis is not systemic, UN Secretary-General António Guterres responded, "Because most of these unsustainable debts are concentrated in poor countries, they are not judged to pose a systemic risk to the global financial system. This is a mirage.

3.3 billion people is more than a systemic risk. It is a systemic failure." Here, on average 38 percent of southern government revenue is claimed by debt servicing, rising in Africa to 54 percent. Such debt servicing equals total spending on health, education, social protection, and climate. In 2023, low-income countries were spending 12 times more on external debt payments than on addressing climate change.[65]

Continuing denial in 2023 by the IMF and World Bank of the gravity of the debt crisis prompted Jean Saldanha, director of the European Network on Debt and Development, to remark,

> By prioritizing lending instruments and market-based solutions for climate action, the IMF and World Bank fail to acknowledge the responsibility of the global north to tackle climate change and fulfill their climate finance commitments to the global south. . . . For justice to prevail the institutions need to deliver genuine climate justice. There is really no time to waste.[66]

Meanwhile, Jayati Ghosh noted that Special Drawing Rights (SDRs), the IMF's reserve asset) are still viable, low-cost ways to strengthen climate finance, *even within* the current institutional framework – especially because IMF quotas disproportionately favor northern countries controlling global reserve currencies. Thus, "[a] new issuance of SDRs would offer immediate relief to countries facing balance-of-payments constraints, particularly those grappling with both debt and climate challenges."[67] Beyond this, noting that the World Bank and IMF "have no vision for decolonizing African economies or addressing the roots of our external debt problems," Kaboub recommends a global South united front committed to collective action on debt, climate finance, financial architecture negotiations, and critically on access to strategic minerals under its "sovereign control."[68]

Such resources could be leveraged for South–South industrial policies instead of exporting raw materials to maintain northern economic hegemony.[69] Unfortunately, the New Climate Institute notes that debt contracts may lock governments into extracting fossil fuels, since approximately three dozen lower-income countries have proven fossil fuel reserves. Some debt contracts, such as resource-backed loans, require repayment directly in natural resources (minerals or oil), or from revenues or natural resource assets as collateral, which arrangements are likely to be undisclosed.[70]

From a historical perspective, Jayati Ghosh raises questions whether the IMF and the World Bank are institutionally appropriate now in a dramatically changed global economy, over eight decades, with "transformation in the relative sizes and significance of national economies, while . . . private financial flows have risen markedly." Here she observes that

> quotas and voting rights are skewed heavily in favour of a few rich economies with a small minority of the world's people. This is now even more difficult to justify, given those states' diminished shares of global output and world trade, which obviously affects their credibility and legitimacy. . . . The IMF's

executive board should be expanded to ensure more representation from global-majority countries, especially from Africa.[71]

Absent unprincipled rulers, debt forgiveness would enable revitalization of public services such as health, education, and retraining schemes for transforming economies. Additional reconfiguration would protect rights of global workers (especially those of women and migrant laborers), peasants and Indigenous peoples, fisherfolk and pastoralists impacted by globalization, and environments (territorial and atmospheric). All of this, and more, requires meaningful and cooperative global governance, especially reversing the terms of public–private partnerships, which typically privilege private initiative, technology, and power to shape global programming. In short, "humanity faces common challenges which require global public investment on a large scale," especially climate, environmental, and social crises. And to accomplish this, Ghosh rehearses well-known reforms: implement unitary taxation of transnationals so that "each country taxes its share of a multinational's profits . . . at the same rate as local firms;" with a global minimum corporate-tax rate "high enough to make a difference;" and ensuring that "countries are maintaining and sharing their national asset registers, so that extreme wealth is taxed appropriately."[72]

Finally, the deglobalization response is ultimately about re-embedding the economy in society, that is, ending the subjection of society to a market logic. It is noteworthy that the WTO's inflexible "liberalization" disallowed buy-local and hire-local provisions in the formation of trade agreements, effectively outlawing social (as opposed to private) control of markets at appropriate scale. As deglobalization advocate Walden Bello claims:

> Contrary to the claims of some critics, deglobalization was never about delinking from the international economy. It was always about achieving a healthy balance between the national economy and international economy, one largely presided over by a state that pragmatically employed tariffs, quotas, and other mechanisms to ensure the survival and health of local industries competing against highly subsidized northern agriculture and industrial corporate giants with deep pockets.[73]

Again, this means privileging public initiative. With respect to food sovereignty, political-economist Jennifer Clapp claims, "One place to start is for governments to shift their support from the large-scale, specialized and export-oriented food system to building infrastructure for more diverse local food production, processing and markets."[74] With the pandemic shutting down many food supply chains across the world, deepening food insecurity (for close to 3 billion people) encouraged a revaluing of domestic agricultural systems by civil society and social movements across the world. The deglobalization thesis outlines appropriate food sovereignty principles: "Local food production must be delinked from corporate-dominated global supply chains, and each country should strive for food self-sufficiency."[75]

Over the past two decades, Bello has championed a "deglobalization paradigm," which, in essence, reverses the World Bank's directive in 1980 redefining development as "participation in the world market." Thus, deglobalization entails the following:

1. Production for the domestic market as the center of gravity of the economy rather than production for export markets
2. Trade policy (quotas and tariffs) to protect the local economy from destruction by corporate-subsidized commodities with artificially low prices
3. Industrial policy to revitalize the manufacturing sector
4. Equitable income and land redistribution, to create a vibrant internal market
5. De-emphasizing growth
6. Development and diffusion of environmentally congenial technology in both agriculture and industry
7. Economic decisions subject to democratic decision making and not left to the market or to technocrats
8. Civil society to monitor and supervise the private sector and the state (to be institutionalized)
9. Promotion of "mixed economy," including community cooperatives, private enterprises, and state enterprises, excluding transnational corporations
10. Replacement of centralized institutions like the IMF and World Bank with regional institutions built on principles of cooperation, transcending the "logic of capitalism."[76]

In short, this is not about dismantling global relations but democratizing them. Global supply chains now effectively erase the undemocratic and profoundly abusive neocolonial conditions under which many commodities are produced. High mass consumption has consequences. For example, in *Cobalt Red*, British Academy Global Professor Siddarth Kara details:

> Of all the tragedies that have afflicted the Congo, perhaps the greatest of all is the fact that the suffering taking place in the mining provinces today is entirely preventable. But why fix a problem if no one thinks it exists? Most people do not know what is happening in the cobalt mines of the Congo, because the realities are hidden behind numerous layers of multinational supply chains that serve to erode accountability. By the time one traces the chain from the child slogging in the cobalt mine to rechargeable gadgets and cars sold to consumers around the world, the links have been misdirected beyond recognition.[77]

To underscore the paradoxes of "development," we return to American political scientist Francis Fukuyama's famous "end of history" notion (as the Cold War subsided with globalization deepening in 1992)—predicting "the universalization of Western liberal democracy as the final form of human government." He claimed: "The spectacular abundance of advanced liberal economies and the infinitely diverse consumer culture made possible by them seem to both foster and preserve liberalism in the political sphere . . . underwritten by the abundance of a modern free market economy."[78] Such reduction of development to abundance via liberalism erases the capitalist world market's structural foundations, based on transnational elite class power mediating cross-territorial investment and trade to promote an "imperial mode of living" for a global minority with the means to participate in "high mass consumption."[79]

CONCLUSION

Is the globalization project over? Not yet. But it appears to be in transition, hopefully to a collectively democratic project of ordering the world: a sustainability project? The series of crises outlined here are not uniformly coordinated so much as expressing a variety of dimensions of the crisis manifesting across time and space. The political distance between the Latin rebellions (over economic sovereignty), the Arab Spring (over austerity), and the southern European uprising (over popular sovereignty) is as striking as their combined revolt against neoliberal capitalism's impact (however distinctive to their regions).

In the meantime, the general crisis is exposing a tectonic shift underway as the West loses ground to non-Western forces—expressed in rising multipolarity and the ascendance of China (see the next chapter). Although this shift is decades in the making, it is already perceptible, and yet it is unclear how it will unfold. Climate and public health emergencies, automation and digitalization, species extinctions, and gross inequalities within and between world regions, particularly the so-called global South and global North, are the challenges that the globalization project has bequeathed to humanity to address.

KEY TERMS

- Arab Spring
- Bolivarian Alternative for the Americas (ALBA)
- BRICS
- Deglobalization
- European Union (EU)
- Group of 20 (G-20)
- Illiberalism
- Millennium Development Goals (MDGs)
- Multipolarity
- Occupy Movement
- South-South Cooperation (SSC)
- Union of South American Nations (UNASUR)

FURTHER READING

Bello, Walden. Counterrevolution. *The Global Rise of the Far Right*. Halifax, NS: Fernwood Publishing, 2019.

Brand, Ulrich, and Markus Wissen. *The Imperial Mode of Living. Everyday Life and the Ecological Crisis of Capitalism*. London & New York: Verso, 2021.

Calhoun, Craig, and Georgi Derluguian, eds. *Aftermath: A New Global Economic Order?* New York: NYU Press, 2011.

Falk, Richard. *Chaos and Counterrevolution: After the Arab Spring*. London: Zed Books, 2015.

Hall, Stuart. "Authoritarian Populism: A Reply." *New Left Review* 1, no. 151 (1985).

Halperin, Sandra. *Re-Envisioning Global Development. A Horizontal Perspective*. London & New York: Routledge, 2013.

Hopewell, Kristin. *Clash of Powers. US-China Rivalry in Global Trade Governance*. Cambridge: Cambridge University Press, 2020.

Hossain, Naomi, and Patta Scott-Villiers, eds. *Food Riots, Food Rights and the Politics of Provisions*. New York: Routledge, 2017.

Pieterse, Jan Nederveen. *Multipolar Globalization. Emerging Economies and Development*. New York: Routledge, 2018.

Taylor, Marcus, and Sébastien Rioux. *Global Labour Studies*. Cambridge, UK: Polity Press, 2018.

7 GLOBAL REORDERINGS

While the previous chapter focused on the socioeconomic and political pitfalls of globalization, this chapter addresses the reworking of international political-economic relations, from the perspective of development strategies. As the UN Secretary-General António Guterres stated, in 2023, "the post-Cold War period is over. A transition is under way to a new global order."[1]

Transitioning from the U.S.-inspired globalization project, which instituted neoliberal market relations as the vehicle of development, entails a broader affirmation of the significance now of socio-environmental circumstances. This refocusing represents recognition of the extreme shortcomings of relying on a market calculus (at the expense of socioecological protections) and also the threatening *combination* of social, health, ecological crises. Here, we examine the elements of ongoing adjustment: from a largely unipolar world, through alternative development trajectories, to green transitions.

In relation to this global moment of truth, in January 2024, journalist Larry Elliot noted, "Washington and Beijing are in a grim struggle for economic supremacy. The gap between north and south is widening, and liberal democracy is being challenged by a new breed of autocrats. The planet continues to heat up [and] there are once again competing visions of what constitutes progress and success." Generally, there is now a growing recognition that reducing consumer prices via efficient global markets is not an optimal development model; rather, with forms of "glocalisation," "there is value in governments knowing that they will not run short of vaccines, protective equipment, computer chips and energy."[2]

This moment has revealed the insecurities of the globalization project, in that it pivoted on a dialectic, or interaction, between a territorial, and an extra-territorial, market logic. Thus,

> Unlike national markets, which tend to be supported by domestic regulatory and political institutions, global markets are only "weakly embedded." There is no global antitrust authority, no global lender of last resort, no global regulator, no global safety net, and, of course, no global democracy. In other words, global markets suffer from weak governance, and are therefore prone to instability, inefficiency, and weak popular legitimacy. This imbalance between the national scope of governments and the global nature of markets forms the soft underbelly of globalization. A healthy global economic system necessitates a delicate compromise between these two.[3]

And such a compromise is outlined by the deglobalization thesis (discussed in the previous chapter) as a deliberate public re-embedding of both global and domestic markets in civil society in the interests of equity, stability, and sustainability.

GLOBALIZATION PROJECT LEGACIES

Before discussing such a realization, it is important to complicate the scenario of state interventions. Not only are global relations here to stay, however modified, but also their patterning does not conform simply to a tidy set of international relations. Reform, therefore, is more complicated, largely because of the relative autonomy of corporate and financial relations. And here we focus on tax havens, global production networks, and the complicated multipolarity system.

Special Economic Zones

Special economic zones formed as a patchwork of (relatively) independent jurisdictions while states in the global North abandoned capital controls in the 1970s and 1980s, establishing an informal international finance system. Offshore or enclave processing zones were formed to supply world markets. That is, "capitalism in the age of globalization hasn't homogenized the world into a flat, monochromatic space" as once expected: "The world now contains more than 54,000 economic enclaves: estates, islands, parks, havens, free ports, bonded warehouses, export processing zones, special economic zones, free-trade zones."[4] Such zones attract investment and/or financial levies, for purposes of profits on export production or tax avoidance schemes, accounting for 10 percent of global wealth, in islands or micro-states. For historian Quinn Slobodian, resort by corporations and the rich to locate their capital in small and exceptional spaces (tax havens) to escape the reach of states is a "radical form of capitalism" evading public accountability, where such an economy of zones and enclaves constitutes a "world without democracy."[5]

China pioneered the enclave model, as premier Deng Xiaoping pursued liberalization in 1979 to develop industrial production in special economic zones in coastal provinces (e.g., Shenzhen) with special laws. A fishing village at the time, two decades later Shenzhen was larger than New York and included Taiwanese electronics manufacturer Foxconn, now producing iPhones there. In the same year (1979), the United States reached its peak of 19.5 million manufacturing jobs and has since surrendered a third of them to such enclave production. And while China exported 4 percent of U.S. manufactured exports in 1980, it is now the world's largest exporter of most of its zonal manufactures, contributing to current protectionism.[6]

Meanwhile, the Cayman Islands have registered addresses for over 18,000 businesses, which benefit from tax evasion in their home states, but pay registration, licensing, and processing fees. Tax havens deprive the United States of $150 billion annually. For the global South, the cost is worse: where 4 percent of U.S. financial wealth is squirreled away offshore, the figure for Latin America is 22 percent, and for Africa 30 percent. It was calculated in 2006 that the global South loses $10 in illicit outflows for each $1 in aid. In short, such "plutocratic secession" constitutes the Fast World elite, whose affinity is for the extra-national world of zones, enclaves, and special jurisdictions.[7] Reigning in this elite to address much-needed civic and environmental needs is a substantial obstacle requiring cooperative multilateral intervention to consolidate global tax policies on such extra-territorial financial transactions.

Global Production Networks

Global production networks were instituted by the 1995 World Trade Organization, with its *raison d'être* articulated by founding Director-General Renato Ruggiero as "writing the constitution of a single global economy," to avoid returning to "a world of national barriers, protectionism, economic nationalism, and conflict."[8] However, the pandemic crisis and rising protectionisms unraveled this vision, with widespread disorder created by the vulnerability of global *supply* chains. The global market's characteristic just-in-time efficiencies (e.g., reduced inventories) were undone by pandemic cautions, and for foodstuffs, and trade protections via export bans.

At this point, the **World Economic Forum** devised a partnership with the 2021 **UN Food System Summit** to deepen transnational corporate power over global governance of the food system. Transnational corporate agrifood relations had evolved, in the financialization era, to reorganize food production and retailing, where "the multinational food industry . . . has encouraged produce from one part of the world to be shipped to another part of the world for processing, before coming back to places near its origin to be consumed."[9] And here such marketing calculations are "introduced in the management of populations and the administration of special spaces," expressing and realizing "*the territoriality of global capitalism.*"[10]

The partial embedding of national territory in global resource circuits expresses accommodation by states to market rule. Such is the legacy of the globalization project, which in turn has promoted forms of multipolarity. And these register an emergent development based in (geo-economic) processes reorganizing the global economy via supply networks formed through varying articulations of corporate and financial deals *with, within* and *across* states. For example "since 2008, leading farm management companies such as Cresud/Brasilagro, Adecoagro, SLC Agrícola, El Tejar, TIAA-CREF, Multigrain/Xingu Agro, and V-Agro acquired collectively over 750,000 ha in Brazil, drawing venture capital from multiple financial partners in Brazil, EU, and especially United States and Japan."[11] Such deals organize a multiplex world, where "the nature of economic interdependence today is denser, consisting of trade, finance, and global production networks and supply chains, whereas . . . multipolarity is mainly trade-based."[12] In other words, the embedding of states in such extra-territorial resource networks complicates national economic renewal.

Multipolarity

Multipolarity was prefigured in the 1961 Non-Aligned Movement (vs. the Cold War and subsequently a U.S.-centered unipolar world). Its recent appearance stems from the Group of 20 intervention in the Doha Round of 2003 to challenge the use, by the United States and other northern powers, of agricultural subsidies at the expense of southern agroexporters. This event was the formative expression of multipolarity, with the new agroexport powers, Brazil, India, and China, "challenging the hegemony of the United States rather than the neoliberal paradigm of the WTO."[13] Insisting on additional liberalization in the North, they each sought some protection for their own small-scale farming systems for domestic political reasons. As political scientist Kristin Hopewell notes, "Domestic tensions are precisely why no state is advancing a purely neoliberal agenda at the WTO. Instead, their negotiation positions reflect these contradictory impulses between liberalization and protection."[14]

Beyond this tension, the BRICS phenomenon represents substantial dissatisfaction with, and challenge to, the global order, identified as it has been with U.S. power. In fact, As UN Secretary-General António Guterres remarked in August 2023 at a BRICS Summit in Johannesburg, "Today's global governance structures reflect yesterday's world," adding that multilateral institutions such as the UN Security Council and the World Bank and International Monetary Fund need reforming to reflect new geopolitical and economic realities since postwar decolonization.[15] By the end of the summit six new members were accepted into the group: Ethiopia, Egypt, Argentina, Iran, United Arab Emirates, and Saudi Arabia.

The Financial Times characterized multipolarity as "the rise of the middle powers," or the "*à la carte world*."[16] Of the eleven states now in the expanded BRICS group, "four can be said to be democracies, four are autocracies, two are monarchies and another a theocracy."[17] As the director of the Global South Program, Sarang Shidore, notes, the Southern states "simply prefer to live in a world in which the United States was a leading, rather than the dominant, power . . . [offering] a chance for the United States to relearn the practice of cooperation [and] let go notions of exceptionalism that do not serve its national interest."[18]

Against the global supremacy of the U.S. dollar, multipolarity is expressed in some local currency trading (de-dollarization); for example, between China, Russia, India, Kenya, Saudi Arabia, and ASEAN nations, Saudi Arabia sells oil in yuan and the UAE sells gas in yuan, while Ghana and other oil producers sell oil in gold instead of dollars, France trades with China in yuan, China and Brazil trade in their own currencies, and India and Malaysia trade in rupees.[19] Nevertheless, the United States remains the center of gravity for global money—in foreign claims on U.S. assets, in the openness and depth and legal stability of U.S. markets, and the U.S. economy's sheer size.[20] Arguably,

> we will see not greater multipolarity, but greater bipolarity. China has replaced Russia as America's main competitor in a new cold war that is less about ideology and more about markets and technology. The $18 trillion Chinese economy has already overtaken that of all 27 European Union countries combined, and China is the largest trading partner to more than 120 countries. Its Belt

and Road Initiative continues to build infrastructure around the world, and the Beijing-based Asian Infrastructure Investment Bank (with a $100 billion capitalization) has 109 members representing 80% of the world's population.[21]

The multipolarity thesis clearly involves a variety of interpretations. But they do not necessarily cancel each other out. Political scientist professor Stephen G. Brooks argues multipolarity is a myth, because "US firms hold a 53% profit share in high-tech industries, compared with a mere 6% for China. China is also only a regional military power, and that will long remain the case, leaving the US as the sole superpower that can command the global commons."[22] Meanwhile, Yu Jie, Senior Research Fellow at Chatham House (London), argues, "China will continue to shift the rest of the world toward greater multipolarity, since it sees that as the best way to manage its stalemate vis-à-vis the United States."[23]

NASCENT DEVELOPMENT TRAJECTORIES

The Chinese Model

As we have seen, China's admission to the WTO in 2001 was an act of Western hubris in assuming it would conform to Northern rules of market liberalization, as it was considered the "workshop of the world" at the turn of the twenty-first century. China joined as a key player, even as its form of state-regulated capitalism was distinct from the neoliberal model. As an export powerhouse, China's pursuit of a strategic ethic of pragmatism, including supporting illiberal governments, and "mutual benefit," informed its **Belt and Road Initiative (BRI)**, an alternative global economic, institutional, digital, and diplomatic network to trade and investment relations in the U.S.–EU nexus. It is a measure of how China's rapid accumulation of wealth is now deployed across the world.

The BRI comprises an extensive network of highways, railways, energy pipelines, and new border crossings: south to Asia and Southeast Asia, east to Latin America, and west through former Soviet republics in Central Asia, and Syria and Iran, to Europe and Africa.[24] It has involved more than 90 projects across 60 countries and has cost $890 billion (compared with the post-WWII U.S. Marshall Plan's $130 billion investment in today's dollars) focused on technology investments.[25] Africa is a source for oil and minerals in particular and an outlet for Chinese goods. In 2009, China surpassed the United States as Africa's largest trading partner and now surpasses the U.S. aid regime with its concentration on direct investment in resources and transport infrastructures for continental developments.[26] Chinese infrastructural development in 155 countries encompasses almost 75 percent of the world's population and more than half of the world's gross domestic product (GDP), as well as the Digital Silk Road, which supplies advanced information technology (IT) infrastructure, including broadband networks, e-commerce hubs, and smart cities to the BRI states.[27]

According to President Xi Jinping, the BRI secures energy supplies from the West "via routes the U.S. military cannot disrupt,"[28] and food supplies from Russia, and Central, South, and Southeast Asia, alongside its Maritime Silk Road, with ports complementing trade routes. These investments and new trade patterns powered global economic growth. World Bank data, from 2008–2021, show "as the world's per capital GDP grew by 30 percent and China's by 263 percent, China accounted for more than 40 percent of all global growth . . . and nearly 60 percent of people worldwide who rose above the $5 a day mark and 70 percent who rose above the $10 a day mark were Chinese."[29]

Alongside the globalization project, China's economic development model has conditioned economic possibilities for other countries. As a commercial and financial hub, new infrastructure pioneer, and universal trading partner, China has reshaped world markets. "[W]hile some thriving countries have succeeded in replicating China's pattern of development powered by manufacturing and urbanization, others have grown as natural resource exporters serving the Chinese boom and surfing what is called the global commodity super-cycle that it produced," resulting in some nations deindustrializing, "leaving them less well equipped to navigate the new landscape on their own."[30] In 2022, of the outstanding debt-service obligations of the 74 lowest-income countries totaling $35 billion, $13.1 billion (37 percent) was owed to China.[31]

The BRI partly addresses the Chinese government's priority for food security for its huge population. China has more than 100 agricultural cooperation agreements with BRI countries, contributing to its Food Silk Road, establishing China as the world's largest food importer, enabled by its transnational agribusinesses.

> COFCO and Beidahuang Group have pursued international competitiveness through huge overseas direct investment, high-profile mergers and acquisitions, and control over critical infrastructure. . . . COFCO has become the world's largest grain trader. . . . Likewise, by acquiring Syngenta, ChemChina has emerged as one of the leading agricultural input and seed providers in the world. . . . These Chinese agribusinesses are increasingly reshaping the global food trade system and challenging the dominance of the leading Western agribusinesses.[32]

China's "going out" global strategy is partly driven by extensive soil erosion, drought, desertification, and the pursuit of "agricultural modernization." While millions of peasant farms remain, critical to Chinese grain reserves, (largely young male) peasants circulate as a reserve army of labor, under a system called *hukou*, whereby migrant workers lack urban rights but retain farmland rights. Until recent retrenchments, they have served as a flexible labor force for the massive industrial sector, as the final assembly station for global commodity chains, accounting for 60 percent of Chinese exports.[33] China has recently upgraded from low-value to high-value products, led by electronics and information technology goods; however, it still assembles components designed and made elsewhere. Thus, an iPhone may have its parts manufactured in various sites, for example, in Korea, Taiwan, or Germany, with final assembly performed by the relatively most underpaid labor, so that the product is marked as "made in China."[34]

Such a development model of state-centered liberalism may be viewed as a hybrid, related to its world-historical positioning. In the short term, China's opening to global capitalism in the 1990s strengthened the Chinese state by enriching a postrevolutionary class and "re-centralization of decision-making, greater coordination of development, and the reassertion of the power over the economy of state-owned financial, energy and industrial enterprises."[35] Over the long term, China's economic growth patterning has recentered some global wealth accumulation from West to East across the twenty-first century, via its strategy of "development cooperation,"[36] in contrast to the Washington Consensus pattern of private and uncoordinated global supply chains. Here, Chinese BRI globalization with collaborating states, leaves "tangible infrastructure for public use as more appealing to local populations than fungible funds which end up being embezzled or misappropriated."[37] Nevertheless, in some cases infrastructure has not spurred economic growth, leaving some countries highly indebted, such that China's role has shifted from being the world's largest bilateral lender in addition to being its largest debt collector.[38]

Such globalization with Chinese characteristics unites a short game operating within an already frayed U.S.-centered global framework, with a long game constructing an alternative organizing principle, namely neo-mercantilism (a form of "economic nationalism") anchored in the BRI framework.[39] By this we mean that the Chinese political-economic model of development has involved pursuit of international self-reliance,[40] where offshore investments enable access to raw materials (food, minerals, fossil fuels), as well as industrial components, to power the expanding domestic economy. President Xi Jinping refers to this dynamic as "dual circulation," where export promotion is matched with expansion of the domestic market, including social welfare programs.[41] Here, Xi recently invoked the goal of "common prosperity" alongside crackdowns on business and the ultra-rich.[42] This policy shift involves a paternalistic role vis-à-vis capital for the state: "increasing its presence in the tech and real estate sectors and aligning private entrepreneurship with the broader interests of the nation."[43]

The question now is whether Chinese state capitalism serves as a (generic) model for state-managed development (with variations across political systems, resource endowments, sustainable practices, wealth distributions, cultural integrity, etc.). As noted earlier, public interventions have emerged to *address* the shortcomings of neoliberal market governance revealed by the pandemic (and climate emergencies). Internationally, we have seen authoritarian trends, whether right-wing or "liberal authoritarianism," strengthen. In particular, while the 2017 World Economic Forum referred to China as the "present champion of economic globalization,"[44] sociologist Salvatore Babones observed, "liberal internationalist embrace of Xi Jinping as a free trader is emblematic of contemporary liberalism's prioritization of economic rights over basic freedoms," *revising "liberalism" in market, rather than human rights, terms.*

Here, President Xi Jinping claimed that when organizing a country's development path, "All roads lead to Rome," implying that a liberal world order can accommodate various forms of government, including one-party dictatorship.[45]

What characterizes this new conjuncture is the rising association of authoritarianism with a renewed focus on shoring up forms of economic nationalism. Such forms vary between West and East, as well as North and South, given relational differentiation of states in a historically asymmetric world economy. Political-economy professor Ho-Fung Hung argues President Xi, in centralizing power, now embraces an aggressive nationalism, a growing surveillance state, and "shifting [the] basis of state legitimation . . . towards nationalist fervour."[46] This strategy echoes in Prime Minister Modi's India.

ENIGMATIC INDIAN NATIONALISM

India's national development profile is a distinctly uneven enigma. Its economy is one of the fastest growing, with GDP rising annually at 6.2% since 2006, and exceeding China's growth in 2021. Public infrastructure spending under Prime Minister Narendra Modi's government has soared, with electricity access for 98% of households and investment in roads, airports, train stations and other projects exploding. By 2022 India was ranked first in per capita internet use, exceeding that of the United States and China combined. It is also in the top five in the world in renewable energy capacity. Journalist Sophie Perryer describes India as a "major exporter of business process outsourcing services, IT infrastructure and software services [and] it is the world's second-largest start-up hub [with] a highly advanced technological infrastructure." This is an outgrowth of India's famed offshore service industry, with "dozens of ambitious 20-somethings . . . crammed in like commuters in a subway car, sitting at long banquet tables in front of well-worn computer screens creating websites for companies in the US and around the world."

Meanwhile, the share of wealth held by billionaires rose from 29% to 43% between 2016 and 2022, while India's richest 1% owned more than 40.5% of total wealth in 2021. Concurrently, between 2018 and 2022, hunger in India rose from 190 to 350 million for citizens among India's almost 1.42 billion. Such a plutocracy is the creation of Prime Minister Modi, with his confidential partnership with the billionaire class, incentivizing them with substantial subsidies and regulatory changes. For Jayati Ghosh, this focus overlooks "the vast majority of micro, small, and medium-size enterprises, which employ most of Indian's workforce," half of which remains employed in low-productivity sectors accounting for 20% of national income.

India's notorious struggle with low job creation is deepening a social crisis, evident in high youth unemployment in a population surge surpassing that of China. With rapid GDP growth, just 48% of Indian males were engaged in paid employment in 2022–2023, compared to just 13% of women, with India having one of the world's lowest workforce participation rates. Former World Bank chief economist Anne Krueger argues India "could benefit from a powerful 'demographic dividend' in the coming years. . . . [But] labor-force skills are in serious need of upgrading." In these depressed conditions, Modi's attempts to corporatize farming in 2020–2021 precipitated a broad social uprising to protect precarious rural households dependent on multiple livelihoods across rural and urban sites. According to scholars Amita Baviskar and Michael Levien, this generated an alliance of farmers, labor unions, Dalit groups, non-Dalit women and families dependent on the Public Distribution System, and various civil society organizations in effective social solidarity, "contesting centralization of illiberal power" at the expense of diverse survival strategies by India's disadvantaged. Such agitation continued in 2024, alongside Modi's ongoing Hindutva "renaissance."

This threat was preceded by a supermarket revolution in the 2000s led by India's Reliance Industries, Walmart, and Amazon Retail. Food policy analyst Devinder Sharma noted, "At stake is the livelihood security of 12 million small shopkeepers, 40 million hawkers and at least 200 million (of the 600 million) small farmers." Such tension symbolizes the distinct worlds in play—that of small-scale Indian family enterprises versus the global reach of exclusive high-growth markets.

Combining Hindu xenophobia (directed violently at India's minority Muslim population, including Kashmiris) and populist claims as a "messiah of development" and consumerism, right-wing Bharatiya Janata Party (BJP) candidate Modi became prime minister in 2014. The BJP's neoliberal "Shining India" media campaign advocated private wealth creation over India's official rhetoric of egalitarian and shared futures. Journalist Pankaj Mishra argues that embracing globalization exposed India to global finance, and "corruption scandals involving the sale of billions of dollars' worth of national resources such as mines, forests, land, water and telecom spectrums have revealed that crony capitalism and rent-seeking were the real engines of India's economy." Renowned author Arundhati Roy terms Modi's model of development "violent Hindu nationalism underwritten by serious corporate money."

Mishra suggests that citizens, long promised "trickle down" development, are increasingly "vulnerable to demagogues promising *national regeneration*. It is this tiger of unfocused fury, spawned by global capitalism in the 'underdeveloped' world, that Modi has sought to ride." This model is utterly failing to deliver basic "health before wealth" to its citizens.

Sources: Bradsher (2006); D. Sharma (2007); Mishra (2015, 2016, 2017, 2023); Crabtree (2018); Guttal (2018); Goel and Kumar (2019); Perryer (2019); Statista (2020); Baviskar and Levien (2021); Krueger (2023); Chakravorti and Dalmia (2023); Zakaria (2023); Roy (2023); Paliwal (2023); Wallace-Wells (NYT 8/2023); Ghosh (2023a, 2023b, 2024a, 2024b).

Economic Nationalism

Current claims of fragmented globalization suggest neoliberal globalization is "not ending so much as it is changing," partly because policymakers overlooked its "adverse distributional consequences."[47] The backlash registered in Britain's vote to leave the European Union and in the U.S. electoral struggle in 2016 between right- and left-wing populist upsurge, led by TV personality Trump and progressive Congressman Sanders, respectively. Rising nationalism is a conjunctural product of grievance (nativist or unionist), the evident vulnerability of globalized supply chains, migrant waves, and deepening geopolitical tensions, especially between the United States and China. Development policy has come to question claims of efficiency associated with global supply chains.

Rather than adopting autarky, governments embrace "friend/near-shoring" and regional and bilateral trade agreements. For example, China's special relationship with Southeast Asia, via the BRI, is changing as ASEAN members encourage different Chinese investments, from infrastructure to technologies, renewable energy, and electric vehicles (EVs). Further, during the recent trade war between the United States and China, firms on both sides of the conflict resiliently rerouted supply chains: "Chinese firms ramped up exports and investments in Vietnam and Mexico, and the US in turn boosted Vietnamese and Mexican imports to replace those from China." Here, trade resiliency worked through alternative "hub-and-spoke" trading networks.[48] And in 2023, the European Union, the United States, India, Saudi Arabia, and the United Arab Emirates joined in planning "their own BRI-style infrastructure project connecting Europe, the Middle East and India," including scientific research cooperation.[49] In the midst of such restructuring of the former multilateral state system, a commitment emerged from a G-7 summit in southwest England in June 2021, to replace the Washington Consensus with the **Cornwall Consensus**, inverting the Washington roadmap from privatization to "revitalizing the state's economic role . . . in the interest of the common good."[50] This preceded talk of a new productivist paradigm modifying, if not replacing, neoliberalism in the United States, with domestic cross-sectoral supply-side measures such as "the embrace of industrial policies to facilitate the green transition, rebuild domestic supply chains, and stimulate good jobs."[51]

Industrial policy is implemented with targeted subsidies, regulations, and tax incentives to reform the economic structure with strategic investments. This was, more or less, the blueprint for President Biden's 2021 policies, where his national security advisor openly rejected core neoliberal assumptions "that markets always allocate capital productively and efficiently" and that "the type of growth [does] not matter." Former World Bank economist Joseph Stiglitz commented, "once one recognizes how flawed such premises are, putting industrial policy on the agenda becomes a no-brainer."[52] Further, he called for "a new twenty-first-century social contract to ensure that all citizens are guaranteed access to health care, education, security in retirement, affordable housing, and a decent job with decent pay."[53]

This sentiment reflects a broad shift by competition authorities across the world from "a purely competition-focused lens to one that incorporates the broader needs of society."[54] In Africa, for instance, competition law and social policy have converged across the continent, over the last 15 years, such that up to 70 percent of states now have appropriate competition laws, addressing not only mergers and acquisitions, but also provisions regarding restrictive agreements, price fixing, and unfair business practices.[55] Between 2021 and 2023 "the South African competition authority has been particularly active, imposing public interest conditions on more than 74 mergers relating to employment," ownership spread, and local production and procurement. And in Tanzania, for example, the competition authority "may consider whether the merger is likely to benefit the public by increasing efficiency in production of distribution, promoting technological or economic progress, increasing efficiency in resource allocation, or protecting the environment."[56]

In relation to such trends, economics professor Mariana Mazzucato recommends,

> [A]s the public sector's capabilities and expertise have been hollowed out, it has become more susceptible to capture by vested interests. The question we should be asking is not how much growth we can achieve, but what kind. To achieve greater economic output that is also inclusive and sustainable, governments will need to embrace their potential to be value creators and powerful forces shaping the economy. Reorienting public organizations around ambitious missions . . . will allow us to tackle the grand challenges of the twenty-first century and ensure that the economy grows in the right direction.[57]

The Fourth Industrial Revolution

Even so, pursuing *competitive* industrial policy, rather than simply private competition, is the dominant strategy in the shift toward economic nationalism. And it corresponds to the arrival of the Fourth Industrial Revolution (4IR).

> The first phase began around 1800 . . . when the steam engine came into use, and was based in Britain, France, and Germany. The second phase, in 1900, saw the advent of electricity, and was centered in the US, the UK, and Germany. The third was the information-technology revolution, beginning in 2000 and concentrated largely in the US, Germany, Japan and Korea. . . . China intended to be at the forefront of the fourth phase, which would center on integrating robots and artificial intelligence.[58]

As we have seen, the Chinese ascent has depended on the development of a transnational infrastructure, the BRI, as an alternative market and investment space to that centered on the global North, along with a national techno-economic strategy to out-distance northern competitors. At the turn of the twenty-first century, China accounted for less than 5 percent of global research and development funding for technological innovation, but by 2020, it was contributing 24 percent, and it now spends the second-largest amount of research and development funds on digital and robotic technologies.[59] Robots deploy "internet of things" tools to create data-intensive processing as sensors, including human–machine interactions, improving production efficiencies to shape and lead markets across the world by reducing labor costs and circulation time for commodities.[60]

This enhancement represents a dramatically new process overtaking the "race to the bottom" phenomenon associated with the globalization project. Former governor of the Reserve Bank of India, Duvvuri Subbarao, observed in 2020, "In the 1990s, global value chains were becoming the cornerstone of manufacturing. Today the global value chain model is eroding because of advances in machine learning, artificial intelligence and robotics."[61] Such advances threaten high- and low-skill jobs across the world that would normally anchor global value chains. Thus, a report from the Steelcase factory (office furniture) in Grand Rapids, Michigan, observed that "industrial robots assisted workers in their tasks. Now workers—those who remain—assist the robots in theirs. In consequence, wages fall and jobs in factories become less abundant and less appealing."[62]

The Chinese government has targeted the robotic industry (along with artificial intelligence [AI] and automation) as strategically important to its industrial and world ascendancy. Even as China, Korea, Taiwan, and Singapore together have led the world with robot adoption, since 2016 China has been the largest market for industrial robots, with its Robotics Industry Development Plan setting a goal of a ten-fold expansion of robotic use by 2025, enabled in part by provincial government subsidies to firms to encourage robotization.[63] Leading Chinese industries for robotics are automotive (44.5 percent), electronics (24.7 percent), metals (13.9 percent), plastics and chemicals (11.5 percent), and food and beverages (2.9 percent). China dominates the global electronics industry to the tune of over 70 percent.[64]

> By 2021, China outstripped the United States with 18 percent more robots per manufacturing worker. This superiority stemmed from government policy, with generous subsidies rather than market forces. China had 322 robots per 10,000 workers, while the United States had 274, as represented in Figure 7.1.

FIGURE 7.1 ■ Industrial Robots per 10,000 Manufacturing Workers (2021)

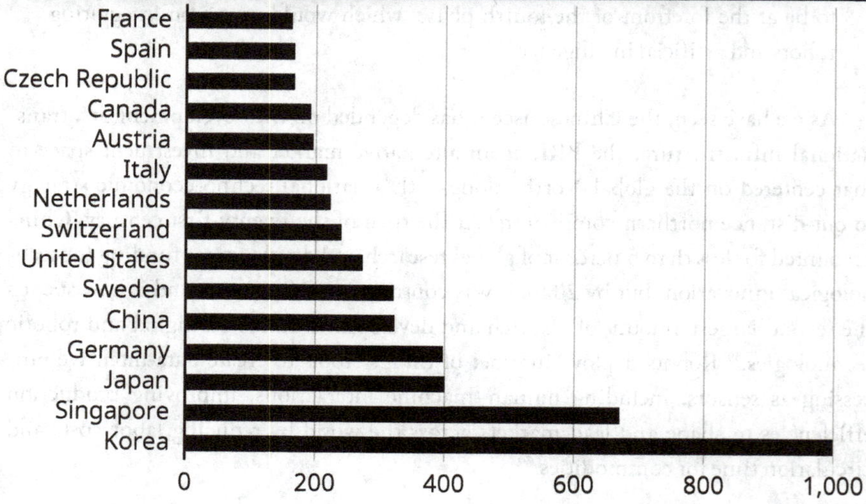

Source: Robert D. Atkinson, "Chinese Manufacturers Use 12 Times More Robots than U.S. Manufacturers When Controlling for Wages," Innovation Files blog post, Information Technology and Innovation Foundation, September 5, 2023, https://itif.org/publications/2023/09/05/chinese-manufacturers-use-12-times-more-robots-than-us-manufacturers-when-controlling-for-wages/.

In 2022, Chinese businesses installed more industrial robots than the rest of the world combined, exceeding its biggest manufacturing rivals, Japan, the United States, South Korea, and Germany.[65]

Automation and AI have global reach and consequence, especially intensifying world unevenness as the 4IR matures. Aside from China, the United States, Germany, Japan, South Korea, Finland, Sweden, and Switzerland spend more than 2 percent of GDP on research and development. Contrastingly, sub-Saharan African states spend on average just 0.4 percent of their GDP, which is also substantially lower.[66] The CEO of *Africa at Work*, Dianna Games, suggests, "Africa is stuck in the second industrial revolution, with governments still prioritising industrial programmes and skills that will be disrupted, and even marginalised, by current technology trends."[67]

Addressing questions whether Africa could leapfrog to the 4IR, Games argues that since Africa holds more than 40 percent of the minerals and metals necessary to address climate change, the continent should focus now on value capture and retention as the substratum of the green transition, starting with infrastructure development. And this would assist African industrialization over time: "The African Union's Agenda 2063 aims to accelerate industrialisation, with the goal of increasing the continent's share of global manufacturing value addition from the current level of about 1.5% to 7% by 2030 and 15% by 2063."[68]

This is in line with the recommendation of the South Centre, namely for southern states to renew the manufacturing paradigm to take advantage of the 4IR technologies: robotics, cyber-physical systems, big data, AI, and machine learning. It identifies challenges such as lack of specialists and infrastructure (now partially supplied by China) and lack of collaboration between academia and industry and among countries. Nevertheless, it notes that some countries "are taking steps to implement the 4IR. Ghana, for example, is preparing to set up Artificial Intelligence (AI) research centers with the help of Google. Similarly, in Pakistan, the President launched [an initiative] for Artificial Intelligence & Computing (PIAIC) aimed to be a center of education and research in AI."[69] Even so, note that "a search driven by generative AI uses four to five times the energy of a conventional web search. Within years, large AI systems are likely to need as much energy as entire nations . . . . [Furthermore], generative AI systems need enormous amounts of fresh water to cool their processors and generate electricity."[70]

Given colonial legacies, leapfrogging is not so much the name of the game. As noted, at the African Economic Conference 2023, by the chief economist for Africa, United Nations Development Programme (UNDP), the 4IR is "not exclusively about industrialization in Africa but it is about how changes in the use of technology could disrupt, revitalize and spark exponential growth,"[71] an acknowledgment of uneven and combined global development. Revitalization and sparking growth can benefit from Africa's distinctively youthful population structure, in addition to addressing the continent's shortfalls in coordination, finance, education, and internet connectivity, and negotiating the international governance of digital technologies, enabling "transformational rather than transactional relations when it comes to the 4IR." With digital governance, the most significant hurdle concerns ensuring fair treatment from the huge digital corporations (e.g., Google, Microsoft, Amazon, Apple) with their extensive data sets and influence over governments and global standards in the digital space, complicating national leapfrogging.[72]

Though Africa has more renewable energy potential than the entire world needs, this raises the question of funding renewable energy projects on the continent, where "the cost of capital is 14 percent in Nigeria, for instance, compared with 1 percent in the United States, and 15 percent in Pakistan. . . . A small fraction of private climate investment goes to the 54 countries of the continent."[73] In fact, while the $100 billion a year promised by the global North in 2009, by 2020, did not materialize, now "an estimated $1.8 trillion a year is needed by 2030 for the world's poorest countries to transition their economies and adapt to climate change, according to a report by an influential panel of experts commissioned by the G20."[74] Whether this materializes remains to be seen.

Meanwhile UN-mediated "biodiversity funding" amounted to "a fraction of the $967 billion needed annually to achieve 2030 targets," which means the funding that countries have promised the Global Biodiversity Framework Fund (GBFF) "is, perhaps literally, a drop in the ocean." Corresponding climate funds are given as loans, to support renewable energy projects, such as manufacturing electric batteries. International donors expect financial returns on such investments. Contrastingly,

> biodiversity funds that support projects to protect wetlands for migratory birds or manage agricultural lands in nature-friendly ways often do not provide returns—at least not in terms of cash. This is partly because current economic systems fail to see the value that a healthy planet provides through biodiversity and ecosystem services.[75]

Green Transition

The **green transition** is of global significance, if not of *equal* significance, across the postcolonial world as the historic extractive region. This transition may account for green industries worth more than $10 trillion globally by 2050.

Nevertheless, Mariana Mazzucato warned in 2024,

> If the false dichotomy between economic prosperity and environmental sustainability persists, the green transition will lack the political support it needs to succeed. . . . *A green, just transition requires a new social contract, which means redefining the typical partnership between government and business.* While profit rates are high globally, investment rates are not, owing to the increasing financialization of both finance and business. In the United States and the UK, only

20% of finance goes into the productive economy; the rest flows into the more speculative finance, insurance, and real-estate domain.[76]

Meanwhile, China has seized the green transition opportunity. After signing an international treaty on climate change at the UN Framework Convention on Climate Change (UNFCCC), in 2015, China embraced green growth, augmenting investment in renewable energy, over the next eight years by 61 percent (minus Environmental, Social, and Governance [ESG] clauses proposed by the EU).[77] By 2024, China had 80 percent of the world's capacity for producing batteries.[78] In addition, China has almost 50 percent of the world's wind power, has nearly half of new solar capacity, and is the world's foremost exporter of EVs.[79] The year 2024 opened with China's largest EV brand, BYD Co., poised to surpass Tesla Inc. In noting the transformation of the auto industry's competitive landscape, the financier of BYD (and Tesla) underscored that instead of size and legacy, an auto company's dominance is "about the speed at which they can innovate and iterate. BYD began preparing long ago to be able to do this faster than anyone thought possible, and now the rest of the industry has to race to catch up."[80]

China's pace-setting is in part due to target-setting, with its updated Made in China 2025 initiative.[81] A parallel was made in 2022 by the Biden administration, with stimulus funding of a $740 billion Climate and Health Care bill and $1.2 trillion for strategic investment in upgraded infrastructure and domestic manufacturing capacities and green energy. Such strategic upgrading included the Biden administration's award, in early 2024, of $1.5 billion to a chipmaker firm, GlobalFoundries, to revitalize semiconductor manufacturing in the United States, enhance worker skills, and upgrade U.S. chip-making for use in EVs and the power grid.[82] Meanwhile, in 2021 the European Commission announced the Global Gateway as the EU's new flagship strategy, investing in infrastructure to counter China's BRI and focusing on five sectors: digital (secure and open internet); climate and clean energy; transport; health (including vaccines and supply chains); and education and research.[83]

On the world scale, western governments view the Made in China initiative as a regression to centralized decision making, with the U.S. Chamber of Commerce claiming it is a "strategy to use state resources to alter and create comparative advantage in these sectors on a global scale," not only remaking China from its low-cost manufacturing "workshop of the world" role to an added-value competitor but also reducing competitive access to China's market.[84] Here, struggle over whether the rules of the game apply to China is complicated by the China paradox where China, as "both a major economic power and a developing country with relatively low per capita incomes," scrambles global trade governance, while the United States counters with tariffs while insisting China should open its markets.[85]

The United States–China standoff highlights the tensions embedded in a transition combining national economic transformation with international competition and continuing offshore access to markets and resources, in a highly unequal world economy. Even in the global North, when President Biden's climate bill passed in 2022—with tax breaks estimated at $369 billion and clean energy technology grants—U.S. battery production incentives were so generous a Norwegian electric battery company chose to move its facility to the United States: "European subsidies still total only perhaps 20 to 40 percent of a firm's investment cost, compared with more than 200 percent in the United States."[86]

This single case symbolizes the ongoing competitive industrial policy reshaping public investment to secure firms and technologies shaping energy futures. Here, "the world has shifted away from decades of emphasizing private competition and has plunged into a new era of competitive industrial policy—one in which nations are offering a mosaic of favorable regulations and public subsidies to try to attract green industries like electric vehicles and storage, solar and hydrogen."[87]

In May 2023, the president of the European Commission, Ursula von der Leyen, stated: "An economic growth model centred on fossil fuels is simply obsolete. . . . We need to decarbonize our economies as quickly as possible." The goal of net zero emissions by 2050 is nevertheless predicated on *continuing* the current profit-centered growth model, while developing "clean technologies," with predictions of a 15-fold increase in EVs by 2050, alongside quadrupling solar panels and wind turbines.[88] Notably, not only are northern governments attempting to develop an edge in green transition technologies, they are also hoping that "rebuilding their manufacturing base will help them mitigate the political and social fallout from deindustrialization and runaway inequality."[89]

Much of this strategic planning in the EU concerns securing access to a variety and superabundance of transition minerals. The EU "is already consuming 25–33% of metals produced globally with just 6% of the world's population. In addition, for most metals the EU is between 75% and 100% dependent on imports, most of which come from China or countries in the global South."[90] Further, "[s]olar photovoltaic (PV) plants, wind farms and electric vehicles (EVs) generally require more minerals to build than their fossil fuel-based counterparts. A typical electric car requires six times the mineral inputs of a conventional car and an onshore wind plant requires nine times more mineral resources than a gas-fired plant."[91]

To reach net-zero emissions by 2050 requires a six-fold increase in mineral inputs, including a 40-fold increase in the supply of lithium, in the estimation of the International Energy Agency.[92] China currently dominates much of the renewable energy supply chains, including metals and minerals. In 2020, almost 100% of rare earths used in the EU came from China. It was also the main supplier of 10 of the 30 minerals that the EU defined as critical at that time. It is not only dependence on China but also the very low share of EU production along the entire cleantech supply chain that makes the EU extremely vulnerable to supply shortages.[93]

Under these conditions, the EU and United States have gone from viewing each other as competitors to starting to revive the old transatlantic relationship in a bid to form a "club" to help tip the balance of critical raw materials access in their favor. Even so, Bolivia,

Argentina, and Chile have over two-thirds of world lithium reserves and, given the global shift to battery-driven electrification and growing Southern opposition to green colonialism, such a partnership is not guaranteed.[94] Nevertheless, the stakes are high, and green colonialism is more than about North–South interrelations. It also includes corporate social engineering to gain acceptance and/or access to valuable resources.

INDONESIA AND "GREEN COLONIALISM"

As the largest producer of nickel in the world, Indonesia contributes over a third of the global supply, critical to building lithium-ion batteries, with a compound made from lithium, nickel, manganese, and cobalt. Such batteries enable EVs to travel greater distances and are popular in Europe and the United States, adopted by auto companies such as Ford, Tesla, and Audi. Notably, Indonesia has banned export of nickel ore to strengthen the value-added component of this supply chain. To attract EV investments, Indonesia plans to build EV industries to benefit from U.S. tax credits, also offering tax incentives to attract EV investments, as well as other mining investments.

Such developments affect the condition of the environment, labor, and Indigenous peoples. In 2020 the Indonesian government passed an Omnibus Law on Job Creation, facilitating access to business licenses for foreign investors. This includes permits to gain access to natural resources and to lease land. The law threatens labor rights and deregulates dozens of other laws. Indonesian lawyer Rachmi Hertante observes, "Criticisms and objections came not only from labour groups, but also from environmental activists, peasant and fisherfolk organisations, students, academics from dozens of universities in Indonesia, and several leading religious organizations who see the law as detrimental to labour rights and the environment. They also say it was passed in an undemocratic process and could not be assessed by the public."

Part of this process includes the "social engineering of extraction," enabling **green colonialism.** A case in point concerns Rio Tinto, a British–Australian multinational company that is mining Indonesian gold. As the world's second largest metals and mining corporation, Rio Tinto is practiced in powerful cross-territorial maneuvers. When activists challenged its mining activity, via alliances with national and international nongovernmental organizations, Rio Tinto responded by forming a network of international business organizations and governance standards emphasizing consultation, sustainability, and stakeholder participation. Such a network enabled the formation of governance mechanisms to "reconstruct the legitimacy of the industry as a whole, not merely of individual corporations." These mechanisms included claiming corporate social responsibility, advocating community development programs and consultative committees, framed by international standards to manage contact with local communities.

Lian Sinclair points out that such "participatory mechanisms provide corporations with the opportunity to enlist community representatives in the service of corporate interests." Here, extraction needs not only physical engineering but also social engineering, entailing behavioral interventions "to 'manage' dissent and 'manufacture' consent," thereby depoliticizing extraction and creating "inclusionary control."

This seems to confirm Alexander Dunlap's conception of infrastructural colonization, which "takes a literal approach to territorial control, landscape and socio-cultural change, exploring the literal colonization of habitats, people, social fabrics and more-than-human networks," where statism represents (neo)colonialism: not simply managing population and territory but managing it in compliance with the paradigm of greening via public–private partnerships, with the emphasis on private power.

What does private management of ecosystems add to our understanding of colonialism?

Sources: Niarchos (2023); Mecca and Siswadi (2024); Sinclair (2020, 2023); Verweijen and Dunlap (2021); Hertanti (2023); Dunlap (2023).

Given that over 80 percent of lithium and over 50 percent of nickel, copper, and zinc mining is underway in Indigenous Peoples' territories, the human, lifeworlds, and land rights question is central to the green transition, especially since mining is a risk to waterscapes, food insecurity, and conflict. Over the past decade, the Business and Human Rights Resource Centre "has recorded 550 allegations of human rights violations directly related to extraction of 'green transition' minerals across the world, particularly in Mexico and Central and South America, and in the African continent. These conflicts involve corporations mining for cobalt, copper, lithium, manganese, nickel and zinc."[95] Mary Robinson, former UN Commissioner for Human Rights, reports:

> In the Democratic Republic of the Congo, the world's largest source of cobalt and a major supplier of copper, mining is associated with child labor, corruption, and widespread violence. Indonesia, the world's top nickel producer, has a weak record on protecting communities from mining pollution. Lithium extraction in Argentina, Chile and Bolivia has pitted local communities seeking to defend scarce desert water resources against mining companies that use water-intensive extraction methods and ride roughshod over land rights.[96]

Robinson adds that the Investor Alliance for Human Rights, involving 200 firms with assets worth more than $10 trillion, proposes strengthening regulatory measures, with human rights and environmental due diligence "consistent with the UN Guiding Principles on Business and Human Rights."[97]

Exemplifying local resistance, the recent Plurinational Observatory of Andean Salt Flats combines affected communities, environmental activists, and scientists from Argentina, Bolivia, and Chile in a transnational movement network. It opposes lithium mining of salt flats, as "socio-natural systems with cultural, scientific, and economic value and models of ecologically sound, democratically articulated forms of development in the region" versus **green transition** extractivism.[98] Meanwhile defense-of-territory countermovements across Latin America mobilize a mix of Indigenous cosmo-visions, place-based identities, and international indigenous rights law to unite grassroots resistances in "a movement for an alternative model of territorial relations."[99]

Such resistance aligns with the 2010 *Cochabamba People's Agreement*, based on a "project for the Universal Declaration on the Rights of Mother Earth." The agreement was made when representatives from 140 countries gathered in Indigenous-led Bolivia to outline an explicitly anti-capitalist, decolonial agenda for the sake of the planet, "to create a vision for the future that would not only safeguard nature but imagine a world under a different paradigm of thinking and being." The Declaration underscored:

> "The capitalist system has imposed on us a logic of competition, progress and limitless growth. This regime of production and consumption seeks profit without limits, separating human beings from nature and imposing a logic of domination upon nature, transforming everything into commodities: water, earth, the human genome, ancestral cultures, biodiversity, justice, ethics, the rights of peoples, and life itself."

Then-President of Bolivia, indigenous leader Evo Morales bluntly stated, "Humanity can either save capitalism or our Mother Earth."[100]

This sentiment also applies to growing concerns regarding the digitalization of agrifood systems. The International Panel of Experts on Sustainable Food Systems (IPES-Food) and ETC Group claim that with biodigital agriculture, "advances in digitalization, automation, synthetic biology, and molecular technologies promise to take the risks—and the people—out of food systems. New players argue that producing protein in petri-dishes, letting artificial intelligence manage the farm or invisibly nudge consumer behaviour are the route to resilience."[101]

Besides rendering the social content of farming cultures redundant, digitalization may well eliminate 300 million farms across the world, forcing migration of well over 1 billion people and the undoing of diverse food webs sustaining 70 percent of the world's population.[102]

Such new "frontiers" include replacing public commons (territories, knowledges, sociality) with an increasingly global land space subject to governance by technology that combines Big Ag and Big Data (e.g., Google, Microsoft, Amazon, Alibaba), and financed by asset managers (with no intimate relation to farmers and landscapes) such as BlackRock, Vanguard, Capital Group, Fidelity, and the Carlyle Group. However, while the digital frontier presents itself as "climate-smart" and sanitizing, it is dominated by most of the world's biggest agrochemical firms.[103] The use of pesticides has risen 81 percent in the past 35 years, spiking in some regions such as South America, where the use of pesticides has increased almost 500 percent.[104] Land (re)colonization is already underway via digital mapping technologies representing a "data grab,"[105] where each square kilometer, every square centimeter, of farmland is being mapped "for soil, nutrients, moisture, and sunshine."[106]

Biodigital technologies in northern large-scale industrial agricultural regions are now selecting land in the global South as a new data frontier. These interventions introduce "precision agriculture," where sensors can generate remote information for managing machinery and applying fertilizer and chemicals to targeted units of land for efficiency and yield increase, with data blockchain consolidation providing "value for seed and chemical firms, agronomists, co-operatives, farm insurance providers, and machinery firms."[107]

Infrastructures to enable the spread of digital surveillance techniques in the South are in their infancy; however, data "from new parts of the world and different types of cultivation systems are crucial to the development of digital technologies and algorithms."[108] And insofar as the precision concept invokes environmentalism, linked to climate-smart agriculture, it serves to legitimize financial and policy support for the biodigitalization of agriculture,[109] thereby discounting agroecological methods, which represent substantive green transition, minus the chemicals, commercial largesse, and elimination of farming cultures.

Agroecological transitions across the world account for 30 percent of farms.[110] For instance, in the south of India the Zero Budget Natural Farming (ZBNF) program multiplies small-scale agroecological farming, *with state support.* La Vía Campesina reported, "The ZBNF movement has achieved massive scale not only because of effective farming practices, but because of a social movement dynamic."[111] Originating in Karnataka state with 100,000 farms, it has been supported in Andhra Pradesh, Tamil Nadu, and Kerala states by millions of farmers.[112]

The question arises whether data can be used collectively or only by large agribusiness and digital corporations, reinforcing a digital divide if not wholesale dispossession over time.

Nevertheless, companies such as East Africa's We-Farm provide farmer-to-farmer digital networks for over a million small farmers in Kenya and Uganda, a program replicated elsewhere by open-source access data firms and network platforms that are enabling farmers' independence from corporate management to share local knowledges.[113] Here, data sovereignty for farming cultures represents natural rather than "green" possibilities on the land.

CONCLUSION

The transitions we have discussed are ongoing, so there is no clear way to predict outcomes. This is especially so since the world is at an inflection point. In the wake of the globalization project crisis, global reordering is expressed in rather chaotic multipolar ambitions to side-step the unipolar U.S.-centered world order with alternative trade agreements and political-economic alliances, including China's meteoric rise and its BRI-centered alternative world ordering. Multipolarity includes threatening groupings of authoritarian states, as well as South-to-South solidarities.

Simultaneously, rising economic nationalism signals protective policy shifts in a destabilized world of swelling migrant labor circuits, vulnerabilities of offshore production systems, and some recognition of deepening class, racial, and gender inequalities. Overlaying the human rights question are the disparate ways in which Fourth Industrial Revolution technologies complicate the development paradigm, or experience, across an uneven and combined world, expressing the contradictions of the green transition. These are manifest in both labor displacement via robotization, and green colonialism as firms, states and social movements exploit the urgency of raw materials extraction, with substantial landscape despoliation.

KEY TERMS

Belt and Road Initiative (BRI)
Cornwall Consensus
Green colonialism
Green transition
Multipolarity
UN Food System Summit (UNFSS)
World Economic Forum (WEF)

FURTHER READING

Ajl, Max. *A People's Green New Deal*. London: Pluto, 2021.

D'Eramo, Marco. *Masters: The Invisible War of the Powerful Against Their Subjects*. Cambridge, UK: Polity, 2024.

Dyer-Witheford, Nick. *Inhuman Power: Artificial Intelligence and the Future of Capitalism*. London: Pluto Press, 2019.

Hung, Ho-fung. *The China Book. Why China Will Not Rule the World*. New York: Columbia University Press, 2016.

Jones, Reece. *Violent Borders. Refugees and the Right to Move*. London: Verso, 2016.

Lange, Steffen, and Tilman Santarius. *Smart Green World? Making Digitalization Work for Sustainability*. Abington, UK: Routledge, 2020.

Lee, Ching Kwan. *The Specter of Global China. Politics, Labor, and Foreign Investment in Africa*. Chicago: University of Chicago Press, 2017.

Leguizamón, Amalia. *Seeds of Power. Environmental Injustice and Genetically Modified Soybeans in Argentina*. Durham, NC: Duke University Press, 2020.

8 DEVELOPMENT CLIMATE, OR THE NATURE OF DEVELOPMENT

Our use of the term *development climate* underscores the ways in which climate change and development are mutually conditioning. There are two aspects to this: (1) Fossil fuel–powered development since the eighteenth century has been the principal contributor to climate change via greenhouse gas (GHG) emissions; and (2) climate change, and related biodiversity loss, now drives reassessment of development's future. Here we examine "business-as-usual" adaptations to the climate crisis, with an emphasis on the ecosystem/agriculture nexus.

In 2002, the UN Framework Convention on Climate Change (UNFCCC) produced a prescient report regarding the risk of climate change to countries of the global South, noting,

"Climate change has the potential to shock the economic, social and ecological fabric of a country, and therefore to limit the ability of Less Developed Countries to reduce poverty and achieve their development objectives."[1] Five years later, the UN *Human Development Report* declared, "Climate change is the defining human development issue of our generation." And a landmark report appeared in 2012, authored by 21 past winners of the prestigious Blue Planet Prize, issuing this statement:

> In the face of an absolutely unprecedented emergency, society has no choice but to take dramatic action to avert a collapse of civilization. Either we will change our ways and build an entirely new kind of global society, or they will be changed for us.[2]

The climatic threshold we face today is a stark challenge to a development paradigm with promises of expanding prosperity. More than ever before, humanity's survival depends on reorganizing markets for environmental protection. This means *reconnecting economic and ecological relations*, privileging the latter. As we have seen, Rostow's vision of development stages lays out a linear progression of maturing economic institutions and practices devoid of environmental context. Nature is conceived as if it were *external* to Economy. Nothing could be further from reality: economic practice is premised on the transformation of Nature, renamed as a "resource," into products for sale, divested of their environment impact.

For example, a recent report on the "true cost of cheap cashmere" detailed the destruction of grassland ecosystems of the Mongolian Plateau in Central Asia, with

27.5 million goats (rather than sheep) emerging as the dominant ruminants, sourcing fibers from their downy undercoat to supply affordable sweaters in the world market. Dr. Allington, a landscape ecologist, finds that while "sheep nibble the tops of grasses but leave the base and roots intact, goats eat plants down to the roots so they cannot regrow, degrading habitat and causing soil erosion." As she notes, "the very essence of what makes cashmere luxurious—softness, warmth and longevity—is compromised, at a huge environmental cost."[3] Affordability may shape "high mass consumption"; however, if, instead of focusing on the goods we consume, we recognize we are also consuming Nature, the centrality of the natural world to modern economy becomes clear. Nature itself is now revealing that we have discounted it to our peril.

This rebuke from the natural world to the modern world has taken hold of our imagination only recently, as deterioration of ecosystems and changing climatic patterns have universally made their presence felt. They are manifest in desertification, drought, uncontrolled wildfires, intense hurricanes and flooding, species extinctions, atmospheric and oceanic warming, and chemical contamination of the land, water, and atmosphere. These disasters also reveal *cumulative limits* to human survival. Paradoxically, while "development" is presented as escaping the past, it is not so simple:

> For every year global warming continues and temperatures soar higher, living conditions on earth will be determined more intensely by the emissions of yore, so that the grip of yesterday on today intensifies—or, put differently, *the causal power of the past inexorably rises,* all the way up to the point where it is indeed "too late." The significance of that terrible destiny, so often warned of in climate change discourse, is the final *falling in of history on the present.*[4]

What is so significant about this perspective is the implication that "improving on the past" (as development promise and goal) has left humanity with a serious predicament. In 1988 U.S. climate scientist James Hanson warned the world in congressional testimony of the greenhouse effect, with a "new climate frontier" of strengthening storms, heatwaves, and droughts. In 2023 he remarked, "There's a lot more in the pipeline, unless we reduce the greenhouse gas amounts. These superstorms are a taste of the storms of my grandchildren . . . . [W]e knew it was coming . . . (and) we are damned fools" for not heeding warnings.[5]

LIFEWORLDS AT ODDS

Nature appears unruly now, problematizing economic definitions of "development." But environmental despoliation has a long history, especially for non-Western peoples subjected to colonization of their lifeworlds. For them, Nature is intrinsic to ways of living and regenerating. But Western construction of a development narrative, premised on a *linear* "economic rationality," consigned such low-input cultures to inferior and racialized redundancy—in the process compromising their ecological practices and the world's likelihood of learning from them. In this moment there is increasing urgency for Western science to learn from the world's Indigenous peoples, who conserve 80 percent of the planet's remaining biodiversity, striving to sustain "living economies," based on "an ethics of care and on values of ecological, gender, and social justice."[6]

Indigenous author Bruce Pascoe's book *Dark Emu, Black Seeds* recovers from settler-colonial erasure the sophistication of Australian Aboriginal peoples' civilization, based in landscape and soil management, underlining the ecological rationality of so-called prehistoric people. He observes, "Aboriginal people are born of the earth and individuals within the clan had responsibilities for particular streams, grasslands, trees, crops, animals and even seasons. The life of the clan was *devoted to continuance*," that is, the sustainable embedding of material needs in ecological relations, represented as "lifeworlds."[7]

This perspective was articulated recently by Indigenous activists at Standing Rock (Dakotas, United States) and in northern British Columbia, where Native North Americans have resisted oil pipeline construction through their ancestral territories: "In Lakota Culture, tribal members are meant to treat the earth in a way that it will allow it to flourish for the next seven generations."[8] These recent protests have a double purpose: to protect Indigenous territories and remaining lifeworlds *as well as* to protect the planet from fossil fuel expansion.[9] Here, the modern world has come full circle, with Indigenous voices rising to protect our common futures.

European colonialism was premised on expropriating native peoples from their habitats, as, for example, represented in white settlement of Australia beginning in 1788. Following imperial orders, Sydney's first governor proclaimed immediate sovereignty over all lands, and their inhabitants as trustees. This proclamation was informed by British philosopher John Locke's doctrine of natural law: grounding rights to landed property in the application of labor to the land. As an 1838 *Sydney Morning Herald* editorial observed of the Aborigines: "This vast land was to them a common—they bestowed no labour upon the land—their ownership, their right, was nothing more than that of the Emu or the Kangaroo."[10]

The basis of this claim to sovereign territory, as landed property, is the cornerstone of European development and its imperial foundations via commercial exploitation of the natural world. As mentioned previously, this "past" inhabits our present as carbon colonialism. Belgian historian, David van Reybrouck, notes, "Today's climate change is deeply colonial: it has been largely caused by the temperate zones from the northern hemisphere and it is most deeply felt in the tropics and the Arctic. You cannot decolonise without decarbonising and vice versa."[11] To accomplish this, the global South needs climate reparations. Currently, IMF loans bring huge debts, and, overall, low-income countries "spend 12 times more on debt repayments than addressing climate change."[12] In mid-2023, the activist organization Focus on the Global South recently denounced false market-based solutions to the climate crises [resulting] in financialization of nature and deprivation of natural resource dependent communities, and greater debt distress.

We demand immediate action to protect the environment and biodiversity through increased debt-free climate finance and cancellation of existing debts, phasing out of fossil fuels, an end to funding plastic production infrastructures[,] . . . reducing emissions to real zero and not net zero, advancing sustainable and climate-resilient agro-ecological systems[,] . . . [and] recognizing the collective governance and management rights of nature-dependent communities.[13]

What is telling here is not only how the West was unable or unwilling to apprehend "ecological rationality," to eventual global jeopardy, but also that capitalist modernity retains this blind spot—whether commercial profits are at stake and/or postcolonial racism endures. A timely correction of such cultural conceit, recently, has been the adoption of Indigenous sustainable fire management practices in California and Australia, where firefighter organizations have entered into partnership with Indigenous practitioners to control burning stimulated by global warming[14]—a humbling, but enlightened, move (under climatic pressure) after centuries of Western hubris.

To the extent that threat to ecosystems, species, and people is now epitomized by climatic emergencies, the world of development faces the need for new principles of equitable sufficiency and sustainability, rather than insatiable consumption of dwindling resources. Growing environmental justice movements across the world have inspired southern governments to raise the issue of "ecological debt" in climate conferences, referring to excessive resource extraction, ecosystem degradation, and the disproportionate occupation of environmental space by the rich countries, via "luxury carbon emissions" in the oceans and the atmosphere.[15]

Such responsibility is represented in "carbon appetites," where humanity's wealthiest 10 percent accounts for almost 50 percent of emissions, the middle 40 percent produce 43 percent, with the remaining 50 percent of the world's population producing about 8 percent of emissions. Relatedly, a 2023 Oxfam report found that "the richest 1% of the population produced as much carbon pollution in one year as the 5 billion people who make up the poorest two-thirds." Insofar as the 2023 COP28 climate convention was led by senior officials "in the top 1% of income earners" and corporate lobbyists heavily invested in carbon assets, it is not surprising that support for continued use of fossil fuels continues. Since the first multilateral Earth Summit of 1992, "60% more emissions are being pumped into the atmosphere and more money, carbon and power is concentrated in ever fewer hands."[16]

Rostow's *terminal* stage of "high mass consumption" is now perhaps a double *entendre*. This is the development challenge faced by the global community, subject to overconsumption by a global minority affluent class. At base, it means giving greater priority—and value—to Nature not produced for sale—such as biodiversity, habitat, and the global commons (air, water, forests, wetlands) and to local knowledges and cultures not centered on commodification as their organizing principle.

However, so far this challenge has been restricted by extending "economic rationality" in the pricing of ecosystems as "natural capital." This concept has been mainstreamed in the disciplinary emergence of "ecological economics" and as development institutions have recognized the significance of the natural world's role in wealth creation. The World Bank, for instance, created a new global partnership in 2010: Wealth Accounting and the Valuation of Ecosystem Services (WAVES), aiming "to promote sustainable development by ensuring that natural resources are mainstreamed in development planning and national economic accounts. WAVES is now part of the broader World Bank umbrella initiative, the Global Program for Sustainability." And this approach involved the World Bank's promotion of neoliberal reforms in countries of the global South, to encourage private-led energy transition, according to a Bretton Woods Project report in 2024.[17]

The question becomes what happens when nature is priced in this somewhat new way? It becomes fractionated into individual elements, eliminating its holistic ecological dimensions. Such accounting of ecosystem "services" in exchange-value terms separates them from their ecological relations, thus preparing them for commercial exploitation.

> Capital is interested in the products of nature, but not in "nature" as such. It does not look at a forest as an ecosystem, but as the sum of so many thousands of marketable pieces of wood. It has a unique way of looking at things: forests are seen as a wood pile, land as real estate and oceans as fish stocks.[18]

By individuating Nature in this way, its overall ecological value is voided. The same goes for pricing "ecosystem services," such as planting tree monocultures for storing carbon and awarding "carbon credits" in place of native biodiverse forests. And carbon credits may claim to contribute to a net zero emissions goal, but recent research shows that 78 percent of the "top 50 emission offset projects" were ineffectual,[19] and they cannot challenge continual promotion of fossil fuels.[20]

Carbon credits (used by firms to offset emissions) and the marketing of "ecosystem services" *substitute* for embedding economic processes in ecological relationships, in service of business as usual. One reason for not *reducing* the value of ecosystems to market prices is that their processes and elements are not independent units. Their value instead lies in their *interdependent* complexity. James Lovelock terms this the **Gaia hypothesis**, whereby Earth is a "physiological system" that "behaves as if it were alive," maintaining the surface temperature of the planet and recycling nutrients (in soil, water, and forests) with the "unconscious goal of regulating the climate and the chemistry at a comfortable state for life."[21] As we are learning, capitalist modernity is sabotaging this system.

THE POLITICS OF CLIMATE CHANGE

Naming this geological age the "**Anthropocene**" emphasizes human impact:

> The harnessing of fossil fuel power seemed, for a couple of centuries at least, to have freed large parts of humanity from the need to be in constant dialogue with nature. . . . Coal and oil, precisely because they were fossilized . . . did not

behave independently—not like wind, or water. . . . Now the cumulative effect of those centuries of burned carbon is in the process of unleashing the most ferocious natural tempers of all.[22]

Author Naomi Klein laments the fact that official recognition of unfolding climate emergency in the late 1980s coincided with the inception of the globalization project and its promotion of transnational capitalism and boundless fossil fuel dependence.[23] Klein argues, "We have not done the things that are necessary to lower emissions because those things fundamentally conflict with deregulated capitalism [and] are extremely threatening to an elite minority that has a stranglehold over our economy, our political process, and most of our major media outlets."[24] "Stranglehold" here refers to the powers accorded to the corporate world to drive economic development, subsidized by governments in the interests of revenues and political legitimacy.

On the other hand, military power inertia, remains, for the United States (and now Russia) "to maintain influence over countries that have fewer resources, such as China."[25] Here "the richest countries . . . are spending 30 times as much on their armed forces as they spend on providing climate finance for the world's most vulnerable countries, which they are legally bound to do. Seven of the top ten historical emitters are also among the top ten global military spenders."[26]

FOSSIL FUELING THE GLOBAL MARKET

Expansion of a deregulated global market, powered by fossil fuels, put the oil industry in a commanding position to slow climate action, concealing its own scientific projections of "catastrophic" consequences from continued extraction of fossil fuels. As early as 1965 the president of the American Petroleum Institute reported to its members fossil fuel carbon emissions could cause "marked changes in climate" by the year 2000. Heading up a long-term denial campaign, including funding politicians, Exxon reportedly redacted climate research through the 1980s, and then a Global Climate Coalition (GCC; primarily oil, coal, and auto industries) formed from 1989 to 2001 to lobby governments and sow public doubt about the science, even as a 1995 GCC *internal* report stated, "The scientific basis for the Greenhouse Effect and the potential impact of human emissions of greenhouse gases such as CO_2 on climate is well established and cannot be denied."

In the meantime, Shell released an educational video in 1991 titled "Climate of Concern," warning "global warming is not yet certain, but many think to wait for final proof would be irresponsible. Action now is seen as the only safe insurance." By the twenty-first century, as global warming showed its face, fossil fuel companies embraced the neoliberal practice of encouraging *personal accountability* for emissions (such as purchasing emissions offsets from plane travel), thereby obfuscating industry responsibility. In 2005 British Petroleum (BP) popularized the idea of the personal *carbon footprint* through a $100 million campaign, creating an online calculator of one's own footprint, then targeted at schoolchildren.

Rebranding itself Beyond Petroleum in 2000, BP embodied an apparent shift in sensibility among oil companies. One commentator noted, "denial-backed delay is no longer sufficient, it seems. They're now hoping to leverage their incumbency, and fossil-fuel wealth, to lay claim to the world's clean-energy future as well." A decade later, in January 2020, the American Petroleum Institute (representing over 600 corporations), launched Energy for Progress, a multimillion-dollar campaign designed as a substitute for decades of disinformation and lobbying to stall climate action. In the same month, the International Energy Agency reported that "renewable energy and carbon capture technologies currently represent just under 1 per cent of the industry's investments."

Meanwhile, massive subsidies of fossil fuel–based energy with public funds have suppressed its cost at the expense of alternative energy sources—expressing the structural power of the oil and gas industry. But this logic is hopefully changing.

Sources: Monbiot (2019: 16); Revkin (2009); M. Harris (2020: 32); Energy for Progress: https://energyforprogress.org/#; Crist (2020: 12).

The world is at a turning point vis-à-vis the role of fossil fuels. Indeed, scientists warn of five climate tipping points, risking crossing of natural thresholds, posing "threats of a magnitude never faced by humanity . . . [triggering] devastating domino effects, including the loss of whole ecosystems and capacity to grow staple crops, with societal impacts including mass displacement, political instability and financial collapse." These include ice sheets collapse in Greenland and the West Antarctic, cumulative permafrost thawing, death of coral reefs, and collapse of the main oceanic current in the North Atlantic (as depicted in the 2004 film *The Day After Tomorrow*).[27]

Meanwhile, the world faces a water crisis, with demand outstripping fresh water supply by 40 percent by 2030, according to the Global Commission on the Economics of Water. Lead author Johan Rockstrom (director of the Potsdam Institute for Climate Impact Research) notes, "The scientific evidence is that we have a water crisis. We are misusing and polluting water, and changing the whole global hydrological cycle, through what we are doing to the climate. It's a triple crisis" of governance: of technology, finance, and equal justice.[28] The task, then, is "to understand the links between water, climate change, and biodiversity loss, and to properly define, value, and govern water as a global common good."[29]

At the 2019 World Economic Forum, the *Global Risks Report 2019* declared humanity was "sleepwalking its way to catastrophe" as extreme weather, failure to act on climate change, and natural disasters topped the list.[30] That year, officials of the Bank of England, the European Central Bank, the U.S. Federal Reserve, and the world's largest asset manager, BlackRock, announced financial adjustments to anticipated global warming, Germany proposed phasing out coal-based energy, and Finland and Copenhagen proclaimed the goal of carbon neutrality by the 2030s.[31]

These initiatives suggest hope, but as teenage activist Greta Thunberg said at the time to the assembled elites at Davos: "I don't want your hope. I don't want you to be hopeful. I want you to panic . . . and act as if the house was on fire."[32] The implicit point, here, is not only that global warming is wreaking havoc across the world but also that to successfully engineer an alternative path is not simply about substituting renewable energy. It is about the additional need for public intervention to coordinate climate change abatement and ecological practices, rather than climate adaptation/mitigation measures being managed with a market calculus via multiple, uncoordinated private initiatives. One other way of thinking about this juncture is that

> [t]hese crises are not about the planet going haywire. They are crises caused by failures to assign and enforce social responsibilities. And the wealthiest, most powerful and most capable societies that have ever existed on this planet are behaving as if they owe nothing for what they have gained at the expense of imperiling life on Earth.[33]

BUSINESS AS USUAL?

A business-as-usual approach to climate change views it as a market opportunity to capitalize on "adaptation," since "the world must adapt to what it has become."[34] Consider container shipping, expanding 400 percent since the early 1990s with no international accounting system for emissions. Journalist Ana Swanson, describing a unique Danish ship powered by green methanol producing 100 fewer tons of GHG daily, "an amount equivalent to the emissions of 8,000 cars," wonders if the greening of container shipping lines is a promising adaptation. Generating nearly 3 percent of emissions, the global shipping industry produces a similar amount of carbon annually as the aviation industry. Container ships today are larger than aircraft carriers, carrying more than 200,000 containers "which would stretch for 75 miles if placed in a row," lowering transport costs and enabling "the modern consumer lifestyle, allowing retailers like Amazon, Walmart, Ikea and Home Depot to offer a vast suite of products at a fraction of their historical cost."[35] While significant emissions reductions is a plus, this raises the issue from where such products come: usually from southern economies providing "cheap" industrial labor as dependent development. Perpetuating such *global* patterning of high mass consumption with green shipping underscores the limits, or paradox, of "green business-as-usual."

Nevertheless, what the world has become combines addiction to high mass consumption, with ever more unconventional oil exploration. For investors, there are opportunities for windfall profits on both counts. Norway's petroleum and energy minister, for example, remarked, "It's important to recognize that [Arctic melt] is also an opportunity."[36] The question is, opportunity for whom, and with what social and political implications?

The melting of Arctic sea ice represents a new carbon frontier of oil and gas reserves and 25 percent of the world's known coal reserves[37] (see Figure 8.1). And, given that states and firms are geared to maintaining market position, such reserves are attractive. The oil industry exemplifies the nexus between private and public (as in government) interests, with fossil fuel companies receiving up to $1 trillion in annual global subsidies, serving government legitimacy needs by maintaining fossil fuel–based economic growth. Structurally, sunk costs for business and governments (well over $100 trillion of unburned carbon and tens of trillions of dollars of infrastructure) are a powerful combination for maintaining conventional energy supplies even as alternative energy sources are available.

Importantly, "business as usual" is not simply about global oil companies like ExxonMobil and Shell, for instance. Seventy-five percent of oil extraction is undertaken

FIGURE 8.1 ■ Arctic Sea Ice in September

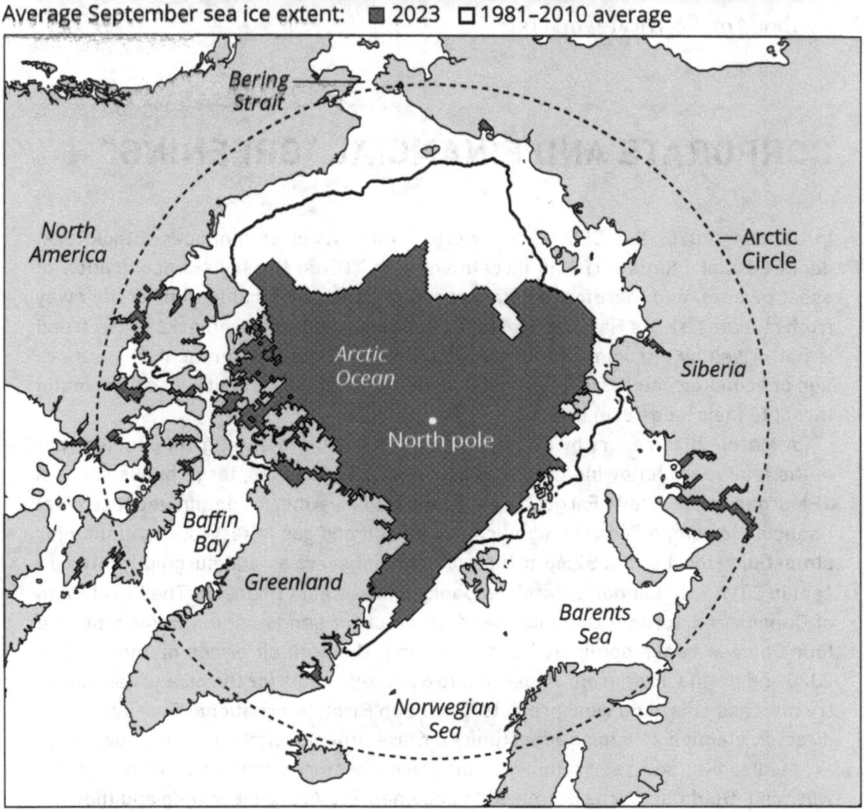

Source: Guardian graphic, "The Climate Crisis Explained in 10 Charts." Original data from Sea Ice Index, National Snow and Ice Data Center. Copyright Guardian News & Media Ltd 2024.

by national oil companies, such as the State Oil Company of the Azerbaijan Republic, Russia's main source of oil.[38] A critical issue here is public liability for the costs of fossil fuel exit, or phaseout—not unlike the bailout of banking sectors following the 2008 financial crisis. Environmentalist Holly Jean Buck notes that the oil industry is already positioned if it faces substantial phaseout pressures—with immunity from climate change lawsuits, some citizens identifying with the industry's contributions to local economic development, and recognition that it has the technology and experience to take the lead in carbon capture and sequestration, at the same time preserving investor confidence. A former head of the U.S. Department of Energy Office of Fossil Fuels, noted in 2018, "These companies are planning for a decarbonized future, however that gets envisioned. And the smart ones are the ones who are out in front. They are going to create their own world and they are not going to be victims to someone else's." And this was in the same year that the new Carbon Capture Coalition was formed in the United States, including fossil fuel companies, agribusiness, heavy industry, think tanks, and unions like the AFL-CIO, the National Farmers Union, and the International Brotherhood of Electrical Workers.[39]

CORPORATE AND FINANCIAL "GREENING"

In January 2020, the CEO of the world's largest asset manager, BlackRock, declared that "climate risk is investment risk." Given the high concentration of asset owners, and therefore of market control, they are unable to diversify away from climate risk. As Harvard professor Rebecca Henderson remarks, "This trend is not driven by altruism or a deep commitment to the environment: it's a function of economic interests . . . climate change is not an externality—it's a profound threat to their long-term returns."

A March 2020 report by an alliance of U.S. environmental groups noted that in the four years following the Paris accords (2016 to 2020), large banks such as JPMorgan Chase, Wells Fargo, Citibank, and Bank of America dominated fossil fuel financing to companies with significant Arctic oil and gas reserves, accounting for almost one-third of the $2.66 trillion of financial services and surging by 40 percent in 2019, with London's Barclays Bank as the largest financier. The Royal Bank of Canada and Toronto Dominion led finance of tar sands mining in Alberta, and four Chinese banks dominated coal financing. But with oil prices plummeting in 2020 and profits down from 20 percent to 6 percent, rates for the oil and gas industry matched solar and wind projects, and Fatih Birol, International Energy Agency director, claimed a historic opportunity for investment switching into renewables.

Meanwhile, several prominent companies gestured toward reducing global warming. Goldman Sachs promised to end financing Arctic oil drilling and thermal coal operations. BlackRock began shifting out of coal investment, but not oil and gas. Microsoft aims to be in a carbon negative position by 2030 and, further, to remove as much atmospheric carbon by 2050 that it has ever emitted. BP aims to be carbon neutral by 2050. Among other airlines, Delta pledged $1 billion toward reducing air travel contributions to global warming over the next decade. Amazon announced investment of $10 billion in "scientists, activists, NGOs—any effort that offers a real possibility to help preserve and protect the natural world." And JPMorgan Chase pledged to end financing oil drilling in the Arctic and reduce loans for coal mining.

A start, a little too late, greenwashing, investor conundrums? Or shaky? In 2024 four of the largest U.S. banks (Citi, Bank of America, JPMorgan Chase, and Wells Fargo, the largest funders of oil, gas, and coal in the world) exited the Equator Principles (standards for financial institutions to address socioenvironmental risks in countries where they finance fossil fuel and mining projects) under pressure from the politics of climate denial (politicians yielding to private interests).

Sources: Carrington, Ambrose, and Taylor (2020); P. Greenfield and Makortoff (2020); M. Harris (2020: 33); R. Henderson (2020); Lakhani and Rushe (2024).

Earlier, in 2006, *Newsweek* reported that "Wall Street is experiencing a climate change," recognizing that "the way to get the green is to go green," articulating the business-as-usual approach of recycling the (market) problem as solution. By 2008, the World Bank was partnering with the UNFCCC's Conference of the Parties (COP) via a Less Developed Countries Fund to administer a **National Adaptation Programme of Action** through its **Global Environmental Facility (GEF)**. The Commission on Climate Change and Development noted the adaptation fund is "the first example of the use of market-based options to generate substantial financial resources to address climate change. The carbon market . . . has the potential to move huge financial flows to developing countries for mitigation and adaptation."[40] Critics term this *carbon imperialism*, whereby the global South is converted into a "carbon dump" (as in sink) to sustain northern lifestyles.[41]

Application of market metrics to natural processes instituted "pricing of ecosystem services"—as in the UNFCCC-established **Reducing Emissions from Deforestation and Forest Degradation** designed to pay farmers and forest dwellers as well as governments to protect forest capacity. Pricing an ecosystem service is designed to incentivize sustainability. However, ecosystem processes are neither singular nor produced for sale. While marketing the environment is an attempt to internalize environmental costs, it is not without hazard, since commodified environmental "resources" become exchangeable. Thus, if conditions change, such as a rising price for resources in a forest (oil, timber, minerals), the original conservation purpose may be overridden by a changed financial calculus. And, of course, for forest dwellers, pricing ecosystem services represents the loss of territorial control, including their spiritual connection to the land.[42]

This scenario fits precisely with Ecuador's 2023 resort to oil drilling in Yasuní National Park, near some of the last isolated Indigenous people on Earth. In 2007, President Correa proposed an internationally subsidized fund for $3.6 billion to keep its Amazonian oil reserves in the ground. Supporters viewed this as a precedent-setting moral victory: a small southern state disregarding a valuable resource in the northern-centered fossil fuel age.[43] It was not to be.

The origins of "ecosystem services" management stem from the first United Nations Earth Summit in 1992 in Rio de Janeiro. It was here that the idea of "global ecology" emerged, which sociologist Wolfgang Sachs called the "rational planning of the planet for Northern Security," when

> the governments at Rio came around to recognizing the decline of the environment, but insisted on relaunching development. As worn-out development talk prevailed, attention centered on the South and its natural treasures and not on the North and its industrial disorder. There were conventions on biodiversity, climate and forests, but no conventions on agri-business, automobiles or free trade. This indicates that UNCED [United Nations Conference on Environment and Development] attempted to secure the natural resources and waste sinks for economic growth in favour of the global middle class, rather than to embark upon a path towards industrial self-limitation and local regeneration.[44]

Southern forests were understood to provide ecosystem services and to be managed as carbon sinks and for biodiversity preservation—bioregions of intrinsic (ecological) value to a northern-led accumulation drive. At the same time, by classifying the atmosphere and biodiversity as a "global commons," the World Bank's GEF overrode protests by the locals, asserting that "everyone has a right of access to them, that local people have no more claim to them than a corporation based on the other side of the globe."[45] Rights are one thing, spatial reach is another, raising the critical question of *how* rights are conceived.

The terms of reference of the current land grabs are similar—namely, that global food security depends on access to land for offshore food (via zoning and capitalization by states, agencies, and transnational corporations). And this process of de-territorialization of agriculture by transnational investment by firms and financiers is undertaken in the name of **sustainable intensification**. Agrifood systems (including transport) account for close to 40 percent of total GHG emissions and are the single largest source of global environmental change. Agriculture is responsible for 80 percent of deforestation in this century, and, of 28,000 species at risk of extinction, it threatens 24,000. "Only 29% of the weight of birds on Earth consists of wild species: the rest is poultry."[46]

SUSTAINABLE INTENSIFICATION PROPOSALS

Sustainable intensification seeks to expand food supplies while conserving land. It means, in relatively neutral terms, "producing more output from the same area of land while reducing the negative environmental impacts and at the same time increasing contributions to natural capital and the flow of environmental services."[47] To the extent that it seeks to enhance "natural capital," sustainable intensification operates within the business-as-usual paradigm. The British Royal Society sets the context:

> Food security is one of this century's key global challenges. Producing enough food for the increasing global population must be done in the face of changing consumption patterns, the impacts of climate change and the growing scarcity of water and land.[48]

Reference here to the challenge of food security omits mention of the present state of affairs, and the legacy of the past, in which capitalist development has steadily displaced farming cultures. Such localized farming systems surviving today actually provide up to two-thirds of the world's food despite being under pressure from continuing dispossession as global agribusiness deepens its command of markets and resources. Much of the industrial agriculture to be sustainably intensified serves an affluent global minority, not the global population. The "food security" trope has fueled the development era, invoking green revolution and biotechnology interventions in the name of feeding the world but also serving strategic political goals, such as government and development agency support for agribusiness technologies. In this context, *agribusiness* often eclipses food security for the world's hungry.

The "food insecurity" trope masks power relations such as displacement of local farming cultures via institutional support of agroindustrial export production. It overlooks how food scarcity has more to do with global provisioning of affluent consumers, whose animal protein preferences corral at least 80 percent of the world's arable land for pasture and feed crops.[49] Climate scientists urge a reversal of livestock production to reduce GHGs, as methane and N_2O (nitrous oxide) contribute more than CO_2 (carbon dioxide) to agriculture's warming effect. Scientist Tim Flannery proposes a "sustainabilitarian diet," cautioning that meat can be produced more sustainably (but not in feedlots). His point is that "[p]lant-animal interactions are at the heart of Gaia's self-regulation. Plants capture the sun's energy, and animals, by feeding upon plants, create and swiftly recycle nutrients that plants need in order to grow."[50]

Sustainable intensification initiatives are underway, with Monsanto's new agricultural technologies (biotech crop-breeding techniques) claiming to lead to "more production on less land, and collectively reduce the amount of resources needed per unit of production."[51] The journal *Nature* advocates a second green revolution for sustainable intensification, but with a more inclusive approach:

> Such a revolution will require a wholesale realignment of priorities in agricultural research. There is an urgent need for new crop varieties that offer higher yields but use less water, fertilizers or other inputs . . . and for crops that are more resistant to drought, heat, submersion and pests. Equally crucial is lower-tech research into basics such as crop rotation, mixed farming of animals and plants on smallholder farms, soil management and curbing waste.[52]

How this realignment of priorities is playing out is indicative of different interpretations of "sustainability." There are two broad approaches: high-input conservation agriculture on less land to preserve biodiversity, and **agroecology**, which restores biodiversity above and below ground with intercropping, agroforestry, cover crops, and mixed farming.[53]

Agroecological methods reflect a growing awareness that Western science must learn from Indigenous people's guardianship of surviving biodiversity. Echoing the developmental disconnection between "past" and present, South African anthropologist Anselmo Matusse emphasizes, "Western scientists and indigenous peoples come with very different world views. [In general] western science is more utilitarian and sees the world in pieces, indigenous knowledge is more about understanding the interconnectedness of things."[54] This latter practice informs modern agroecology, which combines "modern" ecological science with "traditional" Indigenous and peasant knowledges.

SUSTAINABLE INTENSIFICATION IN QUESTION

The high-input technology approach starts from the proposition of a "yield gap" between attainable and potential agricultural yields on southern lands. For example, the World Bank claimed in 2011 that "none of the African countries of most interest to investors is now achieving more than 30 percent of the potential yield on currently cultivated land."[55] The bank's consideration of such conditions, without acknowledging withdrawal of support for most small farming over the preceding three decades (structural adjustment programs), exemplifies how current scarcities can be depoliticized to suit a new agenda. And, in 2010 the European Commission recommended "secure land tenure and use rights" as "prerequisites for higher productivity of smallholder farmers," encouraging governments to prioritize improving "availability and access to food and stimulate the integration of smallholder farmers in production chains."[56]

The G-8 became heavily involved in enabling the new kind of "agriculture for development" advocated in the bank's 2007 *World Development Report*. This report reorients agricultural infrastructure for *sustainable intensification*, advocating "market smart" subsidies "to stimulate input markets" to capture "the benefits of GMOs [genetically modified organisms] for the poor," where "the private sector drives the organization of value chains that bring the market to smallholders and commercial farms."[57] Nobel laureate Wangari Maathai of Kenya's Green Belt Movement avers, "Africa needn't intensify its farming sector so that it takes on the character of the industrial-style agriculture that dominates the West. . . . As we are learning, industrial farming may be efficient, but it has enormous downsides for the environment," and it overwhelmingly feeds livestock.[58]

Within this framework of **value chain agriculture**, integrating farmers into supply chains organized by global firms and investors, agriculture becomes intensified with agri-inputs (transgenic seed, fertilizers, agrochemicals, mechanization), in the controversial name of **climate-smart agriculture** (CSA). In the first decade of the twenty-first century, the number of acres planted worldwide with genetically modified crops increased from 25 million to 400 million.[59] Transgenic crops, representing a new profit frontier, are now claimed to be "climate-smart." Agrochemical and biotechnology firms such as BASF, Monsanto, Syngenta, Bayer, and DuPont have filed over 500 patent documents on "climate-ready genes." This project is represented by a spokesperson for Monsanto, suggesting peasant knowledge is nonadaptive: "I think everyone recognizes that the old traditional ways just aren't able to address these new challenges. The problems in Africa are pretty severe."[60] From this perspective, the premium is on "improving" the land (with external inputs to intensify productivity of commercial, monocultural crops) rather than supporting small-scale mixed farming, which is more likely to sustain soil fertility, as such.

In relation to this, at the World Food Security Summit in Rome (2008), the FAO, the International Fund for Agricultural Development, and the World Food Programme signed a memorandum of understanding with the **Alliance for Green Revolution in Africa (AGRA)**—jointly funded by the Rockefeller Foundation and Bill and Melinda Gates Foundation—to convert Africa's breadbasket regions into a source of food supplies. The Gates Foundation allied with Monsanto, a global biotech corporation, with AGRA committed to introducing imported fertilizers, agrochemicals, and purchased (some biotech-fortified) seeds.[61] These technological packages arrive first via farm input subsidy programs, but with a dependent relation built in, since the seeds have to be purchased anew every year and require commercial synthetic fertilizers. Critics argue the foundation's push to expand high-cost, high-input, chemical-dependent agriculture in Africa exacerbates hunger, worsening inequality and deepening corporate power in the world's most food-insecure region.[62] Senior adviser to the U.S. Institute for Agriculture and Trade Policy, Tim Wise reports,

> Neither the Gates Foundation, nor AGRA itself, nor the donor governments that contribute to AGRA from the global north, have any published evaluation of the effectiveness of that aid. . . . They promised when they launched AGRA that their goal was to double productivity and incomes for 30 million African small-scale farmer households by 2021. There's absolutely no evidence that that's happening.[63]

Under such pressure to produce evidence, the Gates Foundation has now rebranded, eliminating reference to a "green revolution" in Africa.[64]

While the Gates Foundation's emphasis on helping "poor farmers adapt"[65] with technological fixes, African farming cultures have learned over centuries how to tailor their practices to changing environmental conditions. If they are "poor" in commercial terms, their wealth is in their local, environmental knowledge and characteristic experimental science. Across Africa, farmers have not only reversed desertification in southern Niger and Kenya, but also, along the edge of the Sahara, in Nigeria, Niger, Senegal, Burkina Faso, and Kenya, they have employed integrated farming, mixed cropping, and traditional soil and water conservation methods that have increased food production substantially ahead of population growth. Population density has proved essential for farming labor needs, especially with cooperative farming practices and developing and sustaining social networks to exchange labor, seed, cattle, technology, and cash.[66]

While the jury may still be out regarding the stability, durability, and promise of transgenic technologies (beyond feed crops), their application under current commercial conditions has the drawback of overriding small-farmer agroecological knowledge of highly variable local conditions, deploying seed-sharing networks. In response, the International Forum for Agroecology, at Nyéléni, Mali, in 2015, declared:

> Agroecology is political, it requires us to challenge and transform structures of power in society. We need to put the control of seeds, biodiversity, land and territories, waters, knowledge, culture and the commons in the hands of the people who feed the world.[67]

In the summer of 2023, the global trade regime sponsored a new protocol to lock 54 African nations into a proprietary model of food cultivation allowing corporate property rights to override local seed management, including penalties across the African Union for farmers failing "to adopt foreign-engineered seeds protected by patents, including genetically-modified versions of native seeds," in the name of "climate-smart agriculture." As a Ghanaian female farmer claimed, "The companies will try to entice us by saying their seeds are 'better.' Then we'll become dependent on seeds you can't replant. Our seeds are from this soil. It's colonialism to say what seeds we can use and how to use them."[68]

Meanwhile, in 2014, the UN launched the Global Alliance for Climate-Smart Agriculture (GACSA), described as a "voluntary, farmer-led, multi-stakeholder, action-oriented coalition committed to the incorporation of climate-smart approaches within food and agricultural systems."[69] It claims to foster a win-win-win mentality, via intensification, adaption, and mitigation. In this regard, CSA is represented by the UN/FAO and the World Bank as a governance mechanism for promoting improved techniques and inputs rather than a specific technology or practice: "any agricultural technique that—in comparison to standard existing practices—improves one of the triple wins criteria can be designated climate smart."[70] Thus some practices, such as Indian water-harvesting projects, farmer-managed tree regeneration in the Sahel, and other agroecological practices, count in CSA evaluations, but such evaluations are no substitute for rethinking the dominant mode of high-input agriculture, its steady enclosure of local farming systems, rural inequality and the question of land reform, subsidy regimes for corporate agriculture, and food deprivation.

The World Bank assumed leadership in 2015 in promoting CSA, developing profiles of national CSA implementations to establish where investment was needed in achieving the Sustainable Development Goals, promoting the "triple-win" narrative of adopting *intensification*, adaption to climate change via *resilience*, and *mitigation* by reducing emissions. At one level, CSA operates largely as a rebranding exercise, leveraging climate change as a vehicle for accumulation via the intensification of existing technologies.[71]

CSA lacks a participatory mandate to gather farmer knowledge and innovation, which might avert escalation of gender inequality as corporate technological packages sideline seed-sharing practices managed by women farmers.[72] La Via Campesina opposes CSA "as a façade dominated by a corporate oligarchy under which a business-as-usual approach can proceed."[73] As one commentator observes, "Agribusiness corporations that promote synthetic fertilisers, industrial meat production and large-scale industrial agriculture—all of which are widely recognised as contributing to climate change and undermining the resilience of farming systems—can and do call themselves 'climate smart,'"[74] with positive recognition by the World Bank.[75] In keeping with the business-as-usual theme, CSA exemplifies the ease with which power relations come to redefine the role of agriculture in a climate-challenged future as a *technical* resolution.[76]

When GACSA formed, more than 80 civil society organizations (e.g., Institute for Agriculture and Trade Policy, Arab Network for Food Security, World Forum of Fisher People) and farmers' movements (e.g., Campaign for Real Farming [UK], Tamil Nadu Organic Farmer's Federation, Tanzania Organic Agriculture Movement) publicly rejected the initiative, claiming the following:

> The final framework of the Alliance does not contain any criteria or definitions for what can—or cannot—be considered "climate-smart agriculture." Industrial approaches that increase greenhouse gas emissions and farmers' vulnerability by driving deforestation, using genetically modified (GM) seeds, increasing synthetic fertiliser use or intensifying industrial livestock production, are all apparently welcome to use the "climate-smart" label to promote their practices as solutions to climate change.[77]

The civil society claim is that small and medium farmers already have the possibility of climate solutions, "based on agroecological practices and the relocalisation of food systems to effectively fight hunger."[78] This is a key distinction between opposing models of sustainability: sustainable intensification via commercial inputs versus biodiverse, ecological farming methods. Whereas the former has institutional and market power, the latter has staying power, even as CSA sustains agribusiness. Former UN Right to Food Rapporteur Olivier De Schutter, addressing the UN Commission on Human Rights (2011), stated,

> Agriculture should be fundamentally redirected towards modes of production that are more environmentally sustainable and socially just. . . . [Agroecology] helps small farmers who must be able to farm in ways that are less expensive and more productive. But it benefits all of us, because it *decelerates global warming and ecological destruction.*[79]

Continuing research has shown small agroecological farms are substantially more climate-friendly, treating soils with organic fertilizer that absorbs and sequesters carbon more effectively than industrial agriculture, such that 10,000 small- to medium-sized organic farms can "store carbon in the soil equivalent to taking 1,174,400 cars off the road."[80]

Such a case is represented by **system of rice intensification (SRI)**. SRI enhances irrigated rice productivity by altering the management of plants, soil, water, and nutrients, raising "yields to about double the present world average without relying on external inputs."[81] That is, SRI attends to the interrelations among various soil biota (from bacteria to earthworms) with extended root systems, rather than applying external inputs (fertilizer, agrochemicals, transgenic seeds). In 2014, the Indian Bihari government claimed average yields on hundreds of thousands of hectares "were at least 40 percent larger than for conventional rice farming, and possibly far more." By reducing constant waterlogging of rice plants, SRI substantially reduces powerful methane gas emissions, encouraging rice-using companies like Mars and Kellogg's and the agribusiness colossus Olam to set up the Sustainable Rice Platform. Olam CEO Sunny Verghese declared, "The food system is broken. . . . We can't do it overnight but there is a new way of collaborating. Companies must change and reduce their resource intensity. The whole food sector must change."[82] In other words, here is a promising sector amenable to "business as usual."

RENEWABLE ENERGY

Another sector amenable to "business as usual" is renewable energy. Biofuels, for example, have always been part of traditional farming practices. As a so-called transitional fuel in an age of climate uncertainty, they are now an industrial crop (e.g., corn, oil palm, soy, sugar, jatropha). Biofuels, now as "green fuels," are heavily subsidized by governments. The European Union unsuccessfully targeted 2020 as a date by which to supply 10 percent of its fuel needs from biofuels.[83]

Biofuels are controversial. Although their burn is cleaner, their *production* is often carbon intensive. For example, extraction of one ton of palm oil produces 33 tons of CO_2—10 times more per ton of petroleum.[84] A 2022 assessment of the U.S. Renewable Fuel Standard found that the program, "which requires that transportation fuel contain a minimum volume of renewable fuel, and which drives nearly half of global biofuel production—has probably increased greenhouse-gas emissions."[85] The International Energy Agency estimates that by 2030, biofuels will "barely offset the yearly increase in global oil demand," and all renewables, including biofuels, will amount to only 9 percent of global energy consumption.[86] Also, they reduce available food supplies. The World Bank notes that the "grain required to fill the tank of a sports utility vehicle with ethanol (240 kilograms of maize for 100 liters of ethanol) could feed one person for a year."[87]

Production decisions depend on a boardroom financial calculus, often with little concern for allocations between crops for food or fuels and/or environmental integrity. Accordingly, the former UN Human Rights Rapporteur, Jean Ziegler, charged that biofuels are a "crime against humanity."[88] Social movements have renamed biofuels *agrofuels* in recognition of this tradeoff between food and fuel crops, and there have been calls for certification of biofuels to encourage protective socioecological standards.[89] And so Cargill, for example, in its biofuel plantations in Southeast Asia, claims to avoid disturbing peat soils (which store large amounts of carbon) and to protect biodiversity via a no-burn policy on land clearing.[90] Such initiatives follow sustained civil society pressures on such companies with histories of deforestation in Southeast Asia, West Africa, and Brazil.

A study in *Science* claimed that the conversion of rainforests, peatlands, savannas, or grasslands to produce biofuels in Brazil, Southeast Asia, and the United States "creates a 'biofuel carbon debt' by releasing 17 times to 420 times more CO_2 than the annual greenhouse gas reductions these biofuels provide by displacing fossil fuel."[91] Thus, even as biofuels are viewed as a renewable alternative to fossil fuels, they contribute to global warming even though they represent a "green fuel" for Northerners (who pay in cash and taxes) premised on the "export of sustainability" from Southerners (who pay in loss of long-term livelihood and habitat).

In other words, land enclosures for food and renewable energy investments not only support lifestyles of affluent consumers across the world but also threaten small-scale producers' habitats and livelihoods. "Business as usual" may also be inequality as usual.

CONCLUSION: ECOSYSTEM PRIORITY

As the Anthropocene confronts climate emergencies, the question of ecosystem integrity comes to the fore, even as biophysical processes, like many socioeconomic activities, remain unaccounted for. And now the world confronts how to address the staggering carbon footprint of artificial intelligence (AI). It was predicted in 2024 that "billions of devices connected to the internet could be responsible for up to 3.5 percent of global carbon emissions" by 2025.[92] Nature, in all its intrinsic value, does not appear through the conventional development lens and so is easily marginalized and devalued or extinguished; yet these environmental and social resources are central to ecosystem resilience and species survival, including humans.

The landmark 2005 UN **Millennium Ecosystem Assessment (MEA)**, which addresses environmental degradation, states, "Existing national and global institutions are not well designed to deal with the management of common pool resources, a characteristic of many ecosystem services." The dilemma is that national political boundaries cut across ecosystems. Over a thousand biological scientists proposed integrating ecosystem management goals within development planning frameworks at large, noting that "the most important public policy decisions affecting ecosystems are often made by agencies and in policy arenas other than those charged with protecting ecosystems." The MEA identifies poverty reduction strategies that shape development priorities, noting, "In general these have not taken into account the importance of ecosystems to improving the basic human capabilities of the poorest,"[93] where many common pool resources/ecosystems are nurtured by populations often deemed "poor" or "marginal" by development agencies. According to the MEA, these problems, unless addressed, will substantially diminish the benefits that future generations obtain from ecosystems.[94]

The moral of the development climate story, then, is well articulated by former deputy director of the NGO Focus on the Global South, Nicola Bullard, in addressing the dominant development paradigm:

> Perhaps the greatest challenge we face is not so much how we understand sustainability, but rather *how we understand development*. . . . Confronted with collapsing ecosystems, toxic environments, soil depletion, climate chaos, disappearing species, and finite fossil fuels, does sustainability even make sense when there is so little left to sustain? Instead, we should be talking about regenerating and restoring what has been destroyed. . . . What we lack is the imagination to think about how to live differently, how to unravel the power structures that obstruct change, and how to rethink "development."[95]

A healthy place to start is learning to value the multiplicity of ways in which Indigenous and many other communities are already experimenting with renewable practices, working with rather than against Nature. The following chapter addresses this charge.

KEY TERMS

Agroecology
Alliance for Green Revolution in Africa (AGRA)
Anthropocene
Climate-smart agriculture
Gaia hypothesis
Global Environment Facility (GEF)
Millennium Ecosystem Assessment (MEA)
National Adaptation Programme of Action
Reducing Emissions from Deforestation and Forest Degradation
Sustainable intensification
System of rice intensification (SRI)
Value chain agriculture

FURTHER READING

Carton, Wim, and Andreas Malm. *Overshoot. How the World Surrendered to Climate Breakdown.* London: Verso Books, 2024.

Ervine, Kate. *Carbon.* Cambridge, UK: Polity Press, 2018.

Islam, Md Saidul. *Confronting the Blue Revolution: Industrial Aquaculture and Sustainability in the Global South*. Toronto, University of Toronto Press, 2014.

Khan, Naveeda. *In Quest of a Shared Planet. Negotiating Climate from the Global South*. New York: Fordham University Press, 2023.

Pascoe, Bruce. *Dark Emu, Black Seeds: Agriculture or Accident?* Broome, WA: Magabala Books, 2014.

Shapiro, Judith. *China's Environmental Crisis*. Cambridge, UK: Polity Press, 2016.

Taylor, Marcus. *The Political Ecology of Climate Change Adaptation*. London: Earthscan, 2015.

Winders, Bill, and Elizabeth Ransom, eds. *Global Meat: Social and Environmental Consequences of the Expanding Meat Industry*. Cambridge, MA: MIT Press, 2019.

9 PUBLIC AND LOCAL GREEN INITIATIVES

In this chapter, we explore sustainability initiatives and actions on the ground, as counterpoints to relying on "business as usual" and modeling pathways to a green future. These include public, urban, and rural ingenuity, as examples of local and regional initiatives underway, including social movements and grassroots mobilizations proposing remedies to perils of the so-called Anthropocene age.

In addition to improving living standards in such communities, public *participatory* monitoring is an essential first step toward addressing such inequality and vulnerability. One such example is provided by Semarang, Indonesia. A major port city on the low-lying northern coast of the Java Sea, with a population of over five million people, Semarang faces the problem of sea level rise, drought, and extreme temperature fluctuations. The International Institute for Environment and Development report offers a model (democratic) adaptation plan geared to soliciting local input to enhance government responsiveness:

> Using demographic and hazard risk data in conjunction with spatial analyses, we develop a framework for identifying the geographic distribution of potential vulnerabilities. This analysis allows for a community-level, contextualised understanding of vulnerability and can provide a foundation for more effectively fostering adaptive capacity. This localized understanding of needs enhances the capacity of communities to negotiate for resources.[1]

Such participatory governance is quite at odds with neoliberalism's business-as-usual reflex in responses to climatic hazards. A dominant claim is that public services are necessarily inefficient and expensive, whereas the market provides services efficiently and cheaply. The neoliberal way has been to devalue public service, progressively privatized over the past four decades, and individualizing citizen access to private services as "freedom of choice" regardless of inequality of access.

Recently, such a social procedure has been exposed by the universal crisis of *public* health, challenged by mounting climatic emergency. In turn, this has stimulated an ongoing process of reviving public services across the world, in more than 1,600 cities in 45 countries, reducing costs, improving working conditions and service quality, and ensuring greater transparency and accountability. For example, a report published in 2017, *Reclaiming Public Services: How Cities and Citizens Are Turning Back Privatization*, notes, in contrast to private services delivery deference, "In reality, below the radar, thousands of politicians, public officials, workers and unions, and social movements are working to reclaim or create effective public services that address the basic needs of people and respond to our social, environmental and climate challenges . . . most often at the local level."[2]

This report noted that there was an uptick in such approaches since 2008, during the global financial crisis, viewed by many as the turning point in the repute of neoliberal globalization:

> Remunicipalisation is particularly vibrant in Europe. Some 347 cases were found in Germany, 152 cases in France, 64 in the United Kingdom and 56 in Spain. The powerful remunicipalisation tides . . . are just the most visible manifestations of a deeper trend [that] can be seen as a response to austerity policies, a reaction against the excesses of liberalisation and corporate takeover of basic services. . . . Cities are best placed to understand the importance of public services because they deal with the everyday consequences of austerity and privatisation.[3]

Anti-privatization sentiment rose in Latin America at least since the 1980s and then again became highly visible between 2010 and 2015. Progressive presidents were elected in Argentina, Bolivia, Brazil, Dominican Republic, Ecuador, El Salvador, Nicaragua, Uruguay, and Venezuela, having campaigned against privatization failures and for renationalization, to address issues such as private sector mismanagement, inequality, service access, and social programming. For instance, in Ecuador the private pension fund was renationalized, enabling access for nearly one million citizens working in the informal sector, and Bolivia renationalized a French-owned electricity company, allowing $500 million to remain in the public purse rather than disappearing offshore to foreign investors.[4]

PUBLIC GREENING INITIATIVES

Most countries now have green national development plans, although variation along the Environmental Performance Index runs from 82.5 percent to 22.6 percent.[5] Integrating climate change and development, as low-emission development strategies, national transitions differ in content and progress. For example, China's wind and solar capacity surpassed coal in 2024, with 40 percent of installed power generation capacity (coal at 37 percent), exceeding its official target of 1,200 gigawatts by 2030.[6] Meanwhile, India claims a low-carbon growth strategy as part of public planning, titled Green Growth, prioritizing "green industrial and economic transition, environmentally friendly agriculture, and sustainable energy."[7] In the United Kingdom, GDP per capita has risen by 50 percent since 1900, while domestic emissions have halved, and those from offshore purchases have fallen by a third. For Germany, both domestic and offshore emissions have fallen by a third, while per capita GDP has risen by 50 percent. And in France, offshore emissions have fallen by 25 percent while GDP per capita has risen by a third. Further, by 2024,

> Thirty years ago the UK was getting nearly two-thirds of its electricity from coal. This is now less that 2%. The US was getting 55%; this is now less that 20%. Denmark was getting nearly 90%; this is now 10%. [Meanwhile,] renewable energy has grown at an astonishing pace. And not just for the rich. In 2014, Uruguay was getting just 5% of its electricity from wind. Now it's closing in on 50%. The continued plummeting costs of renewable energy technologies and batteries will soon make these choices the default.[8]

Meanwhile, South Australia, an area the size of France and Germany combined, "has been at the forefront of the global energy transition."[9] In 2018, the generation split between fossil fuels and renewables was 50/50, and it expects to reach 100 percent net renewable electricity generation annually as early as 2026–2027. In South Australia, "traditional one-way power systems delivering electricity to homes and businesses are transforming to modern, two-way systems where people can now consume, generate, export and trade energy."[10] Further, the Colombian government is working, through its state-owned oil company, Ecopetrol, to reduce oil extraction and transition to renewable energy. At the 2024 World Economic Forum (WEF) annual meeting in Davos, the president of Colombia, Gustavo Petro, pledged to continue to halt new exploration contracts: "We have decided not to contract any more oil, gas and coal exploration in response to the need to decarbonise our economy." A year earlier, his message to the Davos meeting was this: "We are approaching the point of no return, and that point means the extinction of life. Humanity dies out with capitalism, or humanity overcomes capitalism."[11]

Given the urgency of arresting and/or managing climate change, substantive (democratic) public strategic coordination is essential, rather than expecting a disunited private sector to publicly caretake. This is increasingly embraced in paradigmatic revisions underway among forward-looking economists. One such remedy is the recognition that states can lead, championed by University College of London economics professor Mariana Mazzucato, who proposes refocusing from the corporate sector to the "entrepreneurial state" as driver of development. The publication *Economics After Neoliberalism* includes the proposal that "the government, on behalf of the general public, should retain part ownership of new technologies since so much of innovation relies on public infrastructure (public R&D and subsidies, higher education, the legal regime, etc.)."[12] And this in turn requires renewal of governance functions, since public bureaucracies are not designed to handle the self-organizing needs of a continuing emergency, and working with cross-cutting governance structures.[13] Publicly managed renewable-energy regimes are now emergent. A report from a Californian research team (Stanford and UC–Davis) detailed "how 100 percent of the world's energy, for *all* purposes, could be supplied by wind, water and solar resources, by as early as 2030," including power generation and transport, heating, and cooling systems.[14]

Alternative power sources are a key target of green technology. By 2010 Europe was expanding offshore wind projects to power electricity demand,[15] and Denmark had the largest offshore wind farm, accounting for over 20 percent of its electricity.

The Danes built a grassroots movement, given that wind is "everyone's business," encouraging a national policy of subsidizing wind farms and guaranteeing community participation in the planning process. Wind power machinery prices are declining as a result of these developments, subsidized by governments. With its unique regional supranational governance, Europe planned a renewable power "supergrid" to "connect turbines off the wind-lashed north coast of Scotland with Germany's vast arrays of solar panels, and join the power of waves crashing on to the Belgian and Danish coasts with the hydroelectric dams located in Norway's fjords."[16] The goal is to solve the ultimate criticism of renewable power—namely, that weather is unpredictable and so power delivery is unpredictable. The supergrid combines several different forms of natural energy across a variety of regions, including Germany, France, Belgium, the Netherlands, Luxembourg, Denmark, Sweden, Ireland, and the United Kingdom. EU scientists planned to link solar farms in southern Europe with wind, geothermal, and marine projects elsewhere on the continent and, in a neocolonial initiative, to stray even farther south to capture just 0.3 percent of sunlight in the Sahara and Middle Eastern deserts to power all of Europe's needs.[17]

For the South, solar thermal energy has enormous potential once costs come down. At the household level, plastic solar collectors or cooking stoves are being developed, and in China and Brazil, subsidized solar panels allow water heating and supplementary electricity generation.[18] Meanwhile, the Chinese firm Suntech Power, a global leader in solar energy in over 80 countries, has launched a product called the Solar Home System to serve small, off-grid markets. It is a complete entry-level package for solar electricity generation to power light bulbs and charge cell phones at the household level.[19]

In India and Bangladesh, the Bright Green Energy Foundation has evolved out of Grameen Shakti, a nonprofit organization established to promote and supply renewable energy to millions of rural people, beginning with solar home systems and diversifying into biogas for cooking, electricity, organic fertilizer, and improved cooking stoves to reduce indoor air pollution. Grameen Shakti has involved women in the adoption of renewable energy and has established over 40 technology centers to train women in assembly, installation, and maintenance of solar home systems. Founder Dipal Barua claimed, "Women are the main victims of the energy crisis. They are the ones who suffer most from indoor air pollution, drudgery, and a lack of time because of the onerous tasks of wood-gathering and cooking."[20]

China, with massive government and long-term plans, is the world's leader in clean energy, including compact fluorescent light bulbs, solar water heaters, solar photovoltaic cells, and wind turbines. The executive director of the Environmental Defense Fund observed of the Chinese, "The government realizes green energy technology is the new Industrial Revolution. They say, 'We missed the first one, and we're not going to miss this one.'"[21] This does not mean China will mothball its coal industry and coal-fired plants, as it is at the same time committed to expanding its citizen-consumer population. While it is investing in biomass, wind, and solar power at a record pace, it is also investing in energy sources offshore, such as hydroelectric power in Burma, oil palm in the Democratic Republic of the Congo, natural gas fields in Texas, and oil fields in Sudan.[22]

The International Energy Agency (IEA) predicted China will move from 17 percent of world demand for energy in 2010 to 22 percent by 2035, hopefully sustaining production of clean energy. As the IEA noted, "One point is certain. The center of gravity of global energy demand growth now lies in the developing world, especially in China and India."[23] By the turn of 2024, it was nevertheless clear that the pace of renewable energy deployment globally was still not sufficient to enable deep and permanent cuts to fossil-fueled power. For instance, the United States is experiencing a swelling appetite for more electricity, driven not only by an explosion of data centers and an increasing number of electric cars but also by an increasing number of battery and solar factories and other aspects of the green transition, with some utilities requiring continued fossil fuel access.[24] And in India demand for electricity will skyrocket in coming years as living standards improve (for some) and climate change deepens, with deadly heatwaves escalating air conditioner ownership. By 2050, "India's total electricity demand from residential air conditioners is set to exceed the total energy consumption in the whole of Africa today," according to the IEA.[25]

The pressure is on, according to UN Secretary-General António Guterres, who sounded a grave warning to governments after July 2023 was deemed the "hottest month in the past 120,000 years" (see Figure 9.1). Guterres declared, "The era of global warming has ended. The era of global boiling has arrived."[26]

FIGURE 9.1 ■ Global Average Temperature Change

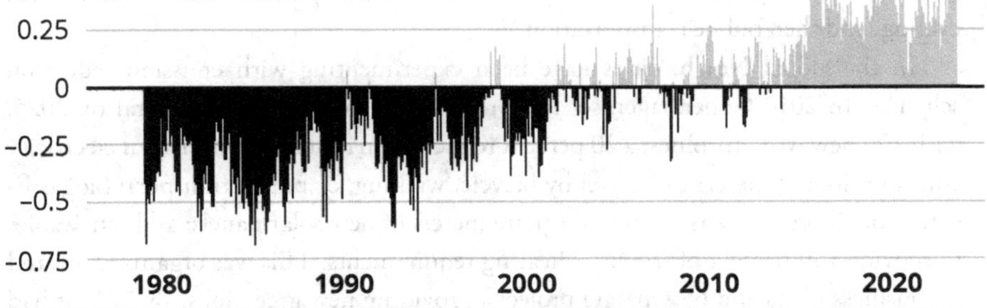

Source: Guardian graphic, "The Climate Crisis Explained in 10 Charts." Original data from Copernicus. Note: first data point is Jan 1979, last is Oct 2023. Copyright Guardian News & Media Ltd 2024.

URBAN INITIATIVES

The 2017 UN-HABITAT report, *Cities and Climate Change*, warned that cities are the "real battle-ground in the fight against climate change." The executive director of UN-HABITAT remarked, "Cities are responsible for the majority of our harmful greenhouse gases (GHGs). But they are also places where the greatest efficiencies can be made."[27]

The "eco-city" phenomenon is still in its infancy and is a moving target since urban planners must transform infrastructures and the built environment as much as citizen habits. This transformation includes addressing rampant inequalities, where a third of urbanites dwell in informal settlements or ghettoes, 90 percent of which are located in the global South,[28] especially as countrysides urbanize, as in vast areas of rural India, Bangladesh, Pakistan, China, Indonesia, Egypt, Rwanda, and other low-income countries. Such sprawling urban peripheries, largely unserviced and beyond regulation, are where most current urban growth is occurring and the most critical environmental hazards can be found.[29] These are insurmountable problems unless there is a substantial about-turn in discriminating against small farming cultures and the emptying of the countryside, and unless public sectors have access to emergency funds from the international financial institutions to address inequality and access to resources such as planned housing, transport, food security, and safe water.

Intermediate targets such as zero waste and carbon neutrality are important goals, requiring changed patterns of consumption and transport in addition to renewable energy regimes. In 2015, the UN convened a network among five emerging eco-cities in Southeast Asia—Cebu in the Philippines, Danang in Vietnam, Iskandar in Malaysia, Map Ta Phut in Thailand, and Pingtan Island in China—to develop a common language of sustainability and set of best practices as a longer-term plan.[30] Meanwhile, the UN's Global Environmental Facility has committed to a public–private partnership, the Sustainable Cities Integrated Approach, initially focusing on China,[31] where "almost 300 eco-cities are either being built or are in the planning stage." The eco-city model includes "a well-planned city layout and public transportation system that makes the priority methods of transportation as follows possible: walking first, then cycling, and then public transportation."[32]

In the global North, cities have been experimenting with emission reduction schemes. In 2010 Copenhagen set itself the goal to be net carbon neutral by 2025, with 100 new wind turbines; a 20 percent reduction in heat and commercial electricity consumption; 75 percent of travel by bicycle, walking, or public transport; biogasification of all organic waste; 60,000 square meters of new solar panels; and renewables to provide 100 percent of the city's heating requirements. This was organized around 22 business plans and 65 separate projects, providing new green jobs. By 2019 it had reduced carbon emissions by 42 percent; 66 percent of trips within the city were by foot, bicycle, or public transport; and 51 percent of heat came from renewables.[33]

Pittsburgh, Pennsylvania, formerly a heavily polluted oil and steel production center, now considers itself a model "green city," as those heavy industries have moved out and offshore. At the turn of the twenty-first century, a coalition of planners, businesspeople, and environmental engineers formed a plan for the city to become a hub of innovation of ecological design.

> Downtown, the skyscraper windows are angled to maximize natural light, heat is piped in from thermal pools deep underground, and solar panels line the roofs far above the bustling sidewalks. The city has a full-time sustainability director charged with shifting its energy sources away from fossil fuels by means of mass transit, urban planning, and municipal procurement policies that place a value on carbon alternatives. The city's water treatment system—channeling water of varying quality, from rain to sewage, into multiple uses—is considered a model for other eco-conscious cities like San Francisco.[34]

Meanwhile, Manchester, home to the industrial revolution, has one of the highest concentrations of solar panels and green office buildings in the United Kingdom. Manchester has introduced consumption-based GHG accounting in a Carbon Literacy Project to reduce the city's ecological footprint. It also has educated employers and homeowners about the benefits (to the city's economy and the planet) of purchasing goods closer to home. This in turn has attracted green investment in the city, both shortening GHG-intensive transport costs and creating new jobs—37,000 between 2007 and 2012.[35] Pittsburgh and Manchester have joined 300 cities around the world in a joint emission reduction commitment. This initiative stems from the Cities for Climate Protection Program, one of three major transnational municipal networks addressing GHG emission reduction. The goal is to address global climate concerns at an urban policy scale. Such collective decentralization includes a resilient transnational network operating at a *multilevel governance* scale. This involves transnational governance and centralized public administration of urban environmental affairs, where green business is subject to urban authority.[36]

Public leadership of urban greening is significant for ensuring democratic distribution of resources. In 2013, the inhabitants of Hamburg restored their power, creating a public energy regime whereby electricity, gas, and heating grids were wrested from private control. In the same year, 25 percent of Germany's electricity came from renewables, wind and solar in particular, supplemented by biogas and hydropower. (In comparison, wind and solar accounted for just 4 percent of total U.S. electricity generation.) Munich plans to be the first large city in the world to use all renewable sources to generate electricity by 2025.[37] While energy privatization reversals are emerging, the countries with the strongest commitments to renewable energy are those with strong, publicly owned electricity sectors (the Netherlands, Austria, and Norway), given that private energy monopolies, beholden to shareholders and high quarterly profits, tend not to prioritize emission reductions.

CIRCULAR ECONOMY

The **circular economy** concept is now shaping how some cities are learning to design out waste and pollution, keeping products and materials in use by systematic recycling and regenerating natural systems. Key to this is overcoming the conventional "linear economy" model of continual throughput of resources (extracted and processed) into goods and services that produce waste and GHGs.

By 2050, two-thirds of us will live in cities. However, our urban centers are grappling with the effects of our current take-make-waste economy. Under this "linear system," cities consume over 75 percent of natural resources, produce over 50 percent of global waste, and emit between 60 and 80 percent of GHGs. A circular economy provides the opportunity to rethink how we make and use the things we need and allows us to explore new ways of ensuring long-term prosperity.[38]

Different cities have distinct ways of operationalizing the circular economy principle. Brazil's innovative city, Belo Horizonte, uses federal funding to finance its Computer Reconditioning Centre, which is integral to the city's digital inclusion, skills development, and waste reduction efforts. Here, citizens from low-income communities are trained to restore donated post-use IT equipment for use by locals via free access to computers and internet, including training in basic digital literacy. To date, 10,446 citizens have been trained in basic technological skills, environmental education, and computer remanufacturing, and Belo Horizonte is regarded as Brazil's most digitally advanced city. Meanwhile, in 2017 Shenzhen was the first city in the world to electrify all public buses (16,000), reducing noise pollution and improving air quality. While e-buses have replaced fuel vehicles, estimated to contribute 20 percent of the city's air pollution, further development is underway to expand renewable energy sources in line with circular economy principles, including improving battery technologies to encourage reuse, charging speeds, and suitability for a wider range of vehicles.[39]

TRANSITION TOWNS

Transition Towns focus on building circular economy infrastructures, emphasizing relocalization: "Unlike most top-down, government-led sustainable development initiatives, the Transition Town movement's success relies exclusively on community volunteers working on a local level."[40] Emerging in the 2000s, it is a movement, or network, by and across communities anticipating peak oil and climate change. By 2019, there were between 2,000 and 3,000 of these groups in 50 countries engaged in processes to manage "energy descent."[41]

The goal is to build social and ecological resilience into local towns and communities (and their governance) by reducing and eliminating fossil fuel dependence and rebuilding local resources via principles of **permaculture**. Sustainable land use design reintegrates humans with their environment, localizing food systems and restoring and emulating natural cycles to replenish ecological relations and reduce waste. The expectation is that work is reduced by its greater productivity in reproducing community (rather than profits) and biodiversity (rather than products). Local currencies enhance local business and new green jobs and recycle wealth through the community instead of repatriating profits to a corporate offshore brass-plate bank. Local markets encourage environmental stewardship and social connection. Education of adults and children is geared toward reestablishing generational and bioregional connection and developing grounded skills, local knowledge, and necessary emotional resilience. As the people of the borough of Southend-on-Sea in the United Kingdom claim,

> Climate Change and Peak Oil can cause us to feel confronted by something overwhelmingly huge that we cannot do anything about. The central message of the Transition Movement is that this state of mind is not the place to start from if we want to achieve something, do something, or create something. Indeed, by shifting our mind-set we can actually recognize the coming post-cheap oil era as an opportunity rather than a threat, and design the future low-carbon age to be thriving, resilient, and abundant—somewhere much better to live than our current alienated consumer culture based on greed, war, and the myth of perpetual growth.[42]

Ultimately, the Transition Town movement is a proactive approach to managing an energy- and climate-challenged future, and, as a movement, it is about alliances across communities rather than a conventional development model that encourages communities and regions to compete with one another. Cooperation along social and ecological justice lines is the underlying organizing principle of the Transition Town movement.

THE COMMONS

The proliferation of alternative conceptions and practices reflects our times, as people rediscover values other than market values in individual and collective attempts to redefine the meaning of development. One key value concept is the **commons**, the source of shared livelihoods and cultural meaning that were enclosed by private property relations during the rise of capitalism. Coauthors J. K. Gibson-Graham claim there is today "a revival of interest in reclaiming and enlarging the commons in the industrialized countries and protecting the yet-to-be completely destroyed or expropriated commons in the 'developing' world." Such a revival is at the same time a rejection of the expansive narrative of privatized development and the rediscovery of local possibility, exemplified in the Transition Town movement and its variants. Gibson-Graham notes,

> The practice of economic development has been dominated by the naturalized universal of the capitalist economy. . . . Development discourse centers on

> the problematic of bringing capitalist economic development to those spaces that are "lacking" its dynamic presence and allure of beneficence. Countless strategies are advocated that will engender (or more proactively "kick start") capitalist industrialization. . . . All strategies are pursued with the promise that increased well-being will trickle down from the capitalist sector and its employees to the wider community. And all are beholden to the conviction that economic growth . . . is unquestionably desirable.[43]

The quest for a new cooperative paradigm echoes across the world, especially in a pandemic and climate change shadow. For instance, in South Korea, as elsewhere, a new desire for a culture of "fairness" confronts the dominant model of ultracompetitive and increasingly corrupt social systems.[44] In West Africa, the concept *Bamtaare* means "harmonious development," integrating community and environment. Ecuador and Bolivia captured the world's imagination in 2008 when their national constitutions reinvented development as "living well" (in Spanish: **buen vivir**, or in Quechua: *sumak kawsay*). *Buen vivir*—the fruit of decades of political struggles and alliances between Indigenous peoples, peasants, afrodescendants, women, environmentalists, and youth—subordinates economy to ecology, human dignity, and social justice. *Buen vivir* includes a spiritual dimension. It complements legal passage of the rights of nature alongside human rights.[45]

Andean cosmology, placing *Pachamama* (planet Earth) at the center of all life, "represents an unprecedented 'biocentric turn' away from the anthropocentrism of modernity."[46] Former Bolivian vice president Alvaro Gardia Linera claimed, "It makes world history. Earth is the mother of all. It establishes a new relationship between man and nature, the harmony of which must be preserved as a guarantee of its regeneration." Of course, good intentions of making world history and actually implementing such a relationship are not the same. The Bolivian Law of Mother Earth also redefines the country's mineral deposits as "blessings," that is, as targets of new conservation measures.[47] Nicola Bullard of NGO Focus on the Global South notes, "The obstacles to be overcome are tremendous. Bolivia is still deeply embedded in an **international division of labor** dating back to sixteenth century colonialism, consigned to providing cheap labor, land, and resources to the rest of the world," despite the mobilization of the Bolivian populace for social and environmental justice.[48]

Nevertheless, for anthropologist Arturo Escobar, this "biocentric turn" exemplifies the civilizational transformation imagined by "transition discourses." Such discourses stem from a variety of social movements and the fields of culture, ecology, religion and spirituality, and alternative science (such as living systems and complexity). They invoke a transition, in eco-theologian Thomas Berry's words, "from the period when humans were a disruptive force on the planet Earth to the period when humans become present to the planet in a manner that is mutually enhancing."[49] Further, the essence of transition discourses is the rejection of the one-world view that informs modern ontology and is reproduced in the currency of globalization. Escobar observes,

> Globalization discourses of all kinds assume that the world is some sort of "global space" that will progressively and inevitably be fully occupied by capitalist modernity. . . . This view of globalization as universal, fully economized, and de-localized is made possible by the immense power of corporations and maintained within manageable levels of dis/order by military might. From its very global conditions are emerging, however, responses and forms of creativity and resistance that make increasingly visible the poverty, perniciousness, and destructiveness of this imaginary.[50]

Escobar's point is that the world contains multiple ontologies or worldviews, forming a "pluriverse," or, as Mexico's Zapatistas claimed, "a world where many worlds fit," beyond capitalist modernity.

RURAL INITIATIVES

Greening initiatives in the countryside are proliferating across the world. One way for us to recognize this development is by seemingly returning to the so-called past, that is, to small- and medium-scale farming systems. Peasant or family farms are represented in the development narrative as relics of premodern times—discounting the fact that they feed up to 70 percent of the world.[51] Their performance is hardly obsolete, as suggested by research that shows "a half-hectare plot in Thailand can grow 70 species of vegetables, fruits, and herbs, providing far better nutrition and feeding more people than a half-hectare plot of high-yielding rice."[52] Where industrial agriculture needs 80 percent of the planet's arable land to feed 30 percent of its people, one hectare of polycultural (small-scale) intercropping produces the same amount of food as one and a half hectares of high-input monoculture cropping.[53] The difference here is between who produces what kind of food. Industrial commodity crops are produced by "agriculture without farmers"[54] with commercial agroinputs (reducing soil nutrients) on land anywhere in principle. In contrast, local polycultures are grown *in situ* by farmers with accumulated knowledge of landscape biodiversity and regional cuisines.

Presently there is deepening conflict between these distinctive food systems—with agribusiness claiming to "feed the world," and small farmers feeding about two-thirds of the world, producing food in place and performing environmental stewardship, where possible. By virtue of the development growth narrative, the former system is institutionally privileged, especially during the neoliberal era, with **World Trade Organization (WTO)** rules favoring transnational food companies' access to the world. WTO rules were a precursor to corporate/financial "land grabbing" in the global South for speculative and productive purposes. More recently, so-called "nature-based solutions" allow northern companies to compensate for their emissions by investing in southern land enclosure for carbon offsetting, such as reforestation and biofuels. Such strategies then transfer responsibility for emission reduction to the global South, meanwhile postponing complete emissions reduction.[55]

As La Via Campesina founding member Nettie Wiebe (professor and farmer from Saskatchewan) remarks, "The difficulty for us, as farming people, is that we are rooted in the places where we live and grow food. The other side, the corporate world, is globally mobile."[56] Thus, in 2012, at the Rio +20 summit, La Via Campesina declared,

> 20 years after the Earth Summit, life on the planet has become dramatically difficult. Expulsion from our lands and territories is accelerating, no longer only due to conditions of disadvantage imposed upon us by trade agreements and the industrial sector, but by new forms of monopoly control over land and water, by the global imposition of intellectual property regimes that steal our seeds, by the invasion of transgenic seeds, and by the advance of monoculture plantations, mega-projects, and mines.
>
> We should exchange the industrial agro-export food system for a system based on food sovereignty, that returns the land to its social function as the producer of food and sustainer of life, that puts local production of food at the center, as well as the local markets and local processing.[57]

Herein lies the key contention: given the power differential between transnational agribusiness and local farmers, marginalization of small-scale farming is the condition for privileging industrial agriculture. As the International Planning Committee for Food Sovereignty (IPC) remarked at the 2008 World Food Summit, in the midst of the global food crisis,

> The serious and urgent food and climate crises are being used by political and economic elites as opportunities to entrench corporate control of world agriculture and the ecological commons. . . . Small-scale food producers are feeding the planet, and we demand respect and support to continue. Only food sovereignty can offer long-term, sustainable, equitable and just solutions to the urgent food and climate crises.[58]

The IPC is the voice of the world's 1.5 billion peasants, family farmers, and Indigenous peoples on 350 million small-scale farms, including forest dwellers, pastoralists, and artisanal fisherfolk. Their food derives from 5,000 domesticated crop species and 1.9 million peasant-bred plant varieties, indicative of the wealth of local farming knowledges.[59] By contrast, industrial agriculture accounts for only 15% of the food that is traded internationally, but accounts for more than 80% of the fossil fuels and 70% of the water used in agriculture. It also uses a narrow genetic base of less than 100 livestock breeds and 150 plant specials. Nevertheless, the industrial agriculture sector benefits from the vast majority of funded research. 96% of all recorded food and agricultural research takes place in industrialised countries and 80% of that research is focused on industrial food processing and retailing.[60]

However, despite lack of access to huge subsidies available to agribusiness, as the UN Committee on World Food Security's High Level Panel of Experts notes, "smallholder agriculture is the foundation of food security in many countries and an important part of the social/economic/ecological landscape in all countries [and the] potential efficiency of smallholder farming relative to larger farms has been widely documented, focusing on the capacity of smallholders to achieve high production levels per unit of land through the use of family labor in diversified production systems."[61]

Much smallholder agriculture has agroecological underpinnings, meaning that its low-input farming practices are guided by natural process, rather than governed by chemical methods. The Rodale Institute, a leader in organic farming research, "found that organic systems use 45 percent less energy, release 40 percent fewer carbon emissions, and have the potential to produce yields up to 40 percent higher in times of drought over conventional systems. Utilizing methods like organic no-till allows the soil to remain undisturbed, capitalizing on its potential to sequester carbon in the ground and return nutrients to our food."[62]

However, industrial agriculture, once an energy converter and provider, is now a heavy energy consumer—the industrial food system expends 10 or more energy calories to produce one calorie of food. Instead of embracing live/biotic carbon, it burns dead carbon in the form of fossil fuels.[63] It is also responsible for up to 80 percent of biodiversity loss. Environmental harm caused by industrial agriculture costs the world $3 trillion each year according to the UN FAO.[64] The reality is that to preserve human civilization and its ecological base, farming the land sustainably means expanding carbon sinks via agroforestry, based on the biodiversity principle, and adopting agroecology as a method of rebuilding soil carbon; both methods reduce carbon in the atmosphere and renew nature in the process.

AGROECOLOGY

Agroecological farming, often identified with the past, is becoming very present in its performance and potential: deploying restorative and regenerative principles by embedding agriculture in ecological cycles. Rather than designate separate spaces to conserve biodiversity and waste sinks, it integrates ecological repair, recycling, and reproduction into farming practice itself: "farming is again being understood, and practiced, as co-production. . . . Farming is not only based on 'economic exchanges,' but also on 'ecological exchange.'"[65]

Further, agroecology's focus on labor-intensive practices has strategic value in expanding rural employment, exercising a multifunctional role in revitalizing the countryside. The *Coordination Paysanne Européene* has noted that "maintaining the number of people working in agriculture is not a sign of economic 'backwardness' but an added value."[66] Recent research shows European agroecological family farming is robust, cooperative (with seed and labor sharing), productive, and with enduring provisioning of urban consumers—embracing "food from somewhere" rather than "food from nowhere."[67]

Rather than a relic, agroecology, defined by the International Panel of Experts on Sustainable Food Systems (IPES), "is the application of the science of ecology (the science of how nature works) to the study, design and management of sustainable food systems, the integration of the diverse knowledge systems generated by food system practitioners, and the *involvement of the social movements* that are promoting the transition to fair, just, and sovereign food systems."[68]

For advocates, any reference to agroecology as a technical "option," where some agroecological methods might be added to conventional agriculture (e.g., climate-smart agriculture), is reductionist, discounting the holism of genuine community-based agroecology, where "knowledge is closely dependent on and intimately linked with the biological, cultural and landscape components of peoples' knowledge systems."[69] Reference to "options" also alludes to growing recognition among agribusinesses and institutional supporters that industrial agriculture is undermining its future via environmental degradation. And this encourages co-optation, also evident in recent claims for climate-smart agriculture, noted in the previous chapter.

While this may suggest business-as-usual manipulation, it also suggests the salience of agroecological practices for long-term resilience. Related to this is the rising legitimacy deficit faced by industrial agriculture and factory farming, and recognition that some greening adjustment is necessary. But the **agroecology** movement is wary about dismissal of its "transformative potential" by development institutions, including the FAO, which instead focus on it as "a way of making industrial agriculture less unsustainable."[70]

Under these trying circumstances, IPES-Food has adopted a "boundary-crossing" approach. It emphasizes positive leverage to avoid "organic/agroecology becoming closed niches, facilitating ongoing exchanges with mainstream actors, and keeping the door open for late adopters [who are] key factors in maintaining momentum and building powerful alliances over time."[71] An example of possible alliance is CRISPR gene editing, which enables scientists in the global South to develop crops "with traits tailored to the needs of local farmers—rather than relying on seeds developed in foreign countries." Kenya's regulations governing such gene-edited crops treats them as conventionally bred crops because they do not use other species' DNA. Nigeria, Malawi, and other African countries, such as Uganda and Ethiopia, are expected to follow suit.[72]

Recently, the UN International Fund for Agricultural Development, responding to food shortages caused by war in Ukraine, encouraged African countries to develop their traditionally diverse cereals, roots, tubers, oil crops, fruit and vegetables. Such "crops have high nutritional and cultural value, are adapted to local tastes and agroecosystems, and can be 'climate smart.'"[73]

This positive gesture implicitly acknowledges the pivotal social movement declaration at the 2015 International Forum on Agroecology Nyéléni in Mali (West Africa), led by La Via Campesina:

> Popular pressure has caused many multilateral institutions, governments, universities and research centers, some NGOs, corporations and others, to finally

recognize "agroecology." However, they have tried to redefine it as a narrow set of technologies, to offer some tools that appear to ease the sustainability crisis of industrial food production, while the existing structures of power remain unchallenged.

> Agroecology is political; it requires us to challenge and transform structures of power in society. We need to put the control of seeds, biodiversity, land and territories, waters, knowledge, culture and the commons in the hands of the peoples who feed the world.[74]

Even so, given its countermovement status, agroecology faces an uphill battle with its solid food security claims. The "yield gap" trope it faces reproduces the prejudice that small-scale farming systems need to raise yields through incorporation into corporate *monocultural* "value chains" for food exports to feed (part of) the world.[75] Lacking subsidies, local farmers nevertheless are endlessly creative: "sowing pigeon peas to shade their soils from a hotter, more scorching sun . . . planting vetiver grass to keep floodwaters at bay . . . resurrecting old crops, like finger millet and forgotten yams, and planting trees that naturally fertilize the soil [and] turning away from one legacy of European colonialism," namely planting grain monocultures and saturating fields with chemicals.[76]

Agroecology's resilient practices are discounted when small farmers are labeled as "traditional," denying their adaptive skills in harnessing the multifunctional role of biodiversity. In the drylands of India's Deccan Plateau—where a variety of rain-fed crops such as sorghum, millets, pulses, and oilseeds are grown—these crops, in combination, solve a wide range of problems faced in Indian agriculture, including soil management, pest control, and minimizing risk and uncertainty. Rural communities like those on the Deccan Plateau have always saved and exchanged their seeds, and women's seed work forms a "localized seed economy" through seed exchanges with ecological, economic, and sociocultural significance. In contrast to seed commercialization (monopolization under patents, the favored method of the development industry),

> The continuous exchange of seeds for local crop varieties circulates genetic resources from one field to another within a village territory and beyond. The dynamic management of genetic resources enhances the stability of traditional agro-systems, increases the adaptation potential of local crops to evolving environmental conditions and limits the risk of genetic erosion. Seed transactions also help ensure that land is not left fallow for lack of seeds, thus avoiding soil erosion and increasing the soil's organic matter content and water retention capacity.[77]

Seed saving minimizes risk, increases crop diversity and nutrition, and provides "self-reliance and bargaining power within the household" for women. It also allows women to select seeds to meet specific individual, environmental, and climatic needs; allows planting at appropriate times; and provides assets—seeds constitute a currency, particularly among women with few resources. It provides the security of a "knowledge commons." Once farmers buy or receive agroindustrial seeds, they are "locked into a production chain where the choices of inputs and the use of the harvest are predetermined by agrochemical and food-processing firms" and depend increasingly on "a network of technical information generated by specialists (agricultural scientists, chemists, genetic engineers, nutritionists, etc.)."[78] In short, control over farming practices relocates from the farming ecosystem to standardized agribusiness techno-fixes designed to sustain productivity and not the ecological base.

This vector is now deploying extensive digital mapping technologies in the form of a "data grab."[79] Across the world each square kilometer, every square centimeter, of farmland is being mapped "for soil, nutrients, moisture, and sunshine."[80] Land (re)colonization in the global South is replacing public commons (territories, knowledges, sociality) with an increasingly global land space subject to data control and now to be governed by technology that combines Big Ag and Big Data (e.g., Google, Microsoft, Amazon, Alibaba), financed by asset managers (BlackRock, Vanguard, Capital Group, Fidelity, and the Carlyle Group). While the digital frontier presents itself as climate-smart and sanitizing, it is dominated by most of the world's biggest agrochemical firms.[81]

The largest study on sustainable farming in Asia has recently been conducted by MASIPAG, a network of peasant farmers and organizations, scientists, and NGOs in the Philippines. It involved a comparison of 280 full organic farmers, 280 farmers converting to organic farming, and 280 conventional peasant farmers. The study showed organic farmers enjoyed greater food security, with more diverse, nutritious, and secure diets and substantially better health. On-farm diversity was substantially higher, with on average 50 percent more crop species than conventional farmers', improved soil fertility, less soil erosion, greater crop tolerance to pests and disease, superior farm management, and higher net incomes.[82]

Sustaining the alternative to a high-tech food system involves two related mobilizations across the world's landscapes. One is cross-class alliances committed to restoring and protecting smallholder rights to land and to produce—now enshrined (in soft law) with the 2018 passage of the UN Rights of Peasants and Other Peoples Working in Rural Areas. Another is transitioning to biodiversified agroecological farming systems, in the words of IPES-Food, "whether the starting point is industrial agriculture or subsistence-style farming," noting,

> the agro-ecological alternative is high-tech and knowledge intensive—it requires complex synergies to be built and sustained between different crop varieties and species, and between different farming systems (mixed crop-livestock systems, for instance) . . . [a growing body of evidence] shows the huge potential of these systems to succeed where industrial systems are failing—namely in reconciling concerns such as food security, environmental and livelihood resistance, nutritional adequacy and social equity.[83]

In its 2018 report titled *Breaking Away From Industrial Food and Farming Systems*, IPES-Food details seven case studies of communities redesigning their food systems *in toto* around agroecological principles. As IPES-Food notes, "The change process can be initiated from a variety of entry points and does not always begin on the farm with input substitution. Transition can also be kick-started by community-building activities, farmer-researcher partnerships, and even by external shocks that make people question the status quo."[84]

Arguably, India's **Zero Budget Natural Farming (ZBNF)** program is one of the world's most successful peasant-based agroecology movements. Beginning in the state of Karnataka with 100,000 farms, it spread to southern states Tamil Nadu, Andhra Pradesh, and Kerala via millions of farmers. A 2017 report of an extensive survey noted that "by adopting ZBNF practices over time 78.7 percent of the farmers saw improvements in yield, 93.6 percent in soil conservation, 76.9 percent in seed autonomy, 87.8 percent in household food autonomy and 85.7 percent in income, while 92.5 percent experienced reduced farm expenses and 92.5 percent a reduced need for credit."[85] It was begun by an agricultural scientist, Subhash Palekar, when as an extensions officer in the 1990s he became disillusioned by the green revolution's detrimental biophysical effects, compared with the ecological methods of Indigenous farmers. At the time farmer suicides were on the rise. "Zero budget" refers to the rejection of credit for purchasing agroinputs, and "natural farming" rejects chemicals. Over time and across space, the ZBNF movement "has organized about sixty massive state-level training camps . . . with an average of one or two thousand farmer participants at each camp, including women, men and youth." Its organizational impetus arose from the Karnataka Rajya Raitha Sangha (KRRS) farmer organization, a member of La Via Campesina.[86]

ZNBF models two rural initiatives that endure across the agrarian world: rejection of "debt farming" and elaboration of countermovement learning, such as mobilization of human resources and agroecological training. Reductions in "debt farming" enable producers to wean themselves off expensive agroinputs (commercial seeds, fertilizer, chemicals). This process has been termed **re-peasantization**, in that it represents deliberate substitution of ecological wealth for commercial wealth via dependency on credit and purchasing external inputs. Rural sociologist Jan Douwe van der Ploeg documents the widespread re-peasantization phenomenon in Latin America and Europe as small-producer resistance to indebtedness and dispossession by corporate value chain agriculture.[87]

As the counterpart to *vertical* power exercised over farmers by agribusiness, rural social movements build on *horizontal* social methodologies practiced by small farmers across time, known as "campesino-a-campesino" exchanges of seeds, ecosystem knowledge, and support. La Via Campesina has recently organized over 40 agroecology training programs and schools across the global South, including in Brazil, Chile, Paraguay, Venezuela, Colombia, Nicaragua, Indonesia, India, Mali, Zimbabwe, Niger, and Mozambique. Peasants learn from peasant experiences through peer-to-peer teaching not only about farming best practices but also about collective organization.As Basque farmer and La Via Campesina strategic leader Paul Nicholson observes,

"[The processes in each continent, in each country, are very different. The objective is not to homogenise these processes. It is clear that the velocity and temporality in each region are very different."[88]

Local organization has payoffs, as an increasing number of countries "are in the process of adopting a framework of legislation for agriculture, food, and nutrition that enshrines rights-based principles of entitlements and access to food in national policies, public policies, laws and constitutions. Constitutional recognition of the right to **food sovereignty** has been achieved in a number of countries, including Ecuador, Bolivia, Nepal and Venezuela," and other countries are following suit.[89] In coming years, it is likely that food supply chains will shorten (regional and national levels) and food systems will embrace more localization, given the food security shocks associated with COVID-19 and the realization that some food supply chains need shortening.

At the *global level*, political advocacy in the United Nations of the agroecological alternative stems from the international coalition of small-scale food producers, represented by the IPC. At the FAO, it works at the global level on behalf of land rights and reform, seed sovereignty, and public support in the UN Committee on Food Security (CFS), offering a unique social movement model for front-line representative activism on a global scale for food sovereignty and producer rights.

At the *ground level*, alongside increasing commercial farmer conversions to ecological practices, nested markets integrating local producers and consumers into solidary economies and small-farmer networks exchanging seed and ecological information deepen the food sovereignty principle in the interstices of the formal economy. This includes a plethora of local food initiatives in rural and urban spaces alike, as food councils form and community supported agriculture and urban gardens proliferate, unemployed/informal workers "return" to the land, and long-ignored Indigenous territorial rights emerge as a new terrain of struggle. Other than entrenched corporate interest, there is no reason why governments cannot support movements toward ecological farming, as with India's ZBNF program transitioning millions of farms to chemical-free agriculture.[90] What *kind* of governments will depend on citizen participation/mobilization, requiring long-term organizing to temper centralization of power, given rising possibility of climate catastrophe in the coming decades.[91]

The **International Assessment of Agricultural Knowledge, Science and Technology for Development (IAASTD)**, a World Bank–sponsored report prepared by over 400 social and natural scientists and development practitioners of various kinds, advocates a role of **multifunctionality** for agriculture in reducing poverty and social/gender inequality, stabilizing rural cultures, and reversing environmental degradation and global warming. Stating that "*business as usual is not an option*," in the face of multiple crises, the IAASTD questions industrial agriculture and transgenic food as solutions since markets fail to adequately value environmental and social harm.[92] In the coming years, IAASTD's roadmap will likely become increasingly salient, as citizens and governments are forced to think outside of the paradigmatic box and intervene to embrace rather than override nature.[93]

CONCLUSION

Perhaps the most important lesson we can draw from this chapter is that many people, cities, and governments are not standing by as business-as-usual proceeds. Such initiatives and experiments have both environmental and social outcomes that alter perception of possibilities in transitioning toward **sustainable development** practices. Whereas some are discrete, many are linked at a multilateral level or through cross-national mobilizations.

Sustainable development cannot occur overnight; nevertheless, we can begin to think of "development" as precisely these initiatives and experiments at different scales. Some involve cleanup and restoration (of entitlements and environments), and others require renewal and rethinking (of species responsibility on Earth). Beyond time and space differentials, shared goals express a common project of humanity in survival mode. This, of course, is not without power struggles over a new development narrative to address extensive social and geographical inequalities and how to deploy technology for healthy outcomes rather than business as usual, with its exclusionary private outcomes and racist heritage.

A different paradigm has a window of opportunity, at this moment of destabilization of the natural world, to go for cyclical regeneration rather than endless growth. Ecological justice and social justice are indivisible, and the ongoing struggles are gaining momentum across the world through solidarist alliances in multiple sites and initiatives.

KEY TERMS

agroecology
Buen vivir
Circular economy
Commons
Food sovereignty
International Assessment of Agricultural Science and Technology for Development (IAASTD)
International division of labor
Multifunctionality
Permaculture
Re-peasantization
Sustainable development
Transition Towns
World Trade Organization (WTO)
Zero Budget Natural Farming (ZBNF)

FURTHER READING

Bjørkhaug, Hilde, Philip McMichael, and Bruce Muirhead. *Finance or Food? The Role of Cultures, Values, and Ethics in Land Use Negotiations*. Toronto, ON: University of Toronto Press, 2020.

Dale, Gareth, Manu V. Mathai, and Jose A. Puppim de Oliveira, eds. *Green Growth: Ideology, Political Economy and the Alternatives*. London: Zed, 2016.

Desmarais, Annette, Priscilla Claeys, and Amy Trauger, eds. *Public Policies for Food Sovereignty.* Abingdon, UK: Routledge, 2017.

HLPE. *Agroecological and Other Innovative Approaches for Sustainable Agriculture and Food Systems that Enhance Food Security and Nutrition. A report by the High Level Panel of Experts on Food Security and Nutrition of the Committee on World FoodSecurity.* Rome: UN/FAO, July 2019.

Kimmerer, Robin Wall. *Braiding Sweetgrass. Indigenous Wisdom, Scientific Knowledge, and the Teachings of Plants.* Minneapolis, MN: Milkweed, 2013.

Ritchie, Hannah. *Not the End of the World. How We Can Be the First Generation to Build a Sustainable World.* New York: Little, Brown Spark, 2024.

Rosset, Peter, and Miguel Altieri. *Agroecology.* Halifax, NS: Fernwood Press, 2017.

SELECT WEBSITES

Declaration of the International Forum for Agroecology, Nyéléni, Mali, 2015: https://viacampesina.org/en/declaration-of-the-international-forum-for-agroecology-mali-2015/

Ellen MacArthur Foundation, *Circular Economy in Cities*: https://www.ellenmacarthurfoundation.org/our-work/activities/circular-economy-in-cities

IAASTD Report, 2008: www.greenfacts.org/en/agriculture-iaastd/

Transition Network: https://transitionnetwork.org/

UN-HABITAT for a Better Urban Future, 2017: https://unhabitat.org/call-for-expressions-of-interest-eoi-for-cooperation-partners-for-agreement-of-cooperation-supporting african-cities-in-inventorying-greenhouse-gas-emissions

UN Millennium Ecosystem Assessment: www.millenniumassessment.org

UN Sustainable Development Goals: https://www.un.org/sustainabledevelopment/sustainable-development-goals

Women Organizing for Change in Agriculture and Natural Resource Management: www.wocan.org

10 TOWARD SUSTAINABLE DEVELOPMENT

What kind of global order emerges in the wake of the globalization project is not yet clear. But its internal tensions certainly condition future possibilities. Such tensions were revealed with the COVID-19 pandemic exposing inequalities (of race, class, and gender) and vulnerabilities of deprived populations, exacerbated by inadequate public service provisions with states having surrendered such capacities to private interest. At this juncture, with the experience of ongoing climatic crises and deteriorating habitats (including soils and water cycles), how sustainable development might successfully proceed overall is in question, even as the previous chapter identified many promising initiatives under way.

This chapter addresses what a sustainable development project might look like. Certainly, at face value, the UN's pursuit of new **Sustainable Development Goals (SDGs)** signals such a direction. We can establish how sustainable development is configured in the SDG framework through a close examination of its goals and targets. This will disclose whether the framework reflects a shift away from the conventional approach to development to address new challenges we face. This cannot be taken for granted, since the SDG framework includes additional commitments to the commercialization of public goods and services.[1]

Under the global austerity regime, governments have steadily defunded public services, including privatizing health care and reducing disease-control capacities. Such discounting of *collective* public authority is mirrored in the contrary responses to the Paris Climate Agreement of 2015 across the state system and the inability so far to effect really consequential cooperation to combat climate emergency, given existing uneven resources and power relations. For example, in early 2024 the London-based nonprofit think tank, Carbon Tracker, in assessing the transition plans of the 25 world's largest oil and gas companies, found that none of them were close to the 2015 Paris Agreement to keep global warming well below 2 degrees above preindustrial levels.[2]

This raises the larger question, what does it take to introduce a distinctive project of development appropriate to these times? It means replacing the economistic concept of "development" with a project steeped in repairing and regenerating our natural foundations and addressing and eliminating social inequalities. Not an easy question to answer, but three (related) parts to it are what gives such projects coherence, what is appropriate to these times, and how best can it be implemented?

INGREDIENTS OF PROJECT COHERENCE

The current and previous projects comprised substantially unequal relations and contributed to cumulative environmental deterioration and accumulation of elite power on a global scale, in the name of Development. As we have seen, a key institution such as the market, so taken for granted, has failed to protect people and Nature. In the current crisis, the forces of the status quo argue for updating market instruments for greening capitalism, whereas progressive countermovements advocate changing the paradigm to prioritize socioenvironmental needs.

It is timely now to revisit the origins of contemporary neoliberalism in Chicago economist Milton Friedman, who, along with Frederick Hayek in the rather exclusive Mont Pelerin Society, initiated the revival of neoclassical economics and its original policy implementation in Chile in 1973, following the coup. In his 1962 book, *Capitalism and Freedom*, Friedman wrote, "Few trends could so thoroughly undermine the very foundations of our free society as the acceptance by corporate officials of a social responsibility other than to make as much money for their stockholders as possible."[3] Accordingly, neoliberal development established a social order depoliticizing the distribution of wealth. Money and markets as the organizing principle of society must appear natural (beyond political reach). This paradigm informed subsequent World Trade Organization rules. As Friedman claimed, "The most important argument for free movement of goods and especially finance was not their direct material benefits, but the *limits they imposed on the autonomy of national governments*"—with the expectation that the threat to governments of capital flight would forestall social development in the public interest.[4]

Alternatively, political-economist Karl Polanyi claimed that allowing the market, which pivots on "fictitious commodities" (human labor, nature, and money) as its organizing principle, the freedom

> [t]o be the sole director of the fate of human beings and their natural environment would result in the demolition of society. . . . Nature would be reduced to its elements, neighbourhoods and landscapes defiled, rivers polluted. . . . No society could stand the effects of such a system of crude fictions even for the shortest stretch of time unless its human and natural substance as well as its business organization was protected against the ravages of this satanic mill.[5]

And no society *is* standing the effects of this belief in such a "self-regulating market" with its calamitous social and ecological consequences. It shows in continual protest, whether in huge urban marches and Indigenous mobilizations and social media expressions, or in rethinking the paradigm of economics that has informed development policy over the past century and a half, or in emergent sustainability policies. Whether and how we may reach a consensus to stabilize and value human and other species' life in terms other than price remains to be seen. There are very powerful private interests wedded to price and profit and potentially very powerful mass countermovements focused on increasingly evident needs for social and ecological protections.

In this closing chapter, we examine the growing recognition of the limits of conventional development thinking and of the need to embed sustainable practices in development futures.

WHAT IS APPROPRIATE TO THESE TIMES?

This question directs our attention to "these times." More than ever we are confronted with the fragility of modern life, that we exist within an encompassing biophysical entity, and that development for these times must first acknowledge that reality. And so, an appropriate conception of development would prioritize Nature, respecting its cycles and processes, which includes the dignity of human and other species' life. We are now well aware of how habitat destruction exposes humans to animal microbes.[6] UN Environment Chief Inger Anderson observed, "Never before have so many opportunities existed for pathogens to pass from wild and domestic animals to people. . . . Our continued erosion of wild spaces has brought us uncomfortably close to animals and plants that harbor diseases that can jump to humans."[7] Growing recognition of such boundary-crossing means *relearning rather than discounting our natural heritage.*

And relearning our natural heritage, at this time of deep global connections among societies, means coming to terms with Earth and its diverse and interrelated ecosystems. Empires and modern states have imposed political boundaries across this system. However, natural cycles and vectors, such as atmospheric processes and viruses, transcend such territorial boundaries. So the question becomes how to institute a new, sustainable project in a world of competing nation-states *within* a biophysical unity. As Barbara Ward, in *Only One Earth*, wrote, "The relentless pursuit of separate national interests by rich and poor alike can, in a totally interdependent biosphere, produce global disasters of irreversible damage."[8] That observation was made half a century ago, and it is only now that people are registering that "we are being invited into a different way of engaging the world."[9]

One possibility, suggested by political scientist John Ruggie, might be establishing a new social episteme such as "global ecology," nurtured by "international custodianship" to shape and secure collective planetary existence: "this episteme would differ in form from modern territoriality . . . insofar as the underlying structural premise of ecology is holism and mutual dependence of parts."[10] According to this framework, each state would act not as protector of individual national interest but as "embodiment and enforcer of community norms" on an international scale. This is not out of the question. We did have a successful example of such collective action from 1987, when countries signed on to the international Montreal Protocol to stem an enlarging ozone hole in the atmosphere centered on Antarctica, followed by a phaseout agreement in 1990, which has seen success. Three decades into the globalization project, with enlarged corporate power, such collective action was more difficult to mobilize, other than through nonbinding agreements to work toward greenhouse gas reduction. In 2006, the UN's Millennium Ecosystem Assessment (MEA) advocated multilateral environmental action:

> International agreements are indispensable for addressing ecosystem-related concerns that span national boundaries, but numerous obstacles weaken their current effectiveness. Steps are now being taken to increase the coordination among these mechanisms, and this could help to broaden the focus of the array of instruments. However, *coordination is also needed between the multilateral environmental agreements and more politically powerful international institutions, such as economic and trade agreements, to ensure that they are not acting at cross-purposes.*[11]

The intent is clear: to champion new development policy frameworks acknowledging and reintegrating human activity with its ecological foundations. Ecological accounting by economists is one thing, but sustainability requires active embedding of economic activity in restorative ecological processes, incorporating values other than price into the development equation. Much of human activity is local, nonmonetized, and diverse, despite the universalizing reach of the market—hence the sensibility expressed in the MEA, advocating "use of all relevant forms of knowledge and information in assessments and decision-making," including those of women farmers. The report suggests that effective ecosystem management requires "place-based" knowledge about the specific dynamics of an ecosystem: "Traditional knowledge or practitioners' knowledge held by local resource managers can often be of considerable value in resource management, but it is too rarely incorporated into decision-making processes and indeed is often inappropriately dismissed."[12]

This is the shortcoming of the development narrative, consigning such embedded local knowledge to "the past" in privileging large-scale technologies of power. The point here is to recognize and respect community-based practices in developing local wealth and security, across all societies, however differentiated. And this enables local initiative geared to human services for improving well-being: shelter, nutrition, health, education, social care, leisure, recreation, creativity and culture, and protection of physical infrastructure and natural wealth. Embedded in communities, such meaningful initiatives may use local currencies, enabling exchange of local skills, goods, and services, keeping community wealth local. Communities routinely (and usually implicitly) exercise self-protection, which we call ecologically sustainable social reproduction, which includes the concept and practice of the commons.

Degrowth Economics

Building on such practices is the concept of **degrowth economics.** This provocative term counters the prevailing orthodoxy of unbridled growth that defines development today. Deploying a dramatic metaphor, economist Serge Latouche argues, "Growth economics . . . destroys societies' immune systems against social ills. And growth needs a constant supply of new markets to survive, so, like a drug dealer, it deliberately creates new needs and dependencies that did not exist before."[13] Latouche proposes that "we have to change our values. We need to replace egoism with altruism, competition with cooperation and obsessive performance with leisure."[14] How to accomplish this comprehensively is the question, even as there is ample evidence that such practices already exist.

Ecological economist Joan Martinez-Alier argues degrowth springs from social movement experiences of cohousing, squatting, neoruralism, reclaiming the streets, alternative energies, waste prevention, and recycling, in addition to citizen science.[15] Degrowth economics spawned an originating Paris Conference (2008) and an allied *decrescita* movement in Italy, spreading to Spain, Canada, the United Kingdom, Mexico, and South America.

At the 2015 Paris Conference, delegates concluded business-as-usual would result in a "process of involuntary and uncontrolled economic decline or collapse" and called for a "paradigm shift from the general and unlimited pursuit of economic growth to a concept of 'right-sizing' the global and national economies," involving "degrowth in wealthy parts of the world" to preserve environmental space for poorer nations. The Second International Conference on Degrowth (2010) in Barcelona advanced a series of practical proposals (e.g., local currencies, ecological taxes, establishment of new jurisdictions for a global commons, universal basic income, decommercialization of politics), concluding degrowth must originate in the rich countries—essentially reversing the linear development narrative. As some point out, if so, then who would purchase the components, gadgets, and clothes produced for export in the global South?

Alternatively, this could be a moment of transition for so-called developing countries to change course, with assistance such as debt forgiveness and historic reparations. This may appear contradictory. For example, a recent article, "The Long, Slow Death of Global Development," argues, "the crux of the problem is this: there is no widely replicable strategy to develop a country—simply put, to turn it from poor to rich—that does not involve an economy becoming highly industrialized."[16]

Such a conclusion reproduces the conventional linear understanding of development, as if there is no other way to eliminate poverty and regain political-economic independence. However, there are alternatives such as reimagining what collective socioecological wealth might look like and regaining a certain cultural independence, such as transcending urban bias, embracing the biocentric turn, and subordinating economy to ecology, human dignity, and social justice.

In relation to degrowth, Tim Jackson, economics commissioner for the British Sustainable Development Commission, articulates a dilemma: "To resist growth is to risk economic and social collapse. To pursue it relentlessly is to endanger the ecosystems on which we depend for long-term survival."[17] A new vision is necessary, based on "rebuilding prosperity from the bottom up," to invest in public/shared goals, assets, and infrastructures. A new, "flourishing" (rather than profit-based) economy would gravitate to service-based activities, ecological/green investment, and a work-time policy that reduces working hours and improves work–life balance, as demonstrated in various country studies.[18] And this, in turn, requires combined forms of short- and long-term (democratic) planning, as centered in the concept of the Green New Deal.[19]

Universal Basic Income

Some ways of valuing this kind of socioeconomic activity draw on the **Universal Basic Income (UBI)** initiative, popularized in Europe (especially Finland), Australia, and the United States in relation to extensive inequality.[20] In the United Kingdom, for example, the 15 million people performing voluntary community work can be recognized with a basic income.[21] In Barcelona's basic income program, almost 1,000 families also participate in "social economy" projects involving employment, housing, and community action to analyze the openness of neighborhoods to creative solutions to poverty. One such program is time banks, where participants trade their abilities and time rather than money. Guy Standing, founder and president of the Basic Income Earth Network, argues,

> There is no reason why a city or country could not afford to have a basic income for everybody. In Britain, tax reliefs for the wealthy and corporations come to about £400bn a year—this by itself could be used to pay for a basic income for everybody. It's not something that is unaffordable—it's a matter of priorities.[22]

In Ontario, the basic income model offers twice the standard amount for welfare, and the director of the Hamilton Roundtable for Poverty Reduction claims it is yielding positive results, the most important being a "restoration of dignity," and that basic income will become the twenty-first century's "preeminent social policy imperative." Given current circumstances, cities across the world are experimenting with basic income programs in order to alleviate social inequalities and provide some financial security. Jim Pugh, cofounder of the Universal Income Project, maintains, "The truth is that most people want to contribute to society. If we can provide them with basic financial security, they'll find a way to do it."[23] Such confidence in UBI contrasts with critiques that it disincentivizes citizens from finding a job and that it is unaffordable. These critiques are found to be largely baseless,[24] rather reflecting asocial perspectives that ignore the unequal structuring of modern societies, where labor has a muted voice compared with the financial power of elites.

UNIVERSAL BASIC INCOME SYSTEMS AT WORK

Variants of the UBI phenomenon are under way in southern countries also, such as Iran, Kenya, Uganda, Togo, Namibia, India, China, Mexico, and Brazil, which, since 2014, has been the only country in the world to legislate all citizens' right to a basic income. The first step toward instituting UBI came in the form of Brazil's Bolsa Família program under President Lula in the first decade of the twenty-first century. Bolsa Família was a program of cash transfers to millions of the poor on the condition that recipients keep their children in school and visit health clinics; it was expanded into unconditional cash transfers. Such a program exemplifies a "human development" principle. The program was extended in 2020, to Maricá, a small city of 160,000, north of Rio de Janeiro. It is the most ambitious city-level response to COVID-19 in Brazil and one of the most notable across a world where suffering from the virus concentrated among deprived populations. Maricá's lowest-income residents, roughly a quarter of the population, had their basic income increased from 130 reals (R$), about US$25, per month to R$300 per month (US$60). Public school children's families received food baskets, with additional support to self-employed workers and small businesses, savings accounts for high school students, free public transportation, massive infrastructure investments, and a sovereign wealth fund for the city to guarantee social programs in perpetuity, paid in a local digital currency.

How do such programs exemplify a "human development" principle?

Sources: Katz and Ferreira (2020); Samuel (2020).

Forms of UBI are responses to current inequalities of access to basic necessities, in addition to precarious employment patterning. This includes the vulnerabilities of workers in the gig economy, where labor rights are largely nonexistent, with employers claiming gig workers are "flexible entrepreneurs." UBI experimentation anticipates automation of jobs increasingly by robotization and artificial intelligence while simultaneously offering possibilities of building community-scale forms of social reproduction.

Here, basic income is a pathway to rehabilitating citizenship, which has been fractured by pervasive neoliberal competitive forces. Foremost expert on basic income, Louise Haagh, claims, "The case for basic income is tied up with the case for democracy and for a form of economic development that is grounded in humanist justice."[25] In this sense, the concept of basic income employs a "moral economy" perspective to restore the UN ideal of the "social contract" at the inception of the development project.

Furthermore, Guy Standing claims,

> Underwritten by taxation on the rich . . . . a basic income would be partial compensation for loss of the commons, which belong to all of us equally, but which have been appropriated by privileged elites and corporations to generate private wealth. In this context, the commons are not just land, waterways, forests, parks, and natural resources, but also the social amenities, public services, and body of ideas and knowledge we inherit as a society. We all deserve a share of the wealth these commons produce.[26]

However, what Standing does not account for is the question of how much contemporary structural inequalities stem from colonial relations, which is why calls for reparations are now so significant.

SUSTAINABLE DEVELOPMENT PROJECT IMPLEMENTATION

At the present time, in the shadow of a combined health, social justice, environmental, and economic crisis, alternatives to neoliberal development on a global scale are appearing in social practices and institutional settings, bearing witness to a *possible* fundamental shift on to a more secure path to the future. As the current global order unravels, an array of social and political forces and experiments prefigure implementation of a sustainable development project. Whether such a project will materialize in a unified way is an open question.

Establishing effective sustainable development first requires epistemic change, as in alternative ways of seeing, and then organizing, the world rather than the dominant "invisible hand" narrative of neutrality and efficiency. This narrative has served neoliberal development on a global scale. It appeals to an individualist philosophy, elevating private interest via the axiom "bad state, good market." And this has enabled private wealth accumulation via the shrinking of the role of states in sustaining programs for public goods and services. When markets fail, jobs disappear, access to goods and services contracts, and protective impulses emerge, demanding public security and oversight during global economic and health crises.

With the crisis of the globalization project intensified by economic recession and alarming inequalities of access to the means of life and health, overdetermined by climate emergencies, the world faces a massive critical juncture. This includes a changing of the guard in the international state system as U.S. leadership shrinks, along with its presumptive liberal world-order. It is expressed in the rise of neo-illiberalism, with the spread of authoritarian nationalist regimes, with an all too common white supremacism shaping their inward-looking economic policy. One prominent French writer's reference to the "reverse-colonization' of white Europe by 'black and brown immigrants'" reveals, ironically, the significance of historic colonial legacies—such as dispossession—in shaping present migration streams and compromising serious international collaborative engagement with the future.[27]

As we have seen, one impulse has been to reinvigorate the nation-state, whether through nativism on the right or against austerity politics by the left, both mobilizations demanding protections, from immigrants or from employment precarity, respectively, driven by joint antipathy to global elite machinations. Such politicization of the nation-state is complemented by shifts in economic theorizing, reflecting a legitimacy crisis of economic globalization. Given the influence of professional economics, we focus on this dimension as a potential paradigm shift toward a managed sustainable development project.

Retheorizing Economics

In the shadow of the 2008 financial and climate crises, the economics discipline engaged in some timely rethinking, anticipating a possible alternative approach to development. In 2018, at a workshop on "new thinking beyond neoliberalism," participants from the newly formed Economics for Inclusive Prosperity network (social scientists, historians, and legal scholars) "agreed that the prevailing neoliberal policy framework had failed society, resulting in monumental and growing inequality." They challenged how economics is often practiced and taught:

> Conservative foundations and think tanks have monopolized the banner of economics in policy circles, pushing the view that there is a steep efficiency-equality trade-off and assigning priority to economic growth. Students often leave their introductory economics courses thinking that "markets always work." Conservatives tend to deploy "economics" as a justification for preferred policies, while liberals are seen as insensitive to the requirements for prosperity.

Contrarily, the network maintains "neoliberalism . . . is not the consistent application of modern economics, but its primitive, simplistic perversion," with its members expressing

> [a] willingness to subordinate textbook economic efficiency to other values such as democratic rule and egalitarian relationships among citizens. These proposals take Polanyi's works to heart: to work well, crucial markets (including markets for labor, land and capital) must be embedded in nonmarket institutions, and the "rules of the game" must be supplied by government.[28]

In 2019, the Not the Nobel Prize, for "fresh economic thinking," was awarded to University College of London economics professor Mariana Mazzucato, whose work refocuses from market rule to the "entrepreneurial state" as development driver. Supposing innovation is best left to the private sector is a myth, she argues, as investors are wary of risk, and this is particularly the case where the world faces the need to replace energy-intensive technologies. Documenting the significance of government investment, she claims, "Every technology that makes the iPhone smart and not stupid owes its funding to both basic and applied research by the State."[29] Her discordant revaluing of the role of public financing encourages Green New Deal visions of an alternative societal organizing principle.[30]

Anthropologist David Graeber commented, "There is a growing feeling, among those who have the responsibility of managing large economies, that the discipline of economics is no longer fit for purpose. It is beginning to look like a science designed to solve problems that no longer exist."[31] And *Guardian* economics writer Andrew Simms suggested, "Something is killing conventional economics and it's probably an inside job. Reliance on abstract mathematics and absurd assumptions has brought the discipline into disrepute. . . . It's because neoclassical economics has so deeply entrenched the notion that markets are better than all other ways of organizing life, that decisions escape rational scrutiny."[32]

Beyond this growing critique of so-called market fetishism, Oxford University economist Kate Raworth notes,

> For over 60 years, economic thinking told us that GDP growth was a good enough proxy for progress, and that it looked like an ever-rising line. But this century calls for quite a different shape and direction of progress . . . the movement that best describes the progress we need is coming into dynamic balance [calling] for a profound shift in our metaphors: from "good is forward-and-up" to "good is in-balance."[33]

Her argument is that the aim of economic activity should be "meeting the needs of all within the means of the planet," a simple but consummate ideal, certainly an improvement on "growth at all costs."[34]

Her model of "doughnut economics" (Figure 10.1) is an effective image, or "compass," to reset the prevailing growth paradigm for sustainable development—where the doughnut ring itself is the "ecologically safe and socially just space" for humanity to strive to be: "between a social foundation that protects against critical human deprivations, and an environmental ceiling that avoids critical natural thresholds."[35] Notably, as reported by the elite World Economic Forum in 2017,

> The hole at the Doughnut's centre reveals the proportion of people worldwide falling short on life's essentials, such as food, water, healthcare and political freedom of expression—and a big part of humanity's challenge is to get everyone out of that hole. At the same time, however, we cannot afford to be overshooting the Doughnut's outer crust if we are to safeguard Earth's life-giving systems, such as a stable climate, healthy oceans and a protective ozone layer, on which all our wellbeing fundamentally depends.[36]

Regarding healthy oceans, Pulitzer Prize–winning scientist writer Elizabeth Kolbert noted in early 2024 that a "startling rise in sea-surface temperatures suggests that we may not understand how fast the climate is changing." In 2023, sea-surface

FIGURE 10.1 ■ Doughnut Economics

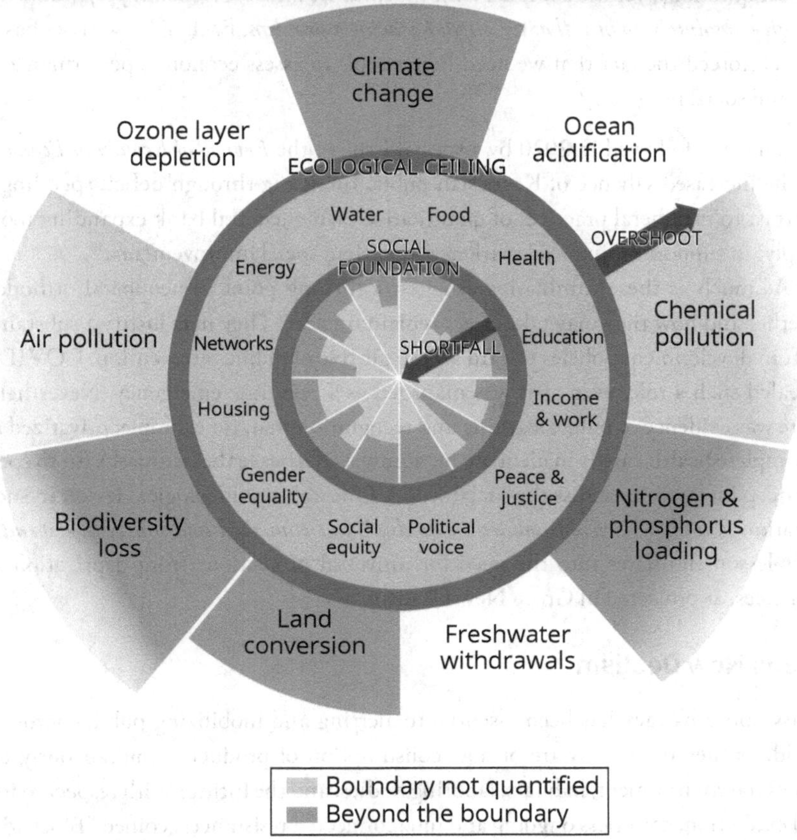

Source: Raworth (2017b).

temperatures set a new record: "the average temperature at the surface of the world's oceans, excluding those at the poles, was just a shade under seventy degrees [and] since the start of 2024, sea-surface temperatures have continued to climb," setting yet another record.[37]

Invoking "the past," Raworth reminds us that civilizations such as the Ancient Greeks, Buddhist, Maori, and Andean cultures practiced thriving in balance, with Ecuador's constitution the first to recognize that Nature (*Pachamama*) "has the right to exist, persist, maintain and regenerate its vital cycles,"[38] underlining the short-sighted Western dismissal of non-Western cultures.

Former World Bank chief economist Joseph Stiglitz opined in 2019:

> The world is facing three existential crises: a climate crisis, an inequality crisis and a crisis in democracy. Will we be able to prosper within our planetary

> boundaries? Can a modern economy deliver shared prosperity? These are critical questions, yet the accepted *ways by which we measure economic performance give absolutely no hint that we might be facing a problem*. Each of these crises has reinforced the fact that we need better tools to assess economic performance and social progress.[39]

This was followed in 2020 by a special issue of the *Review of Keynesian Economics* on the increased salience of Keynesian public financing through deficit spending, in contrast to neoliberal practices of quantitative easing (central bank expanding money supply) in support of financial markets rather than social improvements.[40]

As much as these ruminations suggest a turning point in neoliberal orthodoxy, whether and how they may take effect remain unclear. They may justify a substantive shift in development policies toward a strategic role of public intervention. COVID-19 revealed such a role, even as it was managed as a one-time emergency. Nevertheless, there was evidence of public learning and recognition that, for example, privatized and incomplete health care is inadequate for a universal disease that unmasks (so to speak) the deep inequalities across the social world. One key, nonideological lesson in such a situation is ***humans are not isolated individuals but enmeshed and mutually dependent.*** This lesson translates into the need for universal protections from deprivation and injustices, as projected in Green New Dealism.

Green New Dealism

Grassroots advocacy has been essential to alerting and mobilizing publics across the world, as they become aware of how consumption of products simultaneously consumes the environment, habitats, laboring bodies, and the future. With respect to fossil fuel extraction, countless ongoing and interconnected resistances (coined "Blockadia") warn of the associated peril to planet Earth of extreme extractive projects (such as tar sands drilling in Alberta) and draw attention to the coloniality of the Anthropocene concept, in race, class, and gender terms, insofar as humans at large are not equally responsible for the planetary plunder associated with this geological age.

With the rising climate emergency, countless proposals and practices of greening the economy at different scales (spatial and temporal), have emerged: from biofuels, electric cars, and organic agriculture to wind farms and solar energy. Solar and wind power are gaining traction in response to an increasingly vocal and powerful mobilization of citizens across the world for serious emissions reduction. Energy industry experts view recent expansion of renewables as evidence, suggesting it "may soon seem glacial compared with the changes to come."[41]

Meanwhile, **Green New Deal (GND)** proposals seek to subordinate market rule to social and ecological need, with public intervention. Such proposals have spread from the United Kingdom, through Europe to the United States, Canada, Australia, New Zealand, India, China, and other countries. In South Korea, for example, President Moon Jae-in announced in June 2020, "It's clear the green new deal is the way for us to go. It's necessary to lay out a grand plan for the green new deal to harmonise with the establishment of a digital infrastructure."[42]

These commitments respond to the present moment of climate emergency, with an opportune dimension of social equality: "in the process of transforming the infrastructure of our societies at the speed and scale that scientists have called for, humanity has a once-in-a-century chance to fix an economic model that is failing the majority of people on multiple fronts."[43] In other words, the GND aims not simply to arrest climate change but also to address social inequalities and construct a sustainable model *combining* large-scale social and ecological investments for universal human well-being—something markets in carbon are not equipped to do, even as they may have their place in disciplining private investment.

In 2011 the United Nations Environment Programme (UNEP) critiqued the myth

> that there is an inescapable trade-off between environmental sustainability and economic progress. There is now substantial evidence that the greening of economies neither inhibits wealth creation nor employment opportunities. To the contrary, many green sectors provide significant opportunities for investment growth and jobs.[44]

Current GND proposals recognize the trap of promoting private consumption, shifting development toward public provisioning of jobs and green infrastructure, including housing, resiliency investments in underprivileged communities, and expanding access to a range of social services, including free public university/college education and universal health care. Under these proposals, a coordinated deployment of government finance substitutes for a conventional program centered on carbon taxes for redistribution to the poor and publicly supported private investment in green technologies.

While private interests and market narratives may claim individual rights, citizens are recognizing time is of the essence and collective public measures, including finance on a massive scale, are required. Notably, "handouts to the fossil fuel industry are so extensive that the Stockholm Environment Institute has estimated that as much as half of new oil and gas development would be unprofitable without them."[45] Sociologist Holly Jean Buck suggests that, given integration of fossil fuels with industry in general, nationalization of fossil fuel firms and strategic diversification is critical, such as transforming such firms into *combined energy/carbon removal* companies. Her point is to propose workable measures, including reconditioning fossil fuel firms to gain broad political buy-in for a transition (including maintaining transformed jobs for their workforces).[46] This public fund, generated in a managed fossil fuel industry liquidation, could enable the transfer of pensions invested in fossil fuel companies into renewable and infrastructural investments driving the transition, including upgrading disadvantaged communities, restoring wetlands and clean rivers, and so on.[47]

Reorganizing agriculture along agroecological lines is increasingly recognized as key to sequestering, rather than releasing, carbon. Globally, this means redirecting massive agribusiness subsidies. A recent report found the cost of environmental damage exceeds the value of food produced and that ecologically driven farming would reduce food costs as land health is restored.[48] This means support for small-scale producers and peasant land rights, consolidating local nested markets and stabilizing domestic farming cultures—in line with food sovereignty principles and the IAASTD report.

The U.S. GND proposal includes "working collaboratively with farmers and ranchers in the United States to remove pollution and greenhouse gas emissions from the agricultural sector as much as is technologically feasible . . . by supporting family farming; by investing in sustainable farming and land use practices that increase soil health; and by building a more sustainable food system that ensures universal access to healthy food."[49] This is in line with the proposed European GND, premised on helping ecological farmers stay on the land:

> To end the destructive practices of large agribusinesses, the Common Food Policy would redirect subsidies from corporate landowners to small farmers, and support food sovereignty and sustainable farming methods via low-interest loans and farmer-driven financing. This transformation would be funded by the Green Public Works, a public investment agency mandated to reinvigorate Europe's rural communities and help them produce healthier food for all.[50]

Managed decline of the mass consumption model of development is also mooted. If the wealthiest 10 percent of humanity consumed at the level of the average European, emissions of carbon would reduce by about a third.[51] It is possible that once such groups realize that wealth provides little protection from the socioeconomic and biophysical vicissitudes of climate emergency, recognition of a common purpose might become more palatable.

Multilateralism?

As we have seen, principles of ecological custodianship and social well-being require large-scale, international public intervention with shared democratic forms of governance. However, global disunity and tension mark our times, as U.S. power wanes in the shadow of China's renaissance, nationalism proliferates, and infrastructures of world order fracture. President of the U.S. Council on Foreign Relations, Richard Haass, bemoaned in 2020 "the poor state of global governance. The world today is simply not conducive to being shaped. Power is distributed in more hands, both state and nonstate, than ever before. Consensus is mostly absent. New technologies and challenges have outpaced the collective ability to contend with them."[52]

The solidarity of a United Nations framework is needed more than ever as a protective and proactive response to the new and profound challenges facing the world community. Nationalism is on the rise, and recent experience shows that a united international public front is necessary to rise above competitive national and/or private forces. Here we examine the UN's recent response, in substituting SDGs for the rather ineffectual 2000 Millennium Development Goals.

The UN's 2030 Agenda for SDGs is a comprehensive international initiative addressing multiple dimensions of development across a deeply unequal system of 193 sovereign states. At face value, however, the content, or measures, of development have been broadened to complement economic growth with education, health, gender equity, and environmental health, for example. However, two key problems underscore the SDGs. The conventional assumption of development as a national process remains the bedrock of the SDGs. Sovereign states they are, formally, but they are all embedded to varying extents, and with unequal effects, in a global economy. Colonialism's legacy remains evident in the unequal structuring of the "sovereign" political units of the twenty-first-century global economy. This is now compounded by the SDG framework, which, on closer scrutiny, shows that it is really geared to maintaining economic growth and private privileges, "locking in" commitments to the commercialization of public services and goods as per the World Trade Organization framework.[53] In fact, in December 2023, the associated UN Global Goals organization (formed in 2015) declared, "We reached halftime and we are way down, with only 15% of the goals in track."[54]

The dilemma of an international organization operating with an even hand across the various states is underscored by a critique that the agenda had to be carefully calibrated to avoid upsetting dictatorial regimes, including "this century's worst human rights offenders" such as those of China, Syria, Rwanda, India, Brazil, the Philippines, and Eritrea. The term *human rights* appears only once in a secondary role (in a lengthy text). This is the same for terms valuing basic human freedoms, such as civil liberties, independent judiciary, free and fair elections, and anticorruption.[55] *The Economist* declared the SDGs "worse than useless."[56]

A more analytical evaluation of the SDGs would underscore the shortcomings of *methodological nationalism*: avoiding attention to global processes (historical and contemporary) affecting individual country resource access and distribution. As a global project, development involves cross-border movements of money and migrants (not to mention weather patterns and viruses). Such movements reveal the permeability of territorial boundaries and the need to complicate state-centric development patterning by embedding it in global political-economic-ecological decolonial relations.

A state-centric approach to development is incapable of accounting for such ongoing *global reordering* of landscapes and demographics. To persist with methodological nationalism also misses the complicity of host states in such movements of money and people—vis-à-vis addressing land rights for local producers and human rights for migrants.[57]

The state-centric paradigm includes a long-standing urban-centrism, which assumes depopulation of the countryside for urban-industrial employment. This assumption tends to naturalize rural poverty as the absence of development—rather than recognizing how neoliberal development has actively undermined and withdrawn state support of domestic farming cultures. Thus, the initial SDG proposal in 2013 by the UN's High-Level Panel noted,

> The world is now more urban than rural, thanks to internal migration. By 2030 there will be over one billion more urban residents and, for the first time ever, the number of rural residents will be starting to shrink. This matters because inclusive growth emanates from vibrant and sustainable cities, the only locale where it is possible to generate the number of good jobs that young people are seeking.[58]

Unaddressed here are both the question of land rights for stable domestic farming populations and a routine assumption of urban vitality in an era of joblessness and automation. An assumed future of large-scale high-input agriculture is linked to the UN's High-Level Panel recycling a business-as-usual claim: "Because 'we treasure what we measure,' an important part of properly valuing the earth's natural abundance is to incorporate it into accounting systems."[59] But as noted earlier, commodifying "ecosystem services" cannot achieve sustainable food systems. Paradoxically, SDG2 on Zero Hunger concludes, "The pathway to achieving Zero Hunger should center on place-based, adaptive, participatory solutions that simultaneously attend to local institutional capacities, agroecosystem diversification and ecological management, and the quality of local diets."[60]

The SDGs have evolved from an initial methodological nationalism *analytic* of development toward some recognition of the need for global governance, heightened by the experience of COVID-19. The UN Secretary-General's report remarked, "There is no escaping the fact that the global landscape for SDG implementation has generally deteriorated since 2015, hindering the efforts of Governments and other partners. Moreover, *the commitment to multilateral cooperation, so central to implementing global agreements*, is now under pressure."[61] Further, with conflicts and instability across the world undermining the SDG agenda and "even reversing progress already made," the report then noted, "With developing countries hosting more than 85 percent of the 68.5 million people who were forcibly displaced in 2017, pressures on existing support systems are immense." Here the national design of the SDGs was revealed as incapable of situating displacement as a global-economic phenomenon. And finally, the introduction states,

> Rising income and wealth inequality risk undermining efforts to achieve the SDGs. They threaten to erode social cohesion, entrench insecurity and dampen productivity growth. Rising intolerance in many parts of the world threatens fundamental human rights and human progress. The nexus among inequality, injustice, insecurity and lack of sufficient trust of Governments and institutions can further hinder the necessary conditions for advancing sustainable development.[62]

Reference to the distrust of *extant* governments and institutions underlines neoliberal development's key threat to social health: namely, its antigovernment/antiwelfare narrative in the guise of market efficiency and neutrality. As noted in the SDG 2019 report,

> From climate to disease, from economic downturn to migration and from health to frontier technology, today's challenges require a *strong commitment*

> *to international cooperation and more effective multilateral institutions.* Yet recent trends show some *Governments are retreating from multilateral action and the global public is voicing dissatisfaction with the downsides of globalization*. . . . Global rules must be revised to ensure that they are supportive of the Sustainable Development Goals and conducive to fair globalization.[63]

Reviewing the SDG process does not inspire confidence in a well-managed future, especially when national policy frameworks are tied to austerity measures and/or commercialization of public services and goods. For example, referring to intended support of, for example, child care and the elderly, Louise Haagh notes, "The way the SDGs set more extensive and life-cycle-related targets, at the same time as state powers to implement such goals have weakened, is *deeply ironic*."[64] Such weakening is the consequence of commercialization of public services, such as health care. One of the key problems of the SDG framework is precisely how realization of the goals depends on the private sector. The lesson to be taken from the SDGs initiative is that its shortcomings indicate the urgency of more effective multilateral institutions. The notion of "international custodianship," informed by the Zapatista conception of "a world in which many worlds fit," would be the ideal to which humanity might aspire. While certainly a pipe dream, for now, it is not out of the question that deepening global environmental crises (climate change and pandemics) may well force creation of more effective multilateral institutions. To be effective, they might proactively monitor global public health in the broadest sense (biophysical, social, economic, and political) to enable concerted efforts to protect the natural world, (re)distribute green technologies and material resources across an unequal world, oversee observance of human rights, manage trade relations, and so on.

At the same time the UN Secretary-General refers to "the downsides of globalization" without spelling out what is at issue, other than alluding to dissatisfaction on the part of the "global public" and "Governments." This in itself is indicative of a growing recognition that so-called free markets are economically and socially destabilizing. Thus, urban uprisings have become standard procedure, from the 2011 Occupy movement and Arab Spring protests against majority deprivations, state violence, and profiteering of the ruling elites; through Greek uprisings against EU austerity measures (2014–2015); to similar rolling protests recently in Lebanon, Iraq, Iran, Egypt, Bolivia, India, Algeria, Colombia, Ecuador, Chile, Haiti, Honduras, India, Indonesia, Hong Kong, Sudan, and Zimbabwe.[65] Meanwhile, farmers across the world, in protest mode, are struggling with debt, squeezed by monopolistic retailers and agrochemical firms, with extreme weather, environmental rules (e.g., to reduce nitrogen emissions from intensive livestock farming), and rising energy prices and falling prices for their products, while the big players depend on subsidies.[66]

What seems counterintuitive is that authoritarian movements, and governments, gain energy and support from disaffected classes, long threatened by offshoring of manufacturing jobs, who now constitute a populist mass encouraged by right-wing leaders to perceive climate change (and immigration) as further threatening their livelihoods.

Along with rural disdain for global elites, and identification with ethnonational politics, such authoritarian populism thrives on "a rejection of international collaboration to address climate change . . . [opposing] the legitimacy of a distinctly international political sphere, especially if it has the capacity to discipline (national) capital."[67] This phenomenon has pulled countries such as Brazil, India, Turkey, Egypt, Russia, France, the Netherlands, Italy, England, Canada, and the United States into its orbit.

This backlash against the globalization project, compounded by climate emergency and its national responses, may shape a world future struggling to restore effective and decolonial multilateralism in addressing overwhelming challenges on the global scale. The challenge is to undo inward-looking nationalisms and centralizations of power and strike a balance between "international custodianship" and effective cross-scale subsidiarity to govern renewable forms of development for social justice and human rights. One overwhelming principle deriving from the planetary ecological crisis might be that "if we truly are equal, then we share the Earth."[68]

Subsidiarity

As we have seen, these kinds of remote decisions generate local resistances and demands for representation and voice. This invokes the **subsidiarity** system, adopted partially by the EU, where social and political issues are addressed at the level appropriate to their resolution. It can work as a polycentric governing principle: "a set of nested levels of governance from the most local to the most interconnected, each level taking some responsibility for the overall management of the system."[69] It allows for combinations of centralized and decentralized decision making depending on the nature and/or scale of the problem. Climate change mitigation, for example, requires particular actions at all levels: from international diplomacy for resource redistribution across unequal states, to national public transport systems, to local agroecological stewardship, for example. While the international scale includes an environmental justice dimension, this is also important locally, given how environmental hazards are often sited in lower-income communities.

Meaningful and sustainable development is generally not always possible via centralized decision making at higher levels of governance, which usually involve professional stakeholders (representing nongovernmental organizations, business, politicians, and scientists) rather than citizens, and especially including rural producers and Indigenous peoples. Compared with democratic elections where citizens vote with procedural equality, forms of global governance architecture tend to be unable to give shape "to values of equality," despite claims of inclusiveness.[70] Such values need grounding in their local environments and institutional mechanisms to safeguard, recognize, and include local voices in higher-level decision making. These are certainly not simple processes, but insofar as they respect local voices and rework "development" as culturally appropriate, equalizing via specific resource needs, and are environmentally sustainable, they represent more meaningful and fulfilling goals than endless, unequal growth delivered by a seemingly "invisible hand" (that rarely picks up the check).

A pertinent model of subsidiary governance is that of La Via Campesina, whose global campaigns for food sovereignty and other agrarian questions over the past three decades have "contributed to carving out a new and distinct space for citizen participation in international policymaking."[71] In the aftermath of the 2008–2009 global food crisis, the UN's Committee on Food Security (CFS) opened up space for front-line producer voices in a new Civil Society and Indigenous Peoples Mechanism, "nearly equal to that of official government representatives, including the right to intervene on the floor during CFS plenaries and committee deliberations."[72] This accommodation did not include the right to vote—which agrifood social movements prefer, allowing them to monitor government actions. Agrarian scholars Marc Edelman and Jun Borras observe,

> On most occasions, LVC [La Via Campesina] has employed "inside-outside" strategies and tactics to secure concessions from intergovernmental institutions. While it engages "inside" the spaces of these institutions, it insists on retaining autonomy so it can exercise pressure from "outside" and carry out mobilizations. This dual approach can result in more significant concessions than working just "inside" or "outside."[73]

However, several decades of global neoliberalism have consolidated power for private corporations and financiers, over states, in turn motivating ruling elites to respond to populist upsurges with nationalisms in defiance of international cooperation. It appears likely that this turn will complicate international governance response to deepening climate and public health emergencies. And this phenomenon is further complicated by the recent turn to **multistakeholderism**, as an alternative to multilateralism. As such it appears to include an undemocratic version of subsidiarity—with *select* "stakeholder" representatives of the powers that be.

This "multistakeholder" vision matured during a decade of cascading protests, where citizens were denouncing "a breakdown of the social contract, expressing more and more forcefully a general loss of trust institutions and leaders," in context of "a vacuum of global governance and the rise of various forms of nationalism"—as claimed by the leadership of the World Economic Forum (WEF), that the world is best governed by a self-selected coalition of transnational corporations, governments, and civil society organizations. What became evident in the convening of the UN Food System Summit, in partnership with the WEF in 2021, was the absence of agrarian civil society and Indigenous Peoples' representatives in the stakeholder grouping, suggesting corporate capture of global food system governance. And this was foreshadowed in the WEF's Davos Manifesto (2019), which argued for substitution of neoliberal theorist Milton Friedman's "shareholder capitalism" by "stakeholder capitalism," positioning of "private corporations as trustees of society."[74]

Such an attempt to concentrate governance at the global level, compromising national sovereignties, and possibilities for meaningful *inter*-national cooperation, is a significantly new threshold and may likely slow transitions to a socially just and greening world order. Meanwhile, of additional concern is the deepening power of information technologies, especially "surveillance capitalism" premised on managing individual behavior. Economist Shoshana Zuboff has noted, "Surveillance capitalism moves from a focus on individual users to a focus on populations, like cities, and eventually on society as a whole."[75] In public surveillance technologies, China leads the world: "eight of the 10 most surveilled cities [in the world] are in China," with London and Atlanta the other two.[76] Given the mushrooming of restive citizenries across the world as austerity policies intensify and health and climate emergencies proliferate, repressive political cultures may well multiply, portending widespread state (and private) surveillance in the twenty-first century.

A big question will be to what extent local voices can effectively inhabit and democratize governing institutions. What it means for the possibility of a new, coordinated and just sustainable development project remains to be seen.

CONCLUSION

The previous two chapters have explored the juxtaposition of responses to social, economic, and ecological crises. How development transforms hangs in the balance. Unlike previous projects, guided by time-bound philosophies of power and progress, the present era is confronted with a certain closure of options. We began this chapter with the question of what comes next and have identified significant possibilities in paradigm change toward revaluing public intervention in the general, rather than private, interest as a new development template versus growth *at all costs*. Both the growing interest in universal implementation of UBI and a GND, reflect new possibilities (and limits) to address over time, with subsidiarity as a principle of organization and transparent/democratic procedure.

At the same time, power remains highly centralized in the corporate-financial world, potentially compromising governance at the national and international scales—reflected, for instance, in the shaping of SDGs. The combination of social, economic, and ecological crises strengthens this power where private interests may be viewed as the sole source of crisis management. Meanwhile, mobilized citizenries are resisting and busy formulating alternative understandings and practices of development based on justice, inclusion, local empowerment, and democratic governance. We are in the midst of a highly contested moment. How this will resolve will depend on the success of socioecological protections (with distinctive cultural forms across space) and on a guiding principle of necessity rather than "progress" per se, as climate change and future pandemics threaten.

KEY TERMS

Degrowth economics
Green New Deal (GND)
Multistakeholderism
Subsidiarity
Sustainable Development Goals (SDGs)
Universal Basic Income (UBI)

FURTHER READING

Aronoff, Kate, Alyssa Battistoni, Daniel Aldana Cohen, and Thea Riofrancos. *A Planet to Win. Why We Need a Green New Deal*. London: Verso, 2019.

Caouette, Dominique, and Dip Kapoor, eds. *Beyond Colonialism, Development and Globalization: Social Movements and Critical Perspectives*. London: Zed Books, 2016.

Cohen, Joshua, ed. "Economics After Neoliberalism." *Boston Review, Forum* 11 (2019).

Gaarde, Ingeborg. *Peasants Negotiating a Global Policy Space: La Vía Campesina in the Committee on World Food Security*. London: Routledge, 2017.

Gibson-Graham, J. K. *A Post-Capitalist Politics*. Minneapolis: University of Minnesota Press, 2006.

Jones, Reece. *Violent Borders: Refugees and the Right to Move*. London: Verso, 2016.

Lang, Miriam, Mary Ann Manahan, and Breno Bringel, eds. *The Geopolitics of Green Colonialism. Global Justice and Ecosocial Transitions*. London: Pluto, 2024.

Mann, Geoff, and Joel Wainwright. *Climate Leviathan: A Political Theory of Our Planetary Future*. London & New York: Verso, 2018.

Newell, Peter. *Global Green Politics*. Cambridge, UK: Cambridge University Press, 2019.

Oxfam International. Inequality Inc. *How Corporate Power Divides Our World and the Need for a New Era of Public Action*. 2024.

Robinson, Kim Stanley. *The Ministry for the Future*. New York: Orbit Books, 2020.

Schmelzer, Matthias, Andrea Vetter, and Aaron Vansintjan. *The Future Is Degrowth. A Guide to a World beyond Capitalism*. London: Verso, 2022.

Selwyn, Benjamin. *The Struggle for Development*. Cambridge, UK: Polity Press, 2017.

Shilliam, Robbie. *Decolonizing Politics*. Cambridge, UK: Polity Press, 2021.

Streeck, Wolfgang. *How Will Capitalism End? Essays on a Failing System*. London: Verso, 2016.

Wallace-Wells, David. *The Uninhabitable Earth. Life after Warming*. New York: Tim Duggan Books, 2019.

SELECT WEBSITES

Degrowth: https://www.opendemocracy.net/en/degrowth-case-for-constructing-new-economic-paradigm/

Global Green New Deal: https://www.c40.org/other/the-global-green-new-deal

IPES-Food: http://www.ipes-food.org

UN Sustainable Development Goals: https://sdgs.un.org/goals

GLOSSARY

Agroecology: An increasingly popular method of farming that combines traditional knowledges with contemporary developments in the science of ecology that are designed to promote low-impact and multifunctional agriculture.

Agroecology: An increasingly popular method of farming that combines traditional knowledges with contemporary developments in the science of ecology that are designed to promote low-impact and multifunctional agriculture.

Alliance for Green Revolution in Africa (AGRA): Initiative funded by foundations (e.g., Gates, Rockefeller) to bring green revolution technologies to small farmers in Africa, including (sometimes genetically) modified seeds, fertilizers, agrochemicals and extension advice.

Alliance for Progress: Counterinsurgency organization formed by Latin American states, with U.S. support designed to redistribute resources especially land for development.

Anthropocene: In Earth's geologic time, when human ("development") activity substantially alters the functioning of Earth's ecosystems.

Arab Spring: The early twenty-first century sustained uprising by Arab subjects against authoritarian/ militarized governments for human and civil rights stimulated by conditions of widespread (youth) unemployment, repression, austerity, and basic food shortages.

Belt and Road Initiative (BRI): China's development, in the twenty-first century of a political, economic, diplomatic, and electronic network as an alternative to Western spheres of influence, as an updating of its ancient Silk Road, that formed China's tributary empire.

Biopiracy: A representation of the patenting of biological processes associated with the extraction and insertion of genes in existing organisms, obtaining a monopoly over the use of that genetic resource through genetic modification.

Bolivarian Alternative for the Americas (ALBA): Regional economic bloc, initiated by Venezuela and Cuba, to foster "cooperative advantage" through reciprocal cultural and economic exchanges.

Bretton Woods: The founding site of the international economic system established in 1944, to disperse long-term World Bank development project loans and short-term International Monetary Fund monies to correct national imbalances of payments.

BRICS: Acronym describing the rise and alliance-building among the new middle-income states of Brazil, Russia, India, China, and South Africa.

Buen vivir: Spanish term for living well, anchored in grassroots struggles for human dignity, social justice, and ecologically embedded economic practices.

Central planning: A device by which socialist states guide economic growth through the planned allocation of public and human resources as an alternative to allocation through the market.

Circular economy: Alternative to conventional linear model of throughput of resources—by reusing, sharing, and recycling output products and materials to reduce waste, energy, overconsumption, and emissions, and to encourage sharing.

Climate-smart agriculture: Agricultural intensification, with industrial agroinputs, designed to reduce pressure on land, conserve natural areas, and reduce greenhouse gas emissions.

Colonial division of labor: Specialization between a colony and its metropolitan colonizing country, exchanging primary products for manufactured goods, respectively.

Colonial project: Term describing the organization and practice of colonization as a deliberate political, military, cultural, and economic practice devised to subjugate the non-European world by European imperial powers.

Coloniality: The continuing and persistent logics of Western colonial domination of the non-Western world, expressed in contemporary power structures, at global as well as national scales, shaping political-economic, cultural, and ecological relations. Coloniality augments, for example, the surging migrant streams from the South to North; in conventional accounts, this is disarticulated from the context of coloniality.

Commodity chains: A series of linkages between sites involved in producing part of an overall product for sale on the market.

Commons: Popular term for common property systems, where villagers or communities manage land, resources, and ecosystems in the collective interest.

Comparative advantage: A theorem about how countries specialize in producing and trading what they excel in, relatively, by virtue of their human and natural resources.

Cornwall Consensus: A G-7 decision in 2021 to encourage public initiative in reshaping economies along environmental lines via systematic planning and international cooperation.

Countermovements: Social movements that challenge or resist the dominant paradigm.

Debt regime: A set of rules established by the IMF and the World Bank as conditions to be implemented by indebted nations for further loans and debt rescheduling.

Decolonization: The political process of challenging and overcoming colonial rule and the domination, deprivation and discrimination associated with it. It entails struggles for just repair and restoration even after the formal ending of colonialism.

Deglobalization: Reorientation of economy to domestic needs, rather than export production; democratic oversight of production decisions, deemphasizing uncontrolled growth, and promotion of social justice and green targets.

Degrowth economics: New branch of economic analysis concerned with reduction of energy use (and environmental impact) by reducing consumption, transforming work patterns, and/or recovery of farming practices that produce rather than consume energy.

Dependency analysis: Relational concept explaining historical and contemporary relations between states categorized as "developed" and "developing," emphasizing the colonial division of labor and its ongoing adverse implications.

Development alliance: A multiclass coalition created by states through provision of patronage and social services to support rapid industrialization.

Development paradox: Contradictory relation that questions the claims of, and expresses the various social inequalities, environmental impacts, rights conflicts, cultural/aesthetic outcomes and practices crystallized in, the development process.

Development project: An organized strategy of national economic growth, including an international system of alliances and assistance established within the competitive and militarized terms of the Cold War.

Development states: A centralized bureaucratic state committed to pursuing development in terms of national economic growth.

Economic Commission for Latin America (ECLA): Regional organization of the United Nations that gathers data and prepares reports on Latin American economies; headquartered in Rio de Janeiro.

Economic nationalism: A development paradigm favoring national regulation of economic development protecting domestic economic sectors, employment, and resources, and reducing external dependency.

Environmentalist's paradox: A curious juxtaposition of rising living standards and declining environment health.

European Union (EU): Established in 1992, as a union of fifteen Western European states excluding Norway and Switzerland, the EU seeks to integrate their economies, promoting cooperation and policy coordination, with the Euro as common currency.

Export monoculture: Specialization in production of single crops for export.

Export processing zones (EPZs): Specialized zones established by states to attract foreign investment in export production, with concessions such as cheap unorganized labor, infrastructural subsidies, and tax breaks.

Extractivism: Contemporary model of neoliberal development geared to a race for resources, primarily in the global South, hosted by governments to attract foreign investment for purposes of job creation, social welfare funds, or elite corruption.

First World: A conventional term to refer to the western (capitalist) bloc during the Cold War period.

Food aid regime: The use of food aid by the United States to achieve strategic political objectives in the post-1945 context. It used surplus food produced through subsidies as a strategy to gain political support from states in the global South during the Cold War. As a long-term strategy, the objective was also to capture their markets for U.S. food producers.

Food and Agricultural Organization (FAO): Specialist agency of the United Nations headquartered in Rome; responsible for coordinating reports and developing agricultural production and trade in the developing world.

Food sovereignty: The political/human right of a community or country to determine its own policies regarding food security (adequate supply and appropriate cuisine), and the cultural social and ecological conditions under which it is sustained.

Gaia hypothesis: James Lovelock's claim that planet earth has an in-built self-regulating physiological system that, to date, has enabled a climate sustaining human life. Gaia is the Greek earth-goddess.

General Agreement on Tariffs and Trade (GATT): Agreement signed in 1944 in Havana by the United Nations and implemented in 1947 to monitor and reduce obstacles to free trade among member nations.

Global assembly lines: Dispersal of production processes across sites of relatively low-skilled (feminized) labor predominantly in the global South.

Global division of labor: The subdivision of forms of labor in manufacturing, perishable agricultural commodities, high- and low-end services, through outsourcing of jobs.

Global Environmental Facility (GEF): Organization established by the World Bank under the auspices of UNCED to fund and manage global environmental protection.

Global Green New Deal (GGND): The Global Green New Deal (GGND, 2007) called on governments to allocate a significant share of stimulus funding to green sectors; set out three objectives: (1) economic recovery, (2) poverty eradication, and (3) reduced carbon emissions and ecosystem degradation; and proposed a framework for green stimulus programs as well as supportive domestic and international policies.

Global land grab: Term popularizing land acquisitions, notably in the twenty-first century, geared to growing export crops or biofuels, financial speculation, debt servicing, and offshore food security for food-dependent nations.

Global managers: A group of powerful bureaucrats and officials in the Bretton Woods institutions and the WTO, executives in the transnational corporations and banks, and the bureaucratic elite administering other free trade agreements and global ecology.

Global North: Current term designating a region of so-called "advanced/developed" countries.

Global South: Current term designating a region of so-called "less-developed" countries.

Globalization project: An emerging vision of the world and its resources as a globally organized and managed free trade/free enterprise economy pursued by the largely unaccountable political and economic elite.

Green colonialism: Intensified northern commercial exploitation of materials (minerals), environmental resources (e.g., solar/wind, and forests), Indigenous landscapes, and territories of the global South, in the name of decarbonization.

Green New Deal (GND): Large-scale public planning to rebuild modern economies, production systems, and jobs along sustainable lines, via extensive green infrastructure, low-carbon energy sources, and environmentally sensitive ways of urban and rural living.

Green revolution: A technical package of bioengineered hybrid seeds, requiring chemical and mechanical inputs and irrigation designed to improve agricultural productivity in basic grains such as wheat, maize, and rice.

Green transition: Adoption of decarbonization and sustainable development strategies to shift industrial economies away from fossil fuels and overconsumption of natural resources, to develop renewable energies, low-input agriculture, and regenerate ecosystems.

Group of 7 (G-7): The core group of developed states that meet regularly and effectively set the agenda for global economic management (United States, the United Kingdom, France, Germany, Japan, Italy, and Canada).

Group of 20 (G-20): Formed in 1999 to group industrial and emerging economies (Brazil, China, India, Indonesia, Turkey, and South Africa) to strengthen global economic management.

Group of 77 (G-77): A solidarity grouping of Third World states formed in the mid-1960s, overlapping with the Non-Aligned Movement, now numbering more than 120 nation-states.

Human Development Index: UN term designed to broaden measures of development, in particular regarding education, health and well-being indicators.

Illiberalism: Dilution of the model of liberal democracy that defined the development project, with the deepening of racist, nativist nationalism toward immigrants and social minorities in the twenty-first century.

Import-substitution industrialization: A strategy of protecting domestic industry through tariff and other barriers pursued initially to overcome the specializing effects of the colonial division of labor.

Informalization: The expansion of livelihood activities below the government accounting radar, including a cultural dimension whereby people on the margins develop ingenious social networks of material and emotional support to get by.

Intellectual property rights: Rights to monopolize (in 20-year patents) inventions stemming from scientific discovery usually undertaken by corporate bodies.

International Assessment of Agricultural Science and Technology for Development (IAASTD): UN and World Bank–sponsored report (2008) detailing the relative health of existing agricultural systems and the need to transition away from reliance on industrial agriculture for feeding the world and, instead, support diversified farming systems and local farming knowledges for their multifunctional benefits to society (jobs, local foods) and the environment (restoration of natural soil and hydrological cycles, retention of biodiversity).

International division of labor: Specialization in producing commodities for the world market that divides regions into zones of industrial or agricultural production or high- or low-skilled labor.

International Monetary Fund (IMF): The fund established under the Bretton Woods agreement of 1944 to correct balance of payments difficulties; more recently an agent of structural adjustment.

Land reforms: Mandated changes to patterns of land ownership and/or use, often in contexts where ownership has been highly unequal or unfairly concentrated in the hands of the few.

Maquiladoras: A production zone established on the U.S./Mexican border to assemble imported components with Mexican labor for export.

Marshall Plan: A project of financial aid and export credits organized by the United States to reconstruct postwar Europe and Japan.

Millennium Development Goals (MDGs): UN-sponsored development goals addressing key challenges of the twenty-first century such as hunger and poverty, pandemic disease, environmental damage, gender inequality, global South debt, and universal education.

Millennium Ecosystem Assessment (MEA): UN-sponsored report (2005) regarding the extent of global environmental degradation, in particular the loss of biodiversity and the resulting threat to continued benefits from the planet's ecosystems for future generations.

Multifunctionality (agriculture): Local diversified farming systems perform a variety of social and environmental services, such as stabilizing rural populations, providing various employments, retaining biodiversity, and restoring soil and hydrological cycles and natural pollination (in addition to aesthetic functions of landscape and fresh foods).

Multipolarity: The proliferation of regional trade agreements, as WTO multilateralism and U.S. global hegemony have subsided, alongside the rise of economically powerful states, such as the BRICS.

Multistakeholderism: A term coined by the World Economic Forum in 2019 to evoke a broader constituency at stake in global capitalist governance than Milton Friedman's "shareholder capitalism," even as the WEF referred to corporations as the "trustees of society." This term shaped the UN Food System Summit in 2021, to advance corporate governance of the world food order.

National Adaptation Programme of Action: Institutionalized adaptation measures designed to manage climate change impact on human and ecological systems.

Nation-state: A political unit defined territorially in which state organizations monopolize military power and govern citizens, in the name of development, in return for allegiance to the nation as an "imagined community."

Neoliberalism: A philosophy positing an individual instinct for economic self-interest, justifying elevation of market principles as the organizing logic of society, where private interest trumps the public good.

New International Economic Order (NIEO): A failed initiative pursued by the G-77 countries in 1974 to reform the organization and management of the world economy along more equal and representative lines.

Newly industrializing countries (NICs): Category used to describe middle-income countries of what was then categorized as the Third World that industrialized rapidly and substantially, beginning in the 1960s.

Non-Aligned Movement (NAM): A group of Third World states with progressive and radical leadership that steered an independent course between the two Cold War blocs from the mid-1950s.

Nongovernmental organization (NGO): Private development agency usually geared to financial, educational, empowerment, skill provision, and development training assistance, with varying political impact, and sometimes unaccountable policy influence.

North American Free Trade Agreement (NAFTA): Agreement signed in 1994 between Canada, the United States and Mexico.

Occupy Movement: International youth uprising against deepening socioeconomic inequality, and unemployment, and for social justice and substantive democracy.

Organisation for Economic Cooperation and Development (OECD): The organization of industrialized countries of Western Europe, North America, Japan, Australasia, and now Mexico and South Korea, responsible for gathering data and organizing conferences.

Outsourcing: A reference to the practice of moving parts of a production or value adding chain to contractors abroad, often exploiting weak protections of labor or low environmental standards in order to cut costs and maximize profits.

Permaculture: A holistic (multifunctional) approach to farming that emphasizes sustainable human interaction with ecosystems.

Post-Washington Consensus: The Bretton Woods institutions' move to focus on poverty, suggesting a shift away from the Washington Consensus. However, this has been highly contested.

Poverty Reduction Strategy Papers (PRSPs): Plans for economic and political restructuring prepared by states in partnership with the development agencies, as a way of extending a participatory principle to legitimize the practice of structural adjustment, which lost credibility in the 1990s.

Precariat: Term describing the tenuous condition of a class of unemployed or casually employed workers, generated by rural dispossession, structural unemployment, and outsourcing of jobs.

Privatization: Selling off public property such as national transport systems, public services, or state-owned companies (e.g., energy).

Public Law 480 (PL-480) program: A program instituted by the U.S. government in the mid-1950s to manage the international disposal of agricultural surpluses.

Reducing Emissions from Deforestation and Forest Degradation: A sustainability strategy of "pricing ecosystem services" to reward governments, investors, farmers, and forest dwellers financially for protecting global forests.

Re-peasantization: Contemporary forms of reconstitution of "new peasantries": small and medium-sized farms geared to restoring and sustaining ecological capital as an alternative to high-input agriculture via individual and social farming practices, as well as off-farm activities and forms of agrotourism.

Second World: The designation for those countries belonging to the socialist bloc led by the Soviet Union in the postwar period.

Social contract: The redistributive ethic for securing a rights-based society respecting the dignity of each human being, where states (within cooperative international relations) are responsible for sustaining a just distribution of material and non-material needs.

Social Funds: Emergency funds provided by the World Bank to soften the impact of austerity in the Third World following structural adjustment; these are disseminated through NGOs, often in the form of microcredit.

Social reproduction: Typically feminized forms of social backup to the wage system on the one hand (such as unpaid household labor, public health care, subsistence production), and informal livelihood strategies *in lieu* of public goods.

South-South Cooperation (SSC): The proliferation of political, economic, and diplomatic relations between countries in the global South, as an alternative to a Western-centered international economy.

Structural adjustment: The reallocation of economic resources by a state, typically under conditions laid down by the Bretton Woods institutions to pursue efficiency in the global economy by shrinking government expenditure, reducing wages, removing barriers to investment and trade, and devaluing the national currency.

Subsidiarity: Governance of social and political issues at the appropriate scale, where they can be most effectively and democratically managed.

Sustainability project: An emergent set of quite diverse political, social, and economic initiatives in the twenty-first century driven by the recognition and/or urgency of reducing biodiversity loss, environmental harm, human exposure to pollutants, and greenhouse gas emissions.

Sustainable development: Development practices that meet present needs without compromising the needs of future generations through erosion of the natural resource base.

Sustainable development goals (SDGs): Successor agenda to the Millennial Development Goals in second decade of twenty-first century to reorient UN goals and practices toward redrafting development targets taking on board greater commitments to protecting and restoring environments.

Sustainable intensification: Agribusiness focus on conserving land (soil and water ecosystems) via climate-smart agriculture based in technological interventions to increase output on the same land area.

System of rice intensification (SRI): Method of enhancing irrigated rice productivity without using external agroinputs (chemicals, transgenic seeds, fertilizers).

Technology transfer: The transfer of modern technologies to developing regions.

Third World: A designation for that set of countries belonging to the Non-Aligned Movement and/or the ex-colonies.

Transition towns: Mobilized communities concerned to anticipate "energy descent" by relocalizing economic activity where possible to reduce energy use, recycle waste, develop social cooperation, revalue social reproduction activities, and sustain ecosystems and local economic systems.

Underdevelopment: A concept describing the relational opposite of "development," meaning this is a condition resulting from industrial exploitation through colonial or neocolonial relations.

UN Food System Summit (UNFSS): The 2021 summit in New York City convened by a partnership between the United Nations and the World Economic Forum (WEF) to substitute a select public–private partnership for long-standing multilateralism in governing the global food system, elevating corporate power and practices.

Union of South American Nations (UNASUR): A regional economic integration initiative in as an alliance designed to augment Latin American independence from the United States and the IMF.

United Nations Conference on Trade and Development (UNCTAD): The arm and voice of the Third World in matters of international trade, established in 1964.

United Nations Development Programme (UNDP): An organization of the United Nations that enters into joint-ventures with Third World governments to fund training and other development programs.

United Nations Universal Declaration of Human Rights: The (1948) proclamation of new paradigm of human rights of freedom, equality, life, liberty and security for all, without distinction by race, color, sex, language, religion, political opinion, national or social origin, property, birth, or other status.

Universal Basic Income (UBI): A contemporary social policy to address economic inequality and provide financial security, especially at a time of gig economy, and the need to rehabilitate citizenship.

Urban bias: The stereotyping of rural populations as backward and unproductive, and privileging of urban classes and manufacturing sector to legitimize development strategies.

Value chain agriculture: Incorporation of farming into commodity chains that cross space within or across national territories. The chains include both inputs and outputs: from agribusiness suppliers to processors, retailers, and traders.

Washington Consensus: A set of neoliberal economic policies (trade and financial liberalization, privatization, and macro-stability of the world economy) uniting multilateral institutions, representatives of the United States, and associated G-7 countries that enable corporate globalization.

World Bank: Official title is International Bank for Reconstruction and Development (IBRD); formed in 1944 to channel public funds into large development projects, including infrastructural and energy loans, cash cropping, and, more recently, extractive reserve projects; it acts as a key debt manager via structural adjustment and governance conditions.

World division of labor: A concept accounting for economic specialization across regions linked by migration, trade, and investment relations.

World Economic Forum (WEF): An organization representing political, financial, and corporate elites of the global North, meeting annually in Davos, Switzerland, to monitor and manage the global economy.

World factory: The organization of transnational corporation production across globally dispersed sites serviced by a global labor force.

World farm: A universalized form of agroindustrialization via standardized packages of inputs (seeds, chemicals, machinery) sourcing monocultural crops, factory farms and aquaculture, oriented toward food, feed, fish, and fuel exports.

World Trade Organization (WTO): The organization established in 1995 to regulate the global economy according to the principles of freedom of trade and investment.

World-system analysis: A holistic approach to understanding modern social change as governed by and constituting a historical world-economic system based in an unequal world division of labor, wherein core states and firms exploit peripheral states and peoples for economic advantage.

Zero Budget Natural Farming (ZBNF): A progressive adoption of low-cost methods of agroecological farming in South India by small and medium farmers, spreading via grassroots movements from Andhra Pradesh to supportive neighboring states, with higher crop yields and local food security.

ENDNOTES

CHAPTER 1

1. See, for example, Shilliam (2021).
2. Escobar, Osterwil, and Sharma (2024).
3. Mazzucato (2021).
4. Rodrik (2022).
5. "Why Protecting Indigenous Communities Can Also Help Save the Earth" (2020).
6. Santos (2007).
7. "The Guardian View on Globalisation's Discontent" (2024).
8. Brazil, Russia, India, China, South Africa (the BRICS), and recently Iran, Egypt, Ethiopia, United Arab Republics, Turkey, and Saudi Arabia are an emergent power bloc.
9. Damiano (2024); Lacayo (2024).
10. Romero and Kovaleski (2023); Wang (2023).
11. Travelli (2024).
12. Stiglitz (2024).
13. Quoted in Dehghan (2020).
14. Ibid.
15. World Meterological Association (2023).
16. Kolbert (2024).
17. Alvaredo et al. (2018: 15).
18. Quoted in Esteva (1992: 6).
19. Quoted in United Nations (2006: 3).
20. Hodal (2020).
21. Beuret (2019).
22. Ibid.
23. Quoted in Debroy (2017).
24. Stiglitz (2019).
25. Quoted in N. Klein (2014: 17).
26. Gawande (2020).
27. Quoted in Williams (2017: 24).
28. Cowan and Shenton (1996).
29. Ibid.
30. T. Mitchell (1991: 68–75, 96).
31. A. Smith (1776/1904).
32. Polanyi (1944/2001).
33. Rostow (1960).
34. Singer (1950); Prebisch (1962); Lenin (1916/1997).
35. Frank (1970: 5, 7).
36. Amin (1972: 118); see also Rodney (1972/2018).
37. Rodney (1972/2018).
38. Ibid., 293.
39. Ibid., 300.
40. Wallerstein (1974).
41. Nandy (2002: 115, 111).
42. Huntington (1968: 32–37).
43. Rodale Institute (2019).
44. "Connecting Smallholders to Markets" (2016); McKeon (2018: 2).
45. United Nations Development Programme (2011).
46. Millennium Ecosystem Assessment (2005).
47. E. Wolf (1969); Cooper (1997: 66–67); Davis (2001).
48. Marx (1965).
49. Polanyi (1944/2001).
50. United Nations Development Programme (2009: iii).
51. Brecher, Costello, and Smith (2000).
52. Barnet and Cavanagh (1994: 383); Crossette (1997).
53. Galeano (2000: 25).
54. Selwyn (2018).
55. World Bank (2008: 20).
56. Sen (1999: 74).

CHAPTER 2

1. James (1963); Fanon (1967); Memmi (1967).
2. Shilliam (2014).
3. For a critical discussion, see Hobson (2012).
4. Goody (1996); Hobson (2004).
5. Weber and Weber (2020a); Fanon (1967); Memmi (1967).
6. Watson (2015).
7. Davidson (1992: 83, 99–101).
8. Quoted in Rist (1997: 58).
9. Shilliam (2015, 2020); James (1963); Coulthard (2014).
10. Bunker (1985).
11. Friedmann (1999: 39).
12. Bujra (1992: 146).
13. Quoted in Stavrianos (1981: 247).
14. Day (2010: 25); see also *Better Cotton Initiative*, www.bettercotton.org.
15. McMichael (1984); Tomich (2004).
16. T. Ali (2002: 168). On resistance to the hut and poll tax in colonial Kenya, for example, see Doty (1996: 54, especially endnote 3).
17. Doty (1996: 17, 66, 101, 108, 112).
18. Chirot (1977: 124).
19. Davis (2001: 26, 299, 315).
20. Ibid., 328–29.
21. Ibid., 332–35.
22. E. Wolf (1982: 369, 377).
23. Cooper and Stoler (1997).
24. James (1963).
25. Memmi (1967: 74).
26. Fanon (1967: 254–55).
27. Cooper (1997).
28. Ibid., 66–67.
29. Stavrianos (1981: 624).
30. Quoted in Clarke and Barlow (1997: 9).
31. C. Duncan (1996: 120).
32. International Development Advisory Board (1951: see esp. iii).
33. Adams (1993: 2–3, 6–7).
34. Quoted in Esteva (1992: 6).
35. Quoted in B. Davidson (1992: 167).
36. Esteva (1992: 7).
37. Rist (1997: 79).
38. Ake (1996: 36).
39. Wilder (2015).
40. Cited in Cooper (1997: 79).
41. Rostow (1960).
42. Quoted in Hettne (1990: 3).
43. Bose (1997: 153).
44. D. Lehman (1990: 5–6).
45. Ibid.
46. Cardoso and Faletto (1979: 129–31).
47. Shilliam (2014); Rajagopal (2003); Getachew (2019).

CHAPTER 3

1. Block (1977: 76–77).
2. Quoted in Brett (1985: 106–7).
3. R. E. Wood (1986: 38–61).
4. Rich (1994: 72).
5. Woods (2006: 207).
6. Rich (1994: 58); George and Sabelli (1994: 15); C. Thomas (1985).
7. Rich (1994: 73).
8. Ibid., 75.
9. Weber (2016); Bogues (2011).
10. Adams (1993: 68–69).
11. Quoted in Magdoff (1969: 54).
12. Magdoff (1969: 124); Chirot (1977: 164–65); Taffet (2007).
13. Weber (2016: 155).
14. Quoted in G. Williams (1981: 6–57).
15. Brett (1985: 209); R. E. Wood (1986: 73); Rist (1997: 88).
16. Brett (1985: 209); R. E. Wood (1986: 73).
17. Adams (1993: 73).
18. Weber (2016: 157, emphasis added).
19. Rist (1997: 152–53).

20. C. Thomas (1985).
21. Pilger (2002: 28).
22. Ibid., 26–39.
23. C. Thomas (1987: 148).
24. Ibid., 154.
25. C. Thomas (1987: 146–97); Bogues (2011).
26. The term newly industrializing countries (NICs) was coined by the Organisation for Economic Co-Operation and Development in 1979, and it included four southern European countries: Spain, Portugal, Yugoslavia, and Greece. The common attributes of NICs were rapid penetration of the world market with manufactured exports, a rising share of industrial employment, and an increase in real gross domestic product per capita relative to the First World. See Hoogvelt (1987: 25).
27. Brett (1985: 185–86).
28. Ibid., 188.
29. Knox and Agnew (1994: 347).
30. Hoogvelt (1987: 64).
31. Knox and Agnew (1994: 331). Between 1975 and 1989, this group enlarged to include China, South Africa, Thailand, and Taiwan; Argentina dropped out.
32. Martin and Schumann (1997: 100–101).
33. N. Harris (1987: 102).
34. Grigg (1993: 251).
35. Revel and Riboud (1986: 43–44).
36. Grigg (1993: 243–44); Bradley and Carter (1989: 104). Self-sufficiency measures do not necessarily reveal the state of nutrition in a country or region since a country—for example, Japan—may have a low self-sufficiency because its population eats an affluent diet, which depends on imports.
37. Friedmann (1982).
38. See Magdoff (1969: 135).
39. Dudley and Sandilands (1975).
40. Friedmann (1990: 20).
41. Perkins (1997).
42. Friedmann (1990: 20; 1992: 373).
43. McMichael and Raynolds (1994: 322). The terms peasant foods and wage foods are from de Janvry (1981).
44. Segelken (1995: 5).
45. Wessel (1983: 158).
46. Berlan (1991: 126–27); see also Dixon (2002).
47. Burbach and Flynn (1980: 66); George (1977: 171).
48. Friedmann (1992: 377).
49. Gupta (1998: 53, 58–59).
50. Kloppenburg (1988: xiv).
51. Gupta (1998: 54); Busch and Lacy (1983).
52. Gupta (1998: 54–56).
53. Patnaik (2003: 13).
54. Gupta (1998: 50).
55. Patel (2007: 146–47).
56. Cleaver (1977: 17); Walker (2004: 185).
57. Quoted in Gupta (1998: 4).
58. Shiva (1997: 50–51); Barndt (2008: 38–39).
59. Newman (2006: 1).
60. George (1977: 174–75).
61. Patel (2013).
62. Griffin (1974); Pearse (1980); Byres (1981); Sanderson (1986b); Dhanagare (1988); Raikes (1988); Llambi (1990).
63. Lipton (1977).
64. McMichael and Kim (1994); Araghi (1995).
65. Grigg (1993: 103–4, 185); Araghi (1995).
66. Deere and Leon (2001: 332).
67. Rich (1994: 95, 155).
68. Davis (2006).
69. Prashad (2007: xv)

CHAPTER 4

1. Busan Declaration 2011 (2011: especially pp. 4 and 10).

2. Ricardo (1817/1951).
3. Cerny (1997).
4. Gill (2002).
5. Public Citizen (2004).
6. Harvey (2003).
7. Barnet and Cavanagh (1994: 236).
8. Klare (2002: 14–17).
9. George (1992: 11).
10. Bello (1994: 59); Nash (1994: C4).
11. Rich (1994: 188).
12. Quoted in Bello (1994: 63).
13. Quoted in Saul (2005: 209).
14. Ruggiero (2000: xiii, xv).
15. Roodman (2001: 21).
16. Lissakers (1993: 67).
17. Singh (1992: 141).
18. Quoted in Roodman (2001: 30).
19. Barkin (1990:104–5).
20. George (1988: 41, 49).
21. Quoted in Roodman (2001: 35).
22. Graham (1994); Beneria (2003: 55); Kohl and Farthing (2006: 62, 72).
23. Cheru (1989: 24, 27–28, 41–42); Redding (2000).
24. Rich (1994: 186–87).
25. Singh (1992: 138–39, 147–48).
26. Bello (1994).
27. George (1992: 97).
28. Cox (1987: 301).
29. Calculated from Crook (1993: 16); N. Avery (1994: 95); Hoogvelt (1997: 138).
30. Crook (1993: 9).
31. Crook (1993: 16).
32. Canak (1989).
33. Beckman (1992: 99).
34. J. Sachs (1998: 17).
35. C. Thomas (1987: 1–38); Rist (1997: 130–32).
36. Woods (2006: 168).
37. Wolfensohn (2000).
38. Narayan (2002); Rademacher and Patel (2002).
39. Woods (2006: 168).
40. Fraser (2005: 317).
41. Ibid., 318.
42. Quoted in Weber (2004: 197).
43. Harrison (2004).
44. Quoted in Fraser (2005: 336).
45. Goldman (2005: 229–30).
46. Kagarlitsky (1995); Kolko (1988: 278–96); N. Klein (2007).
47. Quoted in Saul (2005: 209).
48. Ruggiero (2000: xiii, xv).
49. Black (2002: 62).
50. McMichael (1993).
51. Adams (1993: 196–97).
52. Middleton, O'Keefe, and Moyo (1993: 127–29).
53. Quoted in Watkins (1991: 44).
54. Quoted in M. Ritchie (1993: n. 25).
55. Quoted in Wallach and Sforza (1999: x).
56. Quoted in Ransom (2001b: 27).
57. Quoted in Wallach and Woodall (2004: 219).
58. K. Lehman and Krebs (1996); Gorelick (2000: 28–30); Madeley (2000: 75); Carlsen (2003).
59. McMichael (2005).
60. LeQuesne (1997).
61. Dawkins (2000).
62. Tuxill (1999).
63. ActionAid International (2001: 2).
64. Clarke (2001).
65. Ibid.
66. Krajewski (2022: 151).
67. Ibid.

CHAPTER 5

1. Selwyn (2018).
2. Selwyn (2017); Sunil (2021).
3. Levin (2022).
4. UN-Habitat (2022: 73).
5. UM-Habitat (2022: 84).
6. Consider indicatively California's wildfires and its central role in supplying almonds to a world market in which almond milk is advocated as a

"climate smart" alternative to dairy.

7. Bebbington, Fash, and Rogan (2019: 87).
8. Rai and Goldblatt (2020); Rai (2024).
9. Complemented by offshore financial havens—see Palan (2003).
10. Bond (2006: 82–83).
11. Iriart, Waitzkin, and Herhy (2004: para. 18).
12. Iriart et al. (2004).
13. See Gereffi (1994).
14. Canas and Gilmer (2009).
15. H. French (2000: 83–85).
16. J. W. Foster (2005: 215); Macdonald (2005: 31).
17. Fuentes and Ehrenreich (1983).
18. Elson and Pearson (1981: 91).
19. Perrons (2005: 169).
20. W. I. Robinson (2004: 18).
21. Martin and Schumann (1997: 100–101).
22. Friedman (2000: 52); Greenlees (2006).
23. Caulkin (2007); Kala (2015).
24. C. Freeman (2000: 23–48, 65).
25. Harding (2001: 23).
26. Leader (2004); A. R. Müller and Patel (2004); Tripathi (2004).
27. Davis (2006: 172).
28. Watkins (2006).
29. Chan (1996).
30. Eyferth, Ho, and Vermeer (2003).
31. Gereffi (1994).
32. Vasquez (2023).
33. Dugger (2004).
34. Corrado (2011).
35. Moriarty (2022).
36. Bauman (2004).
37. Saul (2005: 146).
38. Kennedy (2001).
39. Davis (2006: 169, 199).
40. Quoted in ActionAid (2004: 11).
41. Via Campesina (2000).
42. Sengupta (2015).
43. Richburb (2022: 29).
44. Hochschild (2003).
45. Montalbano (1991: F1); Ride (1998: 9).
46. World Bank (2014).
47. World Bank (2023).
48. Tan (1991b).
49. Ball (1990).
50. Tan (1991a).
51. Pattisson et al. (2021).
52. Quoted in Perrons (2005: 220).
53. Mize and Swords (2010).
54. Minkoff-Zern (2019).
55. Standing (2013).
56. Scully (2016).
57. Weghmann (2019).
58. World Bank (2020).
59. Davis (2006: 1–2).
60. R. Boyd (2006: 491, 495, 497).
61. D. Harvey (2005: 127); R. Boyd (2006: 493–94).
62. Cited in "China's Forgotten Peasants" (2006).
63. ActionAid (2004: 35–36, 40).
64. Davis (2006: 190).
65. Bond (2006: 58).
66. Ferguson (2006: 194).
67. D. Harvey (2005: 139); Watts (2005–2006: 36).
68. M. Elliott (2007: 23).
69. McGreal (2006–2007: 6); Brautigam (2009).
70. All quoted in H. W. French (2010).
71. Quoted in Muchena (2006: 23).
72. McGreal (2006–2007: 6).
73. C. Lee (2009: 652).
74. Bond (2006: 60).
75. Muchena (2006: 24–25).
76. Bond (2006: 74); Turner (2007).
77. Obi (2019).
78. Byerlee et al. (2011: 16).
79. Scott (2015).
80. UNAC and GRAIN (2015: 3).
81. Quoted in Vidal (2010).
82. Quoted in Daniel (2009: 28).

83. Sanderson (1986a); Raynolds et al. (1993); Raynolds (1994).
84. See Patel (2013).
85. Friedland (1994).
86. FAO (2011).

CHAPTER 6

1. Therborn (2022: 37).
2. Vince (2022).
3. Haagh (2019: 9).
4. Oxfam (2023: 4).
5. H. Stewart (2015: 14).
6. Livingston (2024).
7. Funk (2014: 6).
8. Standing (2013 46–47).
9. Titumir and Kamal (2013: 173, 175); Hill (2018).
10. Standing (2013: 52).
11. Bunting (2010); Standing (2013).
12. Younge (2019).
13. Plecher (2020).
14. Alvaredo et al. (2018: 9, 11).
15. Standing (2013: 29).
16. Savio (2015).
17. Iglesias (2015a: 35).
18. Santos (2015).
19. Beas (2011).
20. Wolfensohn (2000).
21. UNDESA (2010: 11).
22. Credit Suisse ABS (2023: 9).
23. Titumir and Kamal (2013: 173); Wike (2014).
24. Sader (2008: 6).
25. Landsberg (2010).
26. Polanyi (1944/2001).
27. Tran (2011).
28. Ehrenreich (2019).
29. Gleckman (2019, 96).
30. Schwab (2019).
31. Schwab and Malleret (2020, 37, 41, 53).
32. Canfield, Anderson, and McMichael (2021); McMichael (2021).
33. Letter to UN Secretary-General, https://www.foodsovereignty.org/wp-content/uploads/2020/02/EN_Edited_draft-letter-UN-food-systems-summit_070220-4.pdf
34. McCoy (2018).
35. M. Wolf (2010: 7).
36. Ding (2018).
37. Hervieu (2011: 11).
38. Glennie (2011: 44).
39. McMichael (2020: 16).
40. Onyekwena and Ekeruche (2019).
41. Therborn (2011: 52–53).
42. Swanson (2019).
43. Brad Setser, quoted in Farrer and Kuo (2019).
44. Zacharopoulou and Al-Mashat (2023).
45. The White House (2021).
46. Stiglitz (2023).
47. Stiglitz (2022).
48. Hendrikse (2018: 169 italics added).
49. Bello (2020a).
50. Riley (2023).
51. Mishra (2017).
52. Roy (2019).
53. Hendrikse (2021).
54. Slobodian (2018).
55. Crouch (2018: 1).
56. Ibid., 3.
57. Quoted in Williams (2017: 24).
58. Subacchi (2023).
59. Bello (2020a).
60. Suwandi, Jonna, and Foster (2019).
61. Wu (2020).
62. Monbiot (2022).
63. Krueger (2023).
64. Kaboub (2023).
65. Bretton Woods Project (2023).
66. Eurodad (2023).
67. Ghosh (2023b).
68. World Bank (2022).
69. Kaboub (2023).
70. Wolfenden (2023).
71. Ghosh (2024).
72. Ghosh (2023a).
73. Bello (2020b).
74. Clapp (2020).
75. Bello and Feffer (2009).
76. Bello (2020b).
77. Kara (2023: 10).

78. Alvarez (2018).
79. Brand and Wissen (2021).

CHAPTER 7

1. Quoted in Prashad (2023).
2. Elliott (2024).
3. Rodrik (2011: xvi).
4. Quinn Slobodian, quoted in Immerwahr (2023: 22).
5. Immerwahr (2023: 23).
6. Ibid.
7. According to historian Nils Gilman, Immerwahr (2023: 24–25).
8. Ruggiero (2000: xiii, xv).
9. Quoted in Bello (2020a).
10. Ong (2006: 3, 7. Emphasis added).
11. Oliveira (2018: 118).
12. Acharya (2017: 11).
13. Hopewell (2016, 18).
14. Ibid., 180.
15. "UN's Guterres" (2023).
16. Tooze (2023).
17. Shidore (2023).
18. Ibid.
19. Lama (2023).
20. Tooze (2023).
21. Adebajo (2023).
22. Brooks (2024).
23. Yu Jie (2024).
24. Jones and Zeng (2019).
25. Hu (2015).
26. Kaiman (2017).
27. Tortajada and Zhang (2021).
28. McBride et al. (2023: 2, 6).
29. Wallace-Wells (2023).
30. Ibid.
31. Krueger (2023).
32. Tortajada and Zhang (2021).
33. Bobin (2006: 17).
34. Suwandi et al. (2019).
35. Dirlik (2017: 63).
36. Scoones et al. (2016: 8–9).
37. Benabdallah (2019: 100).
38. Bradsher (2023a).
39. McMichael (2020).
40. Ibid., 126.
41. Zhang (2023).
42. Hawkins (2023).
43. Hung (2023).
44. Cited in Zeng (2019: 578).
45. Babones (2019: 59, 69).
46. Hung (2023).
47. El-Erian (2023).
48. Mackenzie and Sahay (2023).
49. "China's Belt and Road Initiative Is Boosting Science" (2023).
50. Mazzucato (2021: 18).
51. Rodrik (2022).
52. Stiglitz (2023).
53. Stiglitz (2019a).
54. Naidu, Tzarevski, and Nxumalo (2023).
55. Coetzer (2023).
56. Naidu et al. (2023).
57. Mazzucato (2023).
58. Quoted in Kolhatkar (2017).
59. Center for Strategic and International Studies (2023).
60. Boles (2023).
61. Subbarao (2020).
62. Kolhatkar (2017).
63. Atkinson (2023).
64. Cheng et al. (2019: 74).
65. Bradsher (2023b).
66. Masters (2021: 367).
67. Quoted in Masters (2021: 366).
68. Games (2023).
69. Asghar et al. (2020: 2).
70. Crawford (2024).
71. African Development Bank Group (2023).
72. Masters (2021: 366, 369, 372, 364).
73. Sengupta (2023).
74. The Economist (2023).
75. "Countries Need to Make Good" (2024). See also Convention on Biological Diversity: https://www.cbd.int
76. Mazzucato (2024, emphasis added).

77. Stewart (2023).
78. Smialek and Swanson (2024).
79. Wallace-Wells (2023).
80. Lee (2023).
81. Institute for Security and Development Policy (2018).
82. Swanson and Clark (2024).
83. Müller, Ghiotto, and Bárcena (2024: 14).
84. Institute for Security and Development Policy (2018).
85. Hopewell (2020: 29, 19, 60).
86. Smialik and Swanson (2024).
87. Ibid.
88. Müller et al. (2024: 4).
89. Roberts and Lamp (2023).
90. Müller et al. (2024: 4).
91. Society for Mining, Metallurgy and Exploration (2024).
92. Robinson (2022).
93. Müller et al. (2024: 10).
94. Stewart (2023).
95. Müller et al. (2024: 8).
96. Robinson (2022).
97. Ibid.
98. Aranoff et al. (2019: 150–151).
99. Copeland (2019, 22).
100. Dearing (2023).
101. IPES-Food and ETC Group (2021: 55, 5).
102. Ibid., 16.
103. Stone (2022: 8).
104. Lappé (2022); also see Leguizamón (2020).
105. Fraser (2019).
106. IPES-Food and ETC Group (2021: 63).
107. Fraser (2019: 899).
108. Stone (2022: 5, 9).
109. Newell and Taylor (2018: 17).
110. Biovision Foundation for Ecological Development & IPES-Food (2020: 4).
111. La Vía Campesina (2018).
112. Rosset and Altieri (2017, 75); Khadse et al. (2018).
113. Prause, Hackfort, and Lindgren (2021).

CHAPTER 8

1. UNFCCC (2002: 26).
2. Quoted in N. Klein (2014: 22).
3. Allington (2023).
4. Malm (2016: 9).
5. Quoted in Milman (2023).
6. Lacayo (2024).
7. Pascoe (2014: 145, italics added).
8. Rivas (2017: 73).
9. Lindeman (2020: 33).
10. McMichael (1984: 41).
11. Oltermann (2024).
12. B. Tucker and Talaat (2023).
13. Anisa (2023).
14. Colman (2022); Nogrady (2024).
15. Martinez-Alier et al. (2016: 14).
16. Watts (2023).
17. WAVES (Wealth Accounting and the Valuation of Ecosystem Services): https://www.wavespartnership.org/; Sward and Le Lannou (2024).
18. Kenis and Leviens (2015: 49).
19. Slawson (2023).
20. Ervine (2018); Buck (2021).
21. Lovelock (2007: 15, 17).
22. N. Klein (2014: 175).
23. Ibid., 18–19.
24. Ibid., 19, 18 (italics added).
25. Hunt (2023).
26. Akkerman et al. (2022: 1).
27. Niranjan (2023).
28. F. Harvey (2023).
29. Mazzucato et al. (2022).
30. Swanborough (2019).
31. M. Harris (2020): 32.
32. "Speeches of Greta Thunberg" (n.d.).
33. Ellis (2023).
34. Funk (2014: 52).
35. Swanson (2023).

36. Quoted in Funk (2014: 45).
37. Ibid., 46.
38. Buck (2019: 198).
39. Ibid., 200–202.
40. R. Klein et al. (2008: 4).
41. Storm (2009).
42. McAfee (2012).
43. Einhorn and Andreoni (2023/2024).
44. W. Sachs (1993: xvi).
45. Hildyard (1993: 34).
46. Monbiot (2022).
47. Pretty, Toulmin, and Williams (2011).
48. Royal Society (2009).
49. H. Ritchie (2024).
50. Flannery (2009: 86–93).
51. Quoted in Abergel (2011: 267).
52. "How to Feed a Hungry World" (2010: 531).
53. Perfecto, Vandermeer, and Wright (2009).
54. Matusse, quoted in Perfecto et al. (2009).
55. Byerlee et al. (2011: xiv).
56. European Commission (2010).
57. World Bank (2007b: 8); Mittal (2009: 5).
58. Maathai (2010: 236).
59. Funk (2014: 249).
60. Weiss (2008: 4). See also Green America (2013).
61. Mittal (2009).
62. Malkan (2024).
63. Schloredt (2019).
64. Wise (n.d.).
65. Quoted in Funk (2014: 247).
66. Lim (2008).
67. La Via Campesina (2015).
68. Zaitchik (2023).
69. United Nations (2014).
70. Taylor (2018: 93).
71. Clapp, Newell, and Brent (2018: 84).
72. A. Collins (2018).
73. Taylor (2018: 90).
74. Gioia (2018: 1403–4); see also IPES-Food (2017: 75).
75. United Nations (2014).
76. Taylor (2018: 93).
77. "Corporate-Smart Greenwash" (2014).
78. Ibid.
79. De Schutter (2011).
80. Altieri (2008); Contiero (2012).
81. Uphoff (2003).
82. Quoted in Vidal (2019).
83. European Court of Auditors (2023).
84. Ibid.
85. Fairley (2022).
86. GRAIN (2007: 6).
87. World Bank (2007a).
88. Quoted in Ferrett (2007).
89. Rainforest Action Network (2018).
90. Cargill (2015: 86).
91. Fargione et al. (2008).
92. "'Tsunami of Data'" (2017).
93. Millennium Ecosystem Assessment (2005: 20).
94. Ibid., 1.
95. Bullard (2011: 141–42).

CHAPTER 9

1. Mulyana et al. (2013).
2. Kishimoto and Petitjean (2017: 11).
3. Ibid., 162–63.
4. Ibid., 37–38, 46, 95–97, 166, 107.
5. Environmental Performance Index (2022).
6. Howe (2024).
7. ClearIAS (2024).
8. H. Ritchie (2024: 83–84, 89–90).
9. Government of South Australia (2023).
10. Government of South Australia (2023).
11. Chavez and Peñaranda (2024).
12. S. Naidu et al. (2019).
13. Florini, LaForge, and Slaughter (2023: 155–57).

14. Quoted in N. Klein (2014: 101–2).
15. Jha (2010).
16. D'Armagnac (2010: 31)
17. Jha (2010).
18. Goldemberg and Lucon (2010:18).
19. Shi (2010: 35).
20. Arthur (2010: 31).
21. Dreyfuss (2010: 14).
22. Krauss and Bradsher (2014).
23. Quoted in Krauss (2010: D7).
24. Popovich (2023); Plumer and Popovich (2024).
25. Madhok (2024).
26. Acciona (2023).
27. UN-HABITAT (2016).
28. Yazdani and Dola (2013: 43).
29. Parnell, Pieterse, and Watson (2009).
30. Dictus (2015: 21).
31. Ishii (2014).
32. Kokkinos (2016).
33. Robertson (2019).
34. Shapiro (2014: 110).
35. Ibid., 119.
36. Cities for Climate Protection Program: https://en.wikipedia.org/wiki/Cities_for_Climate_Protection_program
37. Rydge and Bassi (2014: 1, 14).
38. Ellen McArthur Foundation (n.d.b).
39. Ellen McArthur Foundation (n.d.a).
40. M. Lee (2013).
41. Transition Network: http://www.transitionnetwork.org.
42. Southend in Transition (2007).
43. Gibson-Graham (2006: 188, 166).
44. Harlan (2011: 30).
45. Escobar (2011: 138).
46. Ibid.
47. Vidal (2011: 7).
48. Bullard (2011: 141–42).
49. Quoted in Escobar (2011: 138).
50. Esobar (2011: 139).
51. GRAIN (2022).
52. Quoted in Leahy (2008).
53. W. Wood (2019: 22).
54. La Via Campesina (2009).
55. Pimbert (2023).
56. Quoted in Ainger (2003: 10).
57. La Via Campesina (2012).
58. Declaration of the Terra Preta Forum on the Food Crisis (2008).
59. Rosset and Altieri (2017: 69).
60. Payne et al. (2017).
61. HLPE (2013: 11–12).
62. Rodale Institute (2019).
63. Altieri and Toledo (2011: 596).
64. FAO (2015).
65. "Trucost Reveals the $3 Trillion Environmental Cost of Farming" (2015).
66. Van der Ploeg (2010: 4).
67. Coordination Paysanne Européene (CPE, 2003).
68. Smithers (2019).
69. Quoted in Rosset and Altieri (2017: 2, italics added).
70. Rosset and Altieri (2017: 3).
71. A. Mann (2019: 93).
72. Ledford (2024).
73. Ghanem (2022).
74. Gliessman (2018: 6).
75. World Bank (2017).
76. Sengupta and Farah (2023).
77. ActionAid International (2008: 28).
78. Pionetti (2005: 154).
79. Fraser (2019).
80. IPES-Food and ETC Group (2021: 63).
81. Stone (2022: 8).
82. Lappé (2020).
83. Ibid.
84. Rosset and Altieri (2017: 75).
85. Gliessman (2018: 2).
86. Rosset and Altieri (2017: 76).
87. HLPE (2013: 34).

88. Van der Ploeg (2008); also Da Viá (2012).
89. Rosset and Altieri (2017: 109–10); A. Mann (2019: 94).
90. McKeon (2015: 153); Gaarde (2017: 151).
91. De Schutter and Yambi (2020).
92. Ibid., 17–18.
93. Ibid., 20.

CHAPTER 10

1. Weber (2014, 2017); Weber and Weber (2020b).
2. Noor (2024).
3. M. Friedman (1962).
4. Quoted in J. W. Mason (2018).
5. Polanyi (1944/2001: 73).
6. Shah (2020: 6).
7. Quoted in Carrington (2020).
8. Quoted in Toulmin (2009: 2).
9. Charles Eisenstein, quoted in Buck (2019: 101).
10. Ruggie (1993: 173).
11. Millennium Ecosystem Assessment (2005: 20, emphasis added).
12. Ibid., 24.
13. Latouche (2004: 15).
14. Quoted in Godoy (2010: 19).
15. Martinez-Alier (2010).
16. Oks and Williams (2022: 3).
17. Jackson (2017: 187).
18. Ibid., 200–201.
19. Schmelzer et al. (2022: 295).
20. Dunlop (2017).
21. I. Tucker (2020).
22. Keegan (2018).
23. Ibid.
24. Matthews (2017).
25. Haagh (2019: 137).
26. Standing (2020).
27. Renaud Camus, quoted in Williams (2017: 24).
28. Cohen (2019: 12–13, 14, 25).
29. Quoted in Jackson (2017: 193).
30. Lederer (2019).
31. Graeber (2019).
32. Simms (2019).
33. Raworth (2017a: 53).
34. Quoted in Monbiot (2017).
35. Quoted in Jackson (2017: 141).
36. Raworth (2017c).
37. Kolbert (2024).
38. Raworth (2017a: 54).
39. Stiglitz (2019b).
40. Review of Keynesian Economics (2020).
41. Ambrose (2019).
42. Watts (2020: 28).
43. N. Klein (2019).
44. UNEP (2011: 16).
45. Aronoff et al. (2019: 51).
46. Buck (2019: 204–5).
47. Aronoff et al. (2019: 55).
48. Carrington (2019).
49. Representative Alexandria Ocasio-Cortez and Senator Ed Markey, "House Resolution 109," quoted in Holt-Giménez and Kleiner (2019).
50. Kelleher (2019).
51. Aronoff et al. (2019: 25).
52. Haass (2020).
53. Weber (2014, 2017); Weber and Weber (2020b).
54. Global Goals: https://www.globalgoals.org/resources/
55. Smith and Gladstein (2018: 4–5); Spicer (2020).
56. Quoted in Easterly (2015).
57. For a critical discussion of migration, development and the SDGs, see Suliman (2017).
58. McMichael (2013).
59. Quoted in Sexsmith and McMichael (2015: 587).
60. Blesh et al., (2019: 1).
61. Ibid., i
62. Ibid., ii.

63. United Nations (2019: 39).
64. Haagh (2019: 106, emphasis added).
65. Ehrenreich (2019).
66. Tullis (2023); Cokelaere and Brzeziński (2024).
67. Mann and Wainwright (2018: 45).
68. Mann and Wainwright (2018: 175).
69. Jackson (2017: 191).
70. Kenis and Lievens (2015: 151).
71. Edelman and Borras (2016: 216, 130).
72. Ibid., 134.
73. Ibid., 144.
74. McMichael (2021).
75. Zuboff (2019).
76. Quoted in Naughton (2019).

REFERENCES

Abergel, Elizabeth. "Climate-Ready Crops and Bio-Capitalism: Towards a New Food Regime?" *International Journal of Sociology of Agriculture and Food* 18, no. 3 (2011): 260–74.

Acharya, Amitav. "After Liberal Hegemony: The Advent of a Multiplex World Order." *Ethics & International Affairs*, September 8, 2017. https://www.ethicsandinternationalaffairs.org/2017/multiplexworld-order/.

ActionAid International. "Crops and Robbers." October 2001. https://www.actionaid.org.uk/sites/default/files/doc_lib/crops_robbers.pdf.

ActionAid International. *Power Hungry: Six Reasons to Regulate Global Food Corporations*. Rome: ActionAid International, 2004.

ActionAid International. *Hungry for Solutions? Progress Towards Securing the Right to Food Ten Years After the World Food Summit*. Johannesburg: ActionAid International, 2006. http://allafrica.com/download/resource/main/main/idatcs/00011055:b812889136c5906cdf449b4208ae6687.pdf.

ActionAid International. "We Know What We Need: South Asian Women Speak Out on Climate Change." *ActionAid International*, 2007. http://reliefweb.int/sites/relief-web.int/files/resources/4B96B48680BB519DC12573A1005007A1-actionaid_nov2007.pdf.

ActionAid International. The Time Is NOW: Lessons from Farmers Adapting to Climate Change. 2008. http://www.actionaid.org/publications/time-now-lessons-farmers-adapting-climate-change.

Adams, Nassau A. *Worlds Apart: The North-South Divide and the International System*. London: Zed, 1993.

Adebajo, Adekeye. "Goodbye Multipolarity: Hello Bipolarity." *Wall Street Journal*, December 31, 2023. https://www.livemint.com/politics/policy/goodbye-multipolarity-hello-bipolarity-11704037365561.html.

Adebajo, Adekeye, Ian Bremmer, Stephen G. Brooks, Paula J. Dobriansky, Jorge Heine, Ana Palacio, and Yu Jie. "The Shape of Power in 2024." *Project Syndicate Quarterly. The Year Ahead 2024*, (December 11, 2023): 72. https://www.project-syndicate.org/magazine/multipolarity-non-alignment-global-order-2024-by-adekeye-adebajo-et-al-2023-12.

African Development Bank Group. "African Economic Conference 2023: "Africa Can Leapfrog to the 4th Industrial Revolution with the Right Skills and Policies."" November 20, 2023. https://www.afdb.org/en/news-and-events/african-economic-conference-2023-africa-can-leapfrog-4th-industrial-revolution-right-skills-and-policies-66022.

Agarwal, Bina. "Patriarchy and the 'Modernising State': An Introduction." In *Structures of Patriarchy: The State, the Community and the Household*, edited by Bina Agarwal. London: Zed, 1988.

Ainger, Katherine. "The New Peasants' Revolt." *New Internationalist* 353 (January/February 2003): 9–13.

Ake, Claude. *Democracy and Development in Africa*. Washington, DC: Brookings Institution, 1996.

Akkerman, Mark, Deborah Burton, Nick Buxton, Ho-Chih Lin, Muhammed Al-Kashef, and Wendela de Vries. "Climate Collateral. How Military Spending Accelerates Climate Breakdown." *Transnational Institute*, (2022).

Ali, Tariq. *The Clash of Fundamentalisms: Crusades,*

Jihads, and Modernity. London: Verso, 2002.

Allington, Ginger. "This holiday, consider the true cost of cheap cashmere." *New York Times*, December 16, 2023. https://www.nytimes.com/2023/12/16/opinion/holidays-environment-cashmere.html.

Almeida, Adam. "England's Ludicrous Experiment in Privatised Water Is Coming to a Messy End." *The Guardian*, March 28, 2024. https://www.theguardian.com/commentisfree/2024/mar/28/thames-water-privatised-public-ownership.

Altieri, Miguel. "Small Farms as a Planetary Ecological Asset: Five Key Reasons Why We Should Support the Revitalization of Small Farms in the Global South." *Food First*, January 2008. http://www.researchgate.net/publication/237427498_Small_Farms_as_a_Planetary_Eco-logical_Asset_Five_Key_Reasons_Why_We_Should_Support_the_Revitalisation_of_Small_Farms_in_the_Global_South.

Altieri, Miguel A., and Victor Manuel Toledo. "The Agroecological Revolution in Latin America: Rescuing Nature, Ensuring Food Sovereignty, and Empowering Peasants." *Journal of Peasant Studies* 38, no. 3 (2011): 587–612.

Alvaredo, Facundo, Lucas Chancel, Thomas Piketty, Emmanuel Saez, and Gabriel Zucman. "World Inequality Report 2018." *World Inequality Lab*. https://wir2018.wid.world/files/download/wir2018-full-report-english.pdf.

Alvarez, Maximillian. ""The End of the End of History." In Evil Empire. A Reckoning with Power." *Boston Review*, (2018): 1–2.

Ambrose, Jillian. "Rise of Renewables May See Off Oil Firms Decades Earlier Than They Think." *The Guardian*, October 14, 2019. https://www.theguardian.com/environment/2019/oct/14/rise-renewables-oil-firms-decades-earlier-think.

Amenga-Etego, Rudolf. "Stalling the Big Steal." *New Internationalist* 354 (2003): 20–21.

Amin, Samir. "Underdevelopment and Dependence in Black Africa: Historical Origin." *Journal of Peace Research* 9, no. 2 (1972): 105–20.

Anisa. "People and Nature over Profits for a Just, Inclusive, Transparent and Equitable Future." *Focus on the Global South*, August 23, 2023. https://focusweb.org/people-and-nature-over-profits-for-a-just-inclusive-transparent-and-equitable-future/.

Araghi, Farshad. "Global Depeasantization, 1945-1990." *Sociological Quarterly* 36, no. 2 (1995): 337–68.

Aronoff, Kate, Alyssa Battistoni, Daniel Aldana Cohen, and Thea Riofrancos. *A Planet to Win. Why We Need a Green New Deal*. London: Verso, 2019.

Arthur, Charles. "Women Entrepreneurs Transforming Bangladesh." *Making It* 2 (April 2010): 30–31.

Asghar, Sohail, Gulmina Rextina, Tanveer Ahmed, and Manzoor Illahi Tamimy. "The Fourth Industrial Revolution in the Developing Nations: Challenges and Road Map." *South Centre Research Paper No. 102. Commission on Science and Technology for Sustainable Development in the South*. February 2020.

Associated Press. "Thousands Protest New Argentine President's Austerity Measures." December 20, 2023. https://www.voanews.com/a/thousands-protest-new-argentine-president-s-austerity-measures/7406747.html.

Atkinson, Robert D. "Chinese Manufacturers Use 12 Times More Robots than U.S. Manufacturers When Controlling for Wages." *Information Technology & Innovation Foundation*, September 5, 2023. https://itif.org/publications/2023/09/05/chinese-manufacturers-use-12-times-more-robots-than-us-manufacturers-when-controlling-for-wages/.

Avery, Natalie. "Stealing from the State." In *50 Years Is Enough: The Case against the World Bank and the IMF*, edited by Kevin Danaher, and Muhammad Yunus. Boston: South End, 1994.

———. *The New Authoritarianism. Trump, Populism and the Tyranny of Experts*.

Cambridge, UK: Polity, 2019.

Baird, Vanessa. "Fear Eats the Soul." *New Internationalist October*, (2002): 9–12.

Ball, Rochelle. "The Process of International Contract Labor Migration from the Philippines: The Case of Filipino Nurses." *PhD dissertation, Department of Geography*, PhD diss., Australia: University of Sydney, 1990.

Barkin, David. *Distorted Development: Mexico in the World Economy*. Boulder, CO: Westview, 1990.

Barlow, Maude. *Blue Gold*. San Francisco: International Forum on Globalization, 1999.

Barndt. *Deborah Tangled Routes: Women, Work, and Globalization on the Tomato Trail*. New York: Rowman and Littlefield, 2008.

Barnet, Richard J., and John Cavanagh. *Global Dreams: Imperial Corporations and the New World Order*. New York: Touchstone, 1994.

Bauman, Zygmunt. *Wasted Lives: Modernity and Its Outcasts*. Cambridge, UK: Polity, 2004.

Beas, Diego. "How Spain's 15-M Movement Is Redefining Politics." *The Guardian*, (October 15, 2011): http://www.theguardian.com/commentisfree/2011/oct/15/spain-15-m-movement-activism.

Bebbington, Anthony, Benjamin Fash, and John Rogan. "Socio-environmental Conflicts, Political Settlements and Mining Governance: A Cross-Border Comparison, El Salvador and Honduras." *Latin American Perspectives* 46, no. 2 (2019): 84–106.

Beckman, Bjorn. "Empowerment or Repression? The World Bank and the Politics of African Adjustment." In *Authoritarianism, Democracy and Adjustment: The Politics of Economic Reform in Africa*, edited by Peter Gibbon, Yusuf Bangura, and Arve Ofstad. Uppsala, Sweden: Nordiska Afrikainstitutet, 1992.

Bello, Walden. "The Corporate Food System Is Making the Coronavirus Worse." *Foreign Policy in Focus*, April 20, 2020a. https://fpif.org/the-corporate-food-system-is-making-the-coronavirus-crisis-worse/.

———. ""Never Let a Good Crisis Go to Waste: The Covid-10 Pandemic and the Opportunity for Food Sovereignty" [Issue Brief]." *Transnational Institute*, April 2020b. https://www.tni.org/files/publication-downloads/web_covid-19.pdf.

Bello, Walden, with Shea Cunningham, and Bill Rau. *Dark Victory: The United States, Structural Adjustment and Global Poverty*. London: Pluto Press, with Food First and Transnational Institute, 1994.

Bello, Walden, and John Feffer. "The Virtues of Deglobalization." *Foreign Policy in Focus*, September 3, 2009. https://fpif.org/the_virtues_of_deglobalization/.

Benabdallah, Lina. "Contesting the International Order by Integrating It: The Case of China's Belt and Road Initiative." *Third World Quarterly* 40, no. 1 (2019): 92–108.

Beneria, Lourdes. *Gender, Development, and Globalization: Economics as if All People Mattered*. New York: Routledge, 2003.

Berlan, Jean-Pierre. "The Historical Roots of the Present Agricultural Crisis." In *Towards a New Political Economy of Agriculture*, edited by W. Friedland, L. Busch, F. Buttel, and A. Rudy. Boulder, CO: Westview, 1991.

Beuret, Nicholas B. "Emissions Inequality: A Gulf between Global Rich and Poor." *Social Europe*, April 10, 2019. https://www.socialeurope.eu/emissions-inequality.

Biovision Foundation for Ecological Development & IPES-Food. "Money Flows: What Is Holding Back Investment in Agroecological Research for Africa?" *Biovision Foundation for Ecological Development & International Panel of Experts on Sustainable Food Systems*, 2020. https://www.ipes-food.org/_img/upload/files/Money%20Flows_Full%20report.pdf.

Black, Maggie. *The No-Nonsense Guide to International*

Development. London: Verso, 2002.

Blesh, Jennifer, Lesli Hoey, Andrew D. Jones, Harriet Friedmann, and Ivette Perfecto. "Development Pathways toward 'Zero Hunger'." *World Development* 118 (2019): 1–14.

Block, Fred L. *The Origins of International Economic Disorder: A Study of United States International Monetary Policy from World War II to the Present*. Berkeley: University of California Press, 1977.

Bobin, Frederic. "Mutually Assured Dependence." *Guardian Weekly*, (July 14–20, 2006): 17.

———. "Radical Anti-Colonial Thought, Anti-Colonial Internationalism and the Politics of Human Solidarities." In *International Relations and Non-Western Thought: Imperialism, Colonialism and Investigations and Global Modernity*, edited by Robbie Shilliam. London: Routledge, 2011.

Boles, Christine. "Robotics—an Extension of the Ongoing Digital Transformation." *Forbes*, July 21, 2023. https://www.forbes.com/sites/forbestechcouncil/2023/07/21/robotics-an-extension-of-the-ongoing-digital-transformation/?sh=292be7483b67.

Bond, Patrick. *Looting Africa: The Economics of Exploitation*. Pietermaritzburg, South Africa: University of Kwa-Zulu Natal Press, 2006.

Bose, Sugata. "Instruments and Idioms of Colonial and National Development: India's Historical Experience in Comparative Perspective." In *International Development and the Social Sciences*, edited by Frederick Cooper, and Randall Packard. Berkeley: University of California Press, 1997.

Boyd, Rosalind. "Labour's Response to the Informalization of Work in the Current Restructuring of Global Capitalism: China, South Korea and South Africa." *Canadian Journal of Development Studies* 27, no. 4 (2006): 487–502.

Boyd, Stephanie. "Secrets and Lies." *New Internationalist* 303 (1998): 16–17.

Bradley, P. N., and S. E. Carter. "Food Production and Distribution—and Hunger." In *A World in Crisis? Geographical Perspectives*, edited by R. J. Johnston, and P. J. Taylor. Oxford, UK: Blackwell, 1989.

Bradsher, Keith. "White House Moves to Increase Aid to Mexico." *New York Times*, (January 12, 1995): D6.

———. "China Invested $1 Trillion to Gain Global Influence. Can That Go On?" *New York Times*, October 16, 2023a. https://www.nytimes.com/2023/10/16/business/chinas-belt-and-road-initiative-bri.html.

———. "China's Electric Car Factories Can't Hire Fast Enough." *New York Times*, December 8, 2023b. https://www.nytimes.com/2023/12/08/business/china-electric-vehicles.html?smid=nytcore-ios-share&referringSource=articleShare.

Brand, Ulrich, and Markus Wissen. *The Imperial Mode of Living. Everyday Life and the Ecological Crisis of Capitalism*. London & New York: Verso, 2021.

Brautigam, Deborah. *The Dragon's Gift: The Real Story of China in Africa*. Oxford, UK: Oxford University Press, 2009.

Brecher, Jeremy, Tim Costello, and Brendan Smith. *Globalization from Below: The Power of Solidarity*. Cambridge, MA: South End, 2000.

Brett, E. A. *The World Economy since the War: The Politics of Uneven Development*. London: Macmillan, 1985.

Bretton Woods Project. "New Data Show Global South Is in Worst Debt Crisis Ever, with Another Lost Decade Looming." *Bretton Woods Observer*, December 13, 2023. https://www.brettonwoodsproject.org/2023/12/new-data-show-global-south-is-in-worst-debt-crisis-ever-with-another-lost-decade-looming.

Brooks, Stephen G. "The Shape of Power in 2024." *Project Syndicate Quarterly. The Year Ahead 2024*, (December 11, 2023): 72. https://www.project-syndicate.org/magazine/multipolarity-non-alignment-global

-order-2024-by-adekeye-adebajo-et-al-2023-12.

Buck, Holly Jean. *After Geoengineering. Climate Tragedy, Repair and Restoration*. London: Verso, 2019.

———. *Ending Fossil Fuels. Why Net Zero Is Not Enough*. London & New York: Verso, 2021.

Bujra, Janet. "Diversity in Pre-Capitalist Societies." In *Poverty and Development in the 1990s*, edited by Tim Allen, and Allan Thomas. Oxford, UK: Oxford University Press, 1992.

Bullard, Nicola. "It's Too Late for Sustainability: What We Need Is System Change." *Development* 54, no. 2 (2011): 141–42.

Bunker, Stephen. *Underdeveloping the Amazon: Extraction, Unequal Exchange and the Failure of the Modern State*. Urbana: University of Illinois Press, 1985.

Bunker, Stephen G., and Paul S. Ciccantell. *Globalization and the Race for Resources*. Baltimore: Johns Hopkins University Press, 2005.

Bunting, Madeleine. "Promoting Happiness and Cutting Welfare: What a Devious Combination." *The Guardian*, (November 28, 2010).

Burbach, Roger, and Patricia Flynn. *Agribusiness in the Americas*. New York: Monthly Review Press, 1980.

Busan Declaration 2011. "Fourth High Level Forum on Aid Effectiveness." *Busan, Republic of Korea*, November 29–December 1, 2011. https://overseas.mofa.go.kr/fj-en/brd/m_3241/view.do?seq=669312&srchFr=&srchTo=&srchWord=&srchTp=&multi_itm_seq=0&itm_seq_1=0&itm_seq_2=0&company_cd=&company_nm=.

Busch, Lawrence, and William B. Lacy. *Science, Agriculture, and the Politics of Research*. Boulder, CO: Westview, 1983.

Byerlee, Derek, Klaus Deininger, Jonathan Mills Lindsay, Andrew Norton, Harris Selod, and Meredith Mercedes Stickler. *Rising Global Interest in Farmland: Can It Yield Sustainable and Equitable Benefits?* Washington, DC: World Bank, 2011. http://documents.worldbank.org/curated/en/998581468184149953/Rising-global-interest-in-farmland-can-it-yield-sustainable-and-equitable-benefits.

Byres, Terry J. "The New Technology, Class Formation and Class Action in the Indian Countryside." *Journal of Peasant Studies* 8, no. 4 (1981): 405–54.

Camus, Renaud. *Le grand remplacement*. Plieux: Chez l'auteur, 2011.

Canak, William L. "Debt, Austerity, and Latin America in the New International Division of Labor." In *Lost Promises: Debt, Austerity, and Development in Latin America*, edited by William L. Canak. Boulder, CO: Westview, 1989.

Canfield, Matthew, Molly Anderson, and Philip McMichael. "UN Food Systems Summit 2021: Dismantling Democracy and Resetting Corporate Control of Food Systems." *Frontiers in Sustainable Food Systems* 5 (2021). .

Canas, Jesus, and Robert W. Gilmer. "The Maquiladora's Changing Geography in the Southwest Economy." *Federal Reserve Bank of Dallas*, (2009): 10–14. https://www.dallasfed.org/research/economy/~/media/documents/research/swe/2009/swe0902c.pdf.

Cardoso, Fernando H., and Enzo Faletto. *Dependency and Development in Latin America*. Berkeley: University of California Press, 1979.

Cargill. "150 Years of Helping the World Thrive." *Sky Delta*, (August 2015): 79–86.

Carlsen, Laura. "The Mexican Farmers' Movement: Exposing the Myths of Free Trade." *Americas Program Policy Report*. Silver City, NM: Interhemispheric Resource Center, 2003.

Carrington, Damian. "'Perverse' Payments Must Be Redirected to Measures Such as Capturing Carbon, Report Says." *The Guardian*, September 16, 2019. https://www.theguardian.com/environment/2019/sep/16/1m-a-minute-the-farming-subsidies-destroying-the-world#img-1.

———. "Coronavirus: 'Nature Is Sending Us a Message,'." *The Guardian*, March 25, 2020. https://www.theguardian.com/world/2020/mar/25/coronavirus-nature-is-sending-us-a-message-says-un-environment-chief.

Caulkin, Simon. "If Everything Can Be Outsourced, What Is Left?" *Observer*, (April 1, 2007).

Center for Strategic and International Studies (CSIS). "China's R&D Expenditures Compared to Leading Nations, 2000-2018." *Innovation Lightbulb*, (June 30, 2023).

Cerny, Philip G. "Paradoxes of the Competition State: The Dynamics of Political Globalization." *Government and Opposition* 32, no. 2 (1997): 251–74.

Chan, Anita. "Boot Camp at the Shoe Factory." *Guardian Weekly*, (November 17, 1996): 20–21.

Chatterjee, Partha. *Nationalist Thought and the Colonial World*. Minneapolis: University of Minnesota Press, 2001.

Chavez, Daniel, and Lala Peñaranda. "The Case of Colombia's Ecopetrol." *Transnational Institute*, February 8, 2024. https://www.tni.org/en/article/state-run-oil-companies-and-the-energy-transition.

Cheng, Hong, Ruixue Jia, Dandan Li, and Hongbin Li. "The Rise of Robots in China." *Journal of Economic Perspectives* 33, no. 2 (2019): 71–88.

Cheru, Fantu. *The Silent Revolution in Africa: Debt, Development and Democracy*. London: Zed, 1989.

"China's Belt and Road Initiative Is Boosting Science—the West Must Engage, Not Withdraw." *Nature* 622 (2023): 669–70. https://www.nature.com/articles/d41586-023-03299-6.

Chira, Susan. "Women Campaign for New Plan to Curb the World's Population." *New York Times*, (April 13, 1994): A12.

Chirot, Daniel. *Social Change in the Twentieth Century*. New York: Harcourt Brace Jovanovich, 1977.

Chomsky, Noam. *World Orders Old and New*. New York: Columbia University Press, 1994.

Clapp, Jennifer. "Spoiled Milk, Rotten Vegetables and a Very Broken Food System." *New York Times*, May 8, 2020. https://www.nytimes.com/2020/05/08/opinion/coronavirus-global-food-supply.html.

Clapp, Jennifer, Peter Newell, and Zoe Brent. "The Political Economy of Climate Change, Agriculture and Food Systems." *Journal of Peasant Studies* 45, no. 1 (2018): 80–88.

Clarke, Tony. "Serving Up the Commons." *Multinational Monitor* 22, no. 4 (2001). www.essential.org/monitor/mm2001/01april/corp2.html.

Clarke, Tony, and Maude Barlow. *MAI: The Multilateral Agreement on Investment and the Threat to Canadian Sovereignty*. Toronto: Stoddart, 1997.

ClearIAS. "Green Growth: India's Strategy for Green Energy." Last updated July 31, 2024. https://www.clearias.com/green-growth/

Cleaver, Harry. "Food, Famine and the International Crisis." *Zerowork* 2 (1977): 7–70.

"Climate Summit Launches Efforts toward Food Security for 9 Billion People by 2050." *Climate Summit 2014*, September 23, 2014. http://www.un.org/climatechange/summit/wp-content/uploads/sites/2/2014/05/AGRICULTURE-PR.Pdf.

Coetzer, Jennigay. "Competition Regimes on the Rise in Africa, Ambitious Authorities and the Struggle to 'Keep Up'." *Law.com International*, December 8, 2023. https://www.law.com/international-edition/author/profile/jennigay-coetzer/.

Cohen, Joshua, ed. "Economics after Neoliberalism." *Boston Review, Forum* 11 (July 29, 2019). http://bostonreview.net/print-issues/joshua-cohen-editors-economics-after-neoliberalism.

Cokelaere, Hanna, and Bartosz Brzeziński. "Europe's Farmer Protests Are Spreading: Here's Where and Why." *Politico*, January 31, 2024. https://www.politico.eu/article/farmer-protest-europe-ma

p-france-siege-paris-germany-poland/.

Collins, Andrea. "Saying All the Right Things? Gendered Discourse in Climate-Smart Agriculture." *Journal of Peasant Studies* 45, no. 1 (2018): 175–91.

Collins, Joseph, and John Lear. *Chile's Free Market Miracle: A Second Look*. Oakland, CA: Food First Books, 1996.

Colman, Jude. "Indigenous Knowledge Reveals History of Fire-Prone Californian Forest." *Nature*, June 7, 2022. https://www.nature.com/articles/d41586-022-01232-x.

Committee on World Food Security/High Level Panel of Experts (CFS/HLPE). Agroecological and Other Innovative Approaches for Sustainable Agriculture and Food Systems That Enhance Food Security and Nutrition. Rome: FAO, July 2019. http://www.fao.org/3/ca5602en/ca5602en.pdf.

Conca, Ken. *Governing Water: Contentious Transnational Politics and Global Institution Building*. Cambridge, MA: MIT Press, 2006.

"Connecting Smallholders to Markets." *Civil Society and Indigenous Peoples' Mechanism*, October 15, 2016. https://www.csm4cfs.org/connecting-smallholders-markets-analytical-guide/.

Contiero, Marco. "Outreach on Climate Change and Sustainable Development." *Stakeholder Forum*, 2012. http://www.stake holderforum.org/sf/outreach/index.php/cop17day9home/532-cop17day-9item3.

Cooper, Frederick. "Modernizing Bureaucrats, Backward Africans, and the Development Concept." In *International Development and the Social Sciences*, edited by Frederick Cooper, and Randall Packard. Berkeley: University of California Press, 1997.

Cooper, Frederick, and Ann Laura Stoler, eds. *Tensions of Empire: Colonial Cultures in a Bourgeois World*. Berkeley: University of California Press, 1997.

Coordination Paysanne Européene (CPE). "For a Legitimate, Sustainable, and Supportive Common Agricultural Policy." November 15, 2003. http://www.cpefarmers.org/w3/article.php3?id_article=50.

Copeland, Nicholas. "Linking the Defence of Territory to Food Sovereignty: Peasant Environmentalisms and Extractive Neoliberalism in Guatemala." *Journal of Agrarian Change* 19 (2019): 21–40. .

"Corporate-Smart Greenwash: Why We Reject the Global Alliance on Climate-Smart Agriculture." *Climate Smart Agricultural Concerns*, September 2014. http://www.climatesmartagconcerns.info/rejection-letter.html.

Corrado, Alessandra. "Clandestini in the Orange Towns: Migrations and Racisms in Calabria's Agriculture." *Race/Ethnicity* 4, no. 2 (2011): 191–201.

Coulthard, Glen Sean. *Red Skin, White Masks: Rejecting the Colonial Politics of Recognition*. Minneapolis: University of Minnesota Press, 2014.

"Countries Need to Make Good on Pledged Biodiversity Funds," editorial. *Nature: International Journal of Science* 626 (February 22, 2024): 691. https://www.nature.com/articles/d41586-024-00509-7.pdf.

Cowan, M. P., and R. W. Shenton. *Doctrines of Development*. London: Routledge & Kegan Paul, 1996.

Cox, Robert W. *Production, Power, and World Order: Social Forces in the Making of History*. New York: Columbia University Press, 1987.

Crabtree, James. "The Staggering Rise of India's Super-Rich." *The Guardian*, July 10, 2018. https://www.theguardian.com/news/2018/jul/10/the-staggering-rise-of-indias-super-rich.

Crawford, Kate. "Generative AI's Environmental Costs Are Soaring—and Mostly Secret." *Nature*, February 20, 2024. https://www.nature.com/articles/d41586-024-00478-x.

Crook, Clive. "New Ways to Grow: A Survey of World Finance." *The Economist, Special Supplement*, September 25, 1993, 3–22.

Crossette, Barbara. *"Kofi Annan's Astonishing Facts!" In Human Development Report 1997*. New York: United Nations Development Program, 1997.

Crouch, Colin. *The Globalization Backlash*. Cambridge, UK: Polity, 2018.

Da Vìa, Elisa. "Seed Diversity, Farmers' Rights, and the Politics of Re-peasantization." *International Journal of Sociology of Agriculture and Food* 9, no. 2 (2012): 229–42..

Daly, Herman. "Sustainable Growth: An Impossibility Theorem." *Development* 3–4 (1990): 45–47.

Damiano, Alice. "Sustainable Life." In *Exploring Environmental Violence. Perspective, Experience, Expression, and Engagement*, edited by Richard Marcantonio, John Paul Lederach, and Agustin Fuentes, 135–55. Cambridge, UK: Cambridge University Press, 2024..

Daniel, Shepard. *The Great Land Grab: Rush for World's Farmland Threatens Food Security for the Poor*. Oakland, CA: Oakland Institute, 2009.

Davidson, Basil. *The Black Man's Burden: Africa and the Curse of the Nation-State*. New York: Times Books, 1992.

Davis, Mike. *Late Victorian Holocausts: El Niño Famines and the Making of the Third World*. London: Verso, 2001.

———. *Planet of Slums*. London: Verso, 2006.

Dawkins, Kristin. "Battle Royale of the 21st Century." *Seedling* 17, no. 1 (2000): 2–8.

Day, Elizabeth. "Cotton-Pickin' Trade." *Guardian Weekly*, (December 10, 2010): 25–27.

de Janvry, Alain. *The Agrarian Question and Reformism in Latin America*. Baltimore: Johns Hopkins University Press, 1981.

De Schutter, Olivier. "How Not to Think of Land-Grabbing: Three Critiques of Large-Scale Investments in Agriculture." *Journal of Peasant Studies* 38, no. 2 (2011): 249–79.

De Schutter, Olivier, and Olivia Yambi. "The 2021 Food Systems Summit Has Started on the Wrong Foot—but It Could Still Be Transformational." *Food Tank*, March 2020. https://foodtank.com/news/2020/03/2021-food-systems-summit-started-on-wrong-foot-it-could-still-be-transformational/.

Dearing, Aissa. "Cochabamba People's Agreement: Annotated." *JSTOR Daily*, September 1, 2023. https://daily.jstor.org/cochabamba-peoples-agreement-annotated/.

Debroy, Bibek. "GDP Measure: Let CSO Figure Out Alternative." *Financial Express*, (February 3, 2017).

"Declaration of the Terra Preta Forum on the Food Crisis, Climate Change, Agrofuels and Food Sovereignty." *International Planning Committee for Food Sovereignty*, June 5, 2008. https://climateandcapitalism.com/2008/06/05/terra-preta-forum-demands-justice-for-victims-of-the-food-emergency.

Deere, Carmen Diana, and Magdalena Leon. *Empowering Women: Land and Property Rights in Latin America*. Pittsburgh: University of Pittsburgh Press, 2001.

Dehghan, Saeed Kamali. "The World Is Failing to Ensure Children Have a 'Liveable Planet,' Report Finds." *The Guardian*, February 19, 2020. https://www.theguardian.com/global-development/2020/feb/19/the-world-is-failing-to-ensure-children-have-a-liveable-planet-report-finds.

Dembicki, Geoff. "How a Conservative US Network Undermined Indigenous Energy Rights in Canada." *The Guardian*, July 18, 2022. https://www.theguardian.com/environment/2022/jul/18/conservative-us-network-undermined-indigenous-energy-rights-in-canada.

Dhanagare, D. N. "The Green Revolution and Social Inequalities in Rural India." *Bulletin of Concerned Asian Scholars* 20, no. 2 (1988): 2–13.

Dictus, Jan. "Eco-Cities: Creating a Common Language." *Making It* 18 (2015): 20–21.

Ding, Yinfan. "How Will the BRICS Lead the Global Economy?" *China Focus*, January 3, 2018. https://w

ww.chinausfocus.com/finance-economy/how-will-the-brics-lead-the-global-economy.

Dirlik, Arif. Complicities. *The Peoples Republic of China in Global Capitalism*. Chicago: Prickly Paradigm Press, 2017.

Dixon, Jane. *The Changing Chicken: Chooks, Cooks, and Culinary Culture*. Sydney: UNSW Press, 2002.

Doty, Roxanne Lynn. *Imperial Encounters: The Politics of Representation in North-South Relations*. Minneapolis: University of Minnesota Press, 1996.

Dreyfuss, Robert. "The Greening of China." *The Nation*, (September 20, 2010).

Dudley, Leonard, and Roger Sandilands. "The Side Effects of Foreign Aid: The Case of Public Law 480, Wheat in Colombia." *Economic Development and Cultural Change* 23, no. 2 (1975): 325–36.

Dugger, Celia W. "Supermarket Giants Crush Central American Farmers." *New York Times*, (December 28, 2004, A1, A10).

Duncan, Colin. *The Centrality of Agriculture: Between Humankind and the Rest of Nature*. Montreal: McGill-Queen's University Press, 1996.

Dunlap, Alexander. ""The State as Colonialism" Debating Infrastructural Colonization and the Roots of Socioecological Catastrophe."." *Political Geography* 107 (November 2023): 102980.

Dunlop, Tim. "'Something Big Has to Change': Could Australia Afford a Universal Basic Income?" *The Guardian*, September 7, 2019. https://www.theguardian.com/australia-news/2017/sep/08/something-big-has-to-change-could-australia-afford-a-universal-basic-income.

Easterly, William. "The SDGs Should Stand for Senseless, Dreamy, Garbled." *Foreign Policy*, (September 28, 2015).

Economist, The. "Will Climate Finance Make or Break COP28?" October 25, 2023. https://impact.economist.com/sustainability/circular-economies/will-climate-finance-make-or-break-cop28?utm_medium=cpc.adword.pd&utm_source=google&ppccampaignID=17210591673&ppcadID=&utm_campaign=a.22brand_pmax&utm_content=conversion.direct-response.anonymous&gad_source=1&gclid=EAIaIQobChMIna LE4vC8hAMVOU5HAR1oVgDdEAMYASAAEgKldPD_BwE&gclsrc=aw.ds.

Edelman, Marc, and Jun Borras. *Political Dynamics of Transnational Agrarian Movements*. Halifax, NS: Fernwood Press, 2016.

Ehrenreich, Ben. "Welcome to the Global Rebellion against Neoliberalism." *The Nation*, November 25, 2019. https://www.thenation.com/article/archive/global-rebellions-inequality/.

Einhorn, Catrin, and Manuela Andreoni. "Ecuador Tried to Curb Drilling to Protect the Amazon. The Opposite Happened." *New York Times*, January 14, 2023. updated February 21, 2024. https://www.nytimes.com/2023/01/14/climate/ecuador-drilling-oil-amazon.html?smid=nytcore-ios-share&referringSource=articleShare

El-Erian, Mohammed A. "Fragmented Globalization." *Project Syndicate*, (2023).

Ellen MacArthur Foundation. Case Studies. N.d.a. https://www.ellenmacarthurfoundation.org/our-work/activities/circular-economy-in-cities/case-studies.

Ellen MacArthur Foundation. Circular Economy in Cities. N.d.b. https://www.ellenmacarthurfoundation.org/our-work/activities/circular-economy-in-cities.

Elliott, Larry. "Evil Triumphs in a Disease-Ridden World." *Guardian Weekly*, (February 14–21, 2001): 12.

———. "Globalization Is Not Dead, but It Is Fading: 'Glocalisation' Is Becoming the NewMantra." *The Guardian*, January 21, 2024. https://www.theguardian.com/business/2024/jan/21/globalisation-glocalisation-industrial-policy-green-growth.

———. "The Chinese Century." *Time*, (January 22, 2007): 19–27.

Ellis, Erie C. "1.5 degrees is not the problem." *New York Times*, December 4, 2023. https://www.nytimes.com/2023/12/04/opinion/rich-nations-climate-change-summit.html.

Elson, Diane, and Ruth Pearson. "Nimble Fingers Make Cheap Workers: An Analysis of Women's Employment in Third World Export Manufacturing." *Feminist Review* 7 (1981): 87–101.

Environmental Performance Index. *2020 EPI Results*. New Haven, CT: Yale Center for Environmental Law & Policy, 2022. https://epi.yale.edu/epi-results/2020/component/epi.

Erdenesanaa, Delger. "One Thing Most Countries Have in Common: Unsafe Air." *New York Times*, March 19, 2024. https://www.nytimes.com/2024/03/19/climate/air-pollution-pm25.html?smid=nytcore-ios-share&referringSource=articleShare.

Ervine, Kate. *Carbon*. Cambridge, UK: Polity, 2018.

Escobar, Arturo. "Sustainability: Design for the Pluriverse." *Development* 54, no. 2 (2011): 137–40.

Escobar, Arturo, Michal Osterwil, and Kriti Sharma. *Relationality: An Emergent Politics of Life beyond the Human*. London: Bloomsbury, 2024.

Esteva, Gustavo. "Development." In *The Development Dictionary*, edited by Wolfgang Sachs. London: Zed, 1992.

Esteva, Gustavo, Salvatore Babones, and Philipp Babcicky. *The Future of Development: A Radical Manifesto*. Bristol: Policy Press, 2013.

Eurodad. "An Historic Opportunity Missed: In the Midst of a Development Crisis Gripping Most of the World, the IMF and World Bank Fail to Provide a Response." *press release*, October 14, 2023. https://www.eurodad.org/an_historic_opportunity_missed_in_the_midst_of_a_development_crisis_gripping_most_of_the_world_the_imf_and_world_bank_fail_to_provide_a_response.

European Commission. "An EU Policy Framework to Assist Developing Countries in Addressing Food Security Challenges." *SEC*, (2010): 379. http://eur-lex.europa.eu/legal-content/EN/TXT/?uri=celex:52010DC0127.

European Court of Auditors. "Special Report 29/2023: The EU's Support for Sustainable Biofuels in Transport—an Unclear Route Ahead." December 13, 2023. https://www.eca.europa.eu/en/publications?ref=SR-2023-29.

Eyferth, J., P. Ho, and E. B. Vermeer. "Introduction: The Opening Up of China's Countryside." *Journal of Peasant Studies* 30, no. 3–4 (2003): 1–17.

Fairley, Peter. "How to Rescue Biofuels from a Sustainable Deadend." *Nature* 611 (2022): S15–17. https://www.nature.com/articles/d41586-022-03649-w.

Fanon, Frantz. *The Wretched of the Earth*. Harmondsworth, UK: Penguin, 1967.

Fargione, J., J. Hill, D. Tilman, S. Polasky, and P. Hawthorne. "Land Clearing and the Biofuel Carbon Debt." *Science*, (February 7, 2008).

Farrer, M., and L. Kuo. "'Amazing Deal' or 'Capitulation'? Why the US-China Trade Truce May Not Last." *The Guardian*, December 14, 2019. https://www.theguardian.com/business/2019/dec/15/amazing-deal-or-capitulation-why-the-us-china-trade-truce-may-not-last.

Fernández-Kelly, María Patricia. *For We Are Sold, I and My People: Women and Industry in Mexico's Frontier*. Albany, NY: SUNY Press, 1983.

Ferrett, Grant. "Biofuels 'Crime against Humanity'." *BBC News*, (October 27, 2007).

Fischer, Andrew M., and Servaas Storm. "The Return of Debt Crisis in Developing Countries: Shifting or Maintaining Dominant Development Paradigms?" *Development and Change* 54, no. 5 (2023): 954–93.

Flannery, Tim. *Now or Never: Why We Must Act Now to End Climate Change and Create a Sustainable Future*. New York: Atlantic Monthly Press, 2009.

Florini, Ann, Gordon LaForge, and Anne-Marie Slaughter. "Democratic Governance for the Long Emergency." In *Democracy in a Hotter Time. Climate Change and Democratic Transformation*, edited by David W. Orr. Cambridge, MA: MIT Press, 2023.

Food and Agriculture Organization of the United Nations (FAO). "The Role of Women in Agriculture." *ESA Working Paper No. 11-02 Agricultural Development Economics Division*, (March 2011). http://www.fao.org/3/am307e/am307e00.pdf.

——. *Natural Capital Impacts in Agriculture: Supporting Better Decision Making*. Rome, Italy: UN FAO, June 2015.

Foster, John Bellamy. "Capitalism and Degrowth: An Impossibility." *Monthly Review* 62, no. 8 (2011): 26–33.

Foster, John W. "The Trinational Alliance against NAFTA: Sinews of Solidarity." In *Coalitions across Borders: Transnational Protest and the Neoliberal Order*, edited by Joe Bandy, and Jackie Smith. New York: Rowman and Littlefield, 2005.

Frank, Andre Gunder. "The Development of Underdevelopment." In *Imperialism and Underdevelopment*, edited by Robert H. Rhodes. New York: Monthly Review Press, 1970.

Fraser, Alistair. "Poverty Reduction Strategy Papers: Now Who Calls the Shots?" *Review of African Political Economy* 104/5 (2005): 317–40.

——. "Land Grab/Data Grab: Precision Agriculture and Its New Horizons." *Journal of Peasant Studies* 46, no. 5 (2019): 839–912.

Freeman, Carla. *High Tech and High Heels in the Global Economy: Women, Work, and Pink-Collar Identities in the Caribbean*. Durham, NC: Duke University Press, 2000.

French, Hilary. *Vanishing Borders: Protecting the Planet in the Age of Globalization*. New York: Norton, 2000.

French, Howard W. "The Next Empire." *The Atlantic*, (May 2010).

Friedland, William H. "The Global Fresh Fruit and Vegetable System: An Industrial Organization Analysis." In *The Global Restructuring of Agro-Food Systems*, edited by Philip McMichael. Ithaca, NY: Cornell University Press, 1994.

Friedman, Milton. *Capitalism and Freedom*. Chicago: University of Chicago Press, 1962.

Friedman, Thomas. *The Lexus and the Olive Tree: Understanding Globalization*. New York: Anchor, 2000.

Friedmann, Harriet. "The Political Economy of Food: The Rise and Fall of the Postwar International Food Order." *American Journal of Sociology* 88S (1982): 248–86.

——. "The Origins of Third World Food Dependence." In *The Food Question: Profits versus People?* edited by Henry Bernstein, Ben Crow, Maureen Mackintosh, and Charlotte Martin. New York: Monthly Review Press, 1990.

——. "Remaking 'Traditions': How We Eat, What We Eat, and the Changing Political Economy of Food." In *Women Working the NAFTA Food Chain*, edited by Deborah Barndt. Toronto: Second Story, 1999.

Fuentes, Anna, and Barbara Ehrenreich. "The New Factory Girls." *Multinational Monitor* 4, no. 8 (1983).

Funk, McKenzie. *Windfall: The Booming Business of Global Warming*. New York: Penguin Books, 2014.

Gaarde, Ingeborg. *Peasants Negotiating a Global Policy Space: La Vía Campesina in the Committee on World Food Security*. London: Routledge/Earthscan, 2017.

Galeano, Eduardo. *Upside Down: A Primer for the Looking Glass World*. New York: Picador, 2000.

Games, Dianna. "AIF 2023: Unlocking Value Chains Is Africa's Development Route." *African Business*, November 28, 2023. https://african.business/2023/11/partner-content/aif-2023-unlocking-value-chains-is-africas-development-route.

Gammage, Bill. *The Biggest Estate on Earth: How Aborigines Made Australia*. Sydney: Allen and Unwin, 2012.

Gawande, Atul. "Why Americans Are Dying of Despair." *The New Yorker*, March 16, 2020. https://www.newyorker.com/magazine/2020/03/23/why-americans-are-dying-from-despair.

George, Susan. *How the Other Half Dies: The Real Reasons for World Hunger*. Montclair, NJ: Allenheld, Osmun, 1977.

———. *A Fate Worse Than Debt: The World Financial Crisis and the Poor*. New York: Grove, 1988.

———. *The Debt Boomerang: How Third World Debt Harms Us All*. Boulder, CO: Westview, 1992.

———. *Whose Crisis? Whose Future? Towards a Greener, Fairer, Richer World*. Cambridge, UK: Polity, 2010.

George, Susan, and Fabrizio Sabelli. *Faith and Credit: The World Bank's Secular Empire*. Boulder, CO: Westview, 1994.

Gereffi, Gary. "The Organization of Buyer-Driven Global Commodity Chains: How U.S. Retailers Shape Overseas Production Networks." In *Commodity Chains and Global Capitalism*, edited by Gary Gereffi, and Miguel Korzeniewicz. Westport, CT: Praeger, 1994.

Getachew, Adom. *World Making after Empire: The Rise and Fall of Self-Determination*. Princeton, NJ: Princeton University Press, 2019.

Ghanem, Michel Edmond. "Africa's Forgotten Crops Could Offset Food Insecurity." *Nature*, May 5, 2022. https://www.nature.com/articles/d41586-022-01185-1.

Ghosh, Jayati. "Jayati Ghosh Says More . . ." *Project Syndicate*, (November 7, 2023a).

———. "SDRs Are the Great Untapped Source of Climate Finance." *Project Syndicate*, (December 12, 2023b).

———. "Can the IMF and the World Bank Really Be Changed?" *Social Europe*, (January 29, 2024).

Gibson-Graham, J. K. *A Postcapitalist Politics*. Minneapolis: University of Minnesota Press, 2006.

Gill, Stephen. "Constitutionalizing Inequality and the Clash of Globalizations." *International Studies Review* 4, no. 2 (2002): 47–65.

Gioia, Paula. "Pathway to Resilience, Hands and Hearts for Peasant Livelihoods and Fair Relations between Humans and Nature." *Third World Quarterly* 39, no. 7 (2018): 1403–10.

Glauber, Joseph W., and Xiaorong Xing. "WTO Dispute Settlement Cases Involving the Agreement on Agriculture, 1995-2019." *Discussion Paper No. 01917*. Washington, DC: International Food Policy Research Institute, 2020.

Gleckman, Harris. "How the United Nations is quietly being turned into a public-private partnership." *Open Democracy*, (July 2, 2019).

Glennie, Jonathan. "The Rise of the 'South-South' Aid Agencies." *Guardian Weekly*, (March 4, 2011): 44.

Gliessman, Steve. *Breaking Away from Industrial Food and Farming Systems. Executive Summary*. Brussels, Belgium: IPES-Food, 2018.

Global Wealth Report. 2023. Credit Suisse AG, 2023. https://www.ubs.com/global/en/family-office-uhnw/reports/global-wealth-report-2023.htm

Godoy, Julio. "Vive la Décroissance." *New Internationalist* 434 (2010): 19.

Godrej, Dinyar. "Precious Fluid." *New Internationalist* 354 (2003): 9–12.

Goldemberg, J., and O. Lucon. "Renewable Energy Options in Developing Countries." *Making It* 2 (2010): 16–18. http://www.makingitmaga-zine.net.

Goldman, Michael. *Imperial Nature: The World Bank and Struggles for Social Justice in the Age of Globalization*. New Haven, CT: Yale University Press, 2005.

Goldsmith, James. *The Trap*. New York: Carroll & Graf, 1994.

Goody, Jack. *The East in the West*. Cambridge, UK:

Cambridge University Press, 1996.

Gorelick, Sherry. "Facing the Farm Crisis." *The Ecologist* 30, no. 4 (2000): 28–32.

Government of South Australia. "South Australia's Green Paper on the Energy Transition." *Department of Energy and Mining*, June 2023. https://www.energymining.sa.gov.au/public-consultations/consultation/south-australias-green-paper-on-the-energy-transition.

Graeber, David. "Against Economics." *New York Review of Books*, December 5, 2019. https://www.nybooks.com/articles/ 2019/12/05/against-economics/.

Graham, Carol. *Safety Nets, Politics, and the Poor: Transitions to Market Economies*. Washington, DC: Brookings Institution, 1994.

GRAIN. "Agrofuels. Special Issue." *Seedling*, July 2007. www.grain.org/seedling/?type=68&1=0.

———. "Peasants Still Feed the World, even if FAO Claims Otherwise." *February* 2 (2022). https://grain.org/en/article/6790-peasants-still-feed-the-world-even-if-fao-claims-otherwise.

Green America. ""How Pervasive Are GMOs in Animal Feed?" blog." *Green Business Network*, July 16, 2013. https://www.greenamerica.org/blog/how-pervasive-are-gmos-animal-feed.

Greenlees, Donald. "Outsourcing Drifts to the Philippines after India Matures." *International Herald Tribune*, (November 11, 2006): 1.

Griffin, K. B. *The Political Economy of Agrarian Change: An Essay on the Green Revolution*. Cambridge, MA: Harvard University Press, 1974.

Grigg, David B. *The World Food Problem*. Oxford, UK: Blackwell, 1993.

"The Guardian View on Globalisation's Discontent: It's Not Right for Poor Countries to Fund the Rich, editorial." *The Guardian*, April 24, 2024. https://www.theguardian.com/commentisfree/2024/apr/24/the-guardian-view-on-globalisations-discontent-its-not-right-for-poor-countries-to-fund-the-rich.

Gunawardana, Samanthi J. "'To Finish, We Must Finish': Everyday Practices of Depletion in Sri Lankan Export-Processing Zones." *Globalizations* 13, no. 6 (2016): 861–75.

Gupta, Akhil. *Postcolonial Developments: Agriculture in the Making of Modern India*. Durham, NC: Duke University Press, 1998.

Guttal, Shalmali. "The Changing Face of Food Retail in India." *Right to Food and Nutrition* 10 (2018). https://www.righttofoodandnutrition.org/files/rtfn-watch-2018_eng.pdf.

Gutteres, Antonio. Acciona. "The Era of Global Boiling." 2023. https://www.activesustainability.com/climate-change/global-boiling/?_adin=02021864894.

Haagh, Louise. *The Case for Universal Basic Income*. Cambridge, UK: Polity, 2019.

Haass, Richard. "The Pandemic Will Accelerate History Rather Than Reshape It." *Foreign Affairs*, April 7, 2020. https://www.foreignaffairs.com/articles/united-states/2020-04-07/pandemic-will-accelerate-history-rather-reshape-it.

Halperin, Sandra. *Re-Envisioning Global Development. A Horizontal Perspective*. London & New York: Routledge, 2013.

Harding, Luke. "Delhi Calling." *Guardian Weekly*, (March 15–21, 2001): 23.

Harlan, Chico. "All Together Now." *Guardian Weekly*, (July 15, 2011): 30.

Harris, Malcolm. "Shell Is Looking Forward. The Fossil-Fuel Companies Expect to Not Just Survive Climate Change but Profit from It." *New York*, (March 2–15, 2020).

Harris, Nigel. *The End of the Third World: Newly Industrializing Countries and the Decline of an Ideology*. Harmondsworth, UK: Penguin, 1987.

Harrison, Graham. *The World Bank and Africa: The Construction of Governance States*. London: Routledge, 2004.

Harvey, David. *The New Imperialism*. Oxford, UK: Oxford University Press, 2003.

———. *A Brief History of Neoliberalism*. Oxford, UK:

Oxford University Press, 2005.

Harvey, Fiona. "Global Fresh Water Demand Will Outstrip Supply by 40% by 2030, Say Experts." *The Guardian*, March 16, 2023. https://www.theguardian.com/environment/2023/mar/17/global-fresh-water-demand-outstrip-supply-by-2030.

Hawkins, Amy. "China: The Big Story." *The Guardian Weekly*, (September 15, 2023).

Hendrikse, Reijer. "Neo-illiberalism." *Geoforum* 95 (2018): 169–72.

———. "The Rise of Neo-Illiberalism." *Krisis | Journal for Contemporary Philosophy* 41, no. 1 (2021): 65–93.

Hertanti, Rachmi. "Between a Mineral and a Hard Place. Indonesia's export ban on raw minerals." *Transnational Institute*, June 15, 2023. https://www.tni.org/en/article/between-a-mineral-and-a-hard-place.

Hervieu, Sebastien. "South Africa Gains Entry to BRIC Club." *Guardian Weekly*, (April 22, 2011): 11.

Hettne, Bjorn. *Development Theory and the Three Worlds*. White Plains, NY: Longman, 1990.

Hildyard, Nicholas. "Foxes in Charge of Chickens." In *Global Ecology: A New Arena of Political Conflict*, edited by Wolfgang Sachs. London: Zed, 1993.

Hill, Amelia. "Migration: How Many People Are on the Move Around the World?" *The Guardian*, September 10, 2018. https://www.theguardian.com/news/2018/sep/10/migration-how-many-people-are-on-the-move-around-the-world.

HLPE. *Investing in Smallholder Agriculture for Food Security. A Report by the High Level Panel of Experts*. Rome: FAO, 2013.

Hobson, John M. *The Eastern Origins of Western Civilisation*. Cambridge, UK: Cambridge University Press, 2004.

———. *The Eurocentric Conception of World Politics: Western International Theory, 1760-2010*. Cambridge, UK: Cambridge University Press, 2012.

Hochschild, Arlie Russell. "Love and Gold." *In Global Woman: Nannies, Maids, and Sex Workers in the New Economy*. New York: Metropolitan Books, 2003.

Hodal, Kate. "World's 22 Richest Men Wealthier than All the Women in Africa." *The Guardian*, January 20, 2020. https://www.theguardian.com/global-development/2020/jan/20/worlds-22-richest-men-wealthier-than-all-the-women-in-africa-study-finds?CMP=share_btn_link.

Holt-Giménez, Eric, and Heidi Kleiner. "Food, Climate, and the Green New Deal." *Food First Backgrounder* 25, no. 1 (2019).

Hoogvelt, Ankie M. M. *The Third World in Global Development*. London: Macmillan, 1987.

———. *Globalization and the Postcolonial World: The New Political Economy of Development*. London: Macmillan, 1997.

———. "Globalization and Post-Modern Imperialism." *Globalizations* 3, no. 2 (2006): 159–74.

Hopewell, Kristen. *Breaking the WTO. How Emerging Powers Disrupted the Neoliberal Project*. Stanford: Stanford University Press, 2016.

———. *Clash of Powers: US–China Rivalry in Global Trade Governance*. Cambridge, UK: Cambridge University Press, 2020.

"How to Feed a Hungry World." *Nature* 466 (2010): 531–32. https://www.nature.com/articles/466531a.

Howe, Colleen. "China's Wind Solar Capacity Forecast to Overtake Coal in 2024." *Reuters*, January 30, 2024. https://www.reuters.com/business/energy/chinas-wind-solar-capacity-overtake-coal-2024-industry-body-2024-01-30/.

Hu, Angang. "Embracing China's New Normal." *Foreign Affairs* 94, no. 3 (2015): 8–12.

Hung, Ho-Fung. "Zombie Economy." *New Left Review, Sidecar*, 2023. https://newleftreview.org/sidecar/posts/zombie-economy.

Hunt, Edward. "Drilling Our Way to Climate Doom. The United States Leads the World in Oil and Natural Gas Production." *Foreign Policy in Focus*, (August 16, 2023).

Huntington, Samuel P. *Political Order in Changing Societies*. New Haven, CT: Yale University Press, 1968.

Iglesias, Pablo. "Spain on Edge." *New Left Review* 93 (2015a): 23–42.

Immerwahr, Daniel. "Zoning Out." *New York Review of Books*, (November 23, 2023): 22–25.

Institute for Security and Development Policy. "Made in China 2025." June 2018. https://isdp.eu/publication/made-china-2025/.

International Development Advisory Board. *Partners in Progress: A Report to President Truman (Foreword by Nelson A. Rockefeller)*. New York: Simon and Schuster, 1951.

International Labour Organization. Trade Union Manual on Export Processing Zones. 2014. https://www.ilo.org/sites/default/files/wcmsp5/groups/public/@ed_dialogue/@actrav/documents/publication/wcms_324632.pdf.

——. *ILO Global Estimates on International Migrant Workers: Results and Methodology*. 3rd ed. Geneva, Switzerland: International Labour Office, 2021.

International Monetary Fund. Annual Report 2022. Washington, DC: International Monetary Fund, 2022. www.imf.org/external/pubs/ft/ar/2022/in-focus/debt-dynamics/.

International Panel of Experts on Sustainable Food Systems (IPES-Food). Too Big to Feed. 2017.

IPES-Food and ETC Group. "A Long Food Movement: Transforming Food Systems by 2045." 2021.

Iriart, Celia, Howard Waitzkin, and Emerson Merhy. "Managed Care Goes Global." *Multinational Monitor* 25, no. 10 (2004).

Ishii, Naoko. "From Problem to Solution: Working With Industry for the Global Environment." *Making It* 16 (2014): 28–31.

Jackson, Tim. *Prosperity without Growth: Economics for a Finite Planet*. London: Routledge, 2017.

James, C. L. R. *The Black Jacobins: Toussaint L'Ouverture and the San Domingo Revolution*. New York: Vintage, 1963.

Jha, Alok. "Sun, Wind and Wave-Powered: Europe United to Build Renewable Energy 'Supergrid'." *The Guardian*, January 3, 2010. https://www.theguardian.com/environment/2010/jan/03/european-unites-renewable-energy-supergrid.

Jones, Lee, and Jinghan Zeng. "Understanding China's 'Belt and Road Initiative': Beyond 'Grand Strategy' to a State Transformation Analysis." *Third World Quarterly* 20, no. 2 (2019)..

Kaboub, Fadhel. "Decolonising the Global Economic Architecture: The Prerequisite for a Just Transition." *Bretton Woods Project*, December 13, 2023. https://www.brettonwoodsproject.org/2023/12/decolonising-the-global-economic-architecture-the-prerequisite-for-a-just-transition/.

Kagarlitsky, Boris. *The Mirage of Modernization*. New York: Monthly Review Press, 1995.

Kaiman, Jonathan. "China Says It Built a Railway in Africa out of Altruism, but It's More Strategic Than That." *Los Angeles Times*, August 4, 2017. https://www.latimes.com/world/asia/la-fg-china-africa-ethiopia-20170804-htmlstory.html.

Kala, Anant Vijay. "India's Services Expansion Quickest in 8 Months in February." *Wall Street Journal*, March 4, 2015. http://www.wsj.com/articles/indias-services-expansion-quickest-in-8-months-in-february-1425451528.

Kara, Siddharth. Cobalt Red. *How the Blood of the Congo Powers Our Lives*. New York: St. Martin's Press, 2023. https://www.democracynow.org/2023/7/13/cobalt_red_kara.

Katz, Paul, and Leandro Ferreira. "What a Solidarity Economy Looks Like." *Boston Review*, April 9, 2020. https://bostonreview.net/class-inequality/paul-katz-leandro-ferreria-brazil-basic-income-marica?utm_sou rce=Boston+Review+Email+Subscribers&utm_campaign=c1937602e8-MC_roundup_4_30_20&utm_medium= email&utm_term=0_2cb428c5ad-c19376 02e8-40993701&mc_cid=c1937602e8& mc_eid=04d16a0f00.

Keegan, Matthew. "Benefit of Burden? The Cities Carrying Out Universal Basic Income." *The Guardian*, June 27, 2018. https://www.theguardian.com/cities/2018/jun/27/benefit-or-burden-the-cities-trying-out-universal-basic-income.

Kelleher, Louise. "Green New Deal for Europe: Commission Co-opting the Real Deal." *Agriculture and Rural Convention (ARC), October 2*, 2019. https://www.arc2020.eu/green-new-deal-europe-commission-co-opting-real-deal/.

Kenis, Anneleen, and Matthias Lievens. *The Limits of the Green Economy*. Abingdon, UK: Routledge, 2015.

Kennedy, Bruce. "China's Three Gorges Dam." *CNN*, 2001. http://www.cnn.com/SPECIALS/1999/china.50/asian.superpower/three.gorges/.

Khadse, A., P. Rosset, H. Morales, and B. G. Ferguson. "Taking Agroecology to Scale: The Zero Budget Natural Farming Peasant Movement in Karnataka, India." *Journal of Peasant Studies* 45, no. 1 (2018): 192–219.

Kidron, Michael, and Ronald Segal. *The State of the World Atlas*. London: Pan, 1981.

Kishimoto, Satoko, and Olivier Petitjean. *Reclaiming Public Services: How Cities and Citizens Are Turning Back Privatization*. Amsterdam: Transnational Institute, 2017.

Klare, Michael T. *Resource Wars: The New Landscape of Global Conflict*. New York: Henry Holt, 2002.

Klein, Naomi. *The Shock Doctrine. The Rise of Disaster Capitalism*. New York: Metropolitan Books, 2007.

———. *This Changes Everything: Capitalism vs. the Climate*. London: Allen Lane, 2014.

———. "The Green New Deal. The Fight for Our Lives." *New York Review of Books*, September 17, 2019. https://www.nybooks.com/daily/2019/09/17/the-green-new-deal-a-fight-for-our-lives/.

Klein, R., T. Banuri, S. Kartha, and L. Schipper. "International Climate Policy." *Commission on Climate Change and Development*, (March 2008).

Kloppenburg, Jack R, Jr. *First the Seed: The Political Economy of Plant Biotechnology, 1492-2000*. Cambridge, MA: Cambridge University Press, 1988.

Knox, Paul, and John Agnew. *The Geography of the World Economy*. London: Edward Arnold, 1994.

Kohl, Benjamin, and Linda Farthing. *Impasse in Bolivia: Neoliberal Hegemony & Popular Resistance*. London: Zed, 2006.

Kokkinos, Patricia. "Year 3 Project on Eco-Cities." *Geography Is Easy*, 2016. https://geographyiseasy.wordpress.com/2016/06/22/year-3-project-on-eco-cities/.

Kolbert, Elizabeth. "Why Is the Sea So Hot?" *The New Yorker*, March 15, 2024. https://www.newyorker.com/news/daily-comment/why-is-the-sea-so-hot.

Kolhatkar, Sheelah. "Welcoming Our New Robot Overlords." *The New Yorker*, October 16, 2017. https://www.newyorker.com/magazine/2017/10/23/welcoming-our-new-robot-overlords.

Kolko, Joyce. *Restructuring the World Economy*. New York: Pantheon, 1988.

Krajewski, Markus. "The Impact of Services Trade Liberalization on Human Rights—Revisiting Old Questions in New Contexts." *Trade, Law and Development* 12, no. 1 (2022): 131–57.

Krauss, Clifford. "In Global Forecast, China Looms Large as Energy User and Maker of Green Power." *New York Times*, (November 10, 2010): D7.

Krauss, Clifford, and Keith Bradsher. "China's Global Search for Energy." *New York Times*, May 21, 2014. https://www.nytimes.com/2014/05/22/business/international/chinas-global-search-for-energy.html.

Krueger, Anne O. "China and the Sovereign-Debt Bomb." *Project Syndicate*, (January 13, 2023).

——. "The Coming Debt Crisis." *Project Syndicate*, (December 18, 2023).

La Via Campesina. "Bangalore Declaration." October 6, 2000. https://viacampesina.org/en/bangalore-declaration-of-the-via-campesina/.

——. "A G8 on Agriculture Without Farmers = More Hunger and Poverty." *press release*, April 21, 2009. https://viacampesina.org/en/a-g8-on-agriculture-without-farmers-more-hunger-and-poverty.

——. "The People of the World Confront the Advance of Capitalism: Rio +20 and Beyond." *position paper*, 2012. https://viacampesina.org/en/the-people-of-the-world-confront-the-advance-of-capitalism-rio-20-and-beyond/.

——. "Declaration of the International Forum on Agroecology." February 27, 2015. https://viacampesina.org/en/declaration-of-the-international-forum-for-agroecology.

——. "A Major Breakthrough in Scaling Up Agroecological Farming in Karnataka, India." June 26, 2018. https://viacampesina.org/en/a-major-breakthrough-in-scaling-up-agroecological-farming-in-karnataka-india/.

Lacayo, Ana Victoria Portocarrero. "Care Is the New Radical: Food and Climate Approaches from a Peasant Feminist Perspective." *Journal of Peasant Studies*, (February 11, 2024). .

Lakhani, Nina, and Dominic Rushe. "US Banks Abandon 'Bare Minimum' Environmental Standards Project, Alarming Climate Groups." *The Guardian*, March 5, 2024. https://www.theguardian.com/business/2024/mar/05/us-banks-leave-esg-finance-climate-crisis.

Lama, Fadi. *Why the West Can't Win. From Bretton Woods to a Multipolar World.* Atlanta: Clarity Press, 2023.

Landsberg, Martin. "ALBA and the Promise of Cooperative Development." *Monthly Review* 62, no. 7 (2010): 1–17.

Lappé, Anna. "We Need to Change How We Grow Our Food." *Heated*, April 8, 2020. https://heated.medium.com/we-need-to-change-how-we-grow-our-food-ac75fc494130.

——. "After 60 years, 'Silent Spring' Is Still Changing the World." *Civil Eats*, October 19, 2022. https://civileats.com.

Latouche, Serge. *In the Wake of the Affluent Society: An Exploration of Post-Development*. London: Zed, 1993.

Leader. "Shining Example." *The Guardian*, (April 23, 2004): 3.

Leahy, Stephen. "Reinventing Agriculture." *Inter Press Service*, (April 15, 2008).

Lederer, Katy. "Meet the Leftish Economist with a New Story about Capitalism." *New York Times*, November 26, 2019. https://www.nytimes.com/2019/11/26/business/mariana-mazzucato.html?smid=nytcore-ios-share.

Ledford, Heidi. "CRISPR-Edited Crops Break New Ground in Africa." *Nature*, January 25, 2024. https://www.nature.com/articles/d41586-024-00176-8.

Lee, Chingkwan. "Raw Encounters, Chinese Managers, African Workers and the Politics of Casualization in Africa's Chinese Enclaves." *China Quarterly*, no. 199 (2009): 647–99.

Lee, Danny. "Chinese Carmaker Overtakes Tesla as World's Most Popular EV Maker." *Bloomberg*, December 26, 2023. https://www.bloomberg.com/news/features/2023-12-27/elon-musk-s-tesla-is-losing-ev-race-to-china-s-byd.

Lee, Matilda. "Transition Towns: The Global Movement That Works Local." *Dialogue Earth*, October 10, 2013. https://dialogue.earth/en/uncategorized/6408-transition-towns-the-global-movement-that-works-local.

Leguizamón, Amalia. *Seeds of Power. Environmental Injustice and Genetically Modified Soybeans in Argentina*. Durham, NC: Duke University Press, 2020.

Lehman, David. *Democracy and Development in Latin*

America. Philadelphia: Temple University Press, 1990.

Lehman, K., and A. Krebs. "Control of the World's Food Supply." In *The Case against the Global Economy, and for a Turn toward the Local*, edited by J. Mander, and E. Goldsmith. San Francisco: Sierra Club Books, 1996.

Levin, Sam. "'We Have Failed': How California's Homelessness Catastrophe Is Worsening." *The Guardian*, 2022. https://www.theguardian.com/us-news/2022/mar/22/california-homelessness-crisis-unhoused-and-unequal.

Lenin, Vladimir Ilych. *Imperialism: The Highest Stage of Capitalism*. New York: International Publishers, 1916/1997.

LeQuesne, C. "The World Trade Organization and Food Security." *Talk to UK Food Group*, (London, July 15, 1997).

Lim, L. C. "Sustainable Agriculture Pushing Back the Desert." *Institute of Science in Society*, 2008. www.isis.org.uk/desertification.php.

Lindeman, Tracie. "'Revolution Is Alive': Canada Pipeline Protests Spawn Climate and Indigenous Rights Movement." *The Guardian*, February 28, 2020. https://www.theguardian.com/world/2020/feb/28/canada-pipeline-protests-climate-indigenous-rights.

Lipton, Michael. *Why Poor People Stay Poor: Urban Bias in World Development*. London: Temple Smith, 1977.

Lissakers, Karin. Banks. *Borrowers, and the Establishment: A Revisionist Account of the International Debt Crisis*. New York: Basic Books, 1993.

Livingston, James. "What Was Capitalism?" *Project Syndicate*, February 16, 2024. https://www.google.com/search?q=Livingston+what+was+capitaism&oq=Livingston+what+was+capitalism&gs_lcrp=EgZjaHJvbWUyBggAEEUYOTIJCAEQIRgKGKAB0gEJMTY2MzVqMWo3qAIAsAIA&sourceid=chrome&ie=UTF-8.

Llambi, Luis. "Transitions to and within Capitalism: Agrarian Transitions in Latin America." *Sociologia Ruralis* 30, no. 2 (1990): 174–96.

Lovelock, James. *The Revenge of Gaia: Earth's Climate Crisis and the Fate of Humanity*. New York: Basic Books, 2007.

Maathai, Wangari. *The Challenge for Africa*. New York: Anchor Books, 2010.

Macdonald, Laura. "Gendering Transnational Social Movement Analysis: Women's Groups Contest Free Trade in the Americas." In *Coalitions across Borders: Transnational Protest and the Neoliberal Order*, edited by Joe Bandy, and Jackie Smith. New York: Rowman and Littlefield, 2005.

Mackenzie, Kate, and Tim Sahay. "Trading Order." *The Polycrisis*, September 14, 2023. https://www.phenomenalworld.org/analysis/trading-order/#:~:text=Chinese%20firms%20ramped%20up%20exports,manufacturing%20industry%20in%20Southeast%20Asia.

Madhok, Dishka. "A Coal Billionaire Is Building the World's Biggest Clean Energy Plant and It's Five Times the Size of Paris." *MarketPlace Asia*, March 20, 2024. https://www.cnn.com/2024/03/19/business/india-adani-green-energy-plant-climate-intl-hnk/index.html.

Madeley, John. *Hungry for Trade*. London: Zed, 2000.

Magdoff, Harry. *The Age of Imperialism*. New York: Monthly Review Press, 1969.

Malkan, Stacy. "Critiques of Gates Foundation's Agricultural Interventions in Africa." *U.S. Right to Know*, September 4, 2024. https://usrtk.org/bill-gates/critiques-of-gates-foundation/.

Malm, Andreas. *Fossil Capital. The Rise of Steam Power and the Roots of Global Warming*. London: Verso, 2016.

Mann, Alana. *Voice and Participation in Global Food Politics*. London: Routledge/Earthscan, 2019.

Mann, Geoff, and Joel Wainwright. *Climate Leviathan*. London: Verso, 2018.

Martin, Hans-Peter, and Harold Schumann. *The*

Global Trap: Globalisation and the Assault on Democracy and Prosperity. London: Zed, 1997.

Martinez-Alier, Joan. "Beyond GDP Lies Economic Degrowth." *European Alternatives*, March 2010. http://www.euroalter.com/2010/beyond-gdp-lies-economic-degrowth/.

Martinez-Alier, Joan, Leah Temper, Daniel Del Bene, and Arnim Scheidel. "Is There a Global Environmental Justice Movement?" *Journal of Peasant Studies* 43, no. 3 (2016).

Marx, Karl. *Das Kapital*. Moscow: Progress, 1965.

Mason, J. W. "The Market Police." *Boston Review*, June 1, 2018. http://bostonreview.net/class-inequality/j-w-mason-market-police.

Masters, Lesley. "Africa, the Fourth Industrial Revolution, and Digital Diplomacy: (Re)negotiating the International Knowledge Structure." *South African Journal of International Affairs* 28, no. 3 (2021): 361–77. .

Matthews, Dylan. "The Two Most Popular Critiques of Basic Income Are Both Wrong." *Vox*, July 20, 2017. https://www.vox.com/policy-and-politics/2017/7/20/15821560/basic-income-critiques-cost-work-negative-income-tax.

Mazzucato, Mariana. "A New Global Economic Consensus." *Project Syndicate*, October 13, 2021. https://www.project-syndicate.org/commentary/cornwall-consensus-rebuildingglobal-governance-by-mariana-mazzucato-2021-10?barrier=accesspaylog.

———. "Rethinking Growth and Revisiting the Entrepreneurial State." *Project Syndicate*, August 8, 2023. https://www.project-syndicate.org/commentary/growth-entrepreneurial-state-direction-more-important-than-rate-by-mariana-mazzucato-2023-08.

———. "A Progressive Green Growth Narrative." *Project Syndicate*, January 19, 2024. https://www.project-syndicate.org/commentary/climate-policies-public-investments-will-increase-incomes-productivity-growth-by-mariana-mazzucato-2024-01.

Mazzucato, Mariana, Ngozi Okonjo-Iweala, Johan Rockstrom, and Tharman Shanmugaratnam. "Transforming the Economics and Governance of Water." *Project Syndicate*, September 21, 2022. https://www.project-syndicate.org/commentary/new-economics-and-governance-of-water-by-mariana-mazzucato-et-al-2022-09.

McAfee, Kathy. "The Contradictory Logic of Global Ecosystems Services Markets." *Development and Change* 43, no. 1 (2012): 105–32.

McBride, James, Noah Berman, and Andrew Chatzky. "China's Massive Belt and Road Initiative." *Council on Foreign Relations Backgrounder*, February 2, 2023. https://www.cfr.org/backgrounder/chinas-massive-belt-and-road-initiative.

McCoy, Alfred. "Beijing's Bid for Global Power in the Age of Trump. 'America First' versus China's Strategy of the Four Continents." *TomDispatch.com*, August 21, 2018. https://www.tomdispatch.com/blog/176460/tomgram%3A_alfred_mccoy%2C_will_china_be_the_next_global_hegemon/.

McGreal, Chris. "Continent Waits to See Cost of Lavish Embrace." *Guardian Weekly*, (December 22–January 4, 2006–2007): 6.

McKeon, Nora. *Food Security Governance. Empowering Communities, Regulating Corporations*. London: Routledge, 2015.

McMichael, Philip. *Settlers and the Agrarian Question: Capitalism in Colonial Australia*. Cambridge, UK: Cambridge University Press, 1984.

———. "World Food System Restructuring Under a GATT Regime." *Political Geography* 12, no. 3 (1993): 198–214.

———. "Global Development and the Corporate Food Regime." In *New Directions in the Sociology of Global Development*, edited by Frederick H. Buttel, and Philip McMichael. Amsterdam: Elsevier, 2005.

———. *Food Regimes and Agrarian Questions*. Halifax, NS: Fernwood, 2013.

——. "Does China's 'Going Out' Strategy Prefigure a Food Regime Transition?" *Journal of Peasant Studies* 47, no. 1 (2020): 116–54.

——. "Shock and Awe in the UNFSS." *Development* 64 (October 22, 2021): 162–71. .

McMichael, Philip, and Chul-Kyoo Kim. "Japanese and South Korean Agricultural Restructuring in Comparative and Global Perspective." In *The Global Restructuring of Agro-Food Systems*, edited by Philip McMichael. Ithaca, NY: Cornell University Press, 1994.

McMichael, Philip, and Laura T. Raynolds. "Capitalism, Agriculture, and World Economy." In *Capitalism and Development*, edited by Leslie Sklair. London: Routledge & Kegan Paul, 1994.

Mecca, Bruce, and Azhania N. Siswadi. "How Indonesia Can Win the Global Race on Critical Minerals." *The Diplomat*, February 2, 2024. https://thediplomat.com/2024/02/how-indonesia-can-win-the-global-race-on-critical-minerals/.

Memmi, Albert. *The Colonizer and the Colonized*. Boston: Beacon, 1967.

Middleton, Neil, Phil O'Keefe, and Sam Moyo. *Tears of the Crocodile: From Rio to Reality in the Developing World*. Boulder, CO: Pluto, 1993.

Millennium Ecosystem Assessment. *Ecosystems and Human Well-Being: A Framework for Assessment*. Washington, DC: Island Press, 2005. http://www.millenniumassessment.org/documents/document.358.aspx.pdf.

Milman, Oliver. "'We Are Damned Fools': Scientist Who Sounded Climate Alarm in 80s Warns of Worse to Come." *The Guardian*, July 19, 2023. https://www.theguardian.com/environment/2023/jul/19/climate-crisis-james-hansen-scientist-warning.

Minkoff-Zern, Laura-Anne. *The New American Farmer. Immigration, Race, and the Struggle for Subsistence*. Boston: MIT Press, 2019.

Mishra, Pankaj. *Age of Anger. A History of the Present*. New York: Picador, 2017.

Mitchell, Timothy. *Colonizing Egypt*. Berkeley: University of California Press, 1991.

Mittal, Anuradha. "Introduction." In *Voices from Africa: African Farmers and Environmentalists Speak Out against a New Green Revolution in Africa*, edited by Anuradha Mittal with Melissa Moore. Oakland, CA: Oakland Institute, 2009.

Mize, Ronald L., and Alicia C. S. Swords. *Consuming Mexican Labor: From the Bracero Program to NAFTA*. Toronto: University of Toronto Press, 2010.

Monbiot, George. "Finally, a Breakthrough Alternative to Growth Economics." *The Guardian*, April 12, 2017. https://www.theguardian.com/commentisfree/2017/apr/12/doughnut-growth-economics-book-economic-model.

——. "Salt of the Earth." *The Guardian Weekly*, May 13, 2022. https://www.everand.com/article/574262899/Salt-Of-The-Earth.

——. "What Links Rishi Sunak, Javier Milei and Donald Trump? The Shadowy Network behind Their Policies." *The Guardian*, January 6, 2024. https://www.theguardian.com/commentisfree/2024/jan/06/rishi-sunak-javier-milei-donald-trump-atlas-network.

Montalbano, William D. "A Global Pursuit of Happiness." *Los Angeles Times*, (October 1, 1991): F1.

Moore, Madelaine. *Water Struggles as Resistance to Neoliberal Capitalism—a Time of Reproductive Unrest*. Manchester, UK: Manchester University Press, 2023.

Morgan, Bronwen. *Water on Tap: Rights and Regulation in the Transnational Governance of Urban Water Services*. Cambridge, UK: Cambridge University Press, 2011.

Moriarty, Andrew. "Immigrant Farmworkers and America's Food Production: 5 Things to Know." *FWD.us*, September 14, 2022. https://www.fwd.us/news/immigrant-farmworkers-and-americas-food-production-5-things-to-know/.

Muchena, D. T. "The China Factor in Southern Africa." *Openspace* 1, no. 4 (2006): 22–26.

Müller, Anders Riel, and Raj Patel. "Shining India? Economic Liberalization and Rural Poverty in the 1990s." *Food First Policy Brief No, 10*, (2004).

Müller, Bettina, Luciano Ghiotto, and Lucí Bárcina. "The Raw Materials Rush." *Transnational Institute*, (2024).

Mulyana, Wahyu, Ivo Setiono, Amy Kracker Selzer, Sainan Zhang, David Dodman, and Daniel Schen-sul. *Urbanisation, Demographics and Adaptation to Climate Change in Semarang, Indonesia*. London: International Institute for Environment and Development, 2013.

Naidu, Lerisha, Angelo Tzarevski, and Spheshile Nxumalo. "Africa: The Increasing Focus on Public Interest Concerns in Competition Policy." *Global Compliance News*, June 2, 2023. https://www.globalcompliancenews.com/2023/06/02/https-insightplus-bakermckenzie-com-bm-antitrust-competition_1-africa-the-increasing-focus-on-public-interest-concerns-in-competition-policy_05302023/.

Naidu, Suresh, Dani Rodrik, Gabriel Zucman, and Lenore Palladino. "Economics after Neoliberalism." *Economics after Neoliberalism. Boston Review.* edited by Joshua Cohen. 2019. https://www.amazon.com/Economics-after-Neoliberalism-Boston-Review/dp/1946511455.

Nandy, Ashis. "The Beautiful, Expanding Future of Poverty: Popular Economics as a Psychological Defense." *International Studies Review* 4, no. 4 (2002): 107–21.

Narayan, Deepa, with Raj Patel, Kai Schaft, Anne Rademacher, and Sarah Koch-Schulte. *Can Anyone Hear Us? Voices of the Poor.* New York: Oxford University Press, 2002.

Nash, Nathaniel C. "Vast Areas of Rain Forest Are Being Destroyed in Chile." *New York Times*, (May 31, 1994): C4.

Naughton, John. "The Goal Is to Automate Us: Welcome to the Age of Surveillance Capitalism." *The Guardian*, January 20, 2019. https://www.theguardian.com/ technology/2019/jan/20/shoshana-zuboff-age-of-surveillance-capitalism-google-facebook.

Newell, Peter, and Olivia Taylor. "Contested Landscapes: The Global Political Economy of Climate Smart Agriculture." *Journal of Peasant Studies* 45, no. 1 (2018): 108–29.

Newman, Bryan. "Indian Farmer Suicides: A Lesson for Africa's Farmers." *Food First Backgrounder* 12, no. 4 (2006): 2.

Niarchos, Nicolas. "Hidden Crimes." *New York Review of Books*, November 25, 2023. https://www.nybooks.com/online/2023/11/25/hidden-crimes-nicolas-niarchos/.

Niranjan, Ajit. "Earth on Verge of Five Catastrophic Climate Tipping Points, Scientists Warn." *The Guardian*, December 5, 2023. https://www.theguardian.com/environment/2023/dec/06/earth-on-verge-of-five-catastrophic-tipping-points-scientists-warn.

Nogrady, Bianca. "Indigenous Australian Fire-Stick Farming Began at Least 11,000 Years Ago." *Nature*, March 11, 2024. https://www.nature.com/articles/d41586-024-00693-6?utm_source=Live+Audience&utm_campaign=bee0ed39c0-briefing-dy-20240312&utm_medium=email&utm_term=0_b27a691814-bee0ed39c0-51489900.

Noor, Darna. "World's Largest Oil Companies 'Way Off Track' on Emissions Goals, Report Finds." *The Guardian*, March 22, 2024. https://www.theguardian.com/us-news/2024/mar/22/oil-companies-emissions-goals-report.

Obi, Cyril. "Gunning for Security Governance in a Resource-Rich African State? Interrogating Militarisation in a Democratic Nigeria." *Conflict, Security and Development* 19, no. 6 (2019): 603–21.

Oks, David, and Henry Williams. "The Long, Slow Death of Global Development." *American Affairs Journal* 4, no. 4 (2022): 2–36.

Oliveira, Gustavo de L. T. "Chinese Land Grabs in Brazil? Sinophobia and Foreign Investments in Brazilian Soybean Agribusiness." *Globalizations* 15, no. 1 (2018): 114–33.

Ong, Aihwa. *Neoliberalism as Exception. Mutations in Citizenship and Sovereignty*. Durham, NC: Duke University Press, 2006.

Onyekwena, Chukwuka, and Mma Amara Ekeruche. *The Global South and Development Assistance*. Brookings: Africa in Focus, September 16, 2019. https://www.brookings.edu/blog/africa-in-focus/2019/09/16/the-global-south-and-development-assistance/.

Oltermann, Philip. "End Fossil-Fuel Era to Address Colonial Injustices, Urges Prominent Historian." *The Guardian*, February 15, 2024. https://www.theguardian.com/world/2024/feb/15/end-fossil-fuel-era-to-address-colonial-injustices-urges-prominent-historian.

Oxfam International. "Richest 1% Bag Nearly Twice as Much Wealth as the Rest of the World Put Together over the Past Two Years." January 16, 2023. https://www.oxfam.org/en/press-releases/richest-1-bag-nearly-twice-much-wealth-rest-world-put-together-over-past-two-years#:~:text=The%20richest%201%20percent%20grabbed,half%20of%20all%20new%20wealth

Palan, Ronen. *The Offshore World. Sovereign Markets, Virtual Places, and Nomad Millionaires*. Ithaca, NY: Cornell University Press, 2003.

Parnell, Susan, Edgar Pieterse, and Vanessa Watson. "Planning for Cities in the Global South: An African Research Agenda for Sustainable Human Settlements." *Progress and Planning* 72 (2009): 233–41.

Pascoe, Bruce. *Dark Emu, Black Seeds: Agriculture or Accident?* Broome, Australia: Magabala Books, 2014.

Patel, Raj. *Stuffed and Starved: Markets, Power and the Hidden Battle for the World Food System*. London: Portobello, 2007.

———. "The Long Green Revolution." *Journal of Peasant Studies* 40, no. 1 (2013): 1–63.

Patnaik, Utsa. "Global Capitalism, Deflation and Agrarian Crisis in Developing Countries." *Social Policy and Development Programme Paper No. 15*. Geneva: UNRISD, 2003.

Pattisson, Pete. et al. "Revealed: 6,500 Migrant Workers Have Died in Qatar since World Cup Awarded." *The Guardian*, (23 Feb 2021.https://www.theguardian.com/global-development/2021/feb/23/revealed-migrant-worker-deaths-qatar-fifa-world-cup-2022).

Payne, Adam, Stanka Becheva, and the ILIEA Team. . "Food Sovereignty from the Ground Up." *Farming Matters*, April 2017. https://edepot.wur.nl/416197.

Pearse, A. *Seeds of Plenty, Seeds of Want*. Oxford, UK: Clarendon, 1980.

Perfecto, Ivette, John Vandermeer, and Angus Wright. *Nature's Matrix: Linking Agriculture, Conservation and Food Sovereignty*. London: Earthscan, 2009.

Perkins, John H. *Geopolitics and the Green Revolution: Wheat, Genes and the Cold War*. New York: Oxford University Press, 1997.

Perrons, Diane. *Globalization and Social Change: People and Places in a Divided World*. London: Routledge, 2005.

Pilger, John. *The New Rulers of the World*. London: Verso, 2002.

Pimbert, Michel. "*Financing Agroecological Transformations for Ecological Repair." Centre for Agroecology, Water and Resilience (CAWR)*, Coventry University, November 2023. https://www.coventry.ac.uk/research/areas-of-research/agroecology-water-resilience/cawr-policy-briefs/.

Pionetti, Carine. *Sowing Autonomy: Gender and Seed Politics in SemiArid India*. London: IIED, 2005.

Plecher, H. "Number of Unemployed Persons Worldwide, 2010-17." *Statistica*, March 30, 2020. https://www.statista.com/statistics/266414/unemployed-persons-worldwide/.

Plumer, Brad, and Nadja Popovich. "A New Surge in Power Use Is Threatening U.S. Climate Goals." *New York Times*, March 14, 2024. https://www.nytimes.com/interactive/2024/03/13/climate/electric-power-climate-change.html?smid=nytcore-ios-share&referringSource=articleShare.

Polanyi, Karl. *The Great Transformation*. Boston: Beacon Press, 1944/2001.

Popovich, Nadja. "How Electricity Is Changing, Country by Country." *New York Times*, November 20, 2023. https://www.nytimes.com/interactive/2023/11/20/climate/global-power-electricity-fossil-fuels-coal.html.

Prashad, Vijay. *The Darker Nations: A People's History of the Third World*. London: New Press, 2007.

———. "UN's Vague 'New Agenda for Peace'." 2023. https://www.newagebd.net/article/208972/uns-vague-new-agenda-for-peace#google_vignette.

Prause, Luisa, Sarah Hackfort, and Margit Lindgren. "Digitalization and the Third Regime." *Agriculture and Human Values* 38 (2021): 641–55.

Prebisch, Raul. "The Economic Development of Latin America and Its Principal Problems." *Reprinted in Economic Bulletin for Latin America* 7, no. 1 (1962): 1–22.

Pretty, Jules, Camilla Toulmin, and Stella Williams. "Sustainable Intensification in African Agriculture." *International Journal of Agricultural Sustainability* 9, no. 1 (2011): 5–24. http://www.julespretty.com/wp-content/uploads/2013/09/17.-IJAS-Africa-Sust-Intensification-Pretty-et-al-2011.pdf.

Public Citizen. "The Ten Year Track Record of the North American Free Trade Agreement. The Mexican Economy, Agriculture and Environment." 2004. https://www.citizen.org/wp-content/uploads/nafta_10_mexico.pdf.

Rademacher, Anne, and Raj Patel. "Retelling Worlds of Poverty: Reflections on Transforming Participatory Research for a Global Narrative." In *Knowing Poverty: Critical Reflections on Participatory Research and Policy*, edited by K. Brock, and R. McGee. London: Earthscan, 2002.

Rai, Shirin. *Depletion: The Human Cost of Caring*. Oxford, UK: Oxford University Press, 2024.

Rai, Shirin, and David Goldblatt. "Remedying Depeletion through Social Depletion: A Critical Engagement with the United Nations' Business and Human Rights Framework." *European Journal of Politics and Gender* 3, no. 2 (2020): 185–202.

Raikes, Philip. *Modernising Hunger: Famine, Food Surplus & Farm Policy in the EC and Africa*. London: Catholic Institute for International Affairs, 1988.

Rainforest Action Network. "Agrofuels Are Not Low Carbon." *RAN White Paper*, 2018. https://www.ran.org/wp-content/uploads/2018/06/agrofuels_white_paper.pdf.

Rajagopal, Balakrishnan. *International Law from Below: Development, Social Movements and Third World Reistance*. Cambridge UK: Cambridge University Press, 2003.

Ransom, David. *The No-Nonsense Guide to Fair Trade*. London: Verso, 2001a.

———. "A World Turned Upside Down." *New Internationalist* 334 (2001b): 9–11.

Rapid Transition Alliance. "Transition Towns—the Quiet, Networked Revolution." October 9, 2019. https://rapidtransition.org/stories/transition-towns-the-quiet-networked-revolution.

Raworth, Kate. *Doughnut Economics. Seven Ways to Think Like a 21st-Century Economist*. Business Books, 2017a.

———. "A Doughnut for the Anthropocene. Humanity's Compass in the 21st Century." *The Lancet* 1, no. 2 (2017b): E48–49.

———. "Meet the Doughnut: The New Economic Model That Could Help End Inequality." *World Economic Forum*, April 28, 2017c. https://www.weforum.org/agenda/2017/04/the-new-economic-model-that-could-end-inequality-doughnut/.

Raynolds, Laura T. "The Restructuring of Export Agriculture in the Dominican Republic: Changing Agrarian Relations and the State." In *The Global Restructuring of Agro-Food Systems*, edited by Philip McMichael. Ithaca, NY: Cornell University Press, 1994.

Raynolds, Laura T., David Myhre, Philip McMichael, Viviana Carro-Figueroa, and Frederick H. Buttel. "The 'New' Internationalization of Agriculture: A Reformulation." *World Development* 21, no. 7 (1993): 1101–21.

Redding, Sean. "Structural Adjustment and the Decline of Subsistence Agriculture in Africa." 2000. http://women crossing.org/redding.html.

Revel, Alain, and Christophe Riboud. *American Green Power*. Baltimore: Johns Hopkins University Press, 1986.

Review of Keynesian Economics 8, no. 1. January 2020. https://www.elgaronline.com/view/journals/roke/8-1/roke.2020.8.issue-1.xml.

Ricardo, David. "On the Principles of Political Economy and Taxation, 3rd ed." In *The Works and Correspondence of David Ricardo, Vol. 1, edited by P. Sraffe, with the collaboration of M. M. Dobb*. Cambridge, UK: Cambridge University Press, 1817/1951.

Rich, Bruce. *Mortgaging the Earth: The World Bank, Environmental Impoverishment, and the Crisis of Development*. Boston: Beacon, 1994.

Richburg, Keith B. "Illegal Workers Do Europe's Dirty Work." *Guardian Weekly*, (August 15–21, 2002): 29.

Ride, Anouk. "Maps, Myths, and Migrants." *New Internationalist* 305 (1998): 9.

Riley, Dylan. "Sermons for Princes." *New Left Review* 143 (Sept/Oct 2023).

Rist, Gilbert. *The History of Development: From Western Origins to Global Faith*. London: Zed, 1997.

Ritchie, Mark. *Breaking the Deadlock: The United States and Agriculture Policy in the Uruguay Round*. Minneapolis: Institute for Agriculture and Trade Policy, 1993.

Ritchie, Hannah. *Not the End of the World. How We Can Be the First Generation to Build a Sustainable World*. New York: Little, Brown Spark, 2024.

Ritchie, Hannah, and Max Roser. "Half of the World's Habitable Land Is Used for Agriculture." *Our World in Data*, February 16, 2024. https://ourworldindata.org/global-land-for-agriculture#:~:text=If%20we%20combine%20global%20grazing,for%20humans%20account%20for%2016%25.

Rivas, Josué. "Solidarity in Standing Rock." *World Policy Institute* XXXIV, 4 (2017): 64–74.

Roberts, Anthea, and Nicolas Lamp. "Hockey Sticks & Lamps. Images that Define the Globalization Debate." *Polycrisis*, (August 17, 2023).

Robertson, Derek. "Inside Copenhagen's Race to Become the First Carbon-Neutral City." *The Guardian*, October 11, 2019. https://www.theguardian.com/cities/2019/oct/11/inside-copenhagens-race-to-be-the-first-carbon-neutral-city.

Robinson, Mary. "Supplying the Green Transition Must Be Fast and Fair." *Project Syndicate*, May 12, 2022. https://www.project-syndicate.org/commentary/transition-minerals-respect-for-human-rights-by-mary-robinson-2022-05.

Robinson, William I. *A Theory of Global Capitalism: Production, Class, and State in a Transnational World*. Baltimore: Johns Hopkins University Press, 2004.

Rodale Institute. "Report Finds Agriculture a Leading Cause of Climate Change." August 9, 2019. https://rodaleinstitute.org/blog/report-finds-agriculture-a-leading-cause-of-climate-change/.

Rodney, Walter. *How Europe Underdeveloped Africa*. London: Verso, 2018.

Rodrik, Dani. *The Globalization Paradox: Democracy and the World Economy*. New York: Norton, 2011.

———. "The New Productivism Paradigm?" *Project Syndicate*, (July 5, 2022).

Romero, Simon, and Kovaleski Serge F. "How Invasive Plants Caused the

Maui Fires to Rage." *New York Times*, (August 13, 2023).

Roodman, David Malin. "Still Waiting for the Jubilee: Pragmatic Solutions for the Third World Debt Crisis." *Worldwatch Paper No. 155*. (Washington, DC: Worldwatch, 2001).

Rosset, Peter M., and Miguel A. Altieri. *Agroecology: Science and Politics*. Rugby, UK: Fernwood, 2017.

Rostow, Walt W. *The Stages of Economic Growth: A Non-Communist Manifesto*. Cambridge, UK: Cambridge University Press, 1960.

Rowley, C. D. *The Destruction of Aboriginal Society*. Ringwood, Australia: Penguin, 1974.

Roy, Arundhati. "How to Think about Empire." *Boston Review*, January 3, 2019. https://www.bostonreview.net/articles/arundhati-roy-thinking-about-empire/?utm_source=Boston+Review+Email+Subscribers&utm_campaign=e5056b1339-archive_10_27_23&utm_medium=email&utm_term=0_2cb428c5ad-e5056b1339-40993701&mc_cid=e5056b1339&mc_eid=04d16a0f00.

Royal Society. *Reaping the Benefits: Science and the Sustainable Intensification of Global Agriculture*. London: The Royal Society, 2009.

Ruggie, John Gerard. "Territoriality and Beyond: Problematizing Modernity in International Relations." *International Organization* 47, no. 1 (1993): 139–74.

Ruggiero, Renato. "Reflections from Seattle." In *The WTO after Seattle*, edited by Jeffrey Schott. Washington, DC: Institute for International Economics, 2000.

Rydge, James, and Samuela Bassi. "Global Cooperation and Understanding to Accelerate Climate Action." In *The Global Development of Policy Regimes to Combat Climate Change*, edited by Nicholas Stern, Alex Bowen, and John Whalley. London: World Scientific, 2014.

Sachs, Jeffrey. "The IMF and the Asian Flu." *The American Prospect, March–April*, (1998): 16–21.

Sachs, Wolfgang. *Global Ecology: A New Arena of Political Conflict*, edited by Wolfgang Sachs. London: Zed, 1993.

Sader, Emir. "The Weakest Link? Neoliberalism in Latin America." *New Left Review* 52 (2008): 5–32.

Samuel, Sigal. "Everywhere Basic Income Has Been Tried, in One Map." *Vox*, February 19, 2020. https://www.vox.com/future-perfect/2020/2/19/21112570/universal-basic-income-ubi-map.

Sanderson, Steven. "The Emergence of the 'World Steer': Internationalization and Foreign Domination in Latin American Cattle Production." In *Food, the State, and International Political Economy*, edited by F. L. Tullis, and W. L. Hollist. Lincoln: University of Nebraska Press, 1986a.

———. *The Transformation of Mexican Agriculture: International Structure and the Politics of Rural Change*. Princeton, NJ: Princeton University Press, 1986b.

Santos, Boaventura de Sousa. "Beyond Abyssal Thinking." *REVIEW XXX*, no. 1 (2007): 45–89.

———. "The Podemas Wave." *openDemocracy*, (March 16, 2015).

Sarkar, A. N. "Eco-innovations in Designing Eco-cities and Eco-towns." *SmartCity Journal*, September 13, 2016. https://www.thesmartcityjournal.com/en/articles/eco-innovations-eco-cities-eco-towns#:~:text=Eco%2Dcity%20Development%20Criteria&text=Has%20a%20well%2Dplanned%20city,cycling%2C%20and%20then%20public%20transportation.

Saul, John Ralston. *The Collapse of Globalism and the Reinvention of the World*. New York: Penguin, 2005.

Savio, Roberto. "The Hidden Truths behind the Greek Drama." *The Forum, SID*, 2015. http://www.sidint.net/content/hidden-truths-behind-greek-drama.

Schloredt, Valerie. "Big Ag and the Small-Scale African Farmer." *Yes Magazine*, December 13, 2019. https://www.yesmagazine.org/environment/2019/12/13/african-farmer-big-agriculture/?fbclid=IwAR1HanNiYHNxcjG1TxDpW9dDnCyZ5YSwUIJdXYrx2BiGMZ0Tb0lmlrUsqls.

Schneider, Cathy Lisa. *Shantytown Protest in Pinochet's Chile*. Philadelphia: Temple University Press, 1995.

Schmelzer, Matthias, Andrea Vetter, and Aaron Vansintjan. *The Future Is Degrowth. A Guide to a World beyond Capitalism*. London: Verso, 2022.

Schwab, Klaus. "Why We Need the 'Davos Manifesto' for a Better Kind of Capitalism." 2019. https://www.weforum.org/agenda/2019/12/why-we-need-the-davos-manifesto-for-better- kind-of-capitalism/.

Schwab, Klaus, and Thierry Malleret. *Covid-19: The Great Reset*, Forum Publishing, 2020. http://reparti.free.fr/schwab2020.pdf.

Scoones, Ian, Kojo Amanor, Arilson Favareto, and Gubo Qi. "A New Politics of Development Cooperation? Chinese and Brazilian Engagements in African Agriculture." *World Development* 81 (2016): 1–12.

Scott, Jason. "Chinese Eye Australian Outback in $43 Billion Foreign Farming Policy." *Bloomberg Business*, (August 4, 2015).

Scully, Ben. "Precarity North and South: A Southern Critique of Guy Standing." *Global Labour Journal* 7 (2016): 160–73.

Segelken, Roger. "Fewer Foods Predicted for Crowded Future Meals." *Cornell Chronicle*, (February 23, 1995): 5.

Selwyn, Benjamin. *The Struggle for Development*. Cambridge, UK: Polity Press, 2017.

———. "Poverty Chains and Global Capitalism." *Competition and Change* 23, no. 1 (2018): 71–97.

Sen, Amartya. *Development as Freedom*. New York: Knopf, 1999.

Sengupta, Somoni. "60 Million People Fleeing Chaotic Lands, U.N. Says." *New York Times*, June 18, 2015. http://nyti.ms/1fixgP7.

———. "How Africa Can Help the World." *New York Times*, June 16, 2023. https://www.nytimes.com/2023/06/16/climate/africa-renewable-energy.html.

Sengupta, Somini, and Khadija Farah. "Meet the Climate Hackers of Malawi." *New York Times*, April 27, 2023. https://www.nytimes.com/2023/04/27/climate/malawi-farmers-agriculture.html.

Sexsmith, Kathleen, and Philip McMichael. "Formulating the SDGs: Reproducing or Reimagining State-Centered Development?" *Globalizations* 12, no. 4 (2015): 581–96.

Shah, Sonia. "The Other Pandemic: Habitat Destruction." *The Nation*, (March 16, 2020).

Shapiro, Mark. *Carbon Shock: How Carbon Is Changing the Cost of Everything*. Chelsea, VT: Chelsea Green, 2014.

Sheller, Mimi. *Consuming the Caribbean*. New York: Routledge, 2003.

Shi, Zhengrong. "Everywhere Under the Sun." *Making It* 2 (April 2010): 32–35.

Shidore, Sarang. "With BRICS Expansion, American Power Just Took a Big Hit." *New York Times*, (September 1, 2023).

Shiva, Vandana. *Biopiracy: The Plunder of Nature and Knowledge*. Boston: South End, 1997.

Shilliam, Robbie. "Race and Development." In *The Politics of Development: A Survey*, edited by Heloise Weber, 31–48. Abingdon: Routledge, 2014.

———. *The Black Pacific: Anti-Colonial Struggles and Oceanic Connections*. London: Bloomsbury, 2015.

———. "When Did Racism Become Solely a Domestic Issue?" *Foreign Policy*, June 23, 2020. https://foreignpolicy.com/2020/06/23/racism-ir-international-relations-domestic/.

———. *Decolonizing Politics: An Introduction*. Cambridge, UK: Polity Press, 2021.

Simms, Andrew. "Economics Is a Failing Discipline Doing Great Harm—So Let's Rethink It." *The Guardian*, August 3, 2019. https://www.theguardian.com/commentisfree/2019/aug/03/economics-global-economy- climate-crisis.

Sinclair, Lian. "The Power of Mining MNCs: Global

Governance and Social Conflict." *Elgar On-Line*, (2020): 139–58. https://china.elgaronline.com/edcollchap/edcoll/9781789903225/9781789903225.00015.xml.

Singer, Hans W. "U.S. Foreign Investment in Underdeveloped Areas: The Distribution of Gains between Investing and Borrowing Countries." *American Economic Review, Papers and Proceedings* 40 (1950): 473–85.

Singh, Ajit. "The Lost Decade: The Economic Crisis of the Third World in the 1980s—How the North Caused the South's Crisis." *Contention* 2 (1992): 58–80.

Slawson, Nicola. "Top Carbon Offset Projects May Not Cut Planet-Heating Emissions." *The Guardian*, September 20, 2023. https://www.theguardian.com/us-news/2023/sep/20/first-thing-top-carbon-offset-projects-may-not-cut-planet-heating-emissions.

Slobodian, Quinn. "Trump, Populists and the Rise of Right-Wing Globalization." *New York Times*, October 22, 2018. https://www.nytimes.com/2018/10/22/opinion/trump-far-right-populists-globalization.html.

Smialek, Jeanna, and Ana Swanson. "This Arctic Circle Town Expected a Green Energy Boom. Then Came Bidenomics." *New York Times*, February 13, 2024. https://www.nytimes.com/2024/02/13/business/economy/norway-inflation-reduction-act.html#:~:text=The%20world%20has%20shifted%20away,and%20storage%2C%20solar%20and%20hydrogen.

Smith, Adam. *An Inquiry into the Nature and Causes of the Wealth of Nations, 2 Vols*. London: Dent & Sons, 1776/1904.

Smith, Jeffrey, and Alex Gladstein. "How the UN's Sustainable Development Goals Undermine Democracy." *Quartz Africa*, (June 7, 2018): 1–10. https://qz.com/africa/1299149/how-the-uns-sustainable-development-goals-undermine-democracy/.

Smithers, Rebecca. "European Farms Could Grow Green and Still Be Able to Feed Population." *The Guardian*, February 20, 2019. https://www.theguardian.com/environment/2019/feb/20/european-farms-could-grow-green-and-still-be-able-to-feed-population.

Society for Mining, Metallurgy and Exploration. *Clean Energy Technologies Require Minerals*, 2024. https://www.smenet.org/What-We-Do/Technical-Briefings/Meeting-the-U-S-Minerals-and-Metals-Needs-for-Energy.

Southend in Transition. 2007. https://westclifftransition.wordpress.com/.

"Speeches of Greta Thunberg." *Wikipedia*, n.d. https://en.wikipedia.org/wiki/Speeches_of_Greta_Thunberg.

Spicer, André. "Will Finland Introduce a Four-Day Week? Is It the Secret of Happiness?" *The Guardian*, January 6, 2020. https://www.theguardian.com/money/shortcuts/2020/jan/06/finland-is-planning-a-four-day-week-is-this-the-secret-of-happiness?CMP=share_btn_link.

Standing, Guy. *The Precariat: The New Dangerous Class*. London: Bloomsbury Academic, 2013.

Standing, Guy. "The Case for a Basic Income." *Great Transition Initiative*, November 2020. https://greattransition.org/gti-forum/basic-income standing?gad_source=1&gclid=EAIaIQobChMIj9bykMj-hAMVpEhHAR2LJAtDEAAYAyAAEgKu1vD_BwE.

Starr, Amory. *Naming the Enemy: Anti-Corporate Movements Confront Globalization*. London: Zed, 2000.

Stavrianos, L. S. *Global Rift: The Third World Comes of Age*. New York: William Morrow, 1981.

Stern, Nicholas. *The Economics of Climate Change: The Stern Review*. Cambridge, UK: Cambridge University Press, 2006.

Stewart, Emily Iona. "The EU and US Make a Bid for the World's Critical Raw Materials." *Foreign Policy in Focus*, October 6, 2023. https://fpif.org/the-eu-and-us-make-a-bid-for-the-worlds-critical-raw-materials/.

Stewart, Heather. "Has Globalisation Hit the Wall?"

Guardian Weekly, May 29, 2015. https://fpif.org/the-eu-and-us-make-a-bid-for-the-worlds-critical-raw-materials/.

Stiglitz, Joseph. E. "The Economy We Need." *Project Syndicate*, May 3, 2019a. https://www.project-syndicate.org/onpoint/the-economy-we-need-by-joseph-e-stiglitz-2019-05.

———. "It's Time to Retire Metrics Like GDP. They Don't Measure Everything That Matters." *The Guardian*, November 24, 2019b. https://www.theguardian.com/commentisfree/2019/nov/24/metrics-gdp-economic-performance-social-progress.

———. "The Road to Fascism." *Project Syndicate Quarterly*. Year Ahead 2023. December 12, 2022. https://www.project-syndicate.org/magazine/economic-policy-failures-breeding-politics-of-backlash-resentment-by-joseph-e-stiglitz-2022-12?barrier=accesspaylog

———. "Western Industrial Policy and International Law." *Project Syndicate*, May 31, 2023. https://www.project-syndicate.org/onpoint/industrial-policy-is-back.

———. "What Comes After Neoliberalism?" *Project Syndicate*, June 4, 2024. https://www.project-syndicate.org/onpoint/what-comes-after-neoliberalism.

Stone, Glenn Davis. "Surveillance Agriculture and Peasant Autonomy." *Journal of Agrarian Change* 22, no. 3 (2022): 608–31. .

Storm, Servaas. "Capitalism and Climate Change: Can the Invisible Hand Adjust the Natural Thermostat?" *Development and Change* 40, no. 6 (2009): 1011–38.

Subacci, Paola. "The Great Global Crack-Up." *Project Syndicate*, March 8, 2023. https://www.project-syndicate.org/commentary/global-economy-fragmentation-risks-driven-by-geopolitical-hostilities-by-paola-subacchi-2023-03.

Subbarao, Duvvuri. "India's Economy: When Will the Elephant Dance?" *Knowledge@Wharton*, January 3, 2020. https://knowledge.wharton.upenn.edu/article/indias-economy-when-will-the- elephant-dance/.

Suliman, Samid. "Migration and Development after 2015." *Globalizations* 14, no. 3 (2017): 414–31.

Sunil, W. A. "Sri Lanka: Alton Workers' Action Committee Defends Victimised Colleagues." *World Socialist Web Site*, 2021. https://www.historyofceylontea.com/ceylon-publications/ceylon-tea-articles/sri-lanka-alton-workers-action-committee-defends-victimised-colleagues.html.

Suwandi, Intan R., Jamil Jonna, and John Bellamy Foster. "Global Commodity Chains and the New Imperialism." *Monthly Review*, (March 1, 2019).

Swanborough, Jahda. "6 Things We Learned About The Environment at Davos 2019." *World Economic Forum*, January 25, 2019. https://www.weforum.org/agenda/2019/01/the-environment-was-high-on-the-agenda-in-davos-but-what-actually-happened/.

Swanson, Ana. "Trump Cripples W.T.O. as Trade War Rages." *New York Times*, December 8, 2019. https://www.nytimes.com/2019/12/08/business/trump-trade-war-wto.html.

———. "Shipping Contributes Heavily to Climate Change. Are Green Ships the Solution?" *New York Times*, October 30, 2023. https://www.nytimes.com/2023/10/30/business/economy/shipping-climate-change-green-fuel.html.

Swanson, Ana, and Don Clark. "U.S. Awards $1.5 Billion to Chipmaker GlobalFoundries." *New York Times*, February 19, 2024. https://www.nytimes.com/2024/02/19/business/economy/biden-administration-1-5-billion-chipmaker-globalfoundries.html.

Sward, Jon, and Laure-Alizée Le Lannou. "Gambling with the Planet's Future? World Bank Development Policy Finance, "Green" Conditionality, and the Push for a Private-Led Energy Transition." *Bretton Woods Project*, April 2024. https://www.brettonwoodsproject.org/2024/04/gambling-with-the-planets-future-world-bank-development-policy-finance-green-conditionality-and-the-push-for-a-private-led-energy-transition/.

Swing, William Lacy. "Migration Comes of Age." *Strategic Review*, (July 6, 2015).

Taffet, Jeffrey F. *Foreign Aid as Foreign Policy: The Alliance for Progress in Latin America*. London: Routledge, 2007.

Tan, Abby. "The Labor Brokers: For a Price, There's a Job Abroad—Maybe." *Los Angeles Times*, (October 1, 1991a): H1.

———. "Paychecks Sent Home May Not Cover Human Losses." *Los Angeles Times*, (October 1, 1991b): H2–H3.

Taylor, Marcus. "Climate-Smart Agriculture: What Is It Good For?" *Journal of Peasant Studies* 45, no. 1 (2018): 89–107.

Therborn, Göran. *The World: A Beginner's Guide*. Cambridge, UK: Polity, 2011.

———. "The World and the Left." *New Left Review*, (2022): 1–66.

Thomas, Alan, and Ben Crow, eds. *Third World Atlas*. 2nd ed. Washington, DC: Taylor & Francis, 1994.

Thomas, Caroline. *New States, Sovereignty and Intervention*. Aldershot, Hants, UK: Gower Publishing, 1985.

———. *In Search of Security: The Third World in International Relations*. Boulder, CO: Lynne Rienner, 1987.

Thunberg, Greta. "If World Leaders Choose to Fail Us, My Generation Will Never Forgive Them." *Guardian Weekly*, (September 27, 2019).

Titumir, Rashed Al Mahmud, and Mustafa Kamal. "Growing Together Sustainably: A Zero-Poverty Post-2015 Development Framework." *Development* 56, no. 2 (2013): 172–78.

Tomich, Dale. *Through the Prism of Slavery: Labor, Capital and World Economy*. Lanham, MD: Rowman and Littlefield, 2004.

Tooze, Adam. "Chartbook X Unhedged Debating Multipolarity." October 12, 2023. https://adamtooze.substack.com/p/chartbook-x-unhedged-debating-multipolarity.

Tortajada, Cecilia, and Hongzhou Zhang. "When Food Meets BRI: China's Emerging Food Silk Road." *Global Food Security* 29 (2021): 1–13. .

Toulmin, Camilla. *Climate Change in Africa*. London: Zed, 2009.

Tran, Mark. "Tunisia Offers Wake-Up Call for Development." *The Guardian*, (June 9, 2011).

Travelli, Alex. "What 10 Years of Modi Rule Has Meant for India's Economy." *New York Times*, April 2, 2024. https://www.nytimes.com/2024/04/01/business/india-economy-election.html.

Tripathi, Salil. "Shine On." *Guardian Unlimited*, (May 13, 2004).

"Trucost Reveals the $3 Trillion Environmental Cost of Farming." *Trucost News*, October 15, 2015. https://www.trucost.com/trucost-news/trucost-reveals-3-trillion-environmental-cost-farming/.

"'Tsunami of Data' Could Consume One Fifth of Global Electricity by 2025." *Guardian*, December 11, 2017. https://www.theguardian.com/environment/2017/dec/11/tsunami-of-data-could-consume-fifth-global-electricity-by-2025.

Tucker, Ian. "Automation of Jobs Is One of the Greatest Questions of Our Time." *The Guardian*, January 18, 2020. https://www.theguardian.com/technology/2020/jan/18/automation-jobs-universal-basic-income-daniel-susskind-interview.

Tucker, Bronwyn, and Shereen Talaat. "At COP28, It's Time to Transform the Global Financial Architecture." *Context*, December 4, 2023. https://www.context.news/just-transition/opinion/at-cop28-its-time-to-transform-the-global-financial-architecture.

Tullis, Paul. "Nitrogen Wars." *The Guardian Weekly*, November 24, 2023. https://www.theguardian.com/environment/2023/nov/16/nitrogen-wars-the-dutch-farmers-revolt-that-turned-a-nation-upside-down.

Turner, Mandy. "Scramble for Africa." *The Guardian*, (May 2, 2007).

Tuxill, John. "Nature's Cornucopia: Our Stake in Plant Diversity." *Worldwatch Paper No. 148*, no. 148 (Washington, DC: Worldwatch, 1999).

UNAC and GRAIN. "The Land Grabbers of the Nacala Corridor: A New Era of Struggle against Colonial Plantations in Northern Mozambique." February 2015. http://viacampesina.org/en/images/stories/pdf/ 2015-grain-5137-the-land-grabbers-of-the-nacala-corri-dor.pdf.

UN-HABITAT. "Call for Expressions of Interest (EoI) for Cooperation Partners for Agreement of Cooperation: Supporting African Cities in Inventorying Greenhouse Gas Emissions." December 14, 2016. https://unhabitat.org/call-for-expressions-of-interest-eoi-for-cooperation-partners-for-agreement-of-cooperation-supporting-african-cities-in-inventorying-greenhouse-gas-emissions.

———. *World Cities Report 2022: Envisaging the Future of Cities*. Nairobi, Kenya: UN-HABITAT, 2022.

United Nations. "Localising the Millennium Development Goals: A Guide for Local Authorities and Partners." May 2006. https://www.local2030.org/library/44/Localizing-the-Millennium-Development-Goals-A-guide-for-local-authorities-and-partners.pdf.

———. *Global Alliance for Climate-Smart Agriculture Action Plan*, Climate Summit, 2014. http://www.un.org/climatechange/summit/wp-content/uploads/sites/2/2014/09/AGRICULTURE-Action-Plan.pdf.

———. *Report of the Secretary-General on SDG Progress*. New York: UN, 2019. https://sustainabledevelopment.un.org/content/documents/24978Report_of_the_SG_on_SDG_Progress_2019.pdf.

United Nations Conference on Trade and Development (UNCTAD). *Trade and Development Report 1996*. Geneva: UNCTAD, 1996.

United Nations Department of Economic and Social Affairs. *The Millennium Development Goals Report*. New York: United Nations, 2010. http://www.unfpa.org/public/site/global/lang/en/pid/6090.

United Nations Development Programme. Human Development Report. *Overcoming Barriers: Human Mobility and Development*. New York: Oxford University Press, 2009.

———. *Human Development Report*. New York: United Nations, 2011. http://hdr.undp.org/en/reports/global/hdr2011/.

———. *Towards a Green Economy: Pathways to Sustainable Development and Poverty Eradication*. New York: United Nations, 2011.

United Nations Framework Convention on Climate Change (UNFCCC). *Subsidiary Body for Implementation*. New York: United Nations, 2002. https://unfccc.int/resource/docs/2002/sbi/inf14.pdf.

"UN's Guterres: Today's Global Governance Structures Reflect Yesterday's World." *Reuters*, August 24, 2023. https://www.reuters.com/world/uns-guterres-todays-global-governance-structures-reflect-yesterdays-world-2023-08-24/#:~:text=JOHANNESBURG%2C%20Aug%2024%20(Reuters),universal%20they%20needed%20to%20reform.

Uphoff, Norman. "Higher Yields with Fewer External Inputs? The System of Rice Intensification and Potential Contributions to Agricultural Sustainability." *International Journal of Agricultural Sustainability* 1 (2003): 38–50.

Van der Ploeg, J. D. *The New Peasantries: New Struggles for Autonomy and Sustainability in an Era of Empire and Globalization*. London: Earthscan, 2008.

———. "The Peasantries of the Twenty-First Century: The Commoditization Debate Revisited." *Journal of Peasant Studies* 37, no. 1 (2010): 1–30.

Vasquez, Edith. "Retail Foods." *Report No. GT2023-0005. U.S. Department of Agriculture and Global Agriculture Information Network, July 6, 2023.* https://apps.fas.usda.gov/newgainapi/api/Report/DownloadReportByFileName?fileName=Retail%20Foods_Guatemala%20City_Guatemala_GT2023-0005.pdf.

Verweijen, Judith, and Alexander Dunlap. "The Evolving Techniques of the Social Engineering of Extraction: Introducing Political (Re)actions 'From Above' in Large-Scale Mining and Energy Projects." *Political Geography* 88 (June 2021): 102342. .

Vidal, John. "All Dried Up." *Guardian Weekly*, (March 27–April 2, 2003): 24.

———. "Climate Change to Force Mass Migration." *The Guardian*, (May 14, 2007).

———. "How Food and Water Are Driving a 21st-Century African Land Grab." *The Observer*, (March 7, 2010).

———. "Bolivia Enshrines Rights of Mother Nature." *Guardian Weekly*, (April 15, 2011): 7.

———. "We're Losing Species at Shocking Rates—So Why Is Conservation Failing?" *The Guardian*, (September 18, 2019).

Vince, Gaia. "The Century of Climate Migration: Why We Need to Plan for the Great Upheaval." *The Guardian*, (August 18, 2022).

Walker, Richard. *The Conquest of Bread: 150 Years of Agribusiness in California*. New York: New Press, 2004.

Wallace-Wells, David. "What Can Replace China as a Global Economic Engine?" *New York Times*, August 23, 2023. https://www.nytimes.com/2023/08/23/opinion/columnists/what-can-replace-china-as-a-global-economic-engine.html.

Wallach, Lori, and Michelle Sforza. *Whose Trade Organization? Corporate Globalization and the Erosion of Democracy*. Washington, DC: Public Citizen, 1999.

Wallach, Lori, and Patrick Woodall. *Whose Trade Organization? A Comprehensive Guide to the WTO*. New York: New Press, 2004.

Wallerstein, Immanuel. *The Modern World-System*. New York: Academic Press, 1974.

Walton, John, and David Seddon. *Free Markets & Food Riots: The Politics of Global Adjustment*. Oxford, UK: Blackwell, 1994.

Wang, Claire. "How 19th-Century Pineapple Plantations Turned Maui into a Tinderbox." *The Guardian*, (August 27, 2023).

Watkins, Kevin. "Agriculture and Food Security in the GATT Uruguay Round." *Review of African Political Economy* 50 (1991): 38–50.

———. "The Forgotten Other India." *The Guardian*, (October 3, 2006).

Watson, Irene. *Aboriginal Peoples, Colonialism and International Law: Raw Law*. London: Routledge, 2015.

Watts, Jonathan. "Rivals Awake to a Giant in Their Midst." *Guardian Weekly*, (December 23–January 5, 2005/2006): 36.

———. "Can a Green Generation Remodel a Climate Victim?" *Guardian Weekly*, (June 5, 2020): 28.

———. "The Great Carbon Divide." *Guardian Weekly*, November 24, 2023. https://www.theguardian.com/environment/ng-interactive/2023/nov/20/the-great-carbon-divide-climate-chasm-rich-poor.

Weber, Heloise. "Reconstituting the 'Third World'? Poverty Reduction and Territoriality in the Global Politics of Development." *Third World Quarterly* 25, no. 1 (2004): 187–206.

———. "A Political Analysis of the PRSP Initiative: Social Struggles and the Organization of Persistent Relations of Inequality." *Globalizations* 3, no. 2 (2006): 187–206.

———. "When Goals Collide: Politics of the MDGs and the Post-2015 Sustainable Development Goals Agenda." *SAIS Review of International Affairs* 34, no. 2 (2014): 129–39.

———. "The Political Significance of Badung for Development: Challenges, Contradictions and Struggles for Justice." In *Meanings of Bandung: Postcolonial Orders and Decolonial Visions*, edited by Quynh N. Pham, and Robbie Shilliam. London: Rowman and Littlefield, 2016.

———. "Politics of 'Leaving No One Behind': Contesting the 2030 Sustainable Development Goals Agenda." *Globalizations* 14, no. 3 (2017): 399–414.

Weber, Heloise, and Martin Weber. "Colonialism, Genocide and International Relations: The Namibian-German Case and Struggles for Restorative Relations." *European Journal of International Relations* 26, no. SI (2020a): 91–115.

Weber, Heloise, and Martin Weber. "When Means of Implementation Meets Ecological Modernization Theory: A Critical Frame for Thinking About the Sustainable Development Goals Initiative." *World Development* 136 (December 2020b). .

Weghmann, Vera. "The Making and Breaking of Solidarity between Unwaged and Waged Workers in the UK." *Globalizations* 16, no. 1 (2019): 1–16.

Weiss, R. "Firms Seek Patents on 'Climate Ready' Altered Crops." *Washington Post*, (May 13, 2008).

Wessel, James. *Trading the Future: Farm Exports and the Concentration of Economic Power in Our Food System*. San Francisco: Institute for Food and Development Policy, 1983.

The White House. "Fact Sheet: The Bipartisan Infrastructure Deal." *press release*, November 6, 2021. https://www.whitehouse.gov/briefing-room/statements-releases/2021/11/06/fact-sheet-the-bipartisan-infrastructure-deal/.

"Why Protecting Indigenous Communities Can Also Help Save the Earth." *The Guardian*, October 12, 2020. https://www.theguardian.com/climate-academy/2020/oct/12/indigenous-communities-protect-biodiversity-curb-climate-crisis.

Wilder, Garry. *Freedom Time: Negritude, Decolonization and the Future of the World*. Durham: Duke University Press, 2015.

Wike, Richard. "With 41% of Global Wealth in the Hands of Less Than 1%, Elites and Citizens Agree Inequality Is a Top Priority." *Pew Research Center*, November 8, 2014. http://www.pewresearch.org/fact-tank/2014/11/08/with-41-of-global-wealth-in-the-hands-of-less-than-1-elites-and-citizens-agree-inequality-is-a-top-priority/.

Williams, Gwyneth. *Third-World Political Organizations: A Review of Developments*. Montclair, NJ: Allenheld, Osmun, 1981.

Williams, T. C. "The French Origins of 'You Will Not Replace Us'." *The New Yorker*, December 4, 2017. https://www.newyorker.com/magazine/2017/12/04/the-french-origins-of-you-will-not-replace-us.

Wise, Timothy. "AGRA Retreats from Its Own 'Green Revolution'." *Food Tank*, n.d. https://foodtank.com/news/2022/10/agra-retreats-from-its-own-green-revolution.

Wolf, Eric. *Peasant Wars of the Twentieth Century*. New York: Harper-Collins Paperbacks, 1969.

———. *Europe and the People without History*. Berkeley: University of California Press, 1982.

Wolf, Martin. "Three Years On, Fault Lines Threaten the World Economy." *Financial Times*, (July 14, 2010): 7.

Wolfenden, Tess. *The Debt Fossil-Fuel Trap*. London: Oxford House, 2023.

Wolfensohn, James. "Rethinking Development—Challenges and Opportunities." *UNCTAD Meeting*. Bangkok, February 16, 2000.

Wood, Robert E. *From Marshall Plan to Debt Crisis: Foreign Aid and Development Choices in the World Economy*. Berkeley: University of California Press, 1986.

Wood, Wilbur. "From Dirt to Soil." *The Nation*, (May 20/27, 2019).

Woods, Ngaire. *The Globalizers: The IMF, the World Bank, and Their Borrowers*. Ithaca, NY: Cornell University Press, 2006.

World Bank. *World Development Report*. Washington, DC: World Bank, 1998–1999.

———. *World Development Indicators*. Washington, DC: World Bank, 2006.

———. *Biofuels: The Promise and the Risks. World Bank Policy Brief*. Washington, DC: World Bank, 2007a.

———. *World Development Report*. Washington, DC: World Bank, 2007b.

——. *International Assessment of Agricultural Science and Technology for Development*. Washington, DC: World Bank, 2008. https://projects.worldbank.org/en/projects-operations/project-detail/P090963?lang=es&tab=overview.

——. World Bank. "Migration and Remittances: Recent Developments and Outlook. Special Topic: Forced Migration." *Migration and Development Brief No. 23*, (October 6, 2014). https://openknowledge.worldbank.org/server/api/core/bitstreams/171af48f-d014-5a31-b691-ee5e0c069c6e/content.

——. "Unlocking the Potential of the Agricultural Sector in Egypt" *Promoting Sustainable Investment in Egypt's Food Security Conference, December 5, 2017.* Washington, DC: World Bank Group.

——. "Population Living in Slums (% of Urban Population)." 2020. https://data.worldbank.org/indicator/EN.POP.SLUM.UR.ZS?skipRedirection=true&view=map.

——. "Mineral-Rich Developing Countries Can Drive a Net-Zero Future." June 6, 2022. https://www.worldbank.org/en/news/feature/2022/06/06/mineral-rich-developing-countries-can-drive-a-net-zero-future#:~:text=Over%20two%2Dthirds%20of%20the,Guinea%2C%20Indonesia%2C%20and%20Jamaica.

——. "Remittances Remain Resilient but Likely to Slow." press release, June 13, 2023. https://www.worldbank.org/en/news/press-release/2023/06/13/remittances-remain-resilient-likely-to-slow

World Meterological Association. "Climate Change Is Bad for Health but Climate Services Save Lives." *press release*, November 2, 2023. https://wmo.int/news/media-centre/climate-change-bad-health-climate-services-save-lives.

Wu, Brandon. "The World Needs a New Social Contract, Not More Structural Adjustment." *Foreign Policy in Focus*, April 16, 2020. https://fpif.org/the-world-needs-a-new-social-contract-not-more-structural-adjustment/.

Yazdani, Saeid, and Kamariah Dola. "Sustainable City Priorities in Global North versus Global South." *Journal of Sustainable Development* 6, no. 7 (2013): 38–47.

Yu, Jie. "The Shape of Power in 2024." *Project Syndicate Quarterly. The Year Ahead. 2024*, (December 11, 2023): 72. https://www.project-syndicate.org/magazine/multipolarity-non-alignment-global-order-2024-by-adekeye-adebajo-et-al-2023-12.

Younge, Gary. "Streets on Fire." *The Guardian*, November 23, 2019. https://www.theguardian.com/culture/2019/nov/23/decade-of-protest-occupy-wall-street-extinction-rebellion-gary-younge.

Zacharopoulou, Chrysoula, and Rania Al-Mashat. "Making the International Financial System Work." *Project Syndicate*, October 16, 2023. https://www.project-syndicate.org/commentary/imf-world-bank-annual-meetings-global-financial-architecture-reform-by-chrysoula-zacharopoulou-and-rania-al-mashat-2023-10.

Zaitchik, Alexander. "Seeding Disaster. How Bill Gates and Agribusiness Giants Are Throttling Small Farmers in Africa and the Global South." *The Nation*, October 2–9, 2023. https://www.thenation.com/article/world/new-colonialist-food-economy/.

Zeng, Jinghan. "Chinese Views of Global Economic Governance." *Third World Quarterly* 40, no. 3 (2019): 578–94.

Zhang, Jun. "How China Creates Its Own Market." *Project Syndicate*, (October 30, 2023).

Zuboff, Shoshana. *The Age of Surveillance Capitalism. The Fight for a Human Future at the New Frontier of Power.* New York: Public Affairs, 2019.

INDEX